Making Majorities

EAST-WEST CENTER
SERIES ON

CONTEMPORARY ISSUES IN ASIA AND THE PACIFIC

Series Editor, Bruce M. Koppel

Making Majorities

CONSTITUTING THE NATION IN
JAPAN, KOREA, CHINA, MALAYSIA, FIJI, TURKEY,
AND THE UNITED STATES

Edited by Dru C. Gladney

STANFORD UNIVERSITY PRESS
STANFORD, CALIFORNIA
1998

Stanford University Press
Stanford, California

Printed in the United States of America

CIP data are at the end of the book

A Series from
Stanford University Press and the East-West Center

CONTEMPORARY ISSUES IN ASIA AND THE PACIFIC

Bruce M. Koppel, Editor

A collaborative effort by Stanford University Press and the East-West Center, this series addresses contemporary issues of policy and scholarly concern in Asia and the Pacific. The series focuses on political, social, economic, cultural, demographic, environmental, and technological change and the problems related to such change. A select group of East-West Center senior fellows—representing the fields of political science, economic development, population, and environmental studies—serves as the advisory board for the series. The decision to publish is made by Stanford.

Preference is given to comparative or regional studies that are conceptual in orientation and emphasize underlying processes and to works on a single country that address issues in a comparative or regional context. Although concerned with policy-relevant issues and written to be accessible to a relatively broad audience, books in the series are scholarly in character. We are pleased to offer here the third book in the series, *Making Majorities: Constituting the Nation in Japan, Korea, China, Malaysia, Fiji, Turkey, and the United States*, edited by Dru C. Gladney.

The East-West Center, located in Honolulu, Hawaii, is a public, nonprofit educational and research institution established by the U.S. Congress in 1960 to foster understanding and cooperation among the governments and peoples of the Asia-Pacific region, including the United States.

Preface

THIS volume is based on a conference at the East-West Center sponsored by the former Program for Cultural Studies. I would especially like to thank the director of the Program, Geoffrey White, for encouraging the initial conference and supporting it through the protracted and time-consuming process of bringing this volume to publication. During the conference, staff members at the East-West Center provided tremendous support, especially Anna Tanaka, Sandi Osaki, and Margaret White. Michael Macmillan devoted many hours to an initial copyediting of the volume prior to submission, helping it to achieve a much stronger level of coherence. Elisa Johnston and Carol Wong in the publications office went beyond the call of duty in keeping this volume on track. The editing staff at Stanford University Press, especially Stacey Lynn and the copy editor, Lynn Stewart, helped to shape the final manuscript and clarified many issues of style and content. Several contributors who have participated in many other academic volumes commented on the special attention and thoroughness provided by the copy editor. Finally, I would like to thank the editorial committee of the series on Contemporary Issues in Asia and the Pacific, and especially the series editor, Bruce Koppel, for supporting this project.

A collection such as this, spanning several regions and countries in the wider Asia-Pacific region and drawing together a truly international collection of scholars, represents a collaborative effort that is never completely representative of everyone's views. One of the many debates during and after the conference was over the title. While the participants immediately agreed to the main title of the volume, *Making Majorities*, there was much debate over the subtitle. Since the series in which this volume appears is committed to a comparative, multinational, and cross-regional approach within the Asia-Pacific region, we initially thought to subtitle it "Constituting the Nation in the Asia-Pacific" (there was also disagreement over whether it should be "constituting," "composing," or "constructing" the nation). But given the fact that so much of Asia is left out of the region (and particularly many of the Pacific islands, not to mention other nations bordering the Pacific, such as Chile and Russia), the participants chose to merely list the countries and nations directly discussed, calling into question the nature of the region included in the term "Asia-Pacific."

However, merely listing the regions and countries as we have done (Japan, Korea, China, Turkey, and so on) does an injustice to the minorities that are not mentioned (such as the Kurds), even as it privileges the majorities after whom many of the nations are named. Most difficult is the China/Taiwan issue, where there is severe disagreement on whether one should subsume the other. We finally decided that if we allowed a separate mention of Taiwan in the title, then we would need to do so with other groups, such as the Kurds, Hawaiians, and Indo-Fijians. However, space does not allow us to list all the countries and the peoples or regions discussed that are either part of those countries or claim their own independent status. The length of the subtitle has already encountered objections from both editorial committees. It therefore represents a compromise that may only satisfy the search engines of computer indexes, which prefer such an overabundance of information in a title. The authors themselves have been left to raise the issues regarding their subject and regional areas in their chapters. It is to them that I am most grateful for their patient understanding and commitment to this project.

Contents

Part III
Chineseness

Part IV
Malayness

Part V
Fijianness

Part VI
Turkishness

Part VII
Americanness

Contributors

CHO HAE-JOANG, a cultural anthropologist in training, is a professor in the Department of Sociology, Yonsei University, Seoul. She received her Ph.D. from the University of California, Los Angeles. Her early research focused on gender studies, with special interest in Korean modern history, and her recent work is in cultural studies in the global/local and postcolonial context. She is the author of *Woman and Men in South Korea* (1988), *Reading Texts, Reading Lives in the Postcolonial Era*, three volumes (1992, 1994), and *Children Refusing School, Society Refusing Children* (1996).

SELIM DERINGIL is Professor of History at Bogaziçi University in Istanbul. His undergraduate degree is in European History and Language from the University of East Anglia, Norwich, England (1975). His Ph.D. is from the same institution (1979). He is the author of *Turkish Foreign Policy During the Second World* War (1989) and *The Well Protected Domains: Ideology and the Legitimation of Power in the Ottoman Empire, 1876–1909* (1997).

DRU C. GLADNEY is Senior Research Fellow at the East-West Center and Professor of Asian Studies and Anthropology at the University of Hawai'i at Manoa. His books include *Muslim Chinese: Ethnic Nationalism in the People's Republic* (2d ed. 1996), *Ethnic Identity in China: The Making of a Muslim Minority Nationality* (1998), and *Dislocating China: Muslims, Minorities and Other Subaltern Subjects* (in press).

RICHARD HANDLER was educated at Columbia University and the University of Chicago. He is Professor of Anthropology at the University of Virginia and author of *Nationalism and the Politics of Culture in Quebec* (1988), *Jane Austen and the Fiction of Culture* (with Daniel Segal, 1990), and *The New History in an Old Museum: Creating the Past at Colonial Williamsburg* (with Eric Gable, 1997). He is the editor-elect of *History of Anthropology* and the editor/compiler of *Schneider on Schneider: The Conversion of the Jews and Other Anthropological Stories* (1995).

HSIEH SHIH-CHUNG received his Ph.D. in anthropology from the University of Washington and is a professor at National Taiwan University. He conducted his major fieldwork in the Tai-Lue community, Yunnan, China, and in several indigenous villages in Taiwan. His interests include ethnicity, anthropology of tourism, ethnohistory, interpretive anthropology, and anthropology of northern Southeast Asia.

MARTHA KAPLAN is Associate Professor of Anthropology at Vassar College. She is the author of *Neither Cargo Nor Cult: Ritual Politics and the Colonial Imagination in Fiji.*

JOHN D. KELLY is Associate Professor of Anthropology at the University of Chicago. He is the author of *A Politics of Virtue: Hinduism, Sexuality and Countercolonial Discourse in Fiji.*

LAUREL KENDALL is the curator in charge of Asian ethnographic collections at the American Museum of Natural History. She is the author of *Shamans, Housewives, and Other Restless Spirits: Women in Korean Ritual Life* (1985), *The Life and Hard Times of a Korean Shaman: Of Tales and the Telling of Tales* (1988), and *Getting Married in Korea: Of Gender, Morality, and Modernity* (1996). Her most recent work concerns changes in the Korean shaman world over a twenty-year period.

KEMAL KIRIŞCI is Associate Professor in the Department of Political Science and International Relations at Bogaziçi University in Istanbul. He has contributed articles to a number of journals and books on international migration and Turkey, refugee issues in Turkey, and Turkish foreign policy. He is the author of *The PLO and World Politics* (1986) and the coauthor of *The Kurdish Question and Turkey: An Example of a Trans-State Ethnic Conflict* (1997). He is currently serving a two-year term as a member of the External Research Advisory Committee of the United Nations High Commissioner for Refugees.

ANTHONY MILNER is Professor of Asian History and Dean of the Faculty of Asian Studies at the Australian National University. He is the author of *Kerajaan: Malay Political Culture on the Eve of Colonial Rule* (with V. Matheson, 1982), *Perceptions of the Haj* (1984), and *The Invention of Politics: Expanding the Public Sphere in colonial Malaya* (1995). He is the editor of *Comparing Cultures* (1996) and *Communities of Thought* (1996), among other works.

EMIKO OHNUKI-TIERNEY, a native of Japan, is a Vilas Research Professor at the University of Wisconsin, Madison, and an Associate Researcher at the National Museum of Ethnology, Osaka. She received a Guggenheim Fellowship in 1985. The books she has authored include *Rice as Self: Japanese Identities Through Time* (1993), *The Monkey as Mirror: Symbolic Transformations in Japanese History and Ritual* (1987), *Illness and Culture in Contemporary Japan: An Anthropology View* (1981), *The Ainu of the Northwest Coast of Southern Sakhalin* (1974, reprinted 1984), and *Sakhalin Ainu Folklore* (1969); she is the editor of *Culture Through Time: Anthropological Approaches* (1990).

JONATHAN Y. OKAMURA is a researcher with the Student Equity, Excellence, and Diversity office at the University of Hawai'i and a lecturer in the Department of Ethnic Studies. A social anthropologist by training, he has conducted fieldwork with Hanunuo Mangyans in the Philippines and Filipino immigrants in Hawai'i and has written on the global Filipino diaspora. His recent research in Hawai'i has been concerned with ethnic identity and ethnic stratification.

SHAMSUL A. B. is Professor of Social Anthropology and Dean, Faculty of Social Sciences and Humanities, at the Universiti Kebangsaan Malaysia in Bangi, Malaysia. He researches, lectures, and writes extensively, in both Malay and English, on politics, culture, and economic development in Southeast Asia, with a strong empirical focus on Malaysia. His most well-known book, *From British to Bumiputera Rule* (1986), was a finalist for the Harry Benda Prize of the Association of Asian Studies (United States) in 1988. Currently he is completing a book-length manuscript based on his decade-long research on identity and nation formation in Malaysia.

KOSAKU YOSHINO is Associate Professor of Sociology at the University of Tokyo. He received his Ph.D. from the London School of Economics, studying theories of nationalism. He is the author of *Cultural Nationalism in Contemporary Japan: A Sociological Enquiry* (1992, 1995), *A Sociology of Cultural Nationalism* (1997), and numerous articles on nationalism and national identity in Asia.

Making Majorities

Introduction: Making and Marking Majorities

DRU C. GLADNEY

MAJORITIES are made, not born. This book posits that there are no pure majorities in the Asia-Pacific region or in the West. Numerically, ethnically, politically, and culturally, societies make and mark their majorities and minorities under specific historical, political, and social circumstances. This position sets this volume apart from Samuel Huntington's (1993) influential thesis that civilizations are composed of more or less homogeneous cultures, suggesting instead that culture is as malleable as the politics that informs it. Just as Robert J. C. Young (1995: 29) has argued that the emphasis on "hybridity" supports and is based on a discourse of cultural or racial homogeneity, this volume argues that emphasis on minority/majority rights is based on uncritically accepted ideas of purity, numerical superiority, and social consensus. Emphases upon multiculturalism even become ways of masking serious political, ethnic, and class differences merely in terms of cultural difference, as the cases of Hawai'i (Okamura), Quebec (Handler), Japan (Ohnuki-Tierney, Yoshino), and China (Gladney) illustrate. Affirmative-action policies can isolate, identify, and stigmatize minorities as often as they homogenize, unify, and naturalize majorities.

This book analyzes how majorities and minorities are made and marked across cultural, regional, and national boundaries in the Asia-Pacific region. From Hawai'i to Turkey, this region encompasses an extraordinarily diverse variety of populations and political developments. In the influential collection *What's in a Rim: Critical Perspectives on the Pacific Region Idea*, Dirlik (1993: 5–6) questions the rather recent invention of "the Pacific,"

"Asia," and finally the "Asia-Pacific region and rim." The chapters in this volume examine the notion of "majority-ness" in historical and cross-cultural perspective across a region that is often regarded as composed of relatively homogeneous majorities.

Consider the following statement by Eric Hobsbawm in his landmark study, *Nations and Nationalism Since 1780*: "China, Korea and Japan . . . are indeed among the extremely rare examples of historic states composed of a population that is ethnically almost or entirely homogeneous." Hobsbawm continued: "Thus of the (non-Arab) Asian states today Japan and the two Koreas are 99% homogeneous, and 94% of the People's Republic of China are Han" (1992: 66 and n. 37). For Hobsbawm, and many Western theorists, nationalism has arisen in the West (see Greenfeld 1992). This volume directly challenges this received wisdom regarding European heterogeneity and Asian homogeneity, suggesting that majorities have been constructed historically and politically in each region for very specific and divergent reasons. Following Benedict Anderson's (1991) lead, we argue that just as the nation is an "imagined community," so is the notion of the majority an imagined, and relatively recent, phenomenon.

The chapters in this volume are drawn from a workshop held at the East-West Center that addressed the nature of "homogeneity" in so-called Asian and Pacific states and others frequently identified as such. Besides Japan, China, and Korea, we considered other countries in the region thought to possess such commonalities (what Dominguez calls "samenesses"), including Malaysia, Fiji, Turkey, and, of course, the United States with its so-called white majority. Recent studies have begun to question the construction of majority "whiteness" in America (Dominguez 1986; Frankenberg 1993), but this questioning has rarely been extended to studies of majorities in Asia. It is becoming increasingly necessary to question the nature of "culturalism" before we discuss its "multi" aspects. Who defines the nature of majority culture? When and why? What are minority responses to such majority discourses? How does one become homogeneous? Too often studies of ethnicity and cultural identity have begun their examinations from the margins without pausing to reflect how the center got to its place. The workshop provided an excellent opportunity to reflect on these questions for each region in historical depth as well as comparatively between regions.

The impetus for the workshop stemmed from a series of public lectures on comparative multiculturalism sponsored by the Program for Cultural Studies at the East-West Center. During the series it had become increasingly obvious that the so-called diversity debate revolves around the construction of "minority"/"majority," and that minorities, in general, are defined in terms of an accepted majority. The workshop addressed the nature of national cultures, the construction and representation of majorities, and the relations between stipulated majorities and minorities in each region. Two papers on each region examined the issues of national cultural and majority construction from a number of angles, from both majority and minority perspectives, as well as historically, politically, demographically, and ethnographically. In addition to the solicited papers, we invited three discussants, Professors Arif Dirlik (Duke University), Virginia Dominguez (University of Iowa), and Koichi Maruyama (Kyushu University), to comment on each of the papers and draw out comparative lines of similarity and difference. Vincent Rafael and Geoffrey White were also present as commentator and interlocutor.

Despite increasing awareness in the humanities regarding the political and historical forces that have shaped cultural representation in the West, much of Asia is still viewed as somehow culturally and ethnically homogeneous. Although the relevance of cultural, ethnic, and national identities for a broad range of topics pursued in the humanities and social sciences is widely acknowledged both inside and outside the academy, these perspectives have rarely been brought to bear on the study of Asia, which has generally been treated as a whole or in its constituent nation-state parts (China, Korea, Japan, etc.). The general theoretical discussion of ethnicity and cultural identity has largely been absent from Asian nation studies, and from much of Asian studies in general. In this volume, building on the participants' anthropological, political, and historical research in Asia and the United States, we examine the politics of contemporary culture(s) in comparative perspective by focusing upon (but not limiting ourselves to) issues in Asian and U.S. society where lines of contrast between majority and minority and between cultures are sharply drawn.

The end of the cold war has seen an increasing clash of cultures, not civilizations, in the so-called West and East. In the absence of superpower rivalry, clashes of communal identity—ethnicity, nationality, race, and religion—are more frequent than they were during détente. As a theoretical counterpart to the increasingly complex public debates about cultural and national identities, anthropological metaphors of culture as text have been overtaken by theories that emphasize the social and political manipulations of culture and its representations. Within a society, certain people (often depicted as majorities) and institutions manage the larger part of cultural production and consumption. This is the familiar, Gramscian concern with hegemony. A second politics of cultural representation more particularly concerns anthropology and history. This raises issues of the representation of the minority "other"—or the ethical and political problems inherent in cross-cultural accounts of one culture that are produced by another, observing culture or by a hegemonic state. These representations often involve exoticization and even eroticization of ethnic and cultural groups for political and economic ends, such as national tourism, development funding, and health programs, just as majorities are homogenized for purposes of building electoral coalitions, redistricting, and coalescing interest groups.

There is an increasingly widespread critique of basic assumptions in the humanities and social sciences regarding cultural identity and representation. Concepts of ethnicity, minority, and majority—once utilized by social theorists as unexamined analytic constructs—are increasingly recognized to be socially produced and culturally constituted. This recognition stems in large measure from comparative studies documenting the role of local understandings of culture in the constitution of social identity and political power. At the same time, transnational and multinational companies are increasingly dominating the distribution of global capital that often benefits certain elite groups at the expense of the rest. Many of these transnational companies are run by elites that patronize national and ethnic groups perceived as similar to themselves (Kotkin [1993] regards this as a transnational retribalization).

Increasingly complex and contested debates have emerged over the definitions and uses of concepts of culture, ethnicity, tradition, and history. Universities and colleges across the United States are attempting to deal with the contradictory forces of multiculturalism, economic and political internationalization, and transnationalization with new programs and revised curricula that seek to enhance multicultural and global understanding. Many faculty are involved in ongoing debates within their colleges about the merits and purposes of recognizing within curricula a range of multicultural, physical, and gender diversity. Deliberate constructions of majority and minority cultural traditions are directly implicated in the reproduction of shared conceptions of truth and justice, as well as of existing regimes of power. Notions of majority are increasingly used as idioms of and for political and economic sovereignty, whether in the furtherance of cultural distinctiveness or of national solidarity.

The proliferation of recent publications about the politics of culture and representation indicates a growing and sustained debate over these issues (e.g., Clifford and Marcus 1986; Fischer 1986; Handler 1988). The Asia-Pacific case provides rich material for a comparative analysis of the ways in which accepted categories such as "nation," "ethnicity," "majority," and "minority" are variously constructed. This volume's comparative discussions will provide a perspective from which to consider the categories of identity, Eastern and Western, that exert considerable force in popular and academic representations of majorities and minorities. Three of the key issues addressed are ethnicity, tradition, and history.

The concept of ethnicity, one of the most thoroughly discussed in modern sociology, serves to organize much of Western thinking about the forces that mold identity and structure group relations. Consideration of the constructed character of ethnicity as a product of interaction began with the landmark work of Frederik Barth, Clifford Geertz, and others. This volume moves on to consider a wide variety of cases that show several possible ways for groups to conceptualize group identity and relations. Extensive discussions of the various categories and translations of the term "nation" or "ethnicity" (*minzu* in Chinese, *bangsa* in Malay, etc.) illustrate the often derivative and multivalent discourses of nationalism, to use Partha Chatterjee's (1986) formulation, that have influenced how identities are constructed and represented today in much of Asia.

Definitions of tradition ring with claims to privileged knowledge and authenticity, often displayed in ritual practices and performances that validate those claims. Recent anthropological writings show a small explosion of interest in inventions or constructions of tradition. The seminal book by Hobsbawm and Ranger, *The Invention of Tradition* (1983), marks the beginnings of concerted anthropological and historical investigation of tradition as a historically contingent discourse. This volume suggests how nations and majorities are imagined, invented, and marked in much of Asia.

As discussed by White (1991) and many others, historical discourse is a powerful medium of identity formation. To cite one example from China, the population explosion of the Manchu, from 4.3 million in 1982 to 9.8 million in 1990, illustrates the increasing importance of tracing one's lineage history for contemporary ethnic identification and politics. Clearly, numbers and the building of social coalitions matter. In China, many groups such as the Manchu have attained recognition and population growth only by reclassifying themselves as minorities, a process that involves validating their descent from historical groups and empires once thought totally assimilated. The reinterpretation of national histories and ideologies contributes directly to representational politics in the United States as well as in Asia.

This volume's discussion of increasing discourses of majority and minority allows exploration of a number of questions of more general concern in the humanities and social sciences: How does one become officially "ethnic" in many states in Asia? How are understandings of majority and minority cultures—of shared traditions and pasts—created and shaped in specific political and historical contexts? How does the state shape the way people think of themselves? How do people resist, transform, and appropriate these official representations? What are some of the diverse kinds of historiography used today to reproduce shared identity? And what are some of the political contexts and issues (such as land, language, or citizenship) that evoke and invoke them?

In his recent volume *Minorities at Risk*, Ted Robert Gurr (1993: 11) argues that in the post-cold war period, minorities are becoming increasingly critical to regional and political conflicts, perhaps even more so than superpower relations, which now rarely lead to regionwide conflict. Yet this influential volume, which includes detailed, statistically enumerated descriptions of "proportions of minorities by region" (pp. 28–33), never questions the constructions of the majorities in the regions described. It reproduces vast regions in Asia, such as China and Japan, as homogeneous, with .001 to .050 "minority proportions," while Europe consistently receives minority proportions of up to .601 and 1.00 (evidently, according to Gurr, there are some regions of Eastern Europe where there are no majorities). These policy-driven studies, while useful for identifying which minorities may be subject to increased discrimination, rarely call into question the making of majorities in the region, why it is that, say, some Serbian nationalists were desperately and violently trying to construct a "pure Serbian nation," not by seeking votes but by "ethnically cleansing" the landscape of all those who are not regarded as purely Serbian. In some ways, these discussions of minority rights contribute to the naturalization and homogenization of the majorities, even as they attempt to call attention to the plight of oppressed minorities.

In attempting to denaturalize and question the notion of majority in the Asia-Pacific region, the contributors to this volume have reached several consensuses, despite approaching the subject along very different lines of inquiry. By viewing the issue of majority-ness comparatively and in historical depth, the volume makes the following assertions:

The composition of the nation is not a natural process but is achieved, promoted, and represented through political and cultural means. Thus, Emiko Ohnuki-Tierney's chapter demonstrates that Japanese identity, thought to be homogeneous by Hobsbawm, many other Western scholars, and much of Japanese officialdom, has evolved historically through direct interaction with "significant others," namely, the Ainu aboriginals, the *burakumin*, the West, and other internal and external others who were just as significant for Japanese self-identification as any internal Japanese cultural constructions. Kosaku Yoshino's chapter illustrates that the Nihonjinron ("Japanese person" debate) was encouraged by the business and administrative elite to further uniformity and corporate mentality when it was feared there was too little homogeneity to begin with. The process was, again, in opposition to outsiders, namely, the West.

Numerical majority does not necessarily imply political superiority. This is true in the case of Taiwan, where until recently, Hsieh Shih-chung reminds us, Taiwanese lacked political power and the Nationalists from the mainland defined themselves as representatives of the nation, dominating both

Taiwanese and aboriginals in the political arena. This situation prevails in many regions, such as formerly in South Africa, and currently in Northern Ireland and even Hawai'i, as Jonathan Okamura's chapter suggests, where whites are in a minority vis-à-vis Asians but still exert enormous political and economic clout. Significantly, John Kelly's chapter illustrates that in Fiji, Indo-Fijians have "aspired to minority" status, despite their numerical majority, in order to allay the fears of the Fijian elites. This suggests that numerical majorities do not always hold political power, and that peoples do not always seek to join majorities. Yet numbers always do matter in the construction of majorities, even if the politically powerful are not always numerous. As Bernard Cohn (1987) once argued, the census has played a privileged role in defining group membership, national identities, and majority/minority configurations, even though census categories are often quite arbitrarily created and loosely defined.

Minorities may seek minority status, even in situations in which there is clear discrimination against them. My chapter indicates an ethnoreligious revitalization in China among Muslims and other minorities (such as Tibetans) at a time when China is being increasingly criticized for its human-rights record in minority regions. Though minorities in China now receive certain entitlement programs, they are still regarded as inferior to the so-called Han majority and are expected eventually to assimilate. Kemal Kirişci's discussion of the political plight of the Kurds in Turkey and central Asia in general indicates a growing assertion of Kurdish identity despite decreasing possibilities since the Gulf War of attaining any Kurdish homeland. The Kurds, once regarded as "mountain Turks," have now won recognition as a bona fide minority in Turkey, even though their language is still subject to restriction and criminalization.

Representation is crucial to the making of majorities. Ohnuki-Tierney demonstrates that the Ainu were always represented as wild and animalistic, while the Japanese were depicted as "civilized"; these representations in art and literature clearly marked social and cultural differences. Hsieh notes similar marking of the aboriginals in Taiwan, as Gladney (1994) has noted the exoticization and eroticization of minorities in China. Martha Kaplan shows how the demographic figures for Indo-Fijians are often manipulated and represented in a light that makes them seem to be in either the majority or the minority, depending on the aims of those presenting the figures. Okamura notes similar issues for defining who is in the majority in Hawai'i, where Asians are frequently aggregated as an "ethnic group" or disaggregated as distinct minorities (Japanese, Filipinos, Koreans, Chinese, etc.), depending on political posturing. My chapter notes that the very category of "Han" Chinese majority is of recent origin and masks enormous cultural and linguistic diversity within the Chinese population. There is more diversity between the Cantonese- and Mandarin-speaking populations than there is among Hui and non-Hui nationalities in many areas (particularly regarding urban Hui who no longer believe in Islam but continue to be registered as members of the Hui Muslim minority). In his comments, Dirlik suggested that the early Communists perhaps moved toward a majoritarian discourse in reaction to anarchist factions that threatened to destabilize the country. Richard Handler demonstrates that the representation of minorities in museums and theme parks that seek to convey national culture and origins can be highly controversial, as is the black-slavery exhibit in Colonial Williamsburg. And Laurel Kendall raises the question of who determines which group will speak on behalf of the Korean nation, particularly when much of what is thought to be Korean is embodied in rituals performed by female shamans, who are now even sent on tour by the South Korean government to represent the country.

Majority-ness does not always matter. Cho Hae-joang argues that difference in South Korean society is generally articulated along gender, class, and political lines, rather than ethnic, racial, or religious ones. Selim Deringil argues that in Turkey, being Turkish was not always such a good thing, especially if it implied lower-class status. The Ottomans promoted a cosmopolitan society that comprised culturally different groups, including non-Muslims. In his remarks, Maruyama noted that for transnational and nomadic groups distributed across national boundaries, such as the Kazakhs, Kurds, and Koreans, numerical majority does not matter as much as political recognition and coalition building with cross-border groups.

Religion may define majority-ness as often as other naturalized categories such as culture, race, ethnicity, locality, and language. This is certainly the case in Israel, Dominguez noted in her comments, where the census records religious affiliation only: Jewish, Muslim, Christian, and so forth. In their collection *Asian Visions of Authority*, Keyes, Kendall, and Hardacre (1994: 6–8) have argued that religion, such as state Shintoism in Japan and Islam in Southeast Asia, plays an important role in defining who is included in or excluded from certain configurations of power and authority. In India, Ireland, and especially Malaysia, religion may be the main factor determining one's political or national affiliation (Hindu/Muslim, Protestant/Catholic, Malay Muslim/Chinese, respectively). Shamsul A. B. argues that although it is clearly Islam that is most critical to the construction of Malayness, the exact meaning of "Islam" is not always clear and is frequently manipulated by the various political parties. Anthony Milner suggests that Malay politics is expedient first, Muslim last, but that this is not unique to Malaysia and is indeed typical of many countries where one religion is maintained by the overall majority, such as Italy and Turkey. It is increasingly problematic for Malaysia, however, where scholars have begun to argue that Chinese

Muslims brought Islam from China to Malaysia in the first place, necessitating a reconsideration of common notions of pure Malay Islamic roots.

Given the U.S. interest in the region, and the increasingly problematic notion of what it means to be American in the midst of the growing Asia-Pacific diaspora, this volume should prove to be a timely and useful contribution to sociological, anthropological, historical, and political-economic studies of identity and cultural policy in this changing region. Just as colonialism carried its own culture, representative modalities, and social strictures, as Nicholas Thomas (1992) has argued, so majoritarian discourse influences the way local cultures are configured, counted, and portrayed. Vincent Rafael (1989) has documented how, as a result of "contracting colonialism," postcolonial societies can no longer turn the clock back to precolonial power and social alignments, just as the invention of majorities and stigmatization of minorities is almost impossible to dispel once enshrined in national censuses, demographic charts, and electoral districts.

This volume shows the local history, cultural embeddedness, and political implications of majoritarian discourse, and its consequences for Asia and the United States. Drawing upon experts from within and around the Asia-Pacific region, the volume also provides insights rarely available to Western policymakers and theoreticians. It should provide a useful resource for university seminars, political analysts, cultural theorists, and scholars interested in the changing dynamics of the Asia-Pacific region and the problems associated with this change, as minority voices become increasingly heard and majority-ness even more frequently reasserted.

PART I

JAPANESENESS

1

Culturalism, Racialism, and Internationalism in the Discourse on Japanese Identity

KOSAKU YOSHINO

PREVIOUS studies of nationalism have tended to be confined to the classic cases of "old nationalism" or to the more recent cases of "neonationalism" and ethnic separatism without paying adequate attention to the development of national identity in long-established nations subsequent to the initial period of nation formation. Similarly, the field of race and ethnic relations has been almost entirely confined to multiethnic societies, and racial and ethnic discourse in supposedly homogeneous countries such as Japan has hardly attracted scholarly attention. It was this gap in the study of race, ethnicity, and nation that I wanted to fill in my *Cultural Nationalism in Contemporary Japan* (1992). Japan in the 1970s and 1980s saw a resurgence of cultural nationalism,[1] and this was closely associated with the vast number of publications that Japanese cultural elites produced to define and redefine the distinctiveness of Japanese society, culture, and national character. Discourse of this sort is commonly referred to as the Nihonjinron. This Japanese case offers a number of points that can usefully be considered in the context of more general studies of ethnicity and nationalism.

Despite the general assumption among Japanologists that the Nihonjinron is a case special to Japan, an active concern with national distinctiveness is by no means unique to that country. In fact, reinvention and reassertion of national identity form a theme that is increasingly attracting cultural elites in many other countries where national identity has long been established. The type of nationalism that preserves and enhances national identity in an already well established nation may be called "secondary nationalism," in contrast to "primary" or original nationalism, which is concerned with the creation of that identity. Although the boundaries between primary and secondary nationalism cannot be drawn with any precision because of the difficulty of deciding when national identity is established among significant numbers of a population (and how to define "significant numbers"), a working distinction may be proposed in the above terms.

The creation of national identity in primary nationalism normally centers on a historicist concern with ancestral origin or mythical history, for which reason historians or mythmakers are given an important place. A sense of common ancestral history not only provides a feeling of communal uniqueness but unites successive generations. For example, the tradition of the emperor system (*tennōsei*) in early Meiji Japan combined traditional familism and state Shinto to create the mystique of an imperial lineage unbroken from time immemorial and to stress the unity of Japanese subjects on the basis of the invented historicist vision. A historicist concern is similarly evident in many other examples of primary nationalism.[2] Kedourie (1971: 6) remarks in the context of Indian cultural nationalism in the 1880s that "it is the past of a 'nation' which gives it an identity, a meaning, and a future." Similarly, Kushner (1977: 7) points out with reference to Turkish cultural nationalism (or Turkism) in the 1890s that shared memories of a glorious past are essential for a nation's existence.[3]

By contrast, in secondary nationalism, where a sense of belonging to a historical nation is already taken for granted, the historicist vision becomes less relevant and is largely replaced by a symbolic boundary concern focusing on contemporary cultural differences between "us" and "them." Of course, reinterpretations of history continue to be advanced, but the nation's origin becomes less relevant as a source of national identity. The participants in the Nihonjinron were "pop sociologists" who discussed the cultural and behavioral differences of the Japanese, thereby reaffirming a sense of difference for the contemporary audience. Parallels are found in other long-existing nations. The symbolic boundary process of organizing significant difference between "us" and "them" thus becomes a focal point in the analysis of secondary nationalism.

Various types of "them" are used in this process to rearticulate national identity. One common background for an active concern with national identity (or rather majority identity) in some countries of Western Europe is the increasingly multiracial and multiethnic nature of their societies. For example, Van Heerikhuizen (1982: 120) reports a revived interest in national identity among Dutch intellectuals, attributing it to the "changing composition of the Dutch population" caused by immigrants and migrant laborers. In England, too, race relations aroused discussion, first of immigration, then of the state of the country, and ultimately of "our" English identity (see Wallman 1981: 133). However, racial minorities and foreigners are not the only kind of "them" against which majority (or national) identity is redefined. The presence of foreign cultures within "our" nation also activates the symbolic boundary process. For example, against the "invasion" of Americanism in the field of popular culture, cultural or linguistic nationalism developed in France to defend "very French" realms of French culture. In the non-Western world, reaffirmation of national cultural identity is often a by-product of modernization and Westernization. It may be said that the Nihonjinron worked as a boundary process for Japanese cultural elites to defend and rearticulate "our own realm" in the wake of Westernization. Foreign culture is not necessarily confined to that of the West. In Korea, for example, Japan represented one of the "significant others" against which "Koreanness" was constructed (see Cho Hae-joang's chapter in this volume).

The increasing concern with globalization in the contemporary world is changing people's awareness of the "them" against which "our" cultural identity is defined. With an increase in international contacts, the presence of "them" is not necessarily confined to the actual presence of "foreign" people and culture in a nation. Whether as members of multinational corporations, tourists, or students, people are constantly exposed to cross-national contacts—so much so that they anticipate and sometimes prepare for such contacts even prior to their occurrence. One characteristic of globalization is this readiness to accept cross-cultural contacts as normal; for this reason people willingly prepare themselves with knowledge of cultural differences between "us" and "them."[4] It is this kind of "us" and "them" dialogue that I wish to incorporate in this chapter.

In the following analysis of cultural nationalism in contemporary Japan, an inquiry is first made into the characteristic manners of perception and expression of Japanese identity among "the Japanese." Particular attention is paid to culturalism and "racialism," which characterize the discourse on Japanese identity. The chapter then explores the manners in which the Nihonjinron has affected the perception and expression of the educated sections of the Japanese population. The main concern here is with the way in which the Nihonjinron has been popularized and reproduced for the consumption of ordinary people. Focusing on the marketplace of ideas where theories of cultural differences are reproduced and consumed, it will be found that cultural nationalism in contemporary Japan is generated in close association with reproducers' and consumers' desires to internationalize. The chapter concludes with a reminder that Japanese identity should be understood not as a static entity but within a changing time framework.

Culturalism

National identity is expressed in diverse ways, of which two ideal types deserve especial mention here. First, that identity may be objectified—that is, given concrete forms—or expressed in terms of institutions, customs and practices, rituals and ceremonies, artistic and literary products, and some other forms of artifact. Alternatively, it may be expressed in terms of abstract notions such as cultural ethos, national character, patterns of behavior and thought, *Volksgeist*, and so on. Both expressions are present—albeit in varying degrees—in any nation, but one type sometimes predominates over the other. For example, the English approach tends to be objectifying and institutional. A glimpse at a variety of writings on Britishness, one of the most widely read of which has been Anthony Sampson's *The Changing Anatomy of Britain* (1982), would show us something about the British (or English) tendency to objectify their identity in terms of peculiarly British (or English) institutions. Sampson discusses one British institution after another, including the monarchy, Parliament, the Conservative Party, the Labour Party, trade unions, schools, universities, police, scientists and engineers, the City, farmers, and the press. He quotes Hugh Trevor-Roper, who remarked that "whatever qualities we have as British people [do not] come from the blood or from race" (p. xvii). Trevor-Roper stated that it is *institutions* that form the British national identity.[5]

By contrast, the Nihonjinron do not objectify Japanese identity but express it in terms of holistic culture—described variously as cultural ethos, national character, and patterns of behavior—that is believed to underlie objectified institutions, customs, and practices. The holistic and nonobjectifying approach is compatible with "racialistic" thinking, in which a particular culture belongs exclusively to a particular "race"—a point that will be elaborated on later. By contrast, institutions are not intrinsic to any particular nation and, as such, can be diffused to other nations than that in which they originate. The Nihonjinron approach may best be characterized as that of culturalism. Culture is seen as infrastructural, and social, political, and economic phenomena are viewed as manifestations of a cultural ethos considered unique to the Japanese.

The Nihonjinron particularly emphasized two aspects of Japanese culture or, to be more precise, Japanese social relations. The first concerns the supposedly unique Japanese patterns of communication, which are characterized by a lack of emphasis on logical and linguistic presentation as opposed to the Western patterns, which are supposed to attach utmost importance to the use of dichotomous logic and eloquence (linguistic expression). Essential communication among the Japanese is supposed to be performed empathetically, without the use of direct verbal assertions. Explicit verbal communication is considered unnecessary because of the mutual sensitivity supposedly found in social interactions among the Japanese. This form of culturalism explains everyday occurrences and news in terms of Japanese cultural peculiarities. For example, when a Japanese finds it difficult to make himself understood in conversing in English with a non-Japanese, he may attribute the difficulty to the "uniqueness" of the Japanese, who are supposed to consider it a virtue to say little and rely on nonlogical and nonverbal means to convey ideas, when in fact his poor English is to blame. The same person would probably make whatever efforts were necessary to communicate effectively with another Japanese. Here, culture is used as an excuse, and culturalism conceals the real reason for miscommunication. The nonverbal, nonlogical, and empathetic mode of communicating among the Japanese is a theme that has been touched upon repeatedly by thinkers in modern Japan. Using a typically culturalist argument in his *Bunshō Dokuhon* (Manual of prose composition), novelist Junichirō Tanizaki (1974 [1934]) attributed Japan's losing of the League of Nations debate on the Sino-Japanese conflict to the eloquence of the Chinese and Westerners, who believe in the power of language, and to the Japanese virtue of taciturnity.

The second aspect of Japanese culture much emphasized in the Nihonjinron is groupism or group orientation. Some argue that "interpersonalism" (*kanjinshugi*) is a more appropriate concept to describe Japanese social culture in the sense that it gives the highest value to interpersonal relationships, not to society's unilateral influence or control over individual behavior. Hamaguchi (1980: 37), who coined the term "kanjinshugi," argues that "what it really feels [like] in their everyday life is clearly different from [what is implied by] the term 'groupism' " and that it "cannot be explained in terms of group members' immersion into and loyalty to the organization." The theory of groupism or interpersonalism finds emphasis in the psychological theory of *amae* (dependence), according to which the socialization process in Japan encourages dependence on very close emotional bonds, thereby enabling the persistence of group-oriented social features.[6] Western society, on the other hand, is described as having the opposite characteristics of individualism and independence (self-autonomy). One manifestation of this culturalistic thinking was the well-known argument in the early 1980s that the cause of the trade imbalance between Japan and the United States was a difference in their attitude toward group culture, which resulted in a productivity differential.

Racialism: The Imagining of "Japanese Race"

Since culture is closely associated with "race" in the perception and expression of Japaneseness, it is best to move on to what, for want of a better term, I call racialism. In this chapter, "racialism" refers to the type of thinking that explains aspects of collective identity in "racial" terms and, as such, is intended, as a concept, to be paired with culturalism. "Racialism" as used in this sense has a much wider meaning than "racism."[7] Unlike culturalism, which is explicitly formulated in the Nihonjinron, racialism is vaguely present in the general mental makeup of the Japanese.

A few words of clarification should first be said regarding the controversial notion of "race." The biological concept of race has been refuted for five decades now, yet the construct of race continues to be used in everyday discourse. This social reality has led social scientists to define race by employing social actors' definitions and to use socially constructed races as analytical categories. Borrowing Benedict Anderson's insight regarding nation as "imagined community," it may be said that, like nation, race is imagined in the dual sense that it has no real biological foundation and that the members of a race do not actually know most of their fellow members, "yet in the minds of each lives the image of their communion" (1983: 15). Like nation, race is imagined as limited in that its members perceive its boundaries, beyond which lie other races. And, like nation, race is imagined as a community having a sense of comradeship.[8] A "race" may thus be defined as a human group that perceives itself or is perceived by other groups as different from other groups by virtue of innate and immutable phenotypical and genotypical characteristics. Race has no real biological foundation and is, first and foremost, socially constructed. With this understanding in mind, I will focus on two aspects of what I call racialism in Japan. The first concerns the notion of the "Japanese race" itself, the second the relationship between race and culture in the reconstruction of Japanese identity.

Race is an effective boundary marker because it evokes a strong psychological response. In British and American race relations, race tends to be used for negative categorization of "them," in contrast to ethnicity, which is concerned with positive identification of "us" (see Banton 1983: 106). The Japanese case suggests that race may also be closely concerned with positive identification of the in-group. Race, along with a unique culture, is an important element of Japanese identity. The Japanese historically formed an image of themselves as a racially distinct and homogeneous people. Despite this myth, there is no such entity as the Japanese race in the objective sense; the Japanese, like all other peoples, are the product of a long period of mixture.

In American and British race relations, perception of phenotypical difference is usually the only basis upon which a group is racialized, but the Japanese case suggests that imagination of genotypical difference can also be a basis for racial categorization. Lee and De Vos (1981: 356) observe with reference to the Korean minority in Japan that "although most Koreans are physically indistinguishable from Japanese, they nonetheless continue to be considered racially distinct by Japanese." Socially constructed "race" is used in popular discourse when a person indicates "difference that *seems to be* immutable" (Wallman 1986: 229).[9] A Japanese expresses that aspect of Japanese identity which he or she tends to perceive as being "immutable" or "natural" through the imagined concept of Japanese blood.[10] While not the sort of expression frequently used in everyday speech, it is readily employed when one is called on to explain the "intrinsic difference" of the Japanese. Needless to say, "Japanese blood" is a case of social construction of difference, as a scientifically founded racial classification of the Japanese and non-Japanese is meaningless. But, as Wallman (1986: 229) remarks, the "differences observed and the way they are interpreted say as much about the classifier as about the classified." It is meaningful to analyze how and why this racialized notion is used in the symbolic boundary process to define "us" Japanese.

Using Raymond Firth's distinction between sign and symbol, we may say that "Japanese blood" is not a sign or the abstraction of the object it stands for. By contrast, Firth (1973: 228) understands a symbol as that which "stands for a complex set of emotional and intellectual dispositions," and to which "are assigned meanings of a complex kind of which the individual is by all evidence unconscious or only partly conscious" (Firth 1973: 225; see also Wallman 1981: 121). "Japanese blood" is a symbol that generates, and is generated by, the stable sense of "us" and "our" identity because it represents a complex set of meanings and emotive associations concerning Japanese identity. If ethnicity is a community of people defined by belief in shared culture and history, race focuses upon, and exaggerates, a particular aspect of ethnicity, that is, kinship and kin lineage. The symbol of Japanese blood is strongly associated with the imagined concept that "we" are members of an extended family that has perpetuated its lineage.

The ethnic identity of the Japanese took on a strong racial tone as Meiji cultural and political elites invented the notion of Japan as a family-nation (or family-state) of divine origin. Members of the family-nation were imagined to be related by blood to one another and ultimately to the emperor. Kinship, religion, and race were fused to produce a strong collective sense of oneness. The notion of family-nation, the ideological backbone of prewar and wartime ultranationalism, came under strong attack with Japan's defeat in 1945. Since then, this irrational concept has disappeared from the main ideological scene (except for some right-wing group members). Nonetheless, the nation as "imagined family" (or kin group) has remained alive in the subconsciousness of Japanese people. The racial metaphor of Japanese blood evokes the memory of this kin-oriented, in-group mentality. It was argued earlier that a historicist theme concerning ancestral myth is no longer explicitly stressed in secondary nationalism. A historicist concern with primordial ties continues to be present in this racialized metaphor, however.

Furthermore, the notion of Japanese blood assumes the existence of distinct racial groups, which is predicated upon the assumption of breeding isolation. This assumption enhances the mental distance between "us," the in-group, and others, generating the sense that "we" Japanese people have been formed among "ourselves" and in isolation from others. The symbol of Japanese blood thus facilitates the sentiment that "we" are the product of this special formative experience and possess unique qualities. "Japanese blood" is socially invented not to refer to genetic traits as such but to mold and channel psychological responses concerning "us"-ness and "them"-ness. The symbolic image it generates and the collective sentiment it expresses in it, make it an effective boundary marker.

The preceding discussion should not be taken to suggest that the kind of racialism manifested in the notion of Japanese blood is special to Japan. Racialization of ethnic identity seems fairly widespread in East Asia. The Chinese case offers an interesting comparison. In prominent intellectual Su Xiaokang's definition of China (summarized in Dikötter 1994: 8), Chineseness is primarily "a matter of biological descent, of physical appearance, of congenital inheritance," so that "one will always be 'Chinese' by virtue of one's blood." We find a striking similarity between Japanese and Chinese racial rhetoric, but, unlike the Japanese, the Chinese seem to deemphasize the cultural nature of their identity. Su Xiaokang argues that cultural features, such as "Chinese civilization" and Confucianism, are secondary and can be changed, reformed, or even eradicated—but he says also that cultural features "are thought to be the product of that imagined biological group" (quoted in Dikötter 1994: 8). If culture is the product of a particular race, then, theoretically, it should be equally important. It would be interesting to pursue this comparison further and to identify the contexts in which culture is emphasized and those in which it is deemphasized, but this is too large a topic to be included in this chapter.

Racialism : Race and Culture in Perceptions of Japaneseness

The second aspect of racialism associates unique Japanese culture with the Japanese race. Of course, association of culture with race is not unique to Japan. In fact, genetic determinism is a familiar form of association between race and culture and has often been equated with racism *tout court*—perhaps because social sciences have only concerned themselves with Western cases.[11]

The term "racism" itself is relatively new. Ruth Benedict was one of the first scholars to use it extensively. From the time she wrote *Race and Racism* in 1942 until the late 1960s, when the term began to be used in an expanded sense, racism was equated with the dogma of genetic determinism—that race determines culture. Michael Banton summarizes this doctrine in terms of the propositions that "people's cultural and psychological characteristics are genetically determined" and that "the genetic determinants are grouped in patterns that can be identified with human races in the old morphological sense that envisaged the existence of pure races" (Banton 1970: 17–18). Thus, racism is "the doctrine that a man's behaviour is determined by stable inherited characters deriving from separate racial stocks having distinctive attributes and usually considered to stand to one another in relations of superiority and inferiority" (p. 18). Genetic determinism has been not only a widely held doctrine but also a habit of thinking among "ordinary" people (see Husband 1982: 18).

The Japanese also closely associate their racial and cultural distinctivenesses, but the concept of racism does not adequately describe the type of race thinking that characterizes the discourse of Japanese identity. Japanese thinking suggests that particular cultural traits should belong to a particular group with particular phenotypical and genotypical traits. The main attribute of the sense of Japanese uniqueness is possessiveness. Exclusive ownership is claimed upon certain aspects of Japanese culture. The Nihonjinron are full of examples to illustrate the notion of racially exclusive possession of a particular culture. One common manner of exploring Japanese uniqueness in the Nihonjinron is to infer a "uniquely Japanese" mode of thinking from Japanese words and phrases that are supposed to defy translation, and thereby to suggest that one has to be born a Japanese to be able to grasp the intricacy and delicacy of the Japanese language. For example, Shōichi Watanabe (1974: 8) writes that the spirit of the Japanese language is "as old as our blood." He says that he knows of some Europeans whose Japanese is accurate and quite fluent and that some Korean residents of Japan have won literary awards for their Japanese prose or fiction, but he knows of no foreigner who can write good *waka*, 31-syllable Japanese poetry (pp. 105–6). What he suggests is not that the spirit of the Japanese language is genetically transmitted but that it "belongs exclusively" to the Japanese in the sense that it can be truly appreciated only by them. It may be noted in passing that it would be equally difficult to find Japanese persons in today's Japan who can write good waka.

The notion of racially exclusive possession of a particular culture, which should be distinguished from genetic determinism, is of analytical use for the Japanese case (and perhaps some other cases). My argument is based on an analysis of interviews that I conducted in the late 1980s with schoolteachers and businessmen regarding the extent to which foreigners could acquire the Japanese way of thinking and behaving.[12] The initial reaction of all the respondents was that foreigners, including those born in Japan, could not learn to think and behave like the Japanese. But, as the interviews progressed, the respondents easily switched from one position to another. A quotation from Husband (1982: 18–19) throws light on this situation. Husband remarks that "people experience 'race' as a highly complex body of emotive ideas" and endorses Barzun's (1965 [1937]) position that it is very important to focus on "the ease with which people flow from one proposition to another in sustaining their race-thinking." In my research interviews, for the purpose of contrast, two types of foreigners, phenotypically different (Westerners) and phenotypically similar (Koreans, Chinese, and Japanese Americans), were included for consideration.

The respondents believed that, for several reasons, phenotypically different foreigners (Westerners) could not learn to think and behave like the Japanese. The first reason was the supposedly subtle and implicit nature of Japanese culture—culture in the sense of behavior and ideas. The second was that even if foreigners were somehow to master the subtle Japanese mode of thinking and behaving, they would still not be regarded as having acquired Japaneseness in their behavior because what may be called "role inconsistency" between race and culture obstructs this recognition. As one company manager put it, "We have always been accustomed to the idea that those who speak Japanese should look like the Japanese." Some respondents also suggested that it would make little difference if the foreigners were born and reared in Japan as long as their parents and grandparents were foreigners. As the same company manager remarked, "Their different appearance will remind themselves and us of their difference, thereby making it difficult for them to feel and think like the Japanese and for us to accept them as those who have acquired Japaneseness." This remark typically shows the respondent's "uniracial consciousness," which assumes the unchanging racial and cultural homogeneity of the Japanese. The perceived role inconsistency works as a defense mechanism to preserve that homogeneity.

The association of culture with race may be examined further by considering phenotypically indistinguishable foreigners. Japanese Americans are a case of particular interest here. Most respondents did not foresee any serious obstacles for such American citizens, born and reared in the United States, in integrating culturally in Japan. Most respondents used the phrase *Nihonjin no chi* (Japanese blood) to indicate what they considered to be the immutable aspects of Japanese identity, suggesting that, because Japanese Americans "have Japanese blood," they can eventually learn to behave and think like "us" after an initial effort. The logical question is whether this attitude implies genetic determinism. Here Koreans and Chinese offer an illuminating comparison, because, even though they may be phenotypically indistinguishable, they are classified as "not having Japanese blood," and therefore they are supposed not to be able to "become Japanese" culturally. Respondents' first reactions to the Korean and Chinese cases were, on the whole, very negative, as typified by the remark of one businessman: "No matter how long they live here, I think they will remain Koreans and Chinese. After all, we and they are different *minzoku* [ethnic/racial groups]." Interestingly, however, when their attention was drawn to a number of former Koreans and Chinese who had become naturalized and who then passed as Japanese, including some well-known sports players and entertainers, most respondents had to agree that Koreans and Chinese could "become Japanese" unless reminders of their foreignness, such as names and other signs of their origins, were presented. This seems to contradict the previous point that one has to have Japanese blood to possess Japanese culture.

A lack of logic characterizes race thinking in general. Indeed, logical thinking seems impossible in the Japanese case because, as discussed earlier, the symbol of Japanese blood does not refer to genetic differences as such. The racialized symbol of Japanese blood enhances, and is enhanced by, the sentiment that "we" constitute a kin group whose members have interacted among "ourselves" to perpetuate "our" lineage in isolation from other peoples. This fostered sense of psychological distance between "us" and "them" facilitates the notion that only "we" can share with one another "our" unique modes of thinking and behaving. This type of race thinking may best be called "perceptual association." It would be highly unrealistic to attempt to establish a deterministic relationship between race and culture (i.e., genetic determinism) as regards the respondents' perception of Japanese identity.

It should be noted that the two cultural themes of the Nihonjinron, discussed earlier, and the racial theme concerning the uniracial (*tan'itsu minzoku*) and homogeneous composition of Japanese society, widely assumed in the Nihonjinron, are closely interrelated. The Japanese patterns of communication, which supposedly discourage logical and verbal confrontation, are closely related to the high valuation of consensus and harmony in interpersonal relations, and empathetic, affective, and nonlogical communication is believed to be characteristic of tan'itsu society. What is important here is that the concept of "minzoku" can be interpreted to mean race, ethnic community, nation, or the combination of all these. Racial, ethnic, and national categories rather vaguely overlap in the Japanese perception of themselves. "Tan'itsu minzoku" is a convenient phrase to indicate the oneness and homogeneity of the Japanese people without specifying whether one is referring to racial or cultural features. Such ambiguities surrounding the relation between race and culture underlie what I call perceptual association.

Up to this point, we have discussed the perceptions of Japanese identity among "the Japanese" as a whole without carefully distinguishing the concerns of the cultural elites who "produced" the Nihonjinron (works on Japanese distinctiveness) and those of other educated groups who "consumed" such works. The perceptions of the two groups are similar, partly because the Nihonjinron may have influenced the perceptions of educated Japanese in general and partly because both groups may already have been under the influence of culturalist and racialist modes of thinking that had originated in previous periods. This would be impossible to judge empirically. It would probably be most appropriate to say that, to a much greater extent than previously, culturalism and racialism have been brought into active consciousness with the emergence of the Nihonjinron of the 1970s and 1980s. We shall, therefore, examine the manners in which the Nihonjinron have reinforced the culturalism and racialism of the educated sections of the Japanese population.

It is easy to suppose that the Nihonjinron represent a nationalist ideology that elites consciously produced with the intention of disseminating a culturalist and racialist view of Japanese identity. In fact, the Nihonjinron are commonly identified by critics as such an ideology, invented by elites to manipulate the masses into nationalism by attributing Japan's economic success and its apparent lack of serious social problems (e.g., crime, drugs, social divisions) to the unique virtues of Japanese social relations.[13] It would be grossly simplistic, however, to hold the assumptions associated with classic nationalism and to suppose that cultural and political elites consciously produced nationalist ideology in the form of the Nihonjinron in order to disseminate nationalism among the masses. (It would be impossible to know their intentions, anyway. Some of the major works of the

Nihonjinron were published in the 1970s, and even if we had a chance to talk to the writers, they would probably try to see themselves, retrospectively, as having had right motives.) Rather, I shall argue from the standpoint of consumption of ideas that the view that simplistically assumes ideological manipulation "from above" is inappropriate. There may have been sections of the population who, as is commonly believed, were directly influenced by the Nihonjinron to become more nationalistic, but the number of such people was strictly limited. After all, the Nihonjinron were an elite affair, and my findings suggest that the majority of ordinary educated people tended not to concern themselves directly with abstract theories of society and culture.[14] In order better to understand the relationship of the Nihonjinron to the development of contemporary cultural nationalism, I draw attention to a process whereby ideas of cultural differences are reproduced and consumed in the popular marketplace of ideas.

Internationalism

Earlier in this chapter, I discussed two types of concern that tend to characterize primary and secondary nationalism: a historicist concern with ancestral origin and myth, and a spatial and "sociological" concern with cultural and behavioral differences, respectively. On the basis of this typology, we may make a further generalization. In primary nationalism, the interest of ordinary people (that is, those who are not professional thinkers) in ancestral history is aroused from above. History is taught rather unilaterally to them through the medium of formal education, which is often conducted, as was the case in prewar Japan, through the power of the state. By contrast, the behavioral distinctiveness of a people, an important source of national identity in secondary nationalism, is part and parcel of the everyday life of ordinary people. The role of cultural elites here is to provide those people with perspectives from which to think more systematically about their society and behavior. Ordinary Japanese often consumed the Nihonjinron out of their practical concerns for understanding and solving concrete problems that confronted them in their immediate surroundings. In particular, the Nihonjinron provided those interested in intercultural communication with supposedly useful ideas on cultural differences.[15] It is incumbent on us, therefore, to pay attention to the ways in which the Nihonjinron have been popularized and reproduced to suit the interests of ordinary people.

Of particular importance here is the role of "reproductive intellectuals" (Shils 1972: 22) or "cultural intermediaries" (Bourdieu 1992: 371), who rephrased academics' theories of Japanese society and culture to suit more practical concerns and reproduced them in a form that could be consumed by ordinary people. This was an important channel through which academics' Nihonjinron were disseminated to a wider readership. The majority of my respondents familiarized themselves with academic works on Japanese distinctiveness (such as Nakane's vertical society theory) through reference to them in writings by business elites—an epitome of this type of cultural intermediary. Bourdieu refers to the members of such groups as "new intellectuals" who stand between "classic" intellectuals and the masses. They are popularizers of intellectuals' ideas in contemporary society. Eisenstadt (1972: 18) makes a similar point, remarking that "reproductive" intellectuals—"secondary intellectuals," in his words—"serve as channels of institutionalization, and even as possible creators of new types of symbols of cultural orientations, of traditions, and of collective and cultural identity."

Interestingly, Japanese companies played a nonnegligible role in popularizing and disseminating the Nihonjinron by publishing what may be called "cross-cultural manuals," that is, handbooks, English-learning materials, and glossaries that deal in one way or another with the distinctiveness of Japanese society in the contexts of business and management practices, company employees' everyday lifestyle, "untranslatable" Japanese expressions, and so forth.[16] In these cross-cultural manuals, the Nihonjinron are popularized in such a way that their consumers may apply "theories" of cultural difference to practical issues. Perhaps best illustrative of this point is the type of handbook that combines practical English study with "insights" on cultural differences, both of which are considered necessary tools by many educated Japanese for them to achieve the desired status of a *kokusaijin* (international person). Many of these manuals published by companies were originally intended for, and distributed to, their employees and students (or prospective employees). Although these concerns are especially relevant to business elites working in increasingly multinational corporations—and this is why those elites may be regarded as the role model of reproducers and consumers of these manuals—the concerns are not restricted to business elites and can be expected to be shared by anyone interested in international contacts, such as students and tourists.

The many cultural intermediaries who reproduced the Nihonjinron had, or claimed to have, good intentions: to improve intercultural communication between Japanese and non-Japanese, and to promote the emergence of large numbers of internationally minded Japanese with knowledge about cultural differences and the ability to communicate well in intercultural settings.[17] Many reproducers of the Nihonjinron might best be described as would-be internationalists. Ironically, however, this interest in internationalization and intercultural communication has tended to result in cultural nationalism because of the assumption held by Japanese cultural elites that intercultural communication is made difficult by the unique peculiarities of Japanese patterns of behavior and thought.

It may be useful to elaborate on this point a little further. Wallman understands ethnicity as "the process by which '*their*' difference is used to enhance the sense of 'us' for the purposes of organization or identification" (1979: 3; emphasis added). In the Nihonjinron and their popularized cross-cultural manuals, it is not "their" difference but "our" difference that is actively used to rearticulate Japanese identity. This may seem a small point, but it illustrates the way Japanese elites define Japanese "uniqueness." These elites have long perceived their culture to be on the periphery in relation to the "central" civilizations (first of China, then of the West) and have constructed and reconstructed Japanese identity by emphasizing "our" *particularistic* difference from the *universal* "them."[18] For example, in discussing the nonverbal, nonlogical, and emotive patterns of communication of the Japanese as opposed to the verbal, logical, and rational patterns of Westerners, Japanese elites have assumed "our" patterns to be an exception and "theirs" the norm. These elites have thus tended to see it as natural to adapt themselves to the more "universal" ways of the West.

Conscious recognition of Japanese peculiarities was, therefore, considered the first step toward better intercultural understanding. However, if an attempt to improve intercultural communication is accompanied by an excessive emphasis on Japanese difference and if it neglects those aspects of life common to different peoples, its unintended consequence can be the strengthening of cultural nationalism. In fact, the large increase in publications on Japanese distinctiveness had the effect of emphasizing Japanese difference to the extent that the commonality between Japanese and non-Japanese was neglected. Individually, most writings on Japanese distinctiveness may have had the well-intentioned aim of facilitating intercultural communication. Collectively, they have had the unintended consequence of sensitizing the Japanese excessively to their distinctiveness and thereby creating another obstacle to communication. The resultant racialist assumption that foreign residents cannot understand Japanese people because of the latter's supposedly unique mode of thinking and behaving has actually obstructed foreign residents' adaptation to social life in Japan. In this sense, an interest in intercultural communication and cultural nationalism are two sides of the same coin.

Of course, it would be oversimplifying to attribute cultural nationalism in contemporary Japan solely to an interest in internationalization, and I should hasten to emphasize that this chapter does not aim to furnish an overview of contemporary Japanese nationalism. Nationalism works differently for different groups and for different individuals, and diverse processes are at work in forming it. Nonetheless, a concern with internationalization is one of the most significant factors contributing to the reemphasis of Japanese distinctiveness in contemporary Japan. Scholars who cling to the classic view of nationalism may emphasize the role of the state, which is undoubtedly one agent of cultural nationalism. But precisely because state-initiated nationalism centers on obviously nationalistic ideas and symbols, it fails to elicit voluntary and positive support from large sections of the population. Restraints on any expression of nationalism are still noticeably strong among significant elements of the Japanese population. There have always been large numbers of people whose opposition to nationalism is reinforced by the presence of nationalistic symbols and practices, such as the singing of the Kimigayo anthem and the display of the *Hinomaru* flag, "National Foundation Day," the Education Ministry's control of the content of history teaching, and so on. Writing on similar nationalistic rituals in Britain, Robert Bocock (1974: 98) argues that they "may also make some groups feel less part of the national group in that they are made conscious of the fact that they do not share some of the values which seem to lie behind the group's ritual," such as respect for established authority and military virtues. He cites as examples some groups in Britain who find their sense of separateness from the mainstream society enhanced and their disrespect of established authority and military values reinforced when they witness rituals involving the royal family (e.g., Trooping the Colour, the monarch's Christmas Day speech, the state opening of Parliament). Use of nationalistic symbols has its own unintended consequences. By contrast, internationalization is an agenda that appeals favorably to many sections of contemporary Japanese society that do not wish to see a revival of narrow-minded nationalism of the prewar type. Yet, ironically, efforts to internationalize often end up promoting cultural nationalism.

Changing Perceptions of Japanese Identity

National identity is not a static entity; it should be understood within a changing framework. Three types of changes may briefly be pointed out by way of conclusion. First, discourse on Japanese uniqueness now tends to be identified as problematic in the international political scene, and many cultural elites have become careful not to overemphasize the "intrinsic difference" of Japanese society and culture. Expressions of Japanese identity are changing to reflect this development. Second, and relatedly, use of the idiom "tan'itsu minzoku" is likely to attract strong criticism against the backdrop of the now dominant trend toward demythologization of "uniracial" Japan. The myth of homogeneous Japan is now being challenged in light of the increasing number of migrant workers from Southeast Asia, the Middle East, and other developing regions; this increase makes it unrealistic to refer to Japan (at least urban Japan) as being homogeneous. A critique of the homogeneity myth is also being encouraged by a growing scholarly interest in ethnicity and nationalism. There has been a steady increase in the number of scholars exploring hitherto neglected ethnic phenomena in Japan, such as Okinawa as an "ethnic community."

Third, the notion of racially exclusive possession of Japanese culture is being called into question by the increasing presence on the one hand of foreign-looking foreigners who can speak Japanese just as naturally as "the native Japanese," and on the other of Japanese returnees from abroad (*kikokushijo*) whose behavior and use of the Japanese language appear "unnatural." These cases of "very Japanese" foreigners and "not very Japanese" Japanese have generated a lack of fit between cultural and racial boundaries of difference, thereby causing inconsistency in and inefficacy of the symbolic boundary system that defines Japanese identity. The assumption that those who speak and behave like the Japanese should be racially Japanese, and vice versa, is being challenged through the experience of such "boundary dissonance."[19]

It may be appropriate to conclude with an additional remark on kikokushijo, since the problems they face are symbolic of the issues relating to culturalism, racialism, and internationalism in contemporary Japan. The plight, real or imaginary, of Japanese returnees from overseas has been identified as a social problem in Japan for some time now. While returnees are often reported to undergo a stressful process of readjustment because of their foreignness, that acquired foreignness is also a resource that they can, and often do, exploit to pursue their interests as a new generation of internationalized Japanese in a society where internationalization is a national agenda. We may even suggest that returnee children today are overprotected by, for example, special measures to facilitate their reentry into the Japanese education system, such as exemptions from highly competitive entrance examinations, because of the recent trend to view returnees as a catalyst for positive change in schools and society. Here, a question may be raised as to "whether or not these returning children are international in ways useful to Japanese organizations or in ways helpful to themselves" (White 1992: 37). The mere experience of living in a foreign country does not make one international. For example, children whose overseas experience is limited to southern California probably assume that the Californian lifestyle is the international way. Such an attitude is anticosmopolitan and conducive to the same old process of constructing the Californian way of life as universal and Japanese behavior as peculiar or peripheral in the sense mentioned above. The readjustment difficulty among returnees is not specific to Japan, as many scholars claim. I know of many young men and women in Europe and Asia who, having returned from a long stay abroad, found it difficult to readjust to life back "home." Interestingly, this difficulty is not defined in these countries as a social problem but is simply regarded as a case of unsuccessful readjustment on the part of each individual. This point helps draw our attention to the possibility that the problematization of the returnee issue in Japan may be a process whereby educators, policy-makers, the media, and returnees themselves unconsciously participate in the reinvention of the myth of Japanese uniqueness. Here, too, efforts at internationalizing may paradoxically have the unintended consequence of promoting cultural and racial nationalism, thereby possibly making the situation even harder for returnees.

2

A Conceptual Model for the Historical Relationship Between the Self and the Internal and External Others

THE AGRARIAN JAPANESE, THE AINU, AND THE SPECIAL-STATUS PEOPLE

EMIKO OHNUKI-TIERNEY

THIS chapter examines the development of and representations by the dominant social group and minorities in Japanese society. I argue that the majority-minority discourse within Japanese society must be viewed in the context of the Japanese relations with various foreigners, but especially those who were seen by the Japanese as "superior" in some sense. I propose a model for the construction and representation of alterity as a powerful historical force. It explains the dialectical relationships between the *internal others* (minorities), *external others* (foreigners), and the self or selves of the dominant social group; each relationship is profoundly affected by power inequality. I hope that it serves as a cross-cultural model.

Although the notion of "minorities" and "majority" seems relatively clear-cut at first, it is an enormously complex issue. First, if we take a historical perspective, in many societies minority groups are often not unilinear cloistered groups throughout history. Second, social stratification in general and gender must also be taken into consideration. For example, do women constitute a "caste" group and, if so, how does the "caste system" relate to other systems of stratification, such as class?

The "unmarked majority," as Gladney (1994: 103) puts it, in Japanese society, I believe, is the agrarian Japanese and their "descendants." Importantly, the powerful among the agrarian Japanese were nonproductive members, such as the aristocrats and warriors, many of whom did not directly engage in agricultural production.[1] In contemporary Japan, minorities include the Ainu, Okinawans, *hisabetsu burakumin*, Koreans, Chinese,

Thai and other Asians, Middle Easterners, "Westerners," and so forth.[2] This chapter is about the historical process of construction and representation of two of these minority groups—the Ainu and the hisabetsu burakumin—by the dominant Japanese. I chose these two social groups because I have studied them in some depth.[3] Our investigation must begin with an understanding of the development of "Agrarian Japan" as *the* Japan, followed by a description of each of these two internal others. It concludes with a discussion of the interrelationships among the representations by the agrarian Japanese of themselves and their internal others, and of how the dialectic is affected by the Japanese perception of the external others (Chinese and Westerners).

Agrarian Japan—The Dominant Representation of Japan

Rice as Deities

Wet-rice agriculture was introduced into Japan around 400 B.C.[4] and gradually supplanted the previous hunting-gathering subsistence economy that had begun with the first occupation of the archipelago around 200,000 B.C. Wet-rice agriculture provided the economic foundation for the Yamato state and what later became the imperial family.

The first written account of the meaning of rice in Japanese culture is found in two myth-histories of the eighth century. They were commissioned by the Tenmu emperor, who sought to establish a Japanese identity distinct from that of Tang China (Kawasoe 1980: 253–54), whose influence was engulfing Japan. These myth-histories, the *Kojiki* and the *Nihongi*, dated A.D. 712 and 720 respectively, are replete with references to rice as deities. In one version in the *Kojiki*, Amaterasu (the Sun Goddess) is the mother of a grain soul whose name bears reference to rice stalks. The legendary Jinmu emperor, the so-called first emperor, is the son of the grain soul and, therefore, the grandson of Amaterasu, who sends him to rule the earth.[5] At the time of his descent, Amaterasu gives her grandson the original rice grains that she has grown in two fields in Heaven (Takamagahara) from the seeds of various types of grains[6] given to her by Ukemochi no Kami, the deity in charge of food (Kurano and Takeda 1958; Murakami 1977: 13). The grandson of Amaterasu transforms a wilderness into a land of succulent ears of rice (*mizuho*) and other grains, grown from the original seeds given to him by Amaterasu, whose rays nurture rice and other plants.

In contrast to the creation myths of other peoples, this version of the Japanese creation myth is not about the creation of a universe (see below for other versions of this episode). Rather, it is about the transformation of a wilderness (*ashihara no nakatsu no kuni*) into a land of abundant rice at the command of Amaterasu, whose descendants, the emperors, rule the country by officiating at rice harvest rituals (Kawasoe 1980: 86; Saigō 1984 [1967]: 15–29).

Put another way, the myth-history is an attempt to appropriate rice, introduced from outside Japan, as Japanese rice, grown by Japanese deities. This creation myth codifies a symbolic equation of rice with deities, who in the Japanese view have both positive and negative power (*nigimitama* and *aramitama*). In my interpretation, the soul of the rice grain is not simply equivalent to deities but is identified more specifically as the positive power of divine purity, or the nigimitama.[7] Since human life wanes unless the positive principle replenishes its energy, individuals and their communities must rejuvenate themselves by harnessing the deities' positive power.[8] This they do either by performing a ritual during which they harness the positive power or, alternatively, by internalizing the divine purity by consuming rice. Rice and rice products therefore became the most important food for commensality between humans and deities, on the one hand, and among humans, on the other (Yanagita 1982 [1940]). Even in daily life, rice is the only common dish, distributed usually by the woman of the house, while all other dishes are served individually. "To eat from the same rice cooker" (*onaji kama no meshi o kuu*) therefore is a common expression referring to "us," as opposed to "them."

Rice as Nature, Rice as Past, Rice as Primordial Self

Later in history when the intensification of urbanization prompted cultural construction of nature, rice and rice agriculture became synonymous with "Japanese nature." Thus, although the valorization of the countryside by intellectuals and artists, as epitomized in rice paddies, began earlier, we see its systematic development during the late Edo period when Edo (Tokyo) became the urban center (Harootunian 1988: 23). Nowhere is the construction of the countryside more vividly depicted than in the woodblock prints (*ukiyo-e*) of the time.[9] Rice fields against the background of Mt. Fuji became a common motif to represent "agrarian Japan," that is, "Japan." Travelers, often depicted in these woodblocks, symbolize the transient and changing Japan epitomized by Edo, where they are headed, while rice and rice agriculture stand for Japan in its pristine, unchanging form.[10]

From the perspective of temporal representation, the recurrent motif of rice and rice agriculture in these woodblock prints represents not rice and rice agriculture per se, but something more. At the most obvious level, it signals the four seasons of the year. Flooded rice fields, like rice-planting songs, are the most familiar sign of spring or early summer, the time of birth and growth. Scenes related to rice harvesting represent fall and its joyful harvest at the end of the growing season. These cycles of rice growth became markers of the seasons for all Japanese. The lives of urbanites, fishermen, and all other nonagrarian people were marked by rice and its growth. In addition, agriculture symbolizes the past. The pristine past, representing the primordial Japanese identity, uncontaminated by foreign influences and modernity as represented by the city, is symbolized in the reconstituted agriculture and the rural.[11]

Symbolic equation of the primordial Japanese self with agriculture and countryside continued through the Meiji period (Gluck 1985: 175, 181) and remains strong even today when the Japanese search for nature in the countryside, now nostalgically referred to as *furusato* (old homestead; literally, one's home region). Far from the "reality" of mud, sweat, and fertilizer, rice agriculture was valorized into aesthetics, in much the same way rural France and peasants were idealized by Millet and impressionists, most notably Monet (cf. Brettell and Brettell 1983), and just as English urbanites today construct their "English countryside," often on the cover of chocolate boxes (Newby 1979; R. Williams 1973).[12] Here we see a striking cross-cultural parallel in that urbanization created a need for "the rural" in many societies (Berque 1990). In part for the same reason, it is the post-industrial nations, such as France and Japan, rather than the predominantly agricultural nations, that place obstacles in the way of trade negotiations on agricultural products, as we see today in the GATT negotiations.

In sum, the agrarian cosmology-turned-ideology gave rise to symbolic expressions of rice paddies, ancestral land, and family farmland as *pristine nature*-cum–Japanese land, which, from the temporal perspective, stands for the *pristine past*. Together they stand for the primordial self of the Japanese—all the Japanese.

Summary: Nature in Japanese Culture

As in any culture, there are various natures in Japanese culture, of which the nature represented by rice and rice paddies became the most elevated and articulated for all Japanese. The nature represented by rice has two major characteristics. First, rice as nature represents purity, that is, the purity of the Japanese, as is obvious in the discussion above. Second, since around the seventh century, the dominant representation of nature has become almost exclusively inhabited by plants. Hunting, various forms of rituals involving animals, and meat consumption all became tabooed beginning in the seventh century (N. Harada 1993). Nature ceased to include animals, except animals that are considered messengers from deities.[13]

"Nature without animals" is the other side of the development of Agrarian Japan,[14] which was symbolically equated with the transformation of wilderness into the land of succulent grains of rice. Plants became hegemonic, as it were, writing off from history the hunting that preceded agriculture. This disjunction is somewhat curious,[15] since if we take a purely quantitative approach to time, the period during which Japan's subsistence economy was primarily agriculture lasted a mere two thousand years—far fewer than the preceding periods (50,000 B.P.–250 B.C.), during which Japan's subsistence economy was hunting-gathering.[16] One might argue, on the other hand, that the relatively short duration of the agricultural period does not negate the importance of agriculture because it provided the economic base for the development of Japan as a nation-state. In fact, the very foundation of the imperial system was an agrarian economy and agrarian cosmology.[17] In addition, the prohibition on killing animals had much to do with the introduction and successful development in Japan of Buddhism, which advocated mercy for all living beings. At any rate, for the Japanese in the past as well as today, hunting-gathering, which lasted a very long time, and pastoralism, which never existed, do not hold much fascination. The Japanese vision of nature has little room for wild nature, in sharp contrast to some European cultures, in which hunting and pastoralism have been of great importance, both economically and symbolically.[18]

Internal Others

Although my preamble on Agrarian Japan seems a long detour, it enables us to understand the historical developments and the meanings and values assigned to the internal others, or the minorities, in Japanese society. I propose that the development of Agrarian Japan had two significant consequences. First, it accorded a central position in Japanese society to the settled population, whereby landlessness became transgression. Second, it established a symbolic equation of the self of the dominant Japanese with plants, which in turn gave birth to a symbolic association between the marginalized populations and the negative side of nature represented by "beasts." The first development was responsible for the formation of the social group called hisabetsu burakumin at present, and the second was responsible for the particular nature of the negativity assigned to both the burakumin and the Ainu, on the one hand, and for the initial positioning by the Japanese of Westerners at the external margin, on the other.

The Special-Status People (Hisabetsu Burakumin)

The stereotypical image of what I call the special-status people held until recently by the dominant Japanese was that they engaged in defiling occupations throughout history. While this is in part true, a closer look at the history of special-status people shows that their ancestry consists of heterogeneous people of diverse occupations, some of which the dominant Japanese would no longer associate with them today. Furthermore, there is no clear-cut linear descent line linking the people from one historical period to those of another (T. Harada 1978a, 1978b; Noguchi 1978; Ueda 1978a, 1978c). Most importantly, the meaning and cultural valuation assigned to the occupations and the people who held them have gone through significant transformations over time.

Perhaps the only common denominator of special-status people throughout history is that they have engaged in nonagrarian occupations, including religious, artistic, and artisan specializations. Since they have not been a monolithic group cloistered from the rest of the Japanese throughout history, no single label, even in Japanese, is either appropriate or actually in use to refer to them. I adopted Susan Tax Freeman's suggestion to use the designation "special-status" people,[19] since it is neutral in terms of value and can be both positive and negative, just as the values assigned to the people have been at different historical times. I also use other designations, such as *senmin* (base people), burakumin (settlement people), and so forth, which have been used at different periods in Japanese history. I do not use the latter terms in any derogatory sense. Likewise, I use the terms "outcaste" or, sometimes, "former outcaste" only to refer to the historical fact that, during the Early Modern period, their designated status was below that of the four castes that were believed to constitute Japanese society. The official-legal designation today is "hisabetsu burakumin," which literally means "the people of settlements under discrimination."

Although Japanese society has always been stratified, even during the Ancient period, the late Medieval period was critical in the development of special-status people as a minority in Japanese society. During the first half of the Medieval period, their occupations were quite varied in nature, and they were not clearly demarcated from other occupations, indicating beyond doubt that the special-status people did not constitute a well-defined, separate group within the society. Furthermore, the values assigned to these people and to their occupations were often ambiguous, having both positive and negative meaning and power. For example, since entertainment and performing arts were considered primarily of a religious nature, performers, together with shamans and other noninstitutionalized religious specialists, were considered to be mediators between humans and deities who fetched the positive power of deities on behalf of humans. During the latter half of the late Medieval period, however, while the general dynamics of society and culture continued to be at work, certain occupations of the special-status people came to be viewed as impure; impurity by then had become radical negativity.

If we combine the categories of occupations proposed by Noguchi (1978: 91) and Ninomiya (1933: 74–76, 85–86), the list contains the following occupations for the special-status people during the Medieval period: (1) cleaners of temples, shrines, and their compounds, who also cared for the dead; (2) landscape architects as well as general construction workers; (3) plasterers, carpenters, and arms manufacturers; (4) butchers, tanners, and makers of leather goods; (5) dyers and manufacturers of bamboo articles; (6) entertainers, prostitutes, and diviners; and (7) undertakers and tomb caretakers.[20] Two common denominators of their occupations are readily discernible. First, all of them were nonagrarian. Second, several of them deal with culturally defined impurity.

Medieval society consisted of two systems: one governing "residents," who constituted the core of the agrarian sector of the society, and the other governing "nonresidents." Called the *heimin* (common people), residents were full-fledged members of society who were free in that they were not owned by other individuals and were allowed to be armed and to move freely. They were, however, under obligation to pay taxes. The other class of residents, consisting of two categories (the *genin* and *shojū*), were owned by other individuals and did not have "the right to be taxed" (Amino 1980: 22–23).

"Nonresidents" were also composed of two categories: the *shokunin* (professionals) and the special-status people, then loosely called *eta hinin*. The professionals enjoyed the legally and socially sanctioned privilege of being exempt from taxes, either partially or entirely.[21] In addition to having the right not to pay regular taxes, some of the shokunin were able to cross regional boundaries freely without being checked or assessed taxes, unlike the heimin. Therefore they were able to engage in cross-regional trade of their crafts.[22]

While many eta hinin were without permanent residence, those who resided in a settlement did so at its boundaries, such as along riverbanks, under bridges, or near slopes. Since rivers, hills, and mountains provided natural demarcation lines between settlements, these locations represented places away from the central or main part of the settlement. During the Medieval period, the term *kawaramono* (people of the riverbanks) was therefore applied to people who resided at these places, where no tax was assessed (Yokoi 1982: 335–39). Another term, *sansho*, referred both to these marginal areas and to the people who occupied them. The sansho people held no land and no land tax was levied against them (Noguchi 1978: 89). The term "sansho" literally means "the scattered place"; it contrasts with *honsho*, which means either "central" or "real" place (Yokoi 1982: 337–39). Hayashiya (1980: 130–31) maintains that "sansho" means "nontaxable." In the Japanese society of the time, "nontaxable" also meant "marginal" or other than normal, since tax was levied against land and earnings. Thus the term "sansho" expressed spatial marginality, which in turn was applied to the special-status people who lived on untaxed land, and yet it did not carry an extremely negative meaning as in later times.[23]

In addition to those who were called shokunin, kawaramono, and so on, a number of other types of nonresident population were loosely included in the special-status group. They included *mooto* (outsiders), *kojiki* (beggars), *hijiri* (saints), and the *hinin*. A brief explanation of the hinin category of people during this period succinctly illustrates the nature of the special-status people at the time—marginal without being negative in valuation. A group of people called hinin first appeared during the early phase of the Heian period (794–1185) and became more visible in cities only after the mid-Heian period (Takayanagi 1981: 11–13). Although the literal meaning of the term "hinin" is "nonhuman," during the Medieval period the term referred to those individuals who voluntarily abandoned their society (Morita 1978: 79–80). The hinin included a small number of criminals who were expelled by the society and plain beggars who begged purely for economic rather than religious reasons. But many hinin were hijiri (saints) who primarily for religious reasons decided to leave society (*shukke*) and to reject the demands and responsibilities of their secular life as citizens, such as paying taxes (Kuroda 1972; Morinaga 1967; Takayanagi 1981).[24] Being outsiders to the system, the hijirior itinerant priests stood for an antistructural element in that their abandonment of society symbolically represented a critical stance against the institutionalized religions that were increasingly involved in political power (Kuroda 1972: 44–45).

Institutionalized means to rid themselves of their ascribed status were also available to distinguished artists,[25] providing a positive atmosphere for activities of artists and artisans. The activity of early migrant entertainers and craftsmen undoubtedly seeded the ground for the later efflorescence of folk arts during the latter half of the Medieval period. During later periods, the established arts of architecture, gardening, and the various performing arts of Kabuki, Noh, and *kyōgen* owe much to such people.[26]

The institutionalized means of getting out of one's ascribed status and the multiple system of stratification together provided opportunities whereby talented members of the special-status people gained direct access to centers of symbolic, religious, and political power. Renowned artists and architect-gardeners came under the special tutelage of the imperial court and the powerful warlords.

Formation of Special-Status People as the Internal Other

Flexibility and dynamics were not the only characteristics of the Medieval period. Its other side was the gradual development of occupational specialization, which significantly affected the culturally defined meaning assigned to special-status people. Some of the occupations of special-status people dealing with culturally defined impurity became separated from other types of occupations, and the practitioners of these defiling occupations were subjected to increasing devaluation.

Indicative of the basic transformation of the meaning of the people in these occupations is the steady decrease in status of, and increasing prejudice against, the aforementioned *ryōko*, caretakers of the imperial mausoleums, who claimed the highest status among the senmin during the Ancient period. They became the lowest in social ranking during the Medieval period. The tendency was already under way by the end of the Heian period (Ninomiya 1933: 71) but continued to be formalized throughout the Medieval period. The degradation process is attributed to the intensification of the notion of defilement assigned to corpses, and by extension, to those who handled them (ibid.).

It should be noted here that the concept of the impurity of corpses had always been in the value system of the Japanese: already in the oldest written sources, the *Kojiki* (712) and the *Norito* (927), killing, handling of corpses, and illnesses were all clearly defined not only as impurities but as sins (for details see Ohnuki-Tierney 1984: 35–38). During the Medieval period, with the influence of Buddhism, impure objects and activities extended from human deaths and corpses to dead animals and all activities associated with them. Consequently, many of the occupations of the special-status people came to be regarded as defiling (Yokoi 1982: 267–94). The defiling occupations included those of butchers, tanners, makers of leather goods, falconers, cormorant fishermen, undertakers, caretakers of tombs, executioners, tatami floor-mat makers, footgear manufacturers, and sweepers. All of these occupations involved dealings with culturally defined impurity which derived from death and "dirt." Butchers and falconers handled dead animal bodies, and tanners and makers of leather goods handled hides of dead animals. Undertakers, caretakers of tombs, and executioners were associated with human corpses. The tatami floor mat and footgear are culturally impure because they are touched by feet, the part of the human body that is most defiled because of contact with the ground, that is, "dirt" in a cultural sense. Sweepers remove dirt. (For details on this topic, see Ohnuki-Tierney 1984: 19–50). The special-status people who engaged in these occupations were "the specialists in impurity," as Dumont (1970: 48) would put it; they specialized in dealing with culturally defined dirt/impurity, thereby sparing others the inevitable problems of doing so. Nevertheless, they were seen to be defiled themselves.

A brief history of the term *eta*, a term frequently used for the special-status people from the thirteenth century to the present, illustrates the process whereby these occupations and the people who engaged in them became devalued. Although the interpretation of the term "eta" in different periods of history has been quite controversial among scholars, many agree that the term appeared for the first time in history in the *Chiribukuro* (A dust bag), a document dated 1280 (Morita 1978: 86; Noguchi 1978: 88). Here the term "eta," written in the *kana* (syllabary) and not in characters, referred to the *kiyome* (purifiers; sweepers) and did not carry a derogatory connotation.

By the latter half of the fourteenth century, the pronunciation had changed to "etta." It had already acquired a derogatory connotation and referred to various people, including sweepers, who resided on riverbanks and in other peripheral areas. Significantly, according to the *Ainoshō*, a manuscript dated 1446, two characters were superimposed upon the term previously used only orally: the character for "impurity" was assigned to the sound "e," and the character for "many/much" to "ta." In other words, the term "eta," which referred neutrally to sweepers during the thirteenth century, had become "etta," written in two characters meaning "excessive impurity," by the mid-fifteenth century (Morita 1978: 88–89). In short, by the end of the Medieval period, the meaning of the special-status people engaged in "defiling" occupations was firmly and negatively embedded in the value structure of Japanese culture. All the terms associated with these occupations and people, including "sansho" and "kiyome," had gone through a similar transformation of meaning, receiving strong negative value by the end of the Medieval period (Amino 1980: 9–11).

The establishment of Tokugawa society at the beginning of the seventeenth century signaled major changes in Japanese culture and society that took place during the following three hundred years. Externally, the government tried to eliminate influences from outside, enforcing the closure of the nation by restricting trade and closing ports to most foreigners, and proscribing Christianity. Internally, the Early Modern period (1603–1868) witnessed the development of a "caste society"[27] divided into four castes (warriors, farmers, manufacturers, and merchants, in descending order), plus two social categories outside the system—the emperor at the top and the outcaste at the bottom.

The attempt by the military to take control of the entire nation, partly accomplished through forced settlement of the population for census purposes, had been under way since the latter half of the thirteenth century (Inoue et al. 1978: 169–70). This tendency reached its height at the end of the sixteenth century under the rule of Hideyoshi. In 1582 he recognized land tenure among the special-status people and, at the same time, created two legally defined categories. Thus, while the special-status people had been loosely called "eta hinin," some of them, including those who were previously called "kiyome" and "sansho," were legally defined as *kawata*, while others were defined as hinin (Ueda 1978b: 100–101). The *kawata-eta* alone were defined to have a permanent, hereditary status. Legally, the hinin were placed lower than the kawata-eta, although they were able to move up to the farmer, craftsman, or merchant class under highly specified circumstances. Later, a number of rules were issued in order to place the special-status people under the strict political control of the military government and to regulate their occupations (Ueda 1978b).

In 1710, the actors for Kabuki, Noh, and kyōgen were legally freed from their outcaste status. Other artistic and religious specializations, especially those called *zatsugei* (miscellaneous arts) and *daidōgei* (street performances), were not recognized as forms of art or religion and thus received increasing devaluation (cf. Murasaki 1983: 10).[28]

Marginalizing the emperor and the outcastes by placing them outside of society clearly developed a social structure basically different from that of the Medieval period. Thus, instead of having a multiple structure of stratification in which the emperor-professionals (shokunin) constituted a separate structure, the emperor and the special-status people—including some of the professionals of the Medieval period—belonged to a system that was subordinated to the structure that was considered the core of Japanese society. Many scholars (e.g., T. Harada 1978a; Price 1966: 23; Yokoi 1982: 336) believe that the extreme legal and social discrimination against the special-status people that has persisted until today originated in this period.[29]

The crucial question here is which of the professionals (shokunin) and the religious-artistic specialists (jinin) of the Medieval period came to be included in: (1) the craftsman (*ko*) class; (2) the kawata-eta category and the hinin category respectively; and (3) miscellaneous groups of nonresidents who were not lumped into the two categories of special-status people and enjoyed freedom and mobility. Put the other way, the question is why only certain groups of people became special-status people and why.

Impurity as radical negativity was one important factor. The changing nature of the special-status people during the Early Modern period was also closely related to the development of a value system that stressed agrarian productivity. As the functional ethic, which Bellah (1970 [1957]: 114) calls economic rationalization and aligns with the Protestant ethic, came to govern the moral system of the period, the occupations, including those of special-status people, that were nonproductive in the agrarian sense became devalued.[30] The development of Agrarian Japan with its cosmology turning into ideology thus further contributed to the devaluation of special-status people as not productive.

At any rate, the naturalization process whereby the special-status people and their occupations were viewed as impure and morally inferior was firmly established during the Early Modern period and has persisted until the present.

Modern Period (1868–Present)

When the feudal society came to an end in 1868, the Meiji government made a series of legal reforms, including "emancipation" of the burakumin, the term most often used during the Modern period to refer to the special-status people. The government abolished the law forcing them to wear special clothing and removed restrictions that had confined them to traditional occupations. Noteworthy in recent history is the vigorous liberation movement in the 1920s, known as the Suiheisha movement, through which the special-status people attempted to achieve equality in the society. Their effort for liberalization was severely handicapped by Japan's involvement in wars, and the movement came to an end in 1942 (Akisada 1978).

Despite these efforts, both by the people themselves and, at least to some extent, by the government, the burakumin have remained victims of social discrimination. DeVos and Wagatsuma (1966) referred to them as "Japan's invisible race"; they are invisible because there are no physical characteristics to distinguish them from other Japanese.

Today a minority group in Japan, the hisabetsu burakumin are estimated to number three million people, localized in six thousand communities,[31] with a greater concentration in western Japan, especially in the Kinki district. Many hisabetsu burakumin are employed in small factories connected with their traditional occupations, such as leather and fur processing and butchering. Others are farmers, fishermen, and unskilled laborers. Although many individuals have become economically or socially prominent, the average standard of living is far below that of the non-burakumin. The hisabetsu burakumin have remained mostly endogamous, due to intense prejudice on the part of the non-burakumin. The most common feature of prejudice against the hisabetsu burakumin is the attribution of "uncleanliness" (Donoghue 1966: 138). The Japanese government has made some effort to provide them with special funds for housing and has prohibited job discrimination against them. Japanese society is going through fundamental changes. It is too early to tell whether these changes have affected or will affect the basic symbolic structure of the Japanese and consequently ease, if not eliminate, the prejudice against the burakumin.[32]

The Ainu

The Ainu are a group of people in northern Japan whose traditional life was based upon a hunting-fishing and plant-gathering economy. Although only about eighteen thousand of the Ainu now live in Hokkaido, the northernmost island of Japan, this population was much larger in the past and their homeland included at least southern Sakhalin, the Kurile Islands, northern parts of Honshū (the main island of Japan), and adjacent areas. Despite outsiders' frequent use of the blanket term "the Ainu," Ainu culture was rich in intracultural variations.[33]

Not only was their hunting-gathering economy vastly different from that of their agricultural neighbors (the Japanese, Koreans, and Chinese), they spoke a language of their own, and some of their physical characteristics were thought to distinguish them from their neighbors. The question of Ainu identity continues to press today without a definitive answer.[34]

For all Ainu groups, however, trading with neighboring groups, which included the Aleuts and Kamchadals for those on the central and northern Kuriles, long preceded the systematic encroachment and subsequent colonization by the Japanese and Russians which started in the eighteenth century. Below I sketch primarily events that contributed to the formation of the Ainu as the internal other in Japanese society.[35]

In 1875 the central and northern Kuriles came under the political control of the Japanese government, which made several attempts to "protect" the Ainu, but without success and often with adverse effect upon them. The Kurile Ainu were the hardest-hit victims of the Russians and the Japanese; the last of them died in 1941. Sakhalin south of 50° N had been the homeland of the Sakhalin Ainu, while the territory north of 50° N belonged to the Gilyaks and other peoples. The Sakhalin Ainu, estimated to have been between 1,200 and 2,400 in number during the first half of the twentieth century, most likely moved from Hokkaido, possibly as early as the first millennium A.D., but definitely by the thirteenth century. They were in close contact with so-called native populations both on Sakhalin and along the Amur, such as the Gilyaks, Oroks, and Nanays. Chinese influence too reached the island, probably by the first millennium A.D. It was intensified between 1263 and 1320. This period saw Mongol colonization and the "pacification" of the Gilyaks and the Ainu, who submitted to the tribute system, which further victimized them.[36] With the dwindling of Manchu control over Sakhalin, the tribute system was discontinued at the beginning of the nineteenth century, by which time both the Japanese and the Russians were to take political control of the island and to mobilize its rich natural resources.[37]

The history of contact with outsiders is equally complicated for the Hokkaido Ainu, whose territory once included northeastern Honshu. As the Japanese central government was formed and its force expanded toward the northeast, the Ainu were gradually pushed north away from their territory. Systematic contact between the Ainu and the Japanese started at the end of the sixteenth century with the establishment of the Matsumae clan, which claimed as its territory the southwestern end of Hokkaido and the adjacent areas.[38] In 1799 the Matsumae territory in Hokkaido came under the direct control of the Tokugawa shogunate for the purpose of protecting Japanese interests against Russian expansion southward. Administrative control changed again in 1821 to the Matsumae and then back to the shogunate in 1854 (see Howell 1994). Most drastic and enduring changes took place shortly after the establishment of the Meiji government in 1868. The new government abolished the residential restriction for both the Ainu and the Japanese, who could then live anywhere in Hokkaido. It also encouraged the Japanese to emigrate to Hokkaido in order to utilize its natural resources. The Ainu were enrolled in the Japanese census registers and forced to attend Japanese schools established by the government. Beginning in 1883, the Ainu were uprooted from their settlements, granted plots of land more suited for agriculture, and encouraged to take up agriculture.[39]

Ainu as the Internal Other

Just as the Ainu contacts with the Japanese went through a series of historical changes, so did the Japanese attitude toward them. Since the Ainu homeland is located in what used to be Japan's northern frontier—a hinterland for many Japanese until recently—the Ainu stood outside of the reflexive structure of the Japanese during earlier historical periods. By the eighteenth century, however, the Ainu had clearly become one of the marginalized internal others within Japanese society. Historical agents directly involved in this process were the Japanese governmental officials of different historical periods and the Japanese in the Ainu land. They viewed and represented the Ainu as uncivilized or primitive. But the primitive always have another side—for some Japanese, especially those in parts of Japan distant from the Ainu homeland, the Ainu were and are even today the exotic other. This is especially so with Ainu women, living in "nature," whose "deep-set eyes" had exotic sexuality—a familiar picture in almost every case of colonial-colonized or majority-minority relationship, as articulated by Gladney (1994) and blatantly obvious, but not foregrounded, in Said (1978).

Nowhere is the otherness assigned to the Ainu more vividly expressed than in Japanese paintings of them. For example, in one illustration in *Shōtoku Taishi denryaku* (Biography of Prince Shōtoku), dated 1305, the Ainu are depicted with their hair standing straight up, in striking contrast to the Japanese courtiers and warriors, whose hair is meticulously tied (Sasaki 1990: 162–63, 180; Takakura 1953: 2–3). Or, in one scene in *Seisuiji engi emaki* (Picture scroll for the founding of Seisui Temple) by Tosa Mitsunobu, dated 1517, the Ainu are depicted with pointed ears and pug noses, like *oni* (fiends) or snakes (Sasaki 1990: 164, 182–83).

The Japanese perception and representation of the Ainu are most systematically expressed in a series of Ainu-e[40]—Japanese artists' portrayals of the Ainu and their lives that appeared during a period of a little more than a century, from the beginning of the eighteenth century to the mid-nineteenth century, that is, at the height of Japanese efforts to colonize Ainu territory. The hallmarks of otherness depicted in these paintings include hunting scenes, the bear ceremony, women's tattoos, men's body hair and beards, and Ainu use of jewelry (Izumi 1968a). In contrast to the Japanese, whose deities are primarily plants, the supreme deity of the Ainu is the bear—a sign of Ainu proximity to animals. The association the Japanese made between the Ainu and animals is also seen in their painstaking representations of the bodies of Ainu. The Japanese, who do not have much body hair, often point to the abundant body hair of the Ainu, as well as of Westerners, and use it as "evidence" that these peoples are close to animals.

In these paintings, Ainu eyebrows are frequently drawn together so that there is one continuous thick line of hair above the eyes. Representations of the eyes of the Ainu are quite striking and thus merit special attention. Although by no means uniform in shape throughout the paintings, they are represented in a way that contrasts them with those of the Japanese. For example, the famous series called *Ishū retsuzō* (Portraits of Ainu "chiefs"), produced in 1780 by Kakizaki Hakyō, consists of portraits of Ainu leaders who joined the force of the Matsumae clan at the time of the Ainu uprising called the Battle of Kunashiri and Menashi and is highly political in nature (Takakura 1953: 12–18). Various features used by the artist to mark the otherness of these Ainu include earrings, which the Japanese did not wear. What is striking is that the eyes are all depicted with the pupil surrounded by white on all sides—the type of eye called *sanpakugan*. Sasaki (1990: 193) interprets this to mean that, because sanpakugan is considered to be a *kyōsō*, an inauspicious feature of the face, the Ainu are thus portrayed as inauspicious.[41] Izumi (1968b) notes that, while the eyes in other *Ainu-e* are not all sanpakugan, the eyes of the Ainu both in Kakizaki's paintings and in those by Kodama Teiryō, who drew the Ainu around 1751–63, are "glaring eyes" (*girro to shita me*). Izumi considers these portraits to express the dignity of these leaders. According to Miyata Noboru (personal communication, 1994), the eyes of Japanese shamans are said to become sanpakugan at the time of trance and thus, according to him, the depiction of the Ainu eyes as such simply emphasizes that they are unusual, without discriminatory meaning.

It is worth comparing the Japanese representation of Ainu eyes with that of Japanese eyes and that of animals. At about the same time these *Ainu-e* were drawn, masters of woodblock prints propagated the classical beauty of the Japanese—*hiki-me kagi-bana*—narrow eyes and a narrow but tall nose. This is the technique developed during the Heian period to draw the faces of aristocratic women and men. While it was already known through various paintings, including the picture scroll of the tale of Genji (*Genji monogatari emakimono*), we see a heightened expression in the woodblock prints of Utamaro (1753–1806) and other masters. Noble men and women are drawn with these eyes and nose and fair skin, in contrast to peasants, who are portrayed with rounded eyes, pug nose, and dark skin. Note also that in Japanese visual representations, oni, dragons, and tigers are often depicted with the sanpakugan. The representations of the Ainu are similar to those of fierce and exotic animals, such as dragons and tigers. Dragons are mythical creatures and tigers do not live in Japan. Visual representations of both came from China and became a frequently drawn theme in Japanese paintings.

At the symbolic level, the Ainu therefore represented wild nature in Japanese culture, which had little room for its romanticization, unlike the West. Only in this context can we understand the profound significance of the label *dojin* (the dirt or earth people), a label for the Ainu. The term can mean simply "native people," but it refers more often to "unenlightened natives." Thus, the law to protect the Ainu was titled *Hokkaidō kyū-dojin hogohō* (the protection of the former natives of Hokkaido) (Hokkaidōchō 1934), and it refers to the Ainu as "the former dojin."[42] The Ainu are the only internal other who had been consistently referred to as the dojin, although the term was also applied later to some external others, such as Filipinos and Africans.

How did the Japanese then deal with the dojin? In 1799, when the Japanese government took direct control of the Ainu, it issued "instructions" to the officials in charge of the management of the Ainu. Two of the instructions read (for details, see Takakura 1960: 55–57):

> The Ezo [Ainu] are forbidden to use Japanese but, in areas where the Bakufu has taken over, the use of that language shall be permitted and in fact encouraged so

that the natives will more easily adopt our ways of life. Keep in mind however that they are to use our language and we are not to use theirs.

When the Ezo have become accustomed to our ways and traditions and there are those who wish to follow our customs then permit such to cut their hair and provide them with Japanese clothes. (Takakura 1960: 56)

Most important, however, was the Japanese policy to convert them into agriculturalists and rice consumers. In the same 1799 "instructions," the very first instruction reads:

Teach the Ezo, in due time, how to raise crops and live on cereals and to become used to our way of life. Even before you teach them to cultivate the land, try to *change their diet from meat to grain by telling them that cereals are much better than meat*. Then when the time comes to teach them how to *raise crops their progress will be much faster*. (Takakura 1960: 55; emphasis added)

This instruction is followed by: "When the Ezo are employed as laborers *they should be given rice*" (ibid.; emphasis added). Likewise, when the Meiji government passed the *Hokkaidō kyū-dojin hogohō* (The law for the protection of the former natives in Hokkaido) in 1898, the most important purpose was to encourage agriculture (Takakura 1932: 474).

In sum, the major instrument for the enlightenment of the "primitive Ainu" by the Japanese government during the eighteenth and the nineteenth centuries was to teach them, first of all, agriculture and a rice diet. We see a powerful hegemony of agrarian ideology at work in the colonization of the Ainu.

The Special-Status People and the Ainu as Internal Others

The development of the collective identity of the Japanese, as expressed in "rice as self" and "rice paddies as Japanese land," represents a historical process whereby those social groups who were not anchored to politically defined space became minorities—the internal others—whose presence was written off both from history and from the representation of Japan as Agrarian Japan, in which both symbolic and political centrality accrued to the settled population (warriors and farmers). From the perspective of symbolic structure, the process of naturalization of the agrarian cosmology-turned-ideology was accompanied by the naturalization of culturally constructed impurity and of the centrality of plants, especially rice. The agrarian Japanese were symbolically equated with purity and plants, while those who became the internal other represented animals and impurity. Furthermore, the politico-economic hegemony of the agrarian sector of Japan turned landlessness into transgression.

Note, on the other hand, that the social and symbolic relations of the

Ainu to the agrarian Japanese are in significant ways different from those of the special-status people. The special-status people have throughout history been an integral part of Japanese society. Agrarian Japanese would not have been able to function without their occupations, and they were part of the daily lives of the agrarian Japanese. The Ainu, on the other hand, emerged on the conceptual horizon of most Japanese only during the nineteenth century. Except for emigrés in Hokkaido and traders with the Ainu, most Japanese did not have daily contact with them. They were primitives who were clearly distinct from themselves, or at least the Japanese thought so.

As a corollary, the animals associated with the occupations of the special-status people are domesticated animals: cows, horses, and others. Some of them in their occupations either kill these animals for hides or dispose of their dead bodies. In contrast, the animals assigned to the Ainu were wild animals, from which the agrarian Japanese were afforded some distance.

Lack of distance then is the crucial factor in assigning impurity to the special-status people, but not to the Ainu—a fact that eloquently speaks for the role of special-status people in the reflexive structure of agrarian Japanese. We noted that in earlier times some of them were shamans and entertainers-cum-religious specialists who fetched the divine purity for agrarian Japanese. Later in history they became specialists in impurity who shouldered the impurity of agrarian Japanese, thereby purging them. This resembles the "scapegoat mechanism" by means of which, for example, in the Hitlerite cult of anti-Semitism, the Germans "ritualistically cleansed themselves by loading the burden of their own iniquities upon" the scapegoat, that is, the Jews (Burke 1955: 407). That is to say, the special-status people have always been assigned the role of keeping the Japanese pure; they did so as mediators by bringing in the pure and creative power of deities, and they do so as scapegoats by shouldering the impurity of the dominant Japanese. Mediators and scapegoats therefore carry out a like function, except in a reverse manner, for the maintenance of the purity of the self of the dominant Japanese (for details, see Ohnuki-Tierney 1987: 150–51). As elaborated elsewhere (ibid.: 154–59), taboos, such as impurity, are boundary markers. They separate the special-status people from the agrarian Japanese *precisely because of the proximity of the two.*

In sum, these two internal others stood opposite the agrarian Japanese. For the self of agrarian Japanese, represented by plants and assigned the value of purity, the Ainu stood for wild nature where special-status people stood for the negative side of animality and impurity.

Conclusion: Dialectic Between the Self and Internal and External Others

The particular character of otherness or alterity assigned to the internal others cannot be fully understood through the dialectic between the agrarian self and the internal others alone. This is precisely because the agrarian self/selves are a historical product of the Japanese encounter with the external others.

Japan's history is a series of conjunctures during which internal developments responded to a large degree to flows in world history. These conjunctures have been interpreted through the lens of the Japanese structure of self and other, and they in turn forced the Japanese, or more specifically the agrarian Japanese, repeatedly to reconceptualize their notion of self. Of all the conjunctures, the two that sent the most profound and lasting shock waves throughout the country were Japan's encounter with the high civilization of Tang China between the fifth and seventh centuries, and the encounter with Western civilization at the end of the nineteenth century. The Japanese were propelled to reach for the superior other—to imitate and then surpass the superior qualities of the Chinese and Westerners.

We saw that the birth of the agrarian self itself took place as a result of discourse with the Chinese—in their effort to locate their own identity, the Japanese adopted rice and rice agriculture as their hallmark. In addition, they adopted the Chinese writing system en masse, even though the two spoken languages were totally unrelated, as well as a whole range of other features of Chinese civilization, while at the same time strenuously resisting Chinese civilization in their effort to protect their own Japanese culture and their self.

When the country reopened at the end of the nineteenth century after two centuries of isolation, a similar encounter with another "superior" civilization occurred, this time with the West—with its scientific and technological advances, which the Japanese avidly adopted—in which Japan sought its own image (Pollack 1986: 53). The West became the most important other for the Japanese, who adopted not only Western science and technology but also the day-to-day Western lifestyle, as epitomized by the Meiji emperor with his Western-style hair, clothing, and famous kaiser mustache (Bolitho 1977: 23–41; Taki 1990). As they did with the Chinese, the Japanese strove to distinguish themselves from the Westerners in a symbolic opposition of "us versus them" as "rice versus meat." Thus, one of the othernesses of the Westerners during the early period of encounter was butchering and meat eating, which initially incurred enormous fear of pollution but later was eagerly adopted as *the* marker of Western "enlightenment" (see Ohnuki-Tierney, in press). We recall that butchering and other types of killing of domestic animals were considered by the agrarian Japanese as markers of the burakumin. Rice versus meat then represents the opposition between the agrarian self and the internal other as well as the external other.

Important also was the Japanese encounter with Western "enlightenment" and rationality, which some Japanese intellectuals, especially during the Meiji period, eagerly adopted as hallmarks of civilization (Mertz 1997; Murphy 1994; Ohnuki-Tierney 1993). They even divided the peoples of the world into those who were enlightened (*kaika no hito*), semi-enlightened (*hankai no hito*), and not enlightened (*mikai no hito*) (Mertz 1997). As the Japanese realized that they were behind Westerners in "progress" toward enlightenment, they saw themselves ahead of their internal other—the Ainu. It is this dialectic between the self and the external other that colored the way the Japanese perceived and treated the Ainu. They adopted the unilinear evolutionary theory and anxiously gauged their own progress, for which the primitive Ainu served an important role.

The symbolic meanings assigned to the internal others were intimately related to the way the dominant Japanese saw themselves in relation to the external others. The negativity that the dominant Japanese saw as they reflected upon themselves in their encounter with the external others was then projected upon the internal others, who, in a broad sense, became scapegoats.

From a cross-cultural perspective, an important issue remains—the problem of "boundedness" and "bounding" raised by Virginia Dominguez during the conference that led to this book. As a response to Gladney's (1994) important point about the need to problematize the unmarked majority, the Han of China in his case, John Kelly urges us to think about *the right to be unmarked*—a powerful phrase indeed. Kelly (this volume) evokes Brackette Williams's insistence that we recognize power inequality in the labeling process (Williams 1989: 420). Kaplan (this volume) also expounds on the hierarchically ordered nature of racial/political divisions in Fiji, citing a case of an Indian man who, like agrarian Japanese, paid tax and cultivated land, and who appealed to be classified as a Fijian.

The above sketch of the historical process clearly illustrates that it was the dominant agrarian Japanese who *bound* them when neither social group is physically distinguishable from the agrarian Japanese.[43] The case of the internal others for agrarian Japanese is a classic one of the naturalization of cultural arbitrariness, that is, the marking and bounding of these people as if they were "naturally" marked.

As with many "ethnic groups" in the world, some members of these social groups are calling for their own separate identities, while others are acutely aware of the historical burden of having been marked against their own will. At present, it is illegal in Japan to ask about membership in any of the social groups, and the government has banned disclosure of family registry—a source of identification of membership—unless requested by the individual.

Before we see the globalization of the discourse through our own tinted glasses and assume that all minorities are eager to be marked, we need to examine the historical development of minorities. The three major points I have raised in this chapter may prompt us to examine majority/minority discourse cross-culturally. First, our endeavor must be historicized, because any minority/majority discourse at present is a product of historical development. Second, the model proposed here is general enough to serve to understand cultural construction of alterity, which is almost always characterized by a dialectic process of self and other, including external and internal others. Third, majority/minority relationship is by definition hierarchically ordered, with power inequality according differential access to the process of marking and unmarking a social group.

PART II

KOREANNESS

3

Who Speaks for Korean Shamans When Shamans Speak of the Nation?

LAUREL KENDALL

> But if, by exploits of her hand, woman were to reopen paths into (once again) a/one logos that connotes her as castrated, especially as castrated of words, excluded from the work force except as prostitute to the interests of the dominant ideology . . . then a certain sense, which still constitutes the sense of history, will undergo unparalleled interrogation, revolution.
>
> —Luce Irigaray, *Speculum of the Other Woman*

> Locating "tradition" is locating the politics of meaning in the production of a putative homogeneity.
>
> —Brackette F. Williams, "Nationalism, Traditionalism, and the Problem of Cultural Inauthenticity"

A CHAPTER on female Korean shamans and their rituals might seem an odd inclusion in this volume, but the question of women in general and Korean female shamans in particular adds a dimension to our understanding of how majority discourses come to be framed and how other voices may be appropriated or effaced in this process. In contrast to most of the examples in this volume, the minority in question is not ethnicized, but rather abides as an other that is simultaneously an object within the definition of "us." Like the Japanese (Ohnuki-Tierney, this volume), Koreans describe themselves as a homogeneous people (Cho, this volume): *han minjok*, one people/nation/race, "han" meaning "one," homophonous with the "han" of Han'guk, the Korean nation.[1] As Cho indicates, ethnic minorities do exist within Korea (Chinese, Amerasians, and a very recent population of guest workers from South and Southeast Asia), but those who would define "Korean" do not find it necessary to rationalize the exclusion of these people so much as commonsensical to ignore their existence altogether.

Numerically small and largely invisible—the Amerasians because they inhabit the liminal world that surrounds U.S. army bases—ethnic minorities within Korea do not constitute a significant ethnic other against which "Korean" must be defined and defended. As Cho Hae-joang (this volume) suggests, Korea's significant others have been external, the historical agents of political and cultural domination: Chinese (until the end of the last century), Japanese, and Americans. These are the cast of characters in ethnic jokes and endless comparisons of cultural inventories, from the depth of a bow, to the curve of a roofline, to drinking behavior. As Cho also suggests, precisely because perceptions of historical domination from the outside are a salient feature of Korean historiography, definitions of "Korean" are deemed to be both urgent and problematic.

Women have a contradictory place in this construction. In the discourses of early-twentieth-century Asian nationalisms, images of victimized women, idealized women, women as "good wives and wise mothers" were invoked as signs and symbols of the experience and aspirations of a people (Chow 1991; Mani 1987; Nolte and Hastings 1991). While progressive nationalists, patriots, and reformers throughout Asia spoke of women, their discourses were not intrinsically about women (Chow 1991; Mani 1987). Indeed, experiences and perceptions particular to women were effaced in the process of reinscription. In Gayatri Spivak's (1988) terms, the subaltern could not speak. In Korea as well, conditions of systematic discrimination in both law and social practice have been rationalized as national "tradition": the sanctity of "our women," the preservation of "our families," in opposition to the corrupting influences of the West. The marginal condition of Korean women is handmaiden to the construction of a national "us," a part of the imagining of Anderson's (1983) imagined community. To borrow Emiko Ohnuki-Tierney's phrase (this volume), women constitute an "internal other" in a double sense, internal to the boundaries of the nation, indeed to the most intimate boundaries of experience, and also "internalized," digested into dominant discourses of the self in the production of identity.

The female Korean shamans who are the subjects of this chapter are doubly marginalized, first by gender and second as practitioners of what was once an outcast profession. Over the last decade, the formerly despised shamans have found themselves celebrated as repositories of national tradition, the recipients of frequent media attention (C. Choi 1987, 1991). With this increased visibility, new voices, male voices, "speak for" partially educated female shamans and inscribe shaman practices with new nationalistic meanings. The shamans themselves seem thoroughly complicit in this process. The new respectability accorded shaman rituals reflects a new vision of national identity, constructed in response to changing politics and consciousness. By this process, however, the shamans and their female clients who transact these rituals are seen less as producers of history and culture than as its muted artifacts.

The issue is one of representation, or more specifically, of who is empowered to represent and what is deemed an appropriate subject for representation. It follows that my own musings on how these particular women have come to be objectified in the construction of a majority discourse about Koreanness are similarly problematic, grounded in observations and impressions that are the product of my own position, experience, gender, and the privilege of a Western academic credential. This is the fin de siècle anthropological dilemma that also fuels Richard Handler's discussion (this volume). The best that I can do is to lay out all my cards, explain why I chose to study Korean shamans in the first place and how my early attraction to their world caused me to react so vehemently to things done more recently in their name. My discussion thus begins with an account of a personal journey, told here in the confessional mode of contemporary ethnography, which I do realize is not to every reader's taste. I will then suggest how the appropriation of shaman rituals into a nationalistic majority discourse and the attendant muting of female shamans draws upon local logic as it plays against the unfolding of modern Korean history.

The Anthropologist and the Shamans

"Man is respected and woman abased." "When the hen crows, the house falls down." "In Korea the woman walks ahead of the man—because the roads are mined!" As a Peace Corps volunteer resident in Korea in the early 1970s, I was offered these aphorisms as a test of my cultural relativism and a trial to my patience. My abiding interest in the world of shamans began one cold December day when I was taken to a *kut* (an elaborate shaman ritual) and saw the Korean world turned upside down. Women in brilliant satin costumes spoke with the authority of the gods while other women—strong, wizened matrons—hovered round them, all at the center of the action. The men watched intently from the sidelines. An irate ancestor, speaking through a shaman, pulled the master of the house by the ear and dragged him forward for a tongue-lashing. I said to myself, "I can study this." In this corner of Korean life, at least, my own gender would be not a liability but an asset.

Like many other scholars, I chose a dissertation topic that was not only professionally justifiable but also personally compelling. The emergence of an anthropology of women on American campuses in the 1970s matched my own desire to learn more about the shamans who seemed to defy every stereotype of docile Asian womanhood. In the field, I very quickly learned not to romanticize; shamans' lives are histories of pain and abuse, the work is arduous and uncertain, and relationships among shamans can be fractious and volatile. Suffering and rage are dominant motifs among shamans, clients, and spirits. Women transmit an essentially (although not exclusively) oral tradition from teacher to disciple, perform rituals that balance elements of predictable structure with artistic innovation, and are skilled raconteurs in telling lives and stories that testify to the power of the spirits.[2] I have seen my own early enthusiasm for shamans and their work reflected in some of my students, especially female Korean American students, who are surprised to learn that such formidable and articulate women exist in Korea and that the rich world of belief and practice described in my own and other ethnographies could be enacted by and among women. For this anthropologist, the retrieval of the shaman's world was a feminist act "written against" pervasive assumptions of female subordination and insignificance, in the sense that Abu-Lughod (1991) urges us to "write against culture."

But perhaps I was a romantic after all. Let me describe two recent encounters.

The Tano Kut

Grim thoughts occurred to me when, in the late spring of 1992, I attended a Tano Kut sponsored by a local branch of a national professional association dedicated to improving the situation of shamans and informing the public about Korean culture.[3] Where possible, I avoid staged cultural performances as a professional conceit, and this kut was to be no exception. Since filmmaker Diana Lee and I wanted to record at least one large public display as part of the full spectrum of contemporary shaman practice, and since our invitation came from an apprentice shaman whose work we had already filmed, this seemed like a golden opportunity.

At the Tano Kut, space and time were organized in the manner of a cultural festival rather than a shaman ritual; indeed, the members of the organizing committee consistently referred to it as a *haengsa*, an "event," rather than a shaman's kut, or even a Tano "festival" (Tano *che*).[4] It began with a taped recording of the national anthem, for which members of the audience stood and placed their hands over their hearts. A master of ceremonies introduced members of the festival committee (all men but for one) and distinguished guests (including myself, pinned with a distinguished guest's boutonniere). We sat in a special section where a reviewing stand, a table covered with a banner, had been improvised for the chairman and the committee members. The chairman's remarks echoed the sentiments expressed in the printed program: that the influence of foreign cultures has harmed Korea's own distinct traditions, and that this event was being held to keep the memory of such practices alive. The original local Tano Kut, it was claimed, had disappeared during the colonial period. Once the introductory formalities were complete, the committee and members of the local association gathered for a commemorative photograph.

The kut itself was performed on an open-air stage beside a large apartment complex. As on similar occasions, the stage relegated the spectators to the role of a passive audience while a small group of women from the association, all wearing identical Korean dresses, received the gods' divinations and bowed in unison. The segments of the kut alternated northern and central Korean styles, each performed by a different team of shamans, and as with most contemporary kut, a great deal was left out.[5] The sense of separation, of watching rather than doing, was enhanced by the presence of a loud-voiced man with a microphone who announced each segment, explained its significance, named the participating shamans, and sometimes offered running commentary which, in the climactic moments of a shaman's balancing on knife blades, resembled the frenzied pitch of a football announcer. The invisible fourth wall separating the audience from the stage was breached on a few occasions in self-conscious attempts to evoke the communal atmosphere of a kut: when the announcer urged the very reluctant spectators to come forward and choose divination flags (three men did); when spectators flocked around the two shamans jumping on fodder choppers (*chaktu*) in the flat space in front of the stage; and at the very end of the kut, when the emcee begged spectators to come forward, pay their respects to the spirits, and dance on the stage.[6] When no one came forward, a shaman attempted to rouse the spectators into participation, but she was unable to adjust the microphone. She called for "some man" (*namja*) to come and fix it. I scrawled grouchily in my field notes that her remark was "paradigmatic of the entire day," of men with a microphone imposing their text upon the activities of women who accepted the appropriateness of a new authorization.

We approached the apprentice during a lull in the kut and asked for an explanation of the event, thinking to capture a replay of what she had told us when she invited us to attend. This woman, who on other occasions had seemed to love preening and performing in front of our video camera, misunderstood our intention of interviewing *her*. She led us away and sought out a member of the festival committee, an amateur folklorist with a distinguished mop of white hair, and asked *him* to explain the event on camera. His text, like the stage itself, was removed from immediate experience; he told us how, in the past, women suffered throughout the year but had this one day to enjoy themselves. He then described the sorts of

Tano customs recounted in standard descriptions of Korean folk festivals. One of his colleagues explained to me how members of the Geomancers' Association were active in the festival committee to "help" the members of the Shamans' Association. When I registered surprise,[7] he explained to me that the geomancers have learning (*hak*) while the shamans have inspiration (*yông*), which, he claims, are essentially the same: "We have father virtue [*abôjidôk*] while they have mother virtue [*ômônidôk*]." He spoke of complementarity but implied that the shamans need men's learning to fully understand and convey the significance of their work; learned men provide the text. Thus does a Shamans' Association relegate women to an "auxiliary" (*punyôhoe*), for which our friend the young apprentice, by no means the senior shaman in her community, is the acting chair.

The attitudes expressed by the men at the Tano Kut are echoed among representatives of the several professional associations that now purport to represent the political and cultural interests of shamans.[8] Spokespersons for these groups, usually nonshamans and almost exclusively men, will laud shaman practice as intrinsic to Korean culture while at the same time describing their own work as offering guidance to the illiterate or partially literate practitioners who are incapable of representing their own interests or preserving the pure form of their rituals. Some groups will even invite scholars to lecture the practitioners about the proper form and meaning of kut.

As a distanced spectator I have seen other performances akin to the Tano Kut, and scholars have been putting nationalistic glosses on Korean shaman rituals since the 1920s (Janelli 1986). I had considered these developments interesting, but peripheral to the experiences of the shamans I knew. What disturbed me so much on this occasion (and caused Diana Lee and me to commit our own rebellious act of effacement by intentionally interviewing the head of the Shamans' Association with no tape in the camera) was the totality with which the interpreting voice controlled the act of performance, the degree to which the participating shamans, many of whom had actually financed the kut, accepted this voice as natural. Some of these same shamans were women already known to me as articulate and forthright in their own sphere.

Park Avenue, New York

In the winter of 1994, the Asia Society brought to New York a team of hereditary Korean shamans[9] and musicians from Chin Island who had received the designation "National Treasure" for their performance of the Chindo *sikkim* kut, a ritual to send off dead souls.[10] Within Korea, the group's distant island home conveyed an aura of romanticism and purity of tradition. I had seen this team on several occasions at well-attended performances in Korea. This was their second American tour, and they had become highly skilled at translating their ritual into an abbreviated performance on a proscenium stage. Their appearance on Park Avenue was both exquisite and moving.

The musician Park Byung Chun, the designated leader of the group, was not only a vibrant drummer and dancer, but also an effective, engaging spokesperson. He described through an interpreter the hereditary shaman traditions of southern Korea and the symbolic content of the ritual. He spoke after each performance and gave a lecture demonstration during a two-day symposium on shaman rituals. Park was careful to distinguish himself, a male musician born into a hereditary shaman family, from the shaman women (*mudang*, *munyô*) who danced and manipulated the ritual paraphernalia, even as he was careful to distinguish the women of his team from the charismatic shamans of northern and central Korea. Because the event was billed as a "shaman ritual," the organizers of the symposium thought that it would also be appropriate to hear from the shamans themselves. At the end of Park's remarks, the two senior women of the team were brought on stage. Expressive performers when they did the sikkim kut, they now seated themselves stiffly on two folding chairs and bowed their heads, anxious expressions upon their wrinkled faces. "How did you become a shaman?" the interpreter asked. The oldest woman replied in a halting, quivering voice, "My mother was a shaman [munyô]. I learned to perform from my mother-in-law." Both women seemed to be acutely uncomfortable, and this was the last word we heard from them. Later in the day, the moderator explained to the symposium audience that when she had requested the women's presence, Park had been emphatically opposed, claiming that uneducated women could not represent their tradition to an American audience. No wonder the women had seemed uncomfortable, not only thrust into an unconventional role but bearing the burden of fear that they would embarrass their team and, by extension, the Korean nation. The point, perhaps, is that the tradition had come to be represented, discussed, annotated, rather than merely performed; it had become an icon of cultural knowledge beyond its expressed purpose of sending off a dead soul. (Had I not also played to this assumption when I asked the young apprentice to "explain" the Tano Kut for a documentary film?)

Context and Meaning

Chungmoo Choi has written with great sensitivity and insight regarding the tensions that arise when Korean shaman rituals are transformed into staged entertainments (1987: chap. 2; 1991). I will be concerned here less with the transformed structure and context of performance than with the new meanings imposed upon these staged performances in Korea today and how, in the process of their construction, such meanings almost inevitably render women mute. One obvious point of entry is the neo-Confucian gender dichotomization of woman's sphere and man's sphere as *nae* and *woe*, literally "inside" and "outside," but more accurately characterized as "informal" and "formal" realms of being and expression. "Nae" and "woe" are easily conflated with the anthropologist's "domestic" and "public" (Rosaldo 1974) as a tempting explanation of female subordination and mutedness, but only if the formulation is taken as an opening to discussion, rather than as a given.[11] "Woe," as "formal," connotes a male realm that is most explicitly concerned with public presentations of self, with exhibitions of etiquette and propriety. "Nae," as "informal" and female, is constructed as intimate, a realm of pragmatic management and mundane living, in contrast to—but sometimes the very basis for the maintenance of—the prestigious enactments of culture and ideology, of "face," sustained in the public sphere.[12] I have argued elsewhere that in the ritual realm, men's activities embody idealizations of harmonious families and lineages in the person of respected ancestors, while women address violations of health and harmony by contending with angry gods and restless ancestors, either as housewives who bring their household concerns to shamans, or as the shamans who expel or placate the source of misfortune (Kendall 1985; cf. Janelli and Janelli 1982). By cultural logic, the therapeutic process of a kut to reestablish the harmony of house and household is best transacted between women, as shaman[13] and client, within a realm of intimacy and informality where disharmony, inauspicious events, and violations of propriety can be discussed with humor and pathos. Men retain the face-saving option of denouncing it all as nonsense.

At a country kut, such as I described in the opening chapter of *Shamans, Housewives, and Other Restless Spirits* (1985), the spirits give authority and humor to things already known among the community, to sentiments and family stories that clients, neighbors, and kin may have already revealed to the shamans before the start of the ritual (C. Choi 1989; Kendall 1977). These kut are about life as women live it, with tears and laughter. In contemporary Korea the ground has shifted, and clients living in anonymous apartment blocks hold their kut in the more private settings of isolated rented shrines, far removed from their neighbors and often with no additional kinswomen in attendance. Here, shamans, clients, and spirits share tales of wayward children, drunken spouses, and financial misadventures.

At the other extreme, large public performances, like those described above, address a broad and anonymous community: the citizens of X Town at the Tano Kut, the television-viewing nation, the New York audience, or, on the occasion of the First Conference of the International Society for Shamanistic Research, scholars of the world. Not only are the subjects of more intimate kut less compelling to a broad, anonymous audience, these embarrassing revelations from the private realm are inappropriate for public display. A large public kut thus showcases feats, spectacle, and photo opportunities. Personal stories are swallowed up in a larger national story, idealized, theatrical, and with just a nod to the suffering of women in days gone by. Shaman rituals have come to be about the history of a people, about Korea, in an authorizing process of designating National Treasure teams and "reviving" local rituals with microphone commentary, a process whose dominant voices are almost inevitably those of educated men.

How Shaman Rituals Came to Be About Korea

Shamans and their rituals have only recently been celebrated on public stages and in the media. Shamans have been disdained as lewd women who dance and make bawdy jokes in public and as outcasts who deal with inauspicious, impure, and dangerous forces. Like shamans everywhere, they have been suspected of charlatanry and portrayed as the superstitious antithesis of modernity. My first fieldwork in the 1970s was conducted during a period of repression. In the name of development and enlightenment, petty officials destroyed local shrines and harassed shamans who performed kut (C. Choi 1987; Ch'oe 1974; Walraven 1993). Shamans made pragmatic accommodations by politely offering white envelopes of "cigarette money" to their tormentors (Kendall 1985: 62). These were only the most recent skirmishes in a centuries-long struggle between shamans and Korean officialdom. In dynastic times, Confucian scholar-officials attempted to circumscribe the shamans' activities through legislation. Korean folklore is filled with tales of scholar-officials who successfully unmask shamans' trickery and of scholar-officials who are humbled by the efficacy of shamans' rituals.[14]

Korea's collision with the Western powers and colonization by the Japanese empire between 1910 and 1945 saw the emergence of a new class of intellectuals who faulted Korea's traditions—which they judged to be conservative and unenlightened—for her weakness and humiliation. Confucianism was criticized for fostering oppressive gerontocratic mores and empty ritualism (Robinson 1988: chap. 1). The practices of women and shamans were deemed fundamentally false insofar as belief in the existence of spirits and shamanic powers was unscientific. For the first time, the epithet *misin*—"superstition," but more literally "false belief"—was applied to the activities of women and shamans (Ch'oe 1974). In this, Korea was not unique. Throughout East Asia, popular religious practices were denounced by progressive elites who saw them as a hindrance to social welfare and national strength (Thompson 1975: chap. 8 and Yang 1961: chap. 13 for China; Hardacre 1989 for Japan). Many early progressives marked their rejection of the Korean past by becoming Christian (Clark 1986: chap. 2). The Japanese colonial government, with technologies of social control theretofore unknown in Korea, initiated campaigns against shamans that would be echoed in the Park Chung Hee regime's efforts in the 1970s.

That shamans and their rituals were once a target of the colonial regime enhances their nationalistic aura today. Where a revived ritual, like the local Tano Kut, is described as having disappeared during the colonial period, its history is linked to a story of the widespread and systematic suppression of Korean culture in those same years. This, however, is a fairly recent development. Confucianism was more easily rehabilitated to the needs of twentieth-century Korean intellectual life. As a textual tradition whose exemplars were necessarily learned, Confucianism evoked a past that was "good to think" in a society that affirmed education and social harmony as modernizing projects.[15] In an independent Korea, the idealized past became a *yangban* past, the past of nobles, scholars, and officials, elite and formal, re-created in museum displays throughout the peninsula and perpetuated in official discourses about Korean culture for both domestic and foreign consumption.[16]

Shamans, as despised persons and practitioners of superstition, were initially not so valued. In the 1970s, a research assistant told me that she had initially felt both fear and revulsion at the prospect of associating with shamans. Even in the early 1980s, cultural watchdogs resisted (unsuccessfully) a curator's desire to include shaman paintings in an American exhibition of Korean folk art. In these same years, I consulted with representatives of the Korean Cultural Service over a new display at the American Museum of Natural History. The desired content was to be yangban Korea with not a mention of "superstitious" practices.

At the same time, a contradictory discourse did exist. For several decades, Korean folklore scholars had been writing about shamans and painstakingly recording their work. Modern Korean folklore studies (*minsokhak*) began in the late 1920s as an intellectual response to Korea's situation as a colony of the Japanese empire (Allen 1990; Choi I-H. 1987; Janelli 1986; Robinson 1988).[17] For cultural nationalists, folk traditions would provide symbols of Korean identity and national pride, while an understanding of Korea's "old culture" was seen as essential to the construction of a reformed and strengthened society (Janelli 1986: 30– 31; Robinson 1988: 32; Walraven 1993).[18] Roger Janelli has identified the political underpinnings of early Korean scholarly interests in shamanism. By looking northward and linking local phenomena to the better-known practices of Siberia, cultural nationalists confounded colonialist cultural histories, which constructed Korea as a backwater of Japanese culture (Janelli 1986). By linking contemporary shaman practice to myths of the culture hero Tan'gun as recorded in ancient texts, Ch'oe Nam-sôn precipitated an intellectual tradition that regards shamanism as a unique spiritual force infusing the Korean people (Janelli 1986; Allen 1990; Walraven 1993).[19] These ideas have been echoed in more recent writing (T. Kim 1972: 76) and have come into common parlance among spokespersons for the shaman world (although less often among shamans themselves). Again and again, on recent visits, I have been told that shaman practices (*musok*) are the deep root (*ppuri*) of the Korean people.

Where contemporary practices were constructed as "survivals," scholars valued shamans and their rituals as evidence for ancient and enduring national traditions while maintaining their intellectual distance, as learned men and modern progressives, from the unlettered and superstitious-seeming women who maintained these practices in the twentieth century. More generally, by constructing shaman rituals as national "tradition," folklore scholarship rendered both act and actor in the past tense. The early folklorists would reconstruct an uncolonized, uncorrupted Korean past, and like their colleagues in Europe (Linke 1990), China (ibid.; Hung 1985), and Japan (Yanagita 1970 [1945]), they sought the vestiges of this past in the countryside, an equation that probably first came to seem commonsensical in the emergent urban culture of colonial Seoul in the 1920s.[20]

The Terms of Cultural Revival

The folklore revival of the 1960s and 1970s would be similarly prompted by a nostalgic reaction against rapid industrialization, booming urbanization, and a massive influx of Western popular culture. With the growth and popularization of folklore studies, many educated persons had come to see in shaman practices a pure Korean tradition alive on the peninsula before the arrival of Buddhism and Confucianism. Shamans and their rituals were acceptable where they could be historicized; the new urban middle class could approach them as the subjects of folklore, the lingering relics of a dying tradition. Museum labels seemed always to exaggerate reports of the shamans' demise even as the frozen manikins in cases gave them a place in a larger cultural past. Living in Korea in the early 1970s as a Peace Corps volunteer, I had been amused by the frequent assertion that the shamans had all died out, except for an old crone or two who could still be found in the deep country. In those days, a shaman was my neighbor down a narrow lane in the neighborhood of Seoul's premier Christian university. The sound of drums and cymbals from her kut would resound throughout the night. Yet only a few years later when I began my own research on shamans as a Ph.D. candidate, it seemed perfectly logical, given both anthropological and local perceptions of what I was about, that I should live in a rural village. Even my short journey from intercity bus to country bus, little more than an hour on good days, was sufficient to vest my accounts of shaman practices with ethnographic authenticity. I still scoffed when my interlocutors in Seoul insisted that the relatively youthful and energetic shamans I was observing on a daily basis must necessarily be "dying out." However, the very fact that my observations were made in a rural setting undercut my insistence on the contemporary vigor of my chosen subject; I was living within the landscape of the past.[21]

Chungmoo Choi (1987) has described the contradictory cultural policies initiated under the regime of the late President Park Chung Hee at a moment when "development" and "national culture" hung in the balance. Agents of the New Community Movement (Saemaûl undong) attacked "superstitious" local rituals while folklorists, some in the service of the Ministry of Culture and Information, attempted to protect them (Ch'oe 1974). Some of these same events would eventually be preserved—as endangered cultural relics—under the Cultural Properties Preservation Act. As folk performers, shamans would one day be vested with government stipends to encourage the perpetuation of their art (C. Choi 1987: 65–70; Walraven 1993).[22] Choi sees the cultural policies of the Park regime as a cynical attempt to enhance its legitimacy as protector and defender of the national heritage, even as it initiated profound social and economic changes.

The decade of the 1980s was a critical watershed in Korean thinking about the past. Memories of national humiliation and economic hardship were now circumscribed by Korea's entrance into the ranks of the Newly Developed Nations and by the selection of Seoul as the site of the 1988 Olympics. Viewed from a distance, attributes of "tradition" could be safely enjoyed. In the early 1980s, the Ministry of Culture designated three shaman rituals as Intangible National Treasures (Muhyang munhwaje). Carefully selected shamans were appointed to perform them as Human Cultural Treasures (Ingan munhwaje), and more of both designations would follow. These staged performances, celebrating ritual activities as folk art and reconstructed history, deny the persistence of lived belief and practice. Choi has described some delicious ironies as shamans vie for an official status that enhances their popularity with clients (C. Choi 1987: chap. 2).

The 1980s would see a profound shift in the regard accorded traditional elite culture versus popular culture. This was a decade of debate, argument, and sometimes violent protest, baptized in the blood of the Kwangju Insurrection and culminating in the torrent of popular dissent, labor strikes, and grassroots movements that ushered out the Chun Doo Hwan government in 1987. Things Korean came to be cast in opposition to things Western. The most obvious targets were postwar American patronage, held culpable in the massacre of citizens of Kwangju and more broadly for supporting several decades of dictatorship, and Western-inspired popular culture, seen as having stifled the Korean spirit. But democratically minded social critics were also antielitist, embracing the culture of the masses and scorning the conservative vestiges of the yangban ethos. Nativistic impulses that had fueled Korean folklore scholarship in the 1920s and 1930s and a revival of interest on university campuses in the 1970s (Janelli 1986; Robinson 1988) now blossomed into a broad-based popular culture that drew its idioms from the traditions of downtrodden peasants and outcast shamans (the *minjung*, or masses) (C. Choi 1987; K. Kim 1994).

The Popular Culture Movement (Minjung munhwa undong) claimed that shaman rituals express a uniquely Korean commentary on suffering, life, and death, and that their essential work is the release of han, the unrequited grievances of a historically oppressed people (Commission on Theological Concerns). Among students and other oppositional groups, shaman rituals have been appropriated and transformed into protest theater (C. Choi 1987). At mass demonstrations, sympathetic shamans or self-styled shamanic performers invoke and comfort the souls of students and workers who have died in the cause of social justice (C. Choi 1987: chap. 3; K. Kim 1994; S. N. Kim 1989; Sun 1991: chap. 3). Intellectual enthusiasm for popular religion has mushroomed with performances of kut on university campuses (including Christian universities), the publication of attractively illustrated books on folk traditions, and television appearances by a well-known shaman. Ritual invocations of house and site gods now often mark the opening of a new construction site or building, the anniversary of an organization, or the start of a student demonstration (K. Kim 1994). In the summer of 1991, the First International Congress on Shamanism was held in Seoul, and it was proudly suggested that Korea boasted the most vital living shaman tradition in the world. The process had come full circle, from denial through nostalgic celebration to recognition as a national resource.

Although the Popular Culture Movement has receded, and one hears far less these days about the culture of the masses (Cho, this volume), the developments of the 1980s left their mark upon the shaman world by enhancing the visibility of shaman rituals and securing for shamans a positive identity as cultural icons. Scholars' texts have fed into popular knowledge the claim that shamans are the heirs of an ancient indigenous tradition and that shaman rituals address the unique and profound suffering of the Korean people, thus ensuring that shamans and kut will have a place in the new narratives being constructed. Will female shamans also participate in the construction of these new narratives, or merely be spoken about? Will Korea provide one more example of how the circumstances and practices of women have fueled more abstract discussions of tradition far removed from the terms by which women might understand their own experiences (Mani 1987; Spivak 1988)?

Conclusion: Must Shamans Necessarily Be Silent?

The circumstances that shaped intellectual discourses about Korean shaman rituals, that laid the groundwork for their enthusiastic popularization in recent years, have also necessarily objectified the female shamans who perform them. When first scholars, then popularizers link shaman practices with the myths recorded in ancient texts, contemporary practices are taken as the shreds and patches of something that was once more important, that existed in a purer, more powerful indigenous form long ago. The flesh-and-blood shaman is denied agency, save in a negative sense, as when the folklorist Chang Chu-gun suggests that centuries of ignorant if well-intentioned countrywomen have trivialized a proud religious heritage into a petty preoccupation with good and bad fortune (1974: 137–38). By implication, the essence of shaman practices is beyond the grasp of the practitioners, but within the understanding of masters of textual knowledge. The concerns of women, and their life experiences as refracted through these rituals, are deemed insignificant, the dross that must be cleared away from a shining core.

Even where the Popular Culture Movement looked seriously at the emotional content of contemporary shaman rituals, it folded stories of personal and familial affliction into its own consciousness of class and nation, where suffering is necessarily always a consequence of foreign powers, oppressive regimes, and global capitalism. While many, many ritual expressions of affliction are linked to conditions of poverty and marginalization (e.g., Kendall 1977), and so to the fundamental inequalities of a larger political economy, these themes are more transparent in some kut than in others (e.g., Kim S. N. 1989: chap. 10).[23] In an analysis of the rituals of the oppressed, there is no self-evident space for ritual dramas that deal with drunken and unfaithful spouses, family ambitions, delinquent children, and vengeful ancestral first wives, for dramas cast within the intimate frame of households.

More generally, by equating shaman rituals with "tradition," a folkloric gaze situates shamans and their female clients within the past, and by so doing renders them mute. The valued shamans are "authentic" informants, old women, doddering bearers of an endangered oral tradition that must be safely preserved in the frozen texts of scholars.[24] Innovation jeopardizes authenticity; shamans are not valued as producers of Korean culture but as its passive receptacles.[25] Fixed ritual structures are privileged over the improvised and fluid substance of shaman ritual, the transaction between shaman and spirit performed for specific clients in particular circumstances.[26] To acknowledge the shaman as performer, as innovator and creator of meaning, is to skirt dangerously close to an intellectually troubling issue, the claimed authority of the spirits at the core of shaman ritual. It is also to risk overwhelming the monologic narration of Korean identity with the polyphonous voices of aggrieved humans and spirits.

The privileging of frozen written texts over spontaneous oral performance is by no means unique to Korea (Ong 1982), nor is the privileging of literate men over unlettered women. Within the Confucian world, learned people are regarded as better, more virtuous people. Shamans, like everyone else in Korea, value scholarship not merely as an accomplishment but as a moral quality often denied them in the lives of hardship and deprivation that foretell a shaman's destiny.[27] The respect of the shaman for the scholar has benefited any researcher who chooses to work among them. (Once, at a kut, I took a wicked delight in subverting perceptions of relative worth and authority. When a male client asked me, the scholar, to explain the meaning of the ritual, I insisted that he "ask these women who are my teachers.")

But do the shamans themselves really care that they are "objectified in the service of a majority discourse"? Whatever feminist inclination led me to the shaman world, however much I see gender as implicated in the appropriation of shaman voices, most of the shamans I have encountered in Korea do not derive their primary identity as "women," do not give gender the salience that I would accord it in accounting for why things happen the way they do.[28] Instead, they see their lives as having been defined by an unwelcome calling from the spirits that made them into shamans. As shamans they experience social discrimination and as shamans they have begun to gain respect and recognition. Most of the female shamans I know welcome scholarly and media interest in their profession; once-disdainful relatives and neighbors now show them more respect, and the number of initiates is on the rise (Kendall 1996).[29] Shamans of my acquaintance were particularly impressed when Kim Kumhwa, a well-spoken shaman, the first of their number to hold the title of government-designated Human Cultural Treasure,[30] was featured on a television talk show and addressed respectfully by the moderator as "teacher" (*sônsaeng*). The shaman viewers saw no irony in the bracketing of her remarks with authoritative commentary by scholars.

Shamans grumble about the various professional organizations not because male authorities claim to speak for shamans, but because they are viewed as ineffectual in furthering shamans' interests in the manner of Christian and Buddhist professional associations. I did meet one young shaman who echoed my own feelings in describing the associations as having a "gender problem" (*namnyô munje*),[31] since most of the shamans are women while those who run the associations are nonshaman men. Her remarks are balanced by those of an older shaman, a respected "adviser" (*komun*) in one of the associations. When I asked this woman if it mattered that the administrators were not themselves shamans, she replied that of course the male shamans (*paksu mudang*) are too busy with their own work to run around doing the work of the association, assuming without question that those who do the work of the association would necessarily be men.

But this is not the whole story. The tension between a living shaman practice and a homogenizing, historicizing folkloric tradition is predicated upon gender differences, but it is also about access to the tools of recording and presentation, the means to authorization. While shaman and client are often characterized as "ignorant [unlettered, superstitious] women," the reality is both more complex and more fluid. The shaman practices we know from twentieth-century Korea assume at least a rudimentary ability to memorize the printed texts of chants and to determine auspicious days for rituals using simple charts of Chinese ideographs. Contemporary shamans struggling to master ritual knowledge now have access to inexpensive printed texts of ritual chants and commercial tapes of key songs, both sold in shaman supply shops (*manmulsa*). One may speculate, following a current Korean Buddhist enterprise, that videotaped rituals may not be far behind. Will mass-produced and commercially distributed prompts necessarily standardize local performances and challenge the authority of shaman teachers? The answer seems obvious but is perhaps more ambiguous.

Following demography, shamans are increasingly educated, and some young shamans have attended college. It seems inevitable that shamans should also begin to claim the authority of written texts, tape recorders, and video cameras. What shall be the terms of such mastery? A male shaman has produced an authoritative textbook and runs a school for new initiates under the auspices of the Shaman Anti-Communist Association (Guillemoz 1992), thus subverting the transmission of knowledge from shaman to disciple. At the same time, a shaman of my acquaintance uses her own audiocassettes to undercut the authority of the commercial tapes available to her apprentices in shaman supply shops ("the rhythm is wrong"). When one apprentice recounted a version of the tale of Princess Pari[32] gleaned from a book purchased in such a shop, this same shaman told her, "The book is wrong." A few women have begun to authorize their own practice in published texts. Youngsook Kim Harvey (1979) reported on one such project as early as the mid-1970s (1979). I have recently made the acquaintance of a young shaman who shoots her own videos. Feminist theory would lead us to assume that even with these developments, women must necessarily speak in the preordained terms of someone else's master text (Irigaray 1985). When female shamans author written texts, are these texts distinctive, unique to the perspectives of the practitioners, or do they parrot the style and priorities of what is now a majority discourse—or even the counterdiscourse of sympathetic feminists—just as female ethnographers for so long found it necessary to legitimate themselves by writing in a genre that had little to say about women (Abu-Lughod 1990)?

Afterword: The Anthropologist

I have written to the question "Who speaks for female shamans?" recognizing that my own writing is one more exercise in "speaking for." As so many chest-pounding critics over the last decade have taught us, the very necessity of recording practice is an imposition of prior premises, summations, generalizations, and even doctrine upon the slippery stuff of experience. Words are an imperfect net with which to capture the fluid and all-embracing experience of ritual, the pronouncements, jokes, poetry, dramatic improvisation, percussion, gestures, emotions, and flickers of insight (Kapferer 1983). What shamans and clients transact is, essentially, in what they transact. Any retrieval of "what it all means" is necessarily a selective transformation into literal text. It can be argued that there are more and less "verifiable" and consequently "valid" transformations, that some ethnographies are grounded in more and some in less satisfactory observations and analysis (Sanjek 1990). Even so, the author is necessarily in a position of privilege relative to those described. Those of us who would write an anthropology of women have come to recognize the uncomfortable politics of our "ethnographic authority," of describing those who are seldom empowered to contradict us (Abu-Lughod 1991; Clifford 1983; Visweswaran 1988; Wolf 1992). Spivak's (1988) question, "Can the subaltern speak?" assumes a rhetorical "no." Historian Gail Hershatter (1993) would resist that negative answer in her writing about prostitution in early-twentieth-century China.[33] She affirms that a canny reading of official sources yields not only what her subjects spoke, as utterances entered into the historical record, but how they chose to represent themselves by crafting their explanations of their own experiences and activities in particular ways to secure the limited advantages available to them (p. 119). In a similar vein, but with a very different enterprise, women anthropologists have experimented with new ways of writing that seem better to approximate the worlds our female subjects imagine into being (Abu-Lughod 1993; Behar 1993; Kendall 1988). We have also found it necessary to acknowledge our own interventions, intentions, and feelings (Wolf 1992), as I have tried to do here.

4

Constructing and Deconstructing "Koreanness"

CHO HAE-JOANG

A Boom in "Finding Us"

I SPENT my sabbatical year in northern California in 1994–95. After my arrival in the United States, Western academics persistently asked me the same questions, "What is your opinion of Confucian revivalism?" and "How is the Confucian revivalism in Korea?" These questions were baffling to me because Confucian revivalism is a complex phenomenon and, to my knowledge, has not been a central theme in current discourse among South Korean intellectuals. Later, I discovered active academic discussions in the United States on Asian economic development and common cultural identity in relation to Confucianism (Huntington 1993; Funabashi 1993; Kristof 1993; Chung 1994; Mahbubani 1995).

It is true that a search for a new cultural identity began with the invigoration of the South Korean economy. It is not difficult to find narratives purporting to create a strong national identity or new collective consciousness of various kinds. The new narratives of searching for identity in the 1990s in South Korea are complex, however. As an insider and an active participant in generating these narratives, I feel uncomfortable about the hasty generalizations offered by Western academics and policymakers. In this chapter, I would like to map the contours of emerging narratives on Korean culture and "Koreanness" in the 1990s in South Korea in some detail so as to provide historical and cultural context.

Some popular magical words have emerged in the 1990s. They seem to capture the minds of veterans of the revolutionary 1980s nationalistic-democratization (*minjok-minjung*) movement who are now wandering around disillusioned after the fall of the Eastern bloc, as well as those of conservatives who are relieved to observe the draining of the 1980s revolutionary spirit of anti-Americanism, national reunification, and class struggle. These magical words are "national sentiment" (*kungmin chongso*), "tradition" (*chont'ong*), "finding the root" (ppuri *ch'akki*), "discovering us" (*chagi ch'akki*), "culture war" (*munhwa chonjaeng*), and "commercialization of culture" (*munhwa sangpumhwa*). These words are paired with "international market" (*segye sijang*), "globalization" (*chonjiguhwa*), and "national ability to compete internationally" (*kukga kyongjaeng ryok*).

Phrases such as "new social movement" (*sinsahae undong*), "postmodernism" (*talgundaejuui*), and "new-generation culture" (*sinsedae munhwa*) are gaining popularity, replacing the popular minjung-oriented terminology of the 1980s among intellectuals: "democracy" (*minju*), "class" (*kyegup*), "socialist realism" (*lialism*), and "nation/race" (*minjok*). *Sinto puri* (body and soil are one), which means eating those foods grown in the soil on which one lives, is not just a slogan promoted by the mass media and the farmers' union protesting the Uruguay Round agreement on opening agricultural markets. It appeals to many South Koreans who have a strong yearning for a firm cultural identity. Within the government, a serious search for a cultural identity for a "new nonmilitary state" has begun.

I shall present here new narratives on Koreanness, starting with the demands of businessmen for a theory of a distinctive Korean culture, moving to the Confucian revival movement among the older-generation elite, and then continuing to other popular movements exploring traditional culture among the youth. In conclusion, I will attempt to assess the meaning of the recent search for Koreanness in the context of decolonization and globalization.

On June 3, 1994, the Korean Studies Center of Yonsei University sponsored a workshop entitled "Korean Studies in Globalization: New Narratives on Tradition, Culture and Internationalism." It was organized with multiple and practical goals: promoting interdisciplinary studies among the fields of economics, management science, humanities, and social sciences; orienting business and management people to cultural studies; and persuading the professors of Yonsei to support the establishment of an anthropology department within the university. Professors of philosophy, history, business administration, and economics, as well as businessmen, came to the workshop with high expectations. Six papers were presented by anthropologists, while the discussants were from other disciplines. The first session offered two papers on the rise of new narratives on national identity and tradition.

The second session comprised four papers dealing with issues of South Korean capitalism, business activities, and culture. The session aimed to encourage the encounter between two different fields, that is, economic and management sciences on the one hand and anthropology on the other. From the beginning, however, the session did not go smoothly. The paper presenters, all anthropologists, argued that searching for "national culture" is an outdated and problematic project. Using the example of the Nihonjinron, an anthropologist with a fresh Ph.D. from an American university gave a sophisticated critique of the culturalist approach and concluded that the concept of national culture would soon be discarded. Another anthropologist emphasized the selectiveness of the cultural elements in the process of business negotiation and refuted the existence of "genuine cultural characteristics." A third criticized the way the concept of culture had been used in the field of business anthropology. The professionals in business administration and the businessmen themselves, however, really wanted to hear about national culture from the anthropologists, who they felt should be experts in such things. The commentators, three young professors in international management and a high-ranking businessman from one of the largest firms, could not follow what the anthropologists were saying.

Apparently, the anthropologists were too well acquainted with the latest Western discourse and were ready to deconstruct national character, personality theory, and even the culture concept itself, while the young scholars in business administration were eager to construct those concepts and incorporate them into their fields. The businessman complained about the impotence of scholarly talk, saying: "It is time for Koreans to know about ourselves. There have been many studies of Korean culture, but they are too abstract. They do not make sense to us. If one can make a systematic theory of Korean culture, it will help us a great deal in doing business."

It seems that industries, as they established branches outside Korea, began to realize that they needed help from social scientists. They wanted someone to train their employees to deal with workers from different cultural backgrounds. They wanted to know how the Korean style of management differs from American and Japanese styles. They also wanted to know what was uniquely Korean that they could be proud of. Their bosses wanted to find out which aspects of Korean culture could be wrapped up and sold as value-added products. At the Yonsei workshop, the businessmen wanted to hear a clear-cut lecture from social scientists revealing something essential about Korean character, a systemized definition of Korean people and their culture.

The government, whose biggest concern is increasing economic productivity, is also deeply concerned with the issue of Korean culture and has decided to encourage research on Koreanness with this goal in mind. A document calling for social science research funding published by the Ministry of Education in 1994 expressed this interest:

> We would like to support research projects on Korean culture. We want studies that can promote the understanding of the symbolic and cognitive systems of the Korean people.
>
> Research projects must try (1) to discover the archetypes of Korean culture based on the holistic research of people's lives; (2) to find out cognitive patterns and sentiments universal to our people in order to recover the homogeneity of our national community, particularly in preparation for the reunification of the south and the north; and (3) to establish proper cultural identity, which can be helpful for promoting communication with other nations based on comparative cultural research.
>
> The suggested research fields are (1) how Confucianism, Buddhism, and Taoism have been Koreanized; (2) other traditional beliefs, religious rituals, and Korean views on religion, analyzing the process of how foreign religions were assimilated; (3) the symbolic systems that have persisted in Korean culture; and (4) Korean concepts of beauty and other values, studying folk arts and crafts.

Both the business sector and the government are anxious to have guidelines for representing South Korea that can contribute positively to the rapid expansion of its economy. What they have found, however, is that there are few existing discussions of Korean culture, and that most concepts used in those studies were generated during the colonial era by Japanese colonialists. Business and government sense a need, but neither knows how to satisfy it, nor to whom they should turn.

Confucian Revival

On August 25–26, 1994, the *Dong-a Daily News*, one of the major South Korean newspapers, and the *In-min Daily News*, the major Chinese newspaper, cosponsored a conference entitled "The Thought of Confucius and the 21st Century" in the town of Confucius's birth in Shantung, China. The organizers of the event stated that its purpose was to reestablish cultural communication, reconfirm "the common cultural roots of the two countries," and find out what Confucianism can contribute in the 21st century. The president of the *Dong-a Daily News* expressed a wish for the participants to discover "the Oriental mind and wisdom which will enlighten the 21st century." About two hundred scholars from the two countries participated in the conference, and the event was widely broadcast in both nations.

Many of the participants attempted a critical reevaluation of Confucianism through history, but most seemed to agree that Confucianism has the potential to be the spiritual mainstay of the new century. According to the

Dong-a Daily News (Yoon Chungguk, "Yuhak ūn Todŏksŏng Hoebokŭi Kil," Aug. 27, 1994: 6–7), Confucian humanism, and its attitude toward nature in particular, was seen as providing an alternative paradigm to save the world from moral corruption, excessive materialism, and the destruction of the natural environment. Participants also agreed that Confucianism was not a stumbling block but played a supportive role for successful modernization, which would provide more abundant cultural assets in the future. These messages were clearly sent to readers who only glanced at the newspaper headlines:

> The Spirit of Benevolence and Loyalty [*inui*] Will Be the Future Ethics
>
> "Middle-Way Culture" and Western Science Need to Be Grafted Together
>
> By Respecting Nature, Overcome the Environmental Crisis
>
> All Agreed That Confucianism Is the Way to Recover Morality
>
> Cultivating the Right Personality to Live Together with Others in Harmony
>
> Searching for the Harmony Between Heaven and Humans Is a Universal Lesson
>
> Learning to Live with Nature in Harmony Is the Only Way to Overcome the Crisis of Materialistic Civilization
>
> The Concept of the Limited Universe Will Prevent Moral Corruption

All the participants agreed that Confucian thought must be reinterpreted and adjusted to accord with modern conditions. The Chinese scholars, in particular, were interested in South Korean experiences of economic growth. There was, however, a distinctive difference in the areas of emphasis of the Chinese and South Korean scholars. Believing that South Koreans had preserved Confucian tradition rather faithfully, Chinese scholars wanted to know how Confucianism had contributed to the promotion of economic development.[1] Their South Korean counterparts were much more interested in finding common cultural roots in the East Asian context. In other words, Chinese scholars were interested in Confucianism as a means for capitalistic development, while South Koreans saw it more as a remedy for the evils of that development.

The conference papers were published within two months by the *Dong-a Daily News*. Pyong'gwan Kim, the president of the *Dong-a Daily News*, wrote in the preface that the conference was a success and evoked nationwide response. Kim wrote:

> If the twentieth century was the age of expansion and conflict in the name of Western scientific civilization, the 21st century must be the age of peace through moderation and harmony. This is our wish for the world. Prominent scholars in the world have foreseen that the possibility can be found in Eastern thought, in

Confucianism in particular, and that Asians will play the leading role through their wisdom [*chihye*] and tolerance [*poyongryok*]. (P. Kim 1994: 3–4)

The texts, however, are not all filled with simple slogans and Confucian chauvinism. Some authors attempted careful analyses of the evolution of Confucian thought; others were concerned with the possibility that South Koreans are more materialistic than Westerners. Kim Chung-yol, professor of philosophy, warned that the tragedy of Western civilization may be exploding in Asia rather than in the West because of the excessive speed of Asian environmental destruction and the inability to grasp the cultural crisis (1994b: 13–49). Criticizing the simplistic logic of a hegemonic switchover from the West to the East and lamenting that Asians now are becoming more "Western" than the Westerners, Kim argued that slogans like "the 21st century is the age of the Asia" really mean nothing but the possibility of Asia helping to change the direction of Western civilization. He added, "It would be better not to be awakened at all, if the Asians are going to insist on the binary opposition of the West and the East and want to dominate the other" (1994b: 18).

Cho Sun, a prominent economist who served as a vice-prime minister in the early 1990s, was also critical of the recent trend of identifying Confucianism as the positive driving force for economic growth. He said that, on the contrary, Confucianism creates many impediments to the achievement of a highly industrialized society, namely, nepotism and an excessively family-centered attitude, gender inequality, and authoritarian bureaucracy (1994: 83–84). He believed that practical emphasis must be shifted to improving the common good, cultivating self-reflexivity, and producing real scholars (1994: 87).

The nuances of these examinations of Confucianism are not characteristic of most of the public discourse on this topic. The summaries of the conference that the mass media disseminated were not as sophisticated, and quite a few participants in that conference were ardent Confucian revivalists. This problem was demonstrated in an earlier three-day conference, "The Universality and Particularity of Confucian Culture," organized by the Academy of Korean Studies (Eighth International Conference of the Academy of Korean Studies, June 22–23, 1994). A guest speaker at the opening ceremony of that conference advocated uniting the people of the world who share a common Confucian culture: "According to my calculation, there are 140 million people who participate in Confucian culture. Confucianism will be the leading religion and value system in the coming age."

Similar views were heard from various professionals. Here is a statement made by a professor of management:

> The rapid economic development of East Asia can be explained by its Confucian cultural heritage. Confucianism has a tradition of family-based collectivism; Confucian family ethics have contributed to the accomplishment of social stability by being transferred to the state. In Confucian society, economic growth has been initiated by the highly centralized government that has mobilized the whole nation toward development with a command economy. The government's efforts have been backed up by values like cooperation, solidarity, supremacy of public over private, industriousness, et cetera. . . . If we are to understand the nature of the economy of any society, we have to explore its cultural heritage. People in Confucian culture can and should overcome the limitations of the Western economic system by internalizing the control of physical and material desires. (Kim, Il-gon 1994: 812)

Confucian revivalist voices are gaining strength in everyday contexts, particularly among older men. Here is a letter written by a citizen to a newspaper:

> In the age of high technology, what could be the meaning of Confucianism? Many people tend to think that Confucianism is an obstacle to social development. We often gather together and make a diagnosis of modern society, saying, "Since the Confucian tradition still persists, we cannot have social development." This is not true. We must get over this negative and passive attitude toward Confucianism. Confucianism is the principle of community life which our people have kept for a very long time. We must discover its positive side and revitalize ourselves according to its principles. It is the proper way to re-create our ancestors' tradition. (Lee, K, a resident of Taegu, *Chosôn Daily News*, May 5, 1994)

In the Korean Confucian tradition, performing ancestral rituals was crucial, and through this performance, men reaffirmed their self-identity. In the atmosphere of revitalizing "tradition," some men want to perform more elaborate traditional Confucian rituals, although these desires are often frustrated by the resistance of wives, who must provide the labor necessary for preparing the rituals. Some of the rituals are not confined within extended families but include members of larger lineage groups. It has been increasingly common to reorganize the *munjung* (clans and lineage) as more men have become interested in tracing their ancestors through twenty or thirty ascendant generations, enjoying the feeling of belonging to a group sharing the same surname (H. Cho 1990).[2] This represents a family-level Confucian restoration, led by men who had been away from home physically or mentally and were finally back and wanted to be de facto heads of their households, as their ancestors were in the peaceful years.

There is also a public-scale restoration of Confucianism. Throughout modern South Korean history, Confucianism has been regarded negatively. In the early decades of this century, Korean reformers fiercely criticized Confucianism for its conservatism, elitism, and empty ritualism. Confucianism was blamed for Korea's failure to transform itself into a modern nation-state and also for the relative lack of participation of the traditional Confucian elite in the independence movement during Japanese colonial rule. Although in the years immediately prior to Korea's annexation to Japan Confucian scholars organized the Righteous Armies (*uibyong*) to defend national independence, their resistance as a group quickly subsided after the annexation. In fact, the Japanese colonial government did not attempt to destroy the yangban aristocracy but tried to get its cooperation in disciplining peasants and extracting taxes. Most traditional landlords maintained their status and, in effect, supported Japanese rule by making little attempt at organized resistance.

During the colonial occupation, people of Christian background had more opportunities to get a modern education. Many of them participated in resistance or modernization movements of various kinds, thus gaining power after national independence. A Christian nationalist and pro-American, Syngman Rhee, became the first president of South Korea, with support from the U.S. government. Christianity became a powerful base for religious and political activities in South Korea, while socialism became the basis of North Korean society. It is a historical irony (or inevitability, perhaps) that the minjok-minjung movement, which had been initiated in the 1970s by Christian groups active in human-rights work, prompted a strong anti-Americanism in the 1980s and so undermined the popularity of Christianity among intellectuals. Instead, intellectuals who embraced the movement's goals rediscovered nativistic religions and traditional culture. The Confucian heritage was part of this newly discovered tradition. Confucianists made sure not to lose this chance at restoration, revitalizing their organizations and opening classes on the Confucian classics and calligraphy.

Recent incidents of homicide and of violence within families are another crucial factor underlying the emergence of the current narrative of "going back to Confucianism." The crimes of Park Han-sang, a teenager who was sent to the United States to study and killed his parents for money, and of Chijon-pa, a gang that decided to take revenge upon society by killing the rich using the same method used to kill the captives in the movie *Silence of the Lambs*, shook the whole society and forced people to think about how to recover social morality. The school districts called for teachers to strengthen moral education and suggested giving writing assignments on the topic of filial piety and teaching how to bow properly and to speak in a more polite and honorific manner. The Ministry of Education announced that it would increase the number of days students were permitted to miss classes in order to attend relatives' birthdays, funerals, and weddings.[3] According to the government, the purpose of this measure is to "provide the opportunity to share love and dialogue between family members and kin by increasing the interaction among them in this age of the nuclearization of the family" (*Chosŏn Daily News*, Nov. 12, 1994: 30).

Many Koreans have a strong ambivalence toward Confucian revivalism. Among intellectuals, there is a negative memory of such revivalism under Park Chung Hee's military dictatorship (1961–79); Park promoted the preservation of loyalty and filial piety (*chunghyo*), which can be easily translated into an ethic of compliance and conformity. Eastern philosophy professors were mobilized to preach Confucian values specifically selected to support Park's version of nationalism—that is, "economic growth by any means"—and Park's style of democracy (C. Kim 1994a: 14–16). The younger population, on the other hand, does not take Confucian revivalism seriously, regarding it as an attempt of the older generation to regain power and authority.

In a word, depending on what one wants and where one stands, revitalizing Confucianism has different meanings. It can enhance the relationships among East Asian countries while helping both nations and individuals to regain pride. It can be a means to morally revitalize the society, but also to reinforce paternal authoritarianism at home and in the workplace. Reviving Confucian (yangban) ritualistic tradition may have a value as a tourist attraction, since the yangban culture is elaborate, colorful, and well preserved. And aristocratic culture is "good to think" and even to display with, as Laurel Kendall discusses elsewhere in this volume.

Revival of Popular Folk Culture

The Korean movie *Sŏp'yŏnje*[4] was seen by more than one million people within six months after its opening in 1993. This success, expected by neither director nor producer, was so great that it created the term "*Sŏp'yŏnje* fever." *Sŏp'yŏnje* tells a rather simple story of the tragic fate of a traditional musician's family. The protagonist is an artist who is obsessed with reaching the ultimate state of *sori* (sound) in *p'ansori* (traditional Korean ballad opera). He has two children, a daughter, who is adopted, and a son, whose mother died during childbirth. The artist decides to transmit p'ansori to his two children, but the son runs away to the city, knowing there is no future in being a p'ansori artist and feeling a strong antagonism toward his father. The father and daughter have to live in extreme poverty, but he does not give up his dream. After the son leaves, the daughter refuses to eat or sing. The father, who fears that she might leave him and his art, and intending to implant han in her mind,[5] blinds her with a potion of traditional medicine. In theory, one cannot master the ultimate voice with practice and talent alone. One needs to experience overwhelming suffering and pain. With han in her heart, the blinded daughter begins to practice p'ansori to reach the ultimate state. After her father dies, she becomes a wandering p'ansori performer, as he wanted. As she pursues her profession in poverty, the son works as a traditional medicine dealer in the city. Wanting to meet his sister, he finds her in an inn after a long search, and the two perform p'ansori all through the night. The next day, the two part. The last scene shows the wandering daughter being guided by her own little daughter.

The movie presents Korean traditional music as harmonious with Korean landscapes. Audiences suddenly notice the landscape and realize that its natural beauty and harmony have been destroyed by external powers. In the penultimate scene, the heroine and her brother, who ran away from home cursing traditional music, celebrate their reunion without hugging, crying, or even talking—just singing p'ansori together. This scene is interpreted as a realization of their father's message: "Do not live within han, but sublimate it to form a creative energy."

The historical context of the movie is the period of Japanese colonial rule and American domination. The movie portrays a century of cultural domination, of "forgetting oneself." This simplified version of the cultural history of colonized Korea ends with a simple but comforting message to Koreans: For the last hundred years, Koreans have been swayed by foreign powers; they have been hurting one another in this unbearable situation without knowing why they hate one another. Leaving the memories of the past behind, they are going to end their grudge and return to normality.

What made *Sôp'yônje* such a peculiar success? Here are two student reports on the movie submitted for my class on cultural theory in 1994.

First of all, *Sôp'yônje* made me realize the beauty of p'ansori, which was foreign to me before. I didn't know there was such a moving element in it. In the midst of the invasion of Western culture, we need to reestablish ourselves, and in order to do that, we need to make a new culture based on tradition. This movie showed us what kind of tradition we should seek. I was particularly moved by how the movie evokes sympathy from all the generations. I realized that p'ansori is something that has been with us all the time. Through this movie, I came to think that I should start to find "our" roots in many areas. (Kwonsik, a college senior)

It's been such a long time since I've seen a Korean movie and been moved by the movie. I could feel my shoulders moving up and down when the music flew. It has a simple story with little dramatization and the acting of the stars was not great. Which part of the movie affected me so much? First of all, it was the sori, our music. The sound was not just traditional music. It was more than a sound. I could feel "our sentiment," something we could all feel together. I felt uneasy when Yubong, the main actor, tried to implant an ideology by saying, "These things that are really good are ours!" But still, I think the sentiment permeating the p'ansori communicated with all of us. It made me look for my lost self. Second, the scenery was great. The simple and gentle line of our land was beautifully presented. I could feel peace and comfort with the scenery the actors were traveling through, like a baby who has finally come to lie down in the cradle after a hard struggle walking. After all, the deep consolation came from "Koreanness." Living in a complex, commercialized society without "nationality," I could rarely have such a feeling. The movie aroused nostalgia for what was mine. I will be very happy if this movie can stimulate awareness of our tradition. *Sôp'yônje* proved to me that "Koreanness" can move me, and therefore, I cannot but be a Korean. (Ilgwon, a college junior)

Of course, Korean spectators read the narrative of *Sôp'yônje* in diverse ways. For most South Koreans in their fifties and older, for example, the movie evokes nostalgia. In the course of rapid urbanization, they are the ones who have deserted the soil where they were born and forgotten where they grew up. *Sôp'yônje* provides a space for them to indulge their nostalgia and cry over their guilt for abandoning home. On the other hand, for Koreans in their twenties, who are much more familiar with Western pop, rock, and blues, *Sôp'yônje* attracts curiosity as an exotic production. All get the message, however, that they must think about their own tradition and what they have. As one can read from the students' reports, the desire and joy of finding self-identity and tradition prevail. The movie's unprecedented popularity definitely has to do with the general mood of searching for a new identity in the 1990s. Youngsters particularly seem to take comfort in knowing that there is still something of "ours" left with which all Koreans can identify. Many young Koreans assume that they are in tune with p'ansori in a way foreigners would not be.

It is interesting to think of this search for sori in the context of the lucrative "world music" market—a music of "other places" is consumed and enjoyed as a global pleasure, both exotic and accessible, because music is assumed to be apprehensible across language barriers. The student's assertion that foreigners cannot understand "our" music is worth noting in this regard. It indicates a disjuncture and a tension between the strong nationalistic ideology that exists in South Korea now and the global market force. "*Sôp'yônje* fever" brought many Koreans to buy p'ansori tapes and to attend private schools to play Korean drum or flute and to explore martial arts or folk dances. *Sôp'yônje*-related items became hot commercial products and reinforced the revival of tradition. Buddhist temple rooms for Zen meditation now attract more and more people, while tearooms selling traditional tea and decorated like traditional houses or temples attract youngsters. New stores selling gifts reinvented from traditional arts and crafts and clothing designs modified from traditional styles are profiting near university campuses.

In the 1990s, narratives on culture and identity are flourishing. The hegemonic discourse of Koreanness is being created in haste by the government, businessmen, and the mass media, and is typically presented by older-generation middle-class men. While the self-contemptuous characterization of Chosenjin (a Japanese word for Koreans)[6] lingers, glorification of the Korean cultural heritage is gaining popularity among ordinary people. What is clear from new narratives on Koreanness in the 1990s is that there is a nationalistic attempt to regain national pride and capitalistic spirit in expanding into international markets.

Whose "Koreanness"? Beyond Nationalistic and Capitalistic Narratives

Where does this strong new tide of searching for oneself come from? Does it have anything to do with the democratic transition from the military regime to a civilian government? Did it happen because the South Korean economy has made people proud to be in one of the newly industrialized countries? Will this emerging interest in constructing Koreanness in the 1990s lead to various new social movements that can contribute to making a smooth social transformation into a more self-reliant state and a more democratic society?

First of all, I want to look at the internal logic underlying the revival of tradition. Politically, new narratives have been formulated with high hopes in response to the establishment of the new civilian government in 1992. Ordinary people who had kept silent under the authoritarian regime began to speak their minds under the civilian government. Various self-interest groups are forming and have participated in creating this new discourse. The civilian government and the media are actively engaged in mobilizing and controlling popular voices, in some ways intervening deeply in the formulation of narratives on Koreanness.

Many people living in contemporary South Korea think that their society is no longer exclusively the site of heroic struggles for independence from foreign invaders or for democratic rights suppressed by the military regime. Neoconservative voices are entering the space that was filled in the 1980s with revolutionary minjok-minjung narratives. In particular, those who felt "oppressed" by the ideological minjung narrative, mostly the middle class, have begun to raise their voices. Many South Koreans who lived through the 1980s seem to realize suddenly that they too are victims. Many cultural nationalists now believe that national traditions and values have been the principal resources for Korean economic development and that the revival of traditional culture is the only way to maintain themselves in a competitive materialistic age of "cultural wars."[7]

As Laurel Kendall described in her paper on Korean wedding ceremonies, when the Korean culture was viewed negatively as one of backward customs and values, the traditional wedding was called the "old style" (*kusik*) and the Western wedding the "new style" (*sinsik*) (Kendall 1994: 165–66). The old was to be replaced by the new as an inevitable development. But recently, some of the population have denigrated the "new style" as the "Western-style wedding" (*soyangsik*) in opposition to "our style" (*urisik*). In Kendall's analysis, the oppositions, old style/new style and Western style/our style, reflect two distinct stages in recent Korean history. Finding "our tradition" celebrates a uniquely Korean triumph of the will, a triumph that has been measured by the gross national product of a newly industrialized country and acknowledged internationally in the choice of Seoul as the site of the 1988 Olympics (ibid.: 166). Many Koreans now feel that a full circle has been drawn and that they are finally back "home," ready to recover their ancestral ways. It looks as if the paradox discussed by Chatterjee (1986: 2) of the colonized subject who must reject ancestral ways, which are seen as obstacles to progress, and at the same time cherish them as marks of identity against the colonizer, has been resolved.

Are South Koreans indeed back home? Chatterjee's recent study (1993) is quite illuminating here. He maintains that one characteristic of anticolonial nationalism is its emphasis on autonomy and difference from the colonial world. Specifically, he states, anticolonial nationalists created a special domain of sovereignty by dividing the world of social institutions and practices into two domains—the material and the spiritual. The spiritual was "an 'inner' domain bearing the 'essential' marks of cultural identity" (p. 6). Nationalists declared the spiritual domain their sovereign territory and refused to allow the colonial power to intervene in it. By insisting on and displaying the marks of "essential" cultural difference, they tried to maintain national autonomy.

Korean anticolonial nationalism was a typical example of this process. Ch'oe Nam-sôn, a prominent nationalist at the turn of the century, warned that Korea should not suffer the fate of Egypt and India, where aliens not only ruled but also monopolized the cultures. Ch'oe wrote:

> We must become independent, first in our minds. We must be independent ideologically and academically. We must realize a complete independence and an absolute self-determination by way of our spirit in order to respect ourselves, and to allow our thoughts to become manifest among ourselves and to permit our academic abilities to search for our own identity. We must establish Korean studies with our own hands. We must create a Korean encyclopedia alive with Korean blood and Korean breath. (Quoted in Allen 1990: 792)

Another popular early nationalist, Sin Ch'ae-ho, attempted to write a separatist, particularistic Korean history. As a strategy for strengthening the nation, Sin emphasized a spiritual rebirth embodied in it. Sin believed that heroes in history personified the spirit of the nation. Biographies of Admiral Yi Sunsin, Ch'ae Yong, and other historical patriots were written to provide role models exemplifying the best qualities of the Korean national spirit. They were heroes of defensive warfare and of unflagging loyalty and purity of spirit, patriotic examples for Korean youth to follow (Robinson 1984: 134).

At the height of anti-Americanism in the 1980s, modern patriots searching for national unity found in early nationalists such as Sin Ch'ae-ho kindred souls. A discourse on "self" was revived as a violent reaction to the hegemonic discourse of the dominant "other." It is noteworthy that the theme of a revival of national spirit, an intensified consciousness of Korea's glorious past and racial uniqueness, has been tenaciously maintained by the moral intellectuals in spite of all the drastic institutional changes of more than a century.

Postcolonial people tend to think that they have managed to put the period of colonialism behind them, but often this is not true. As Chatterjee (1993: 11) has stated, the root of postcolonial misery lies "not in our inability to think out new forms of the modern community but in our surrender to the old forms of the modern state." The totalizing, epistemic, and moral discourse of antinationalism persists as an autonomous form of the imagination of the community, but "overwhelmed and swamped by the history of the postcolonial state."

We can also think about the external logic behind the burgeoning of the new narratives. They are stimulated by the economic circumstances, the desire to survive in the world of globalization. Government and business efforts toward "making things uniquely Korean" stem directly from several perceived needs: to improve the Korean image internationally, to teach how one should interact in intercultural settings, and to get ideas about how to commercialize Korean culture in the expanding global market.

President Kim Young Sam proposed his "globalization project" on the day that he returned from a trip to some other Pacific Rim countries. The president described the concept of globalization as "a search for universal values and the common good for all the people on earth." He said that globalization should be differentiated from internationalization in its emphasis on cooperation rather than competition. He then added that globalization is more positive and a "higher" concept, and he urged Koreans to bring Korea to the fore in the context of globalization. Later he redefined globalization as "a survival strategy in the harsh international order and, at the same time, a vision for our next generation to play a central role in world management."

Kim's invocation of globalization is not embraced by all South Koreans. A newspaper columnist, Chang Myungsoo ("Kukjewa wa Segehwa"

[Internationalism and globalism], *Han'guk Daily News*, Nov. 23, 1994: 5), arguing that it is really internationalization that South Korea is going through now, expressed uneasiness about the attempt to bypass this step. In fact, she wrote, South Korea is about to internationalize in order to survive the harsh competition of the global market. The word "globalization" confuses South Koreans.

This is the intersection where global capitalism and nationalism meet. Dirlik provides an insight here in interpreting the new cultural nationalism in the context of global capitalism:

> What is intriguing about cultural nationalism is that its assertion coincides with the "internationalization" of the economies in these societies, and their increased incorporation politically and culturally in global networks. Cultural nationalism seems to represent, on the one hand, a cultural self-assertion against an earlier Eurocentric conceptualization of global culture, and, on the other hand, an effort to contain the disruptive social and cultural consequences of globalization. In nature, it bears a strong resemblance to Orientalist essentialization of East Asian societies, but this time it is the East Asians themselves who produce these representations. (1995: 1–2)

Among academics and political elites, there is an attempt to regain national pride and create a new Asian network through Confucian revival. Interestingly, this effort has been stimulated and encouraged more by outside forces, including the United States, Singapore, and Japan, than by inside intellectuals. For example, an article by Samuel Huntington (1993) created a stir among the large population of South Koreans who had a great interest in politics. Han Sung-ju, the minister of foreign affairs, asked ministry officials to read and discuss the Huntington article. The mass media found this assignment rather interesting and stirred up a big public debate over Huntington's argument on the "clash of civilizations." The overall consensus was that Huntington, and Western political scientists, for that matter, were oversensitive to, and overdefensive about, the rise of the Asian economy. People liked the idea of Asian civilization, although some did not like Huntington's idea of excluding Japan as a non-Confucian civilization and others were puzzled by his ideas about a Confucian-Islamic connection. Huntington's article surely stimulated Korean middle-aged and older male intellectuals to think over the concept of "culture area" and reminded them of the "East Asian coprosperity sphere" proposed by Japan in the 1930s.

Within the Asian context, Lee Kuan Yew, the former prime minister of Singapore and the foremost promoter of "Confucian capitalism," seems to have been quite successful in influencing South Korean elites as well as the Western academic community. I think, however, that much of this interest in Confucian revival comes from Westerners and East Asians who take an exoticizing perspective of the East, orientalizing East Asia and seeing the strengths of an essentialized difference, as Dirlik has stated. Who will benefit from this? As Koo (1993: 248) predicted, based on his study of state and civil society, in this new drift of socioeconomic change the winner, not only of economic power but also of political and cultural power, is most likely to be the capitalist class. Noticeably, this class is no longer confined by the nation-state boundary.

What is distressing here is that I found an interesting echo in the early nationalist narrative (Em 1995: 21). Eager to explain their historic failure and strengthen the nation against invasion, early nationalists, including Sin Ch'ae-ho (1880–1936) and Ch'oe Nam-sôn (1890–1957), who were heavily influenced by the Chinese intellectual Liang Qichao, absorbed social Darwinism as an intellectual framework for understanding the international politics of their time (Allen 1990: 789; Robinson 1984: 130). As early as 1906, Ch'oe stated his dream of future world domination by Korea: "How long will it take us to accomplish the goal of flying our sacred national flag above the world and having peoples of the five continents kneeling down before it? Exert yourselves, our youth!" (quoted in Allen 1990: 790).

Thinking that national vigor was imperative for societal survival, early nationalists launched the "self-strengthening movement," which was predicated on the proposition that Korea had either to struggle successfully in a competitive world or to perish (Robinson 1984: 130). The paradigm inherent in this movement was survival of the fittest and natural selection. South Korea's postcolonial state has never severed itself from this ideology. Apart from the unabashedly nationalistic discourse by moral intellectuals, an autonomous discourse on development, progress, unilineal evolution, and the survival of the fittest has often predominated over the moralist discourse.

The new narratives of the 1990s thus do not appear new when they are compared with those of the early twentieth century. What does this similarity imply? It is too early to state any conclusion or prediction about the direction of recent cultural nationalism, although I can draw one apparent conclusion from the discussion: Koreans' narratives, even on culture and identity, have been notably political in nature. They also show a totalizing tendency to essentialize Koreanness. This is quite understandable if one digs deeper into South Koreans' experiences in their national history as victims of the modernizing world.

In the late nineteenth century, the Korean state was in no position to lead in the creation of a national identity, as had the German state and the Japanese Meiji state. Korean nationalists had to struggle against both Confucian historiography and the orientalist historiography of Japan and the West. Writing against Confucian historiography was necessary in order to be modernized, whereas writing against Japanese and Western perspectives was necessary for maintaining national autonomy (Em 1995: 16). Just as modern Japanese historiography emerged as a response to the orientalism of the West, Koreans under Japanese rule had to write a counter-hegemonic history against the Japanese historiography, to invent "a historiography which insisted that Korea has always had a distinct culture and society" (ibid.: 24). While the elites of imperial Japan were busy generating discourses in order to make "modern national subjects" out of peasants and women and to appropriate "others" into their hegemony, the elites of colonized Korea struggled to resist that hegemony by insisting on cultural essence and the glorious past (Tanaka 1993). When the former regime exercised power to facilitate and to produce the "modern," the anticolonial nationalists exercised power to tie the nation to an autonomous realm of resistance discourse. A solid defensive subjectivity based on binarism was formed through colonial modernization even after the postcolonial era.

As a strategy to defend the nation/home, Koreans had to generate a powerful and totalizing discourse on a fixed identity and historiography. The theoretical basis of the early nationalist discourse was cultural evolutionism and cultural essentialism based on binarism. The new nationalistic voice in the 1990s, despite being generated in a quite different socioeconomic setting, does not deviate much from this. While challenging Western hegemony in the name of traditional culture, this voice is chauvinistic in its desire to be powerful and totalizing in its adherence to an essentialized tradition. It does not allow room to reflect on power/knowledge/history, and it oppresses minority voices at home. The nationalists are particularly anxious to push women back to the domestic sphere. They are not ready to listen to the minority voices within the nation, and they are out to become themselves one of the majority voices in the world.

I can see the strategic value of the essentialization of identity in the colonized condition. But do the Korean nationalists know that it is effective only for defending oneself from outsiders? The ideology persists that Korean blood, citizenship, and national boundaries must be intact and that national identity must supersede all the other aspects of identity, such as gender, class, generation, and locality (including regional identity and expatriate identity). Space for culture, language, communication and reflexivity, and civil society has been erased. Obviously, South Koreans can never construct a new Korea without deconstructing this chauvinistic and frozen Koreanness. Can South Korea be sustained without allowing space for multiple agents in the age of transnationalism and global capitalism? Has the basic structure of the world changed since the nineteenth century?

Epilogue

In February 1995, Oe Kenzaburo and Kim Chi-ha met. Oe is a Japanese novelist, a highly respected intellectual, and the winner of the 1994 Nobel Prize for literature, and Kim is a Korean poet who was a political prisoner and a symbolic figure in the democratic struggles in the 1970s. In the 1970s Oe joined a hunger strike to demand the unconditional release of Kim from prison. Oe respected Kim and even mentioned Kim in his Nobel lecture. What Oe told Kim at this meeting is worth citing here:

> I have a feeling that you are completing a universe. This is quite different from my thinking. I did not try to construct a world. I have been trying to empty myself by diffusing my world. I read your writings when I was wondering whether there can be the universe in me, a small town of me. I don't think the center of the world is moving toward Asia. In all the towns in the world, there is a center. (J. Choi, "Oe Kenazburo ûi Chokuk Pipan" ["Oe Kenzaburo's Critique of His Own Fatherland"], *Han'gyere Weekly*, Feb. 16, 1995: 79)

Kim expressed the view that East Asia will become the new center of the world, but Oe disagreed, saying, "Everywhere is the center and the periphery." Any narrative has a meaning only when it is historically and culturally located. Although I, as a feminist, share Oe's perspective, I cannot simply ignore the poet's wish. Some aspects of the new narratives on Koreanness are annoying to me in their chauvinism and irrationality. I feel, however, that I should not reject them entirely.

When I wrote a critique of *Sôp'yônje* (Cho 1994), I did not criticize the film for effacing women's capacity to voice their own will and desire. I was fully empathetic with Heh-rahn Park (1994), who wrote an insightful criticism of the movie, expressing feelings of frustration and estrangement from the exalting spectators. As she pointed out, in that movie male characters, portrayed as having intractable superegos, are juxtaposed with female characters who are mere receptacles, existing only to rescue the fragile male ego and fulfill its desires. Instead of highlighting this point, however, I emphasized that I was happy to have a film that made me think about "ourselves." I applauded the film and the director's "enlightenment spirit," which urged us to construct narratives of "our lives" in the context of modern history. I was happy to have a "text" to write about. I was telling myself that it represented not a nationalism mainly of resistance to external powers, but a new nationalism with which to build a healthy modern society. Any society caught in the worldwide modernist project cannot and should not skip the stage of building a nation from the inside. Building a "civil society" to make a nation from the bottom up is a crucial process in modernization.

South Korea, having been a "historic failure" for a long time, needs to build a civil society now. Having said this, I fear it sounds fatuous; almost all nations are historic failures in the modern world anyway, some may say. Postmodern failure, however, should be distinguished from modern failure. For the first time in modern history, South Koreans are ready to generate a public discourse on themselves. Having been subalterns in the world system for a long time, Koreans are about to enter the modern era, constructing Koreanness, not deconstructing it.[8]

Decolonization is not an easy matter to people who have given up the language with which they can discuss their problems, who have buried the history of their everyday lives. This process of decolonization has started, however, and its significance should not be underestimated. Wars have been raging against a cultural amnesia. Koreans in the boundary zone have finally begun to ask: Who is Korean, and whose Koreanness are we talking about?

PART III

CHINESENESS

5

On Three Definitions of Han Ren

IMAGES OF THE MAJORITY PEOPLE IN TAIWAN

HSIEH SHIH-CHUNG

WHAT is an ethnic group? This is a critical question for social scientists interested in theory of ethnicity, ethnic politics, sociocultural construal or bioracial orientation of ethnicity, and ethnic-cultural survival. Numerous definitions appear in anthropological and sociological works. Charles F. Keyes (1976) maintained that shared descent is the most critical factor giving rise to a sense of identity. In a later argument (1981), he added pragmatic need in group social life as another important dimension in emphasizing identity and organizing ethnic action. Pierre L. Van Den Berghe, taking a sociobiological approach (1978, 1981), echoed Keyes's theory of blood superiority. Not recognizing the strong possibility of pseudo- or imagined brotherhood, he contended that kin selection under the principles of both biological nepotism and ethnocentrism becomes a basic condition in formulating an ethnic group. George DeVos (1982), in addition, emphasized "subjective sense" or "self-perception" by the form of any key association, such as racial uniqueness, territoriality, economics, religion, aesthetic cultural patterns, and language. His point is supported by James McKay and Frank Lewins (1978), who proposed "a sense of belonging" as a crucial trait in defining an ethnic group. These efforts to describe the scope of a homogeneous people called an ethnic group give the impression of stable and clear boundaries. A particular ethnic group seems to be recognized or identified easily by objective observation.

Etically, a scholar may establish that an ethnic group exists or has existed somewhere by finding shared traits such as language or religion, as suggested by DeVos. Emically, members of this recognized group may, in public or in response to an interviewer's inquiry, claim brotherhood with the other community residents, as in Keyes's example of *chat* Thai (ethnic Thai), a conceptualized identification vocabulary that is shared by all Thai people. Most scholars agree with Keyes's interpretation of "chat," or ethnics, which "constrains social action, but . . . does not determine all action" (1976: 204), although ethnic groups that seem to have effectively maintained member unification can be clearly distinguished by researchers, and probably also by natives. Social scientists have long studied ethnic action, as well as the definition of the ethnic group and its nature (cf. Southall 1976; Geertz 1973; Barth 1969; Berreman 1982; Keyes 1973; Trosper 1981; Eidheim 1969). Studying social life or ways of playing among members of an ethnic group has the same purpose: understanding what this particular group is and how its people identify each other as members.

Michael Moerman (1965) has discussed who the Lue of northern Thailand are, suggesting that historical memory of the Lue state in Sipsong Panna (now Xishuangbanna Dai Autonomous Prefecture, southern Yunnan, China) is a key element shaping people's identity. Judith A. Nagata (1974) has attempted to figure out what a Malay is, pointing out that the membership of the ethnic Malay group changes with the situation. Keyes, decades after these publications, has rethought the nature of Lue identity (1992), taking the name "Lue" as an example of "situational meanings." I would suggest applying this concept to the Lue as their communities in present-day Laos, Thailand, and China face both national and transnational impacts.

These scholars have worked on discovering the principles of receiving ethnic membership. In this, they have followed the tradition of defining an ethnic group and studying its nature. They each have tried to clarify the meaning of a particular ethnic name. Although we know how academic experts define ethnic groups, the natives' or ethnic members' definitions and descriptions of themselves are missing from anthropological knowledge. We do not know the characteristics of the members of a particular ethnic group as seen through their own eyes. Also lacking are systematic analyses of opposing viewpoints among members of the same ethnic group. In this chapter, I will describe an ethnic phenomenon in Taiwan to illustrate the manipulation of a variety of interpretations of ethnic identity by members of different groups.

Interaction between the indigenous people of Austronesian heritage and the Han Taiwanese / Chinese and relationships between the minority people and the state have only recently become of interest to anthropologists in Taiwan. Huang (1989) and Hsu (1989) consider *Ren tong de wu ming* (Stigmatized identity, Hsieh 1987a) to be the first work on the ethnicity of the indigenous people of Taiwan. Since its appearance, a number of researchers have taken up the subject. Mu-chu Hsu (1989, 1991), Mao-t'ai Chen (1992), Ts'ui-p'ing Ho (1993), Hsiao-yen P'eng (1994), and Hsieh (1987b, 1990, 1992a, 1992b, 1992c, 1994a, 1994b) are important contributors.

The greater part of this work has concentrated, however, on the minority or indigenous side of the relationships between minority and majority. In other words, recent anthropological findings have given us an understanding of the nature of the ethnic identity of the indigenous people, the reasons they initiate ethnic-political movements, the expectations of particular minority groups for their own futures, and the formation of the inferiority of indigenous social status. The majority side, on the other hand, seems to have been neglected. We do not know who the majority are, how they define themselves, what they feel about themselves while in contact with the indigenous people, and how they interpret the immigration history of the Han. It is obvious that ethnic phenomena in the context of the indigenous people, the Han, and the state are still not completely clear. This chapter is an attempt to call attention to aspects of the majority side.

In the main nonacademic literature related to indigenous society, there are at least three kinds of definitions of the Han people, or Han *ren* or Pingdiren, that is, people who live in the plains area, as opposed to the mountainous homeland of the indigenous people, or Mountain People (Shandiren). The first kind is proposed by the Han politicians who are responsible for indigenous affairs. The second refers to the viewpoints of indigenous resistance intellectuals. The third comes from a group of Han humanists who are critical of Taiwan's political environment.

In the following sections, I will describe how these different interpreters (Han politicians, indigenous activists, and Han humanists) identify or define the history of the relationships between the Han and the indigenous people, the ethnic or national characters of the Han majority and the Taiwan indigenes, and the nature of Han Chinese culture. Then I will discuss the meanings of these distinguishing interpretive discourses. My purpose is to try to uncover the mechanism shaping the present ethnic phenomena in Taiwan.

Han Ren as a Supporter, Protector, and Curer

Since the Kuomintang (KMT, or Nationalist Party) government fled from the Chinese Communist Party (CCP) in mainland China and set up a refugee regime in Taiwan in 1949, the previous occupation by the Japanese (1895–1945) has been seriously criticized for causing the present "backward" Taiwan and "enslaved" Taiwanese. The KMT government, which is mostly composed of Han Chinese mainlanders, is characterized as the savior of the island. This "salvation" has been much more evident in indigenous tribal areas than in Han Taiwanese communities.

In 1960, an investigative team sent out by KMT headquarters published a report titled *Nong, yu min, kuang gong, Shan Bao sheng huo fang wen bao gao* (A report of the general lives of farmers, fishermen, miners, and Mountain People). The author wrote of the Mountain People, that is, indigenous people: "Lives of the Mountain People are poor and backward in comparison with the Han in the plain. One of the main reasons was Japanese political domination and economic exploitation" (Zhong Guo Guo Min Dang 1960: 84). Pai-yuan Yang, an official who served in the provincial government of Taiwan, even insists on blaming Japanese domination for the "laziness, superstition, alcoholism, and conservatism" found in Mountain People's everyday lives (1968: 163). Another governmental publication, celebrating the sixtieth anniversary of the founding of the republic, maintained that the government had faced a mountain society long dominated by the Japanese police and characterized by ignorance, cultural backwardness, difficult living conditions, and discrimination in every sphere (Tai Wan Sheng Zheng Fu 1971: 23).

In short, the Japanese were bad and had failed, and the indigenous people had experienced a sorrowful history and had encountered a crisis of survival. This dogmatic view gave the KMT every reason to formulate a salvation policy that would get rid of all the badness left by the Japanese and supply the Han ren's goodness to the minority people. The KMT politicians have focused entirely on the improvement of people's social lives and biological character.

In 1953, the KMT government formulated two policies under the names of *Cu jing shan di xing zheng jian she ji hua da gang* (A principle of promoting mountainous administration of Taiwan Province) and *Tai Wan sheng shan di ren min sheng huo gai jing yun dong ban fa* (Methods of improving the lives of the Mountain People in Taiwan Province). It also put forward the slogan "Making the mountain plainized," which means Hanizing the indigenous people.

In 1962, the government replaced this slogan with a new aim, "urging the Mountain People to agglomerate into the general society" (Tai Wan Sheng Zheng Fu 1971: 27). According to the report of the KMT investigative team, the government has been endeavoring to improve the lives of the Mountain People, including their economic life, education, clothing, food, housing, and customs. The government asks the indigenous people to adopt rice cultivation and abandon growing taro and potatoes using slash-and-burn techniques. The most important educational strategy is to force the learning of Mandarin. The public wearing of most traditional clothes is prohibited. Some kitchen facilities and utensils, such as chopsticks, tables, and cooking ranges, have been introduced to indigenous families. In addition, officials sent by the government ask people to divide their houses into separate rooms. Attempts are made to reform all "harmful and unhealthy" customs. Major emphasis is placed on ending drunkenness, destroying superstition, strictly forbidding witch doctors, unifying the dates of various supernatural rituals, and urging the adoption of collective marriage under the supervision of local officials (Zhong Guo Guo Min Dang 1960: 40–41; Tai Wan Sheng Zheng Fu 1971: 23–34; S. Huang 1966: 140–46).

It is clear that state agents and officials and Han politicians regard almost all of the traditional ways of living of the indigenous people as without value. All official documents and patriotic writers have concluded that there has been an "unbelievable improvement of the mountain society" (Zhong Guo Guo Min Dang 1960: 41; S. Huang 1966: 138; Kuo 1985: 1; cf. Hsieh 1992c: 103–4). Pai-yuan Yang (1968), representing the state, cites the following evidence that the Mountain People have entered into "civilized spheres": poverty has been transformed into well-to-do conditions, former (uncivilized) folkways have become historical memory, laziness has been reformed, backward marriage customs have been abolished, modern clothes are worn, old burial ways are no longer followed, and the entire content of the "culture of Three Principles" (the KMT's highest dogma) has been accepted. Yang believes that a new paradise has been founded in the mountainous areas.

Since the middle of this century, the state's propagandists have intensively advertised the achievements of the KMT in indigenous affairs (see Hsieh 1992c: 103–4). The most popular words in the statements of KMT representatives are "improvement," "establishment," "modernization," "protection," and "preferential treatment." Viewed another way, the opposite of the indigenous people is the "modernized," "civilized," "correct," "capable," and "highly moral" Han people. The Han people, especially the political elites and representatives of the state, thus become a group of all-round teachers, kind protectors, and respectable saviors. In other words, the KMT government manipulates powerful media and the educational system to shape a positive image of its treatment of the Mountain People. This heroic image seems to be very different, however, from that perceived by indigenous young intellectuals. I will describe this view in the next section.

Han Ren as Devil

In 1984 indigenous college youngsters initiated a panethnic political movement for the purpose of calling attention to the long, sorrowful history of the indigenes and regaining lost rights (Hsieh 1987a, 1987b, 1992b). Most of the earlier writers and leaders had focused on bringing to light the misfortune of the indigenous people, including both residents in home tribes and urban immigrants, by calling meetings and holding demonstrations. Recently, some radicals have wished to negotiate with the government about the possibility of indigenous autonomy (Hsieh 1992b; Kao 1994). No matter what ideology or strategy the indigenous activists have followed, however, the most important element has always been criticism of the Han people. To them, "Han ren" means "devil." They identify as devilish features of the Han ren discrimination, greed, deceit, rudeness, exploitation, unfairness, killing, ignoring, chauvinism, selfishness, insidiousness, insincerity, utilitarianism, invasion, and immorality. The critical magazine *Lieren Wenhua* (*Hunting Culture*), carried on by a group of young indigenous resistance elites from 1990 to 1992, expressed typical views of these negative features of the Han ren.

Bawan Danaha (1992), in an article published in *Lieren Wenhua*, maintained that the head-hunting behavior that had existed in indigenous societies in the past was a reaction to Han ren's longtime cheating. Walis Yugan, editor in chief of *Lieren Wenhua* (1992: 53), and another primary school teacher, Kaliduoai Kabi (1991), wrote of invasion and being defrauded of reservation land in mountainous areas. Kabi said that bribed officials colluded with profiteers in forming a group of powerful local despots whom the villagers had no way to resist. Monaneng, a famous indigenous blind poet, wrote in the poem *Shan Di Ren* (The Mountain People) about Han ren's deceit causing enslavement of his people (see Jilufugan 1991: 14). To the indigenous elites, "hoodwinking" seems to be in the natural character of the Han ren. The indigenes have been fooled ever since the Han arrived on the island. Even the KMT government, controlled by Han politicians, continues to deceive the indigenous people. For example, on Orchid Island, where the Yami people have lived for more than eight hundred years, the government built a storage facility for nuclear waste, but deceived the residents by claiming that it was a military port (Baluer and Laigelake 1992: 41). In another case, the central government decided to build a huge cement factory at the village of Heping, Hualian County, but never negotiated with the villagers, most of whom are members of the Atayal tribe ("Yuan Zhu Min shi jian ti" 1991).

Chauvinism is another frequent accusation. The editors of *Lieren Wenhua* pointed out that the Han chauvinists compel the indigenous people to migrate to urban areas ("Yuan Zhu Min shi jian fen xi" 1991: 7). Yijang Baluer and Lawagao Laigelake, the previous two chairmen of the Alliance of Taiwan Aborigines (ATA), the first nontraditional resistance organization in indigenous society, complained angrily about the double pressures of Han chauvinism, suffered only by indigenes, and autocratic domination of the KMT government, which was widely endured by all residents of Taiwan (1992: 36). In the early 1990s, the indigenous elites asked to change their ethnic name from Shanbao, which means "mountain siblings," to Yuanzhumin, which means "the people who originally lived here," in the revised constitutional law. The KMT rejected this proposal. Chung-han Ts'ai, one of the six indigenous legislators in the Legislative Yuan, subsequently wrote in *Lieren Wenhua*: "Please do not manifest the superiority of Han chauvinism again and again to grant something to the other party that he does not need. It really hurts us indigenous people" (1992: 15). Another group of anonymous indigenous youngsters at that particular moment collectively deemed that "history will become a curse to Han chauvinism" ("Yuan Zhu Min ku qi le" 1992).

Other features of the Han ren are also associated with natural, ethnic, or national character. Bihao Lamang, a resistance leader, pointed out that an avaricious and brutal character is usually hidden under the surface of self-defined "civilization" and "progress" (1991; cf. "Lan yu yuan yun de qi shi" 1991). Several writers charged that the Han ren's "culture of eating delicacies for strengthening one's own body" had caused the extinction of wild animals in the mountainous areas. Han ren therefore are regarded as immoral people ("Shei shi sha shou?" 1992; I Sing 1992: 20). In addition to such selfishness, Bawan Danaha wrote, the Han ren never think about the minority people: "The humble and good-natured indigenous people are not unable to learn things well; it is instead because the Han people have ignored the value of indigenous existence." (The "it" here refers to the fact that the resource of education is much scarcer in tribal areas than in the plain area.) He regarded the majority group as insidious, prejudiced, disdainful, insulting, and irrational (1991: 39–40). Yijiang Xilan unhesitatingly put all the blame on the KMT's "despicable look" when lamenting the miserable condition of the indigenous people (1992: 27).

In short, the accusations of the indigenous resistance elites include all Han ren, whether land invaders, blood-sucking capitalists, ignorant representatives of the government, or selfish people in general. The Han and indigenous people form a dual frame in terms of moral standards. The former are devilish in character and corrupt in behavior; the latter are pure in character and innocent in behavior. The resistance elites emphasize this contrast as a powerful strategy to further their own ethnic-political movement. It therefore seems to me that an approach resembling racialism, that is, one that assumes all Han ren possess a particular kind of biological nature and practice a universal cultural behavior, is unavoidable.

Han Ren and Original Crime

At about the same time that indigenous voices were beginning to speak out, a group of Han humanists, most of them journalists, social critics, writers, or newspaper editors, also expressed support for the indigenous resistance movement. Besides shouting encouragement, these pen-holders have spent considerable energy on self-reflection and confession of Han ren's responsibility for the tragic state of the indigenous people.

When an indigenous dance team was organized in early 1991, Chin-fa Wu, a self-proclaimed old friend of the indigenes, with a friend from America, went to see it. His friend commented, "They will become the best dancers in the world. They are the real voice of Taiwan. We Han ren owe them too much, actually." This comment brought tears to Wu's eyes. He wrote later that this was his "first time in tears for the culture of Taiwan" (1993: 33). T'ien-chun Hung, a reporter who has written more than twenty articles in several newspapers concerning indigenous history and the future, once said, "I am ashamed of being unable to reward the indigenous people. I have received a lot from the spirits of indigenous people, after all" (1993: 50). Hung's colleague Chia-hsiang Wang feels that he himself bears the cross of guilt for Han ren's treatment of the indigenous people and regrets that he is in no position to help face the miserable circumstances of the indigenous world (1993b: 62). Wang not only mentions his debts to indigenes (1993b: 88) but even realizes that to be a Han brings a measure of self-disgust (1993c: 226). Hsun Chiang, a painter and university professor, has called for self-criticism and introspection regarding the faults of previous years (1993: 168). Yu-feng Chen has straightforwardly urged accepting and tolerating cultures alien to Han Formosans in order to ameliorate the unfortunate situation created by the Han—who are alien to indigenous Formosans (1993: 104).

In another article, Hsun Chiang suggested a strategy to promote Taiwanese self-examination, that is, "to appreciate and respect indigenous arts, an invention by such an uncorrupted people" (1992: 59). But Chin-fa Wu seemed less optimistic. He thought indifference and ignorance about their past savage behavior was still evidenced in the contemporary daily lives of most Han Taiwanese (1992).

Chih-wu Chen, an architecture professor, maintained the same view as Wu, pointing out that "ugly Han chauvinism" and racial discrimination toward the indigenous people continue to stand at the core of Han culture (1991). Mei-hui Lin, an occasional visitor to a Bunun tribe in southern Taiwan, criticized Han people's feeling of superiority after she had returned to her urban hometown. Lin, facing a frustrated indigenous intellectual talking about his stories, was conscious of a great, deep-rooted fault supposedly shared by all Han ren (1991).

It is obvious from these descriptions that these Han humanists believe Han ren should compensate for the present miserable situation of the indigenous people because of their inborn "original sin," that is, their chauvinism, discrimination, and invasion and occupation. A dual frame is also found in this particular philosophy of the relationship between Han ren and the indigenous people. The indigenous people seem to become a highly valued or supermoral symbol or standard. Han ren, on the contrary, are responsible for the majority of the sinful consequences of the multiethnic experiences of Taiwan. Han ren dominate Taiwan at present because indigenous ancestors paid a huge price that Han ren now have to repay. The indigenous people are asking to live satisfying and dignified lives, and that goal ought to be fully supported by Han ren, who owe much to them. Repayment among descendants of historical payments made between these two ethnic entities is an inner principle in the minds of Han humanists, I would suggest.

Conclusion

As discussed above, most representatives of the Han-KMT government are confident that Han ren are saviors, curers, and protectors for the indigenous people. To them, Han ren are without question a "model people" full of kindness, generosity, intelligence, and capability. Indigenous people, on the other hand, are a "salvaged people." To the indigenous resistance elites, however, Han ren are alien invaders with an insatiable desire for private gain who have turned the lives of the indigenous people into tragedy. Han ren are a "devilish people," the opposite of the innocent" indigenous people, and many Han humanists are ashamed of being Han ren because of their people's dishonorable record of relations with the indigenes. Han ren, by their definition, are a "sinful people," and the opposite indigenes might suitably be called "moral people."

In fact, all of these definition makers are constructing various types of people. The frame of "model people" versus "salvaged people" tells us of a process of cooperation, amalgamation, or adjustment in culture, nation-state identity, and ethnic or national character. The "devilish people" versus "innocent people" set suggests a process of historical conquest and contemporary domination between two peoples with different natures, one aggressive and one peaceful. The final contrast of "sinful people" and "moral people" also expresses ethnic or national character. Each of these types of people has been formulated by a principle of quasi racism. The KMT politicians and agents racially recognize that they themselves are "civilized" in nature and judge the indigenous people "uncivilized." Because the latter have to be taught and directed by the former for a very long time, they are beyond doubt innately or biologically backward, although some KMT Han have refused to state overtly that they consider the Mountain People's intelligence to be inferior (cf. Yang 1968: 163).

The resistance elites' accusations toward the Han people are based on the recognition of unchangeable evil features within the Han ren's body. The racially bad character of the Han people causes painful lives in indigenous communities. Under the Han humanists' interpretation, too, the original sin shared by all Han ren represents a kind of natural object existing in the body of the Han ren, a load with which all Han are born. Han ren, according to these humanists, should repay the indigenous peoples to release their own congenital responsibility.

To summarize, people in Taiwan have used various kinds of dual frames to interpret ethnic relationships between Han ren and the indigenous people. Those frames have indicated universal elements, such as history, culture, or ethnic or national character. In reality, however, racist points of view occupy the minds of most frame constructors. Therefore, the most baffling problem in ethnic affairs in Taiwan today probably is the operation of latent racism. People hate racism, but they have been unwittingly controlled by it.

Many scholars (for example, Keyes [1981], Nagata [1981], and Trosper [1981]) contend that members of the same ethnic group, in addition to sharing a common cultural inheritance, will pursue common social interests. Keyes (1992: 45–49) therefore disagrees with calling those people who identify themselves as "Lue" a unique ethnic group, because different "sub-Lue" in Laos, China, and Thailand not only never give evidence of motivation for practical cooperation, but also cognize different meanings of the term "Lue."

In the case of Taiwan, however, we have found that two or more mutually antagonistic interpretations of one's own group may coexist. Han humanists do not readily agree with Han administrators in describing characteristics of the Han people. When one asks KMT officials or social critics, "Who are the Han?" or "What is a Han?" their answers will be totally opposed to humanists' replies to the same questions.

Lao Lue, Sipsong Panna Lue, and Thai Lue may be forming three independent ethnic groups within their nation-states. Han Taiwanese / Chinese, however, all share the same ethnic name, Han ren, live under the same regime, and have practices similar to those of each of the three Lue ethnic groups: exclusiveness and ignorance or perhaps criticism of other groups.

Majority people, such as Han, might be categorized as an ethnic group, but difficulties with members' identity, loyalty, and self-definition seem to be very complicated. It is probable that defining so-called ethnic groups in terms of the understanding of the majority side instead of the minority position will drive us toward a new and challenging era in academic studies.

6

Clashed Civilizations?

MUSLIM AND CHINESE IDENTITIES IN THE PRC

DRU C. GLADNEY

> The great divisions among humankind and the dominating source of conflict will be cultural. Nation states will remain the most powerful actors in world affairs but the principal conflicts of global politics will occur between nations and groups of different civilizations. The clash of civilizations will dominate global politics. The fault lines between civilizations will be the battle lines of the future.
>
> —Samuel P. Huntington, "The Clash of Civilizations?"

> Dialogue here is not the threshold to action, it is the action itself. It is not a means for revealing, for bringing to the surface the already ready-made character of a person; no, in dialogue a person not only shows himself outwardly, but he becomes for the first time that which he is—and, we repeat, not only for others but for himself as well. To be means to communicate dialogically. When dialogue ends, everything ends. Thus dialogue, by its very essence, cannot and must not come to an end.
>
> —Mikhail Bakhtin, *Problems of Dostoevsky's Poetics*

THE epigraphs to this chapter express two fundamentally different views of identity, one absolute and oppositional, the other interactive and interdependent. For Huntington (1993b), culture defines the fault lines along which civilizations are bound to conflict in the post-cold war world; for Bakhtin (1984 [1963]), culture and all aspects of identity are relational, defined and redefined in interaction with an other in a contingent social sphere. While both theorists take culture seriously, they approach the subject from diametrically opposite positions, one essentialist, the other contextual. In this chapter, through examining the fault lines distinguishing two "cultures" in China, those of the Muslims and the Chinese, I will argue that Huntington's view of culture and civilization is fundamentally misguided and entirely unhelpful for understanding cultural nationalism and ethnic conflict in the modern world, thus joining a growing number of critics of Huntington's thesis.[1] I will then suggest that Bakhtin's approach, when adapted to understanding cultural identity formation, can yield a much more powerful theory of cultural and ethnic conflict and accommodation in the context of contemporary nation-states, thus contributing to a growing literature of support for the wider relevance of Bakhtin's theory of dialogism to the study of social relations (see Rahim 1994).

The case of the Muslim Chinese, known as the Hui in China, is particularly critical to the "clashed civilizations" thesis. Huntington singles out Confucian and Islamic civilizations as being fundamentally different from each other and posing the greatest threat to the West. In all, Huntington identifies "seven or eight major civilizations" in the contemporary world: Western (including both European and North American), Confucian, Japanese, Islamic, Hindu, Slavic-Orthodox, Latin American, "and possibly African" (1993b: 25). The greatest threat to the West, Huntington predicts, will come from the Islamic and Confucian civilizations, and the possibility of their forming an anti-Western alliance is his greatest fear. This was spelled out most fully in an earlier article, "The Islamic-Confucian Connection" (1993a: 19–23), in which he argued that the fundamental differences distinguishing European, Confucian, and Islamic (often glossed as "Arab") civilizations will lead to inevitable conflict and misunderstanding. Consider, for example, the following statement:

> European communities, in turn, will share cultural features that distinguish them from Arab or Chinese communities. Arabs, Chinese and Westerners, however, are not part of any broader cultural entity. They constitute civilizations. A civilization is thus of the highest cultural grouping of people and the broadest level of cultural identity people have short of that which distinguishes humans from other species. It is defined both by common objective elements, such as language, history, religion, customs, institutions, and by the subjective self-identification of people. (ibid.: 24)

What of the Muslim Chinese, however, who claim descent from intermarriages between Arabs (and other Muslims) and Chinese in China over the course of the last twelve hundred years? This, of course, raises the subsequent question of biculturalism and multiculturalism. If civilizations are defined by cultures that are fundamentally different from each other, what of those caught in between, at the interstices of culture, language, history, religion, customs, and institutions, or in the transnational diaspora moving between these so-called civilizations? If Rey Chow (1993) is correct that the shifting cultures of the diaspora most characterize the postmodern condition, and that writing that diaspora is now our most daunting challenge, then the situation described by Huntington must apply only to the modern or premodern condition, where one might still imagine cultures and civilizations in relative isolation from each other—though even this does require some imagination. Huntington's theory also becomes problematic when we consider that many of the most recent clashes since the cold war, particularly those involving Islam, have been within cultures and civilizations rather than between them.[2]

The Muslim Chinese and similarly interdependent groups (and in today's world, few are not so) evidence the need for a more developed theory that takes into account not only the heterogeneity of culture, but also the contingency of identity in the modern nation-state. Such a theory is particularly critical for the next step of negotiation, which is not between cultures or civilizations, but between nation-states in a multipolar, decentered post–cold war world. This is precisely the step that Huntington's remarkably facile theory of cultures and civilizations does not allow us to take. His theory is surprisingly essentialist and dichotomous in a world where cultures are increasingly fuzzy, interdependent, and mutually enmeshed.

It is interesting that earlier studies of the Muslim Chinese took an absolutist position similar to Huntington's: that these people had to choose between two fundamentally opposite civilizations, Islamic or Chinese. Raphael Israeli (1978, 1984) has repeatedly argued that Muslims in China, due to their diasporic predicament, had two choices: rebel against the Chinese order and establish their own Islamic state, or assimilate. In fact, they did neither. This chapter will seek to suggest why.

Becoming Ethnic in the People's Republic

Upon the founding of the People's Republic of China, an interesting dialogue began between representatives of the state apparatus and those who saw themselves as "nationalities."[3] More than four hundred groups who, in the terms of Max Weber's definition of ethnicity (1978 [1956], 1: 389), "entertained a subjective belief in their common descent" applied to the representatives of the Chinese government for recognition as official minority nationalities.

After protracted negotiations that involved an enormous program of state-sponsored investigations by Chinese anthropologists, linguists, and local officials, 54 groups succeeded in convincing the state that they were legitimate ethnic groups. The legal ratification of their ethnic status effectively excluded up to 350 other applicant groups from recognition (Fei 1981: 60). The Han were officially designated as the majority group of China, now constituting 91 percent of the total population. In the 40 years since this process began, only one other group, the Jinnuo (recognized in 1979), has convinced the state of its viable existence; fifteen groups are currently official applicants, and over 749,341 people were listed as "unidentified" in the 1990 census (*Renmin Ribao*, Nov. 14, 1990: 3).

In a discussion of the process of ethnic identification in China, Fei Xiaotong, the prominent Chinese social anthropologist, outlined the Marxist-Stalinist criteria for recognition by the state as an ethnic group. In order to be identified, a group must convince the state that it possesses a common language, locality, economy, or psychological makeup, which Stalin glossed as "culture." I write "convince" here because, as I will demonstrate below, these so-called objective criteria for ethnic identification are inherently negotiable: they are used by both sides in the debate for legitimacy. Fei Xiaotong's description of the process of identifying several questionable nationality groups assumes these four criteria and generally begins with the study of the groups' linguistic history (Fei Xiaotong, "Minorities Hold Key to Own Prosperity," interview in *China Daily*, Apr. 28, 1987, pp. 4, 67).

These four criteria are still viewed as normative for defining nationalities in a socialist society such as China (Jin 1984: 67).[4] It is remarkable that the "objective" criteria outlined by Huntington (1993b: 24) above exactly mirror Stalin's nationality criteria. For ethnic identification in China, the state defines what traditions qualify as language, locality, and culture—no matter what group's subjective belief in its existence as a people, or in the legitimacy of these cultural traditions. The Chinese state imagines what qualifies as cultural tradition for the communities in question, and the communities must respond to that depiction in terms of their own traditional notions and imaginations of identity. These often conflicting imagined identities are then negotiated in each socioeconomic setting, revolving upon symbolic representations of state, self, and other.

I will argue in this chapter that ethnic identity in China, and I think other similar contexts, is not merely the result of state definition, and that it cannot be reduced to circumstantial maneuvering for utilitarian goals by certain groups. Rather, I propose that it is best understood as a dialogical interaction of shared traditions of descent with sociopolitical contexts, constantly negotiated in each political-economic setting. This approach will also be seen to shed light on majority-minority relations in China and on the ways in which ethnic minorities are not at all marginal to the construction of Chinese national identity.

The Enigmatic Hui: In Search of an Ethnic Group

I went to China in the fall of 1983 to begin study of the Hui, one of the 55 officially identified minority nationalities. According to the state definition, the Hui are a single minority nationality, the second largest minority group in China, the most populous of ten Muslim nationalities (with almost half of the twenty million Muslims in China), and the most widely distributed of any minority (Huizu Jianshi 1978; Gladney 1991: 10). The other nine Muslim nationalities in China speak mainly Turkic-Altaic (in one case Indo-European) dialects and are concentrated in China's northwest. The Hui are distinguished from other Muslim minorities by the lack of their own language. They speak the largely Han Chinese dialects of the peoples across China with whom they live; hence they have been referred to in the literature as the "Chinese Muslims" (Israeli 1978).

Unlike many of the other minority nationalities of China, the Hui are distinguished negatively: they generally do not have their own language, dress, literature, or music, or the other cultural trait inventories by which more "colorful" minorities are demarcated. Cultural differences between disparate Hui communities far exceed their distinctions from the non-Hui among whom they live. When I arrived in Beijing I set out to carry out my rather narrowly defined proposal: an in-depth social study of an urban Muslim community concentrated mainly in one neighborhood, totaling over 200,000 Hui. However, it was not long before my informants and Hui advisers assigned to me said that if I wanted to really understand the Hui I would have to travel to where they are "typical," such as, I was told, the northwest.

During my year of fieldwork in Beijing, I went on two trips through the northwest and the southeast. I then relocated to the Ningxia Hui Autonomous Region in the northwest and spent a second year conducting further study of a Hui Sufi community. I later returned for three months to the southeast coast to examine another lineage community, and I have since made trips to other prominent so-called Hui communities in Yunnan, Tibet, Qinghai, and Xinjiang. The problem was that the more I traveled, the less I found that tied all of these diverse peoples together into one ethnic group. The following vignettes are drawn from an earlier work (Gladney 1991), which seeks to go into each community in much more ethnographic detail. I present them here to illustrate the diversity found among the Hui across China and to support my argument regarding the dialogic construction of the identity of the minority Hui vis-à-vis the majority Han.

A Northwestern Sufi Community

In Na Family Village (Najiahu), located along the upper reaches of the Yellow River in China's northwest corner, I sat among over a hundred Hui Sufis as they chanted the local *dhikr* (monotheistic formulae). Tightly wedged between two fervent devotees, and being swayed from side to side in my spot in the back of the room, I thought it was no wonder that the local Han sometimes referred to them as the fundamentalistic "shaking-head religion" (*yao tou jiao*) or "shakers." As members of a central Asian Naqshbandiyya Sufi brotherhood, the Hui chant the dhikr according to the specific dictates of their order. Villagers respond to the call to prayer issued daily from the roof of the three-hundred-year-old Ming-dynasty mosque around which the flat-roofed adobe houses are clustered; they regularly present alms to the mosque and follow the advice of the imam in arranging marriages or resolving disputes.

Although they speak a local dialect of Northern Mandarin and have no distinct language of their own, they make use of Islamic names within the village, recite Quranic texts in Arabic, and pepper their speech with Arabic and Persian words known as Huihui *hua* (Hui speech). As members of a strict Sufi *tarikat* known as the Khufiyya, they rarely marry outside of their order, and never to Han or members of rival Sufi groups (see Gladney 1991, app. A). This village is similar to many other isolated Muslim communities in the northwest, which often claim descent from Turkish or Mongolian Muslim ancestors. In the words of Robert Ekvall (1939: 19), who lived in and traveled throughout the northwest in the 1930s, these are still "little Moslem worlds" in the midst of a Han Chinese state. As one local villager explained her identity to me: "I am Hui because I am a Muslim, and my parents were Muslims." For these Hui, it is in dialogue with their Islamic heritage that they locate their unique identity.

A Hui Community in Oxen Street, Beijing

As China's largest urban minority (67 percent of all minorities in Beijing, 87 percent in Shanghai and Tianjin), the Hui often live clustered together around mosques in ethnic enclaves or former ghettos. Hui Qing Zhen (Chinese for *halal*, lit. "pure and true") restaurants can be found in every midsized town and city across China. Ma Baoguo, a youth who runs a small Hui noodle stand on the outskirts of Beijing, is one of 200,000 Hui in the capital city. Young Ma differs markedly from his northwestern Hui coreligionists: little concerned with Islamic doctrinal issues or maintaining the Muslim religious life, he concentrates his energies on running his restaurant. When we met he had never heard of the various Hui Islamic orders that proliferate in the northwest, and he only goes to mosque twice a year, during the Ourban and Ramadan holidays.

In constant dialogical interaction with his Han majority neighbors, Ma distinguishes himself from them, and is often distinguished by them, because of one thing only: he doesn't eat pork. He has taken a Han wife; his parents initially opposed this marriage, but they acquiesced when they were assured that their grandchild would be raised—and registered—as a

Hui. When I asked Ma about his Hui identity, he said: "I am Hui because I maintain the Hui way of life: I don't eat pork and like many Hui, I am good at doing business. Although I am a secular Marxist and don't believe in Allah, I go to mosque twice a year on our official 'minority nationality holidays' in honor of my ancestors, who I think came from the West [Xiyu *ren*] several generations ago."

A Hui Community on the Southeast Coast

In Quanzhou, a town on the coast of southern Fujian Province, a sign above the entrance to the courtyard off a narrow alleyway read in Chinese "Musilin *zhi jia*" (Muslim family). Below the Islamic insignia, two traditional Door Gods made of faded paper guarded the entryway, while poetic Chinese quatrains welcomed the new lunar year. When I entered the courtyard, the host gave the traditional Islamic greeting, *a-salam calaykum*, as incense smoke from a shrine to a local deity rose into the air behind him. My host explained the apparent contradiction between his Hui Muslim identity and his patronage of a Chinese god by reference to descent:

> I am Hui because my earliest ancestor was an Arab (Ahlabo *ren*), and our name was changed in the Ming dynasty [fourteenth century]. We have our family genealogy to prove it. Under the oppressive policy of the Han Chinese feudal government at that time, we Hui were forced to give up our Muslim ways, wear Han dress, adopt Han customs, and not follow Muslim dietary restrictions. But we are still Hui because we are descended from foreign Muslim ancestors. We remember our ancestors were Muslim by not giving them pork during veneration [*baizu*] with the other offerings, lest we ruin their mouths [*huai kou*].

This man is one of nearly 60,000 Hui thinly distributed along China's southeastern coast who, because they no longer maintain Islam as the other Hui in China do, were not recognized as Hui in the 1950s. In addition to folk religionists, Buddhists, Daoists, and Marxist secularists, there are several hundred Christians among these Hui who converted in the late 1930s. They tried to convince the state that they considered themselves Hui, but they lost the debate; they did not fit the state's interpretation of the Stalinist cultural criteria at that time. In 1979, however, after highly politicized negotiations with the state, during which they provided genealogic proof of their ancestry, they were officially recognized as belonging to the Hui.

This legitimation was strongly influenced by the visits by certain foreign Muslims to prominent Islamic archaeological sites in Quanzhou, including early tombs and a mosque (Gladney 1987). Kuwaiti businessmen were so impressed with the Chinese state's treatment of these Muslim coastal communities dating back to ancient days that they heavily funded the Fujian

International Airport in Xiamen and a large hydroelectric-dam project outside Fuzhou. For these Quanzhou lineages, fitting into the state-imagined notion of Hui identity has led to a resurgence in those cultural, generally Islamic, practices associated by the state with the Hui. In 1989, these Hui began keeping the Ramadan fast by not eating pork, and they obtained funds to build, next to their old lineage hall, a new mosque (called a prayer hall, *libaisi*, because stricter Muslims objected to their calling it a mosque unless all of the Hui in the village stopped eating pork). They also arranged for an imam to come from Inner Mongolia and have sent twelve young men and one woman to Huhehot to train to become clerics.

Hui Communities in China's Minority Areas

The Hui nationality also includes many groups in minority border areas who are indistinguishable in language, dress, and customs from their minority neighbors. In one Bai nationality (*minjia*) village north of Erhu Lake in Yunnan Province, I interviewed five Hui women who were training to become imams. They wore traditional Bai dress and spoke only the Tibeto-Burman Bai language, yet they were studying Arabic and Islamic doctrine in a non-Bai Hui mosque in southern Yunnan. A Malay-Austronesian–speaking fishing community I visited on the coast of Hainan Island in the South China Sea is also registered as Hui. When speaking Mandarin, they call themselves Hui. When speaking their own language, however, they refer to themselves as Utsat (Pang 1992). There are also Tibetan Muslims in Lhasa and Mongolian Muslims in the Alashan Banner district of Inner Mongolia; these are recognized by the state not as Tibetan or Mongolian Muslims, but as Hui, because there is no other special category for them.

Hui Identity and State Recognition

These communities not only differ radically from one another in language, locality, economy, and culture, but also have widely divergent visions of their past and future worlds. They subscribe to totally different imagined communities, in Benedict Anderson's (1983) terms, as well as dwelling in different social worlds. Nevertheless, they are recognized by the state as one nationality, and they now use that designation in conversations with other Hui and non-Hui. In this chapter I argue that this masking of ethnic identity and rise of new ethnic collectivities in China is related to power relations and authority.

Past anthropological approaches to ethnicity and religion were ill equipped to deal with ethnic identity in the modern nation-state. Most anthropological ethnicity theory in the West has been generated out of rather isolated studies of tribes or groups of peoples, generally in small-scale developing nations, especially in Africa and South and Southeast Asia. Most of these theories have been found to be cumbersome for the understanding of ethnicity in large, centralized, authoritarian nation-states, such as China and the former USSR, or even in plural societies, such as the United States and the nations of Western and Eastern Europe. Yet it is precisely in these areas that the resurgence of ethnic identity and interethnic conflict has become most pronounced in recent years. Examples are the Tibetan problem in China, the violent disintegration of Yugoslavia, and the tensions between different groups of Muslims in central Asia (and recently between Azerbaijanis and Armenians).

One reason for the limitations of traditional ethnicity theories in the West is that they have been mired in what Carter Bentley (1987: 25) described as "antinomous posturing" over the primordialist-circumstantialist debate—sparring over whether ethnicity is either purely cultural or expressly situational. While it is clear that the Hui cannot be identified as an ethnic group according to cultural traits of language, locality, or even religion, as the case of the Quanzhou Hui demonstrates, a purely socioeconomic or politically motivated situationalist approach, as found in Frederik Barth, Emmanuel Wallerstein, Abner Cohen, and others, cannot account for why the Hui and other ethnic groups have continued to exist in dysfunctional situations. Particularly during the radical periods of recent Chinese history, such as the Cultural Revolution, I can find no instances where the Hui rejected their ancestry: if anything their identity became more pronounced, leading to several large-scale uprisings.

Most theorists now conclude that ethnicity cannot be reduced to a means-ends calculus or primordial attachment but must involve a combination or dialectical interaction of two main aspects of identity: culturally defined notions of descent and sociopolitical circumstance (Keyes 1981: 28). An important consideration for understanding ethnic identification is the role of the state in defining who will be minority and who majority in the modern nation-state, and identifying the context and content of these statuses. In contrast to Huntington, this definition has as much to do with perceived cultural differences as it does with political expediency.

State Definition, Minority Identity, and Majority Nationalism

In every modern nation, identity is manipulated and made meaningful according to internal and external dialogues between state policy and interpretations of identity. However, China and other authoritarian regimes differ from pluralistic nations in that national identity is not optional: one is born into a nationality and is registered as such, or one is not. Unauthorized association of unrecognized minorities are still illegal; compare the situations of the Irish in Chicago or the Jews in New York, who have political power despite not being officially designated as underprivileged minorities in the United States. Only such designated minorities and Native Americans are parallel to the minority nationalities of China and the former Soviet Union. Unrecognized groups are not *ethne* for the Chinese state, no matter how much they themselves think they are.

Ethnic identities are not absent outside of the officially recognized nationalities. Unrecognized peoples live very ethnic lives. Subei people are stigmatized in Shanghai (see Honig 1992); Danmin (boat people) are ridiculed on the southeast coast; and Chinese Jews, even though they may only number 80 so far, are becoming a political force because of international attention and the formation of the Society for the Study of Chinese Jewry. There are also differences among Cantonese, Sichuanese, and Hunanese that have until now been discounted as regional, because these people are all assumed to be Han. While these groups are well recognized as ethnic outside of China, their failure to be counted among the nationalities within the state's domain has never been challenged.

These extranationality associations cast doubt on the notion of the Han. The assumption that 94 percent of China is one ethnic group is accepted by Chinese and most Western scholars;[5] this in itself should give us pause—perhaps we have been taken in for very political reasons. Fred Blake's (1981) important study, *Ethnic Groups and Social Change in a Chinese Market Town*, identified a plethora of ethnic groups defined by language, place, and occupation, including Hakka, Cantonese, and Hokkien. While only one of these groups is recognized as a minority nationality in China, no one has objected to his depiction of them as vibrant ethnic groups. This is perhaps because of their living in the New Territories under Hong Kong's jurisdiction.

Research on the rise of Russian nationalism has been popular since the 1970s in Soviet studies conducted by both foreigners and the Soviets themselves (see Dunlop 1983; Yanov 1987). It is the lack of fit of "Russian" and "Soviet" that has led to so much of this discussion (Allworth 1980: 18). As yet no larger studies of the creation of Han nationalism have emerged—mainly because it is assumed, by sinologists perhaps indoctrinated in the dominant tradition created and maintained by the regime currently in power, that "Han" is generally equal to "Chinese." Studies of Chinese nationalism address all Chinese as if they are alike, rather than considering questions of fit, as the Soviet studies have done. Perhaps the traditional Confucian preoccupation with order and harmony in a society held tenuously together by proper relationships may be one reason why these categories have never been challenged. The very Confucian practice of the "rectification of names" (*zheng ming*) is of primary concern to Chinese ethnographers: once the Han and all of the minority nationalities have been identified or named, order is restored and all is well with the realm. It is not surprising that Engels's *Origin of the Family, Private Property, and the State* is so popular in China, since it makes clear that the state's primary role is to bring order among conflicting classes.

The notion of "Han ren" (Han people) has existed for many centuries, referring to the descendants of the Han dynasty, which had its beginnings in the Wei River valley. However, I submit that the notion of "Han *zu*" or "Han *min*" (Han nationality) is an entirely modern phenomenon, arising with the shift from empire to nation. The notion of a unified Han nationality that comprises 94 percent of China's population gained its greatest popularity under Sun Yatsen. Sun advocated the idea that there were five peoples of China (*wuzu gonghe*), the Han, Man (Manchu), Meng (Mongolian), Zang (Tibetan), and Hui (a term that included all Muslims in China, now divided into the Uygur, Kazakh, Hui, etc.). This recognition served as the main platform for his Nationalist revolution, which overthrew the Qing empire and established the People's Republic. Sun and other nationalists believed that one must have peoples if one is to have a people's revolution. The critical link between Sun's Five Peoples policy and his desire to unify all of China is made crystal clear in his discussion of nationalism, the first of his Three People's Principles (Sanmin Zhuyi). Sun wrote:

> The Chinese people have shown the greatest loyalty to family and clan with the result that in China there have been family-ism and clan-ism but no real nationalism. Foreign observers say that the Chinese are like a sheet of loose sand. . . . The unity of the Chinese people has stopped short at the clan and has not extended to the nation. . . . China, since the Ch'in and Han dynasties, has been developing a single state out of a single race, while foreign countries have developed many states from one race and have included many nationalities within one state. . . . The Chinese race totals four hundred million people; for the most part, the Chinese people are of the Han or Chinese race with common blood, common language, common religion, and common customs—a single, pure race. (1924: 2, 5)

It is apparent that the Stalinist four principles, most recently reinstated by Huntington (1993b: 24), had a substantial influence on this nascent policy of Han nationalism. The overriding purpose of the rhetoric is clear: a call for the unity of the Chinese nation based on a common charter of descent.

This Nationalist policy was later changed by Chiang Kaishek when he presided over the first national congress of the Chinese Hui People's

National Salvation Association in Chongqing. At that time he declared that all non-Han groups within China are subvarieties of an ancient Chinese race. This policy was more fully stated in Chiang's treatise, *China's Destiny*:

> As to the so-called Mohammedans [Huijiao tu] in present-day China, they are for the most part actually members of the Han clan [minzu] who embraced Islam. Therefore, the difference between the Hans and Mohammedans is only in religion and different habits of life. In short, our various clans actually belong to the same nation, as well as to the same racial stock. Therefore, there is an inner factor closely linking the historical destiny of common existence and common sorrow and joy of the whole Chinese nation. That there are five peoples designated in China is not due to differences in race or blood, but to religion and geographical environment. In short, the differentiation among China's five peoples is due to regional and religious factors, and not to race or blood. This fact must be thoroughly understood by all our fellow countrymen. (1947: 39–40)

Under this policy the Hui were not considered a separate minzu (people, nationality), but a religious group with special characteristics, and were to be referred to as Huijiaoren or Huijiao tu. Hence, in Taiwan the Hui (and other Muslims grouped with them) have never attained a special nationality status (Pillsbury 1973). Interestingly, both the rationales and the purposes of Sun Yatsen's and Chiang Kaishek's nationality discourses are the same: national unity. Moreover, in Sun's Five Peoples policy we see the basis of the later Communist minority-nationality platform.

The origins of Sun's Five Peoples policy are unclear. It is not surprising that he made use of the term "minzu" ("nation," "nationality," "people," and "ethnic group" are all legitimate English glosses of the multivocal Chinese term). "Minzu" is not a native Chinese term—it derives from the Japanese term for people or nation, "minzoku." Whether it had gained earlier currency in China is not important. What is critical is that it proved particularly useful to Sun Yatsen (who lived and studied many years in Japan) in his efforts to engender support for a nationalist movement.

It is also not surprising that Sun should have turned to the idea of the Han as the all-embracing national group, including the Sino-linguistic speech communities as well as those of all the regional peoples. Sun was Cantonese; traditional northern suspicions of southern radical movements dating back to the Song dynasty (ninth century) were of course well known to him. This repeated historical pattern and the traditional antipathy between the Cantonese and other northern peoples would have posed enormous barriers to his promotion of a nationalist movement. Sun found a way to rise above deeply embedded north-south ethnocentrisms. His employment of the term "Han" was a brilliant attempt to mobilize non-Cantonese, especially Northern Mandarin speakers and the powerful Zhejiang and Shanghainese merchants, into one overarching national group. The Han were seen to stand in opposition to the other, rather insignificant minorities on their borders, as well as the Western imperialists. Only by drawing together under the idea of the Han people could they prevent the dismemberment of the Chinese state. Naturally, neither the Nationalists in Taiwan nor the Communists on the mainland challenged this generic ethnonym. It proved too fundamentally useful. It is surprising, however, that this concept of the Han as one ethnic group making up 94 percent of China's population has never been doubted by non-Chinese scholars.

By contrast, I recently asked a Han colleague when he first realized he was a Han. No monocultural individual, he grew up in the cosmopolitan Manchurian city of Harbin, long a center of Sino-Soviet trade and northeastern ethnic diversity, and populated by Russians, Manchurians, Koreans, Mongols, Olonqen, Daur, Hezhe, and Hui. Yet this intellectual, now conducting postdoctoral research at Harvard, grew up without ever realizing that he had a distinct nationality. "The first time I knew I was a Han," he told me, "was when I was seventeen years old and I registered for work. I filled out the form and the man there told me to write 'Han' in the blank category for nationality [minzu]. I didn't know what to write." It was when he applied for a job in the state-controlled sector that this Han fully realized his official ethnic status. It had had little meaning for him until that time. Attention to personal habitus cannot ignore the context of state hegemony and power.

The importance of international relations to ethnic identity should also be emphasized. To preserve positive relations with foreign Muslim governments, the Chinese have only been harsh toward their Muslim groups when the most radical politics prevailed. Those extreme-left radicalisms, as political theorists have shown, often coincided with insecure international borders. When China felt threatened by encroaching rival powers (e.g., during the Vietnam War), leftist radicalism prevailed (e.g., the Cultural Revolution). Now that no one challenges the legitimacy of the Chinese nation-state—even Tibet has been accepted as part of China by the United Nations—and the Soviet threat has fallen in upon itself, China can afford to have a more open policy toward its minorities. If outside threats should arise, so presumedly would minority policies harden—just as resentment toward Japanese in America bears a direct relation to the perceived economic or political threat Japan poses to American interests.

Ethnicity and the Nation-State

E. K. Francis (1976: 114), in his lengthy and profound analysis of interethnic relations, was one of the first to argue that the rise of ethnic identities and interethnic conflict was a phenomenon of the modern nation-state—as nation-states were built on the ashes of former empires, ethnic identities became more salient for social interaction and discourse. David Maybury-Lewis (1984: 221), in his discussion of ethnicity in plural societies, has argued that it was the French Revolution's ideal of equality and participation in governance that formed the basis for the idea of the modern nation-state. Even though Rousseau would have opposed the recognition of ethnic groups for fear that they would interfere with individual representation, the "social pact," which Rousseau argued "established equality among all citizens" (1968 [1762]: 49), allowed for the possibility of such recognition. Hobbes's famous dictum, "Nature hath made men so equal" (1962 [1651]: 141), was couched in the awareness of the differences separating them, which he encouraged the state to resolve without the necessity for war as a final means of adjudicating inequity and exploitation. The recognition of equality rests on the admission of difference.

Lloyd Fallers, one of the few anthropologists to analyze the "anthropology of the nation-state," notes that "the logic of populistic nationalism . . . encourages scrutiny to discover and eradicate diversity and thus exacerbates diversity" (1974: 3). "Since sovereignty in the modern nation-state is vested in the people, rather than in a monarch legitimated by descent or religious charisma," Charles Keyes (1984: 15) perceptively argues, "the subjects of the modern nation-state must be integrated into the people."[6] Indeed, Ernest Gellner (1983: 55) proposes that "nationalism engenders nations, not the other way around." It is culture, or, I would argue, cultural expression, that is manipulated and invented for the sake of the nationalist interests of either the state or the community in question.

If culture did not exist, Gellner has suggested, nationalist movements would have had to invent it. Huntington argues that if the cold war no longer exists, culture itself needs to be invented, or at least resurrected, to explain political conflict. As I shall argue below, these "inventions of tradition" (Hobsbawm 1983: 4), whether cultural or political, are better understood as negotiations over, and reinterpretations of, symbolic representations of power and identity—an unceasing process that becomes particularly salient when the nation-state takes upon itself the task of legislating national identity, ethnicizing minorities as a means for homogenizing majority.

National identity becomes particularly critical during modern state-incorporation, where citizenship may be imposed rather than sought. In this case, actual participation in the government process is not as crucial as the idea that such participation should take place in the modern nation-state. The precise nature of the group itself becomes a matter for negotiation and genesis.

The vast majorities of these instances of ethnogenesis occur in the context of incorporation into and identity within a larger nation-state, often dominated by elites appealing to a single ethnic or interest group. These ethnic identities form and reform according to articulated hierarchies of alterity with the particular oppositional power in question (see Gladney 1996). Sir Edmund Leach (1954) was the first anthropologist to argue that ethnic identity is formed as the result of power oppositions: the Kachin in highland Burma only acted ethnically when in opposition to the Shans. Evans-Pritchard's (1940) classic study of the Nuer determined the unique expansive-contractive nature of hierarchical segmentary lineages among acephelous nomadic societies. When the Nuer were confronted with an outside power, they unified and organized to a high degree of political complexity in order to respond to the challenge. When the threat subsided, they diversified and atomized. Ethnic identities are often seen to coalesce and crystallize in the face of higher-order oppositions. Although Huntington (1993b: 22) admits that people and their cultures change as they interact and move across cultures, and that there are different "levels" of culture, he continues to reify culture as a static object, one somehow unaffected by the power relations of the modern state. In the modern era, it is often the nation-state itself to which cultural groups find themselves in dialogical opposition.

The Dialogic Nature of Cultural Identity

I propose that cultural identity and ethnogenesis in the modern nation-state are a process of dialogical interaction between self-perceived notions of identity and sociopolitical contexts, often defined by the state. This is in contrast to Huntington's notion of culture and civilizations that are held constant across time and space, isolated from and uninfluenced by neighboring civilizations, despite centuries of interaction. In each of these examples of Hui ethnogenesis we see at least two levels of discourse, articulated internally and externally. I return to Bakhtin, whose study of Dostoyevsky posed fundamental questions of self and society, identity and ideology: "The endlessness of the external dialogue emerges here with the same mathematical clarity as does the endlessness of internal dialogue. . . . In Dostoevsky's dialogues, collision and quarrelling occur not between two integral monologic voices, but between two divided voices (one of those voices, at least, is divided). The open rejoinders of the one answer the hidden rejoinders of the other" (Bakhtin 1984 [1963]: 253, 254).

In the composition of ethnic discourse and identity, we find an internal dialogue between the social actors over their traditional interpretations of ancestry, no matter how that is marked symbolically, and an external dialogue with those to whom the group is in significant opposition: other ethnic groups or the broader state as it is represented at the local level. As the dialogue at each level changes, so does their self- and other-definition. This dialogue is a "prolonged conversation," as Jean Comaroff (1994: 309) noted in a very different context—continually revived and altered during the course of shifts in discursive power. What is unique in the modern era, however, is that groups are now in dialogue with, and in opposition to, not only other groups, tribes, ethnicities, or whatever you wish to call them, which have always existed; now the group confronts and is confronted by the state, whose general policies are articulated by its representatives at the local level.

I suggest that the process is one of dialogue and interrelation, not dialectics, in that new identities do not always emerge antithetically to the old: new identities may surface, old ones may be reinvented, and all will be in constant dialogue with one another. Dialectical change implies a negation of the prior subject with the resolution of a new synthetic form. Strict Hegelian dialectics invoke notions of unidirectional change and progress. However, ethnic identity and change are often a convoluted process of dynamic interaction with prior notions of identity and environment—a setting in constant flux due to migration, power relations, and state policy. This dialogical process is seen especially in Hui ethnogenesis and the emergence of a higher-order collectivity. The question of state interaction and incorporation—the creation or reinvention of their traditions by the Chinese nation-state—is particularly relevant to the emergence of the modern Hui people.

The Ethnogenesis of a Muslim Minority: From Hui jiao to Hui min

Official histories and minority-nationality maps to the contrary, before their identification by the state in the 1950s, the Hui were not a united ethnic group in the modern sense of the term. Like many other groups, the Hui only emerged in the transition from empire to nation-state. The people now known as the Hui are descended from Persian, Arab, Mongolian, and Turkish Muslim merchants, soldiers, and officials who settled in China from the seventh to the fourteenth century and intermarried with Han women. They largely lived in isolated communities, and the only thing that some, but not all, had in common was a belief in Islam. Until the 1950s, Islam in China was known simply as the "Hui religion" (Hui *jiao*); any believer in Islam was a "Hui-religion disciple" (*Huijiao tu*). When necessary, some of these believers were further described using the terms "Hui who wore turbans" (*zhuantou* Hui), referring to the present-day Uygur; "Hui with colored eyes" (*semu* Hui), meaning central Asian Turkic peoples; and other local ethnonyms. This usage derives from Chinese attempts to generalize about the central Asian peoples on its northwestern borders; the people in the settled oases-based kingdom with which the Tang dynasty had most interaction called themselves Uygur, and the term in Chinese became Huihe or Huigu. By the Yuan dynasty all Muslims were referred to in Chinese as Huihui (Leslie 1986: 195–96). The specific official labels for the Hui people and the other nine Muslim minorities were only legally established after the founding of the People's Republic.

Djamal al-Din Bai Shouyi, a famous Hui Marxist historian, was the first to argue persuasively that "Islam" should be glossed in Chinese as Yisilan *jiao* (Islam), not Hui *jiao* (Bai 1951).[7] He noted that the Hui believed not in their own religion, but in a world religion of Islam, and therefore are Muslims in religious terms. In ethnic terms they are the Hui people, not Hui-religion disciples. In Marxist terms, he identified a process of indigenization of a world religion to a local context, which for the communities now known as the Hui had been going on for twelve hundred years; this process was studied by Weber and later followers of his method. Muslim groups identified by Chinese linguists attempting to use the groups' own languages derived their Chinese ethnonyms from that language family; thus the Uygur, Kazakh, Tadjik, Uzbek, Kyrgyz, and Tatar were identified. In this identification, the Chinese were heavily influenced by the prior Soviet identification of these peoples in Soviet central Asia.[8] Bai Shouyi went on to identify the Muslim peoples not identified by language or locality as a catchall residual group known as Hui *min*, not Hui jiao. Thus the official category of the Hui was legitimated.

More problematic are three other identified Muslim groups, the Dongxiang, Baoan, and Salar, located primarily in the Hexi corridor of the Gansu-Qinghai Tibetan plateau, in a region now largely included in the Linxia Hui Autonomous Prefecture. Each of these groups speaks a combination of Turkic, Mongolian, and Han Chinese dialects and is thus defined mainly by locality; for example, the Dongxiang (East Township) derive their name from the eastern suburb of old Hezhou (Linxia), where they were concentrated. The question remains, however, why these groups received separate identifications, when other groups, such as the Mongolian Hui, Tibetan Hui, Bai Hui, and Hainan Hui, are all identified as Hui despite their separate localities and languages. It is not because the Hui populations are too small; the Tatar number only 4,127, and there were 9,027 Bao in 1982, while there are at least 6,000 Hainan Hui (Pang 1992), as well as large but uncounted populations of Mongolian, Tibetan, Dai, Yi, and Miao Hui (see Ma W. 1986). Chinese minority publications proudly proclaim the recognition of such insignificant groups as the Hezhe, despite their only possessing a population of 1,476 in 1982, up from 300 at the time of the revolution and 450 at the time of their identification in 1953 (Zhongguo 1981: 57–68; Banister 1987: 322–23).

It is clear that a strict interpretation of Stalin's four identification principles would not have yielded the ten Muslim groups identified in China today. Instead, we find a combination of political, strategic, and pragmatic concerns in the early recognition of these groups. This is not surprising, given Walker Connor's (1984) thesis that the early Bolsheviks' main concern in resolving the nationality question was not ideological or theoretical purity, but strategic survivability: ethnic policy was created on the ground in order to enlist the support of the nationalities in the building of the new nation-state. For China, this policy was formed most critically on the Long March.

During the Long March, the Chinese Communist leaders became acutely aware of the vibrant cultural identity of the Muslims and other peoples they encountered on their long trek from the southwest to the northwest, which took them through the most concentrated minority areas. Edgar Snow (1938) and the recent chronicler Harrison Salisbury (1985) graphically described the desperate plight of the Long Marchers, harried on one side by the Japanese and the Nationalists, and on the other by the "fierce barbarian tribesmen."[9] The fathers of the yet-to-be-born Chinese nation were faced with extermination or promises of special treatment to the minorities, specifically including the Miao, Yi (Lolo), Tibetan, and Hui. The first Hui autonomous county was set up in the 1930s in southern Ningxia as a demonstration of the early Communists' goodwill toward the Hui. In a chapter entitled "Moslem and Marxist," Snow (1938) records several encounters with militant conservative Hui Muslims and subsequent strong lectures to Eighth Route Army troops to respect Hui customs lest they offend them and provoke conflicts. Mao in 1936 issued an appeal to the Northwest Hui to support the Communists' cause, even mentioning the renaissance of Turkey under Atatürk as an example for China's Muslims (in Forbes 1976: 77; Lindbeck 1950). One slogan that Snow (1938: 320) observed posted by Hui soldiers training under the Communist Fifteenth Army Corps was "Build our own anti-Japanese Mohammedan Red Army." Perhaps Chairman Mao was more sensitive to the Muslim issue since his brother had been killed in Xinjiang in the 1930s due to interethnic and intra-Muslim factionalism. Party documents that have come to light from the Long March reveal that Chairman Mao explicitly promised self-determination to the minorities until the year 1937, offering them not only privileges, but also the right to secede, which minorities still had under the former Soviet constitution.

However, this right was withdrawn by 1940, and instead limited regional "autonomy" was offered (see Schwarz 1971). The transition in Chinese terminology from "self-determination" (*zi zhu*) to "autonomy" (*zi zhi*) is slight, but for the minorities it represented a major shift in policy.

Since the founding of the PRC, international considerations—particularly the desire for third-world, often Muslim, investment—have encouraged favoritism toward minorities, so that goals of pluralism and assimilation have constantly shifted depending on local and international politics. Chinese Marxists were surprised that these created groups did not fade away with land reforms, collectivization, and erosion of class-based loyalties. Ethnicity persists as a vertical phenomenon that cuts across class and socioeconomic stratification, and it has maintained its salience despite the land-reform campaigns and other efforts to reduce class-based differences in the Chinese and Soviet societies.

That the state employed a Stalinist cultural definition is very important for our understanding of how local ethnic communities responded to policies of incorporation. Walker Connor (1984) has shown that whereas the original creation of ethnic groups was a strategic temporary recognition of ethnic difference in order to solicit support for the revolutionary process, it later led to the hardening of ethnic boundaries—the creation of identities, which serve as the basis for many of the new nations that have recently grown, hydralike, out of the head of the former Soviet empire. After reviewing the resurgence and reinterpretation of so-called traditions, Eric Hobsbawm emphasized their relevance "to that comparatively recent historical innovation, the 'nation', with its associated phenomena: nationalism, the nation-state, national symbols, histories and the rest. All these rest on exercises in social engineering which are often deliberate and always innovative. . . . The national phenomenon cannot be adequately investigated without careful attention to the 'invention of tradition'" (1983: 13–14).

Attention to the creation of culture has become a preoccupation since Hobsbawn and Ranger's important volume (1983). What I am arguing for in this chapter is the examination of the unique process involved in the creation not only of culture, but of "cultures" by authoritarian regimes, a process that the case of the Hui clearly reveals.

Labeling Cultures

The state in China has assigned national labels to the peoples identified by it—labels that I have shown to be quite arbitrary and defined primarily by the state. Nevertheless, it can be argued that over the last forty years, these labels have taken on a life of their own. Like material commodities, which

Appadurai (1986: 3–10) convincingly argues gain enduring sociopolitical value beyond their original intent, these state designations have contributed to a growing sense of minority nationalism. Bernard Cohn (1971) has recorded the continued use of the rather arbitrarily assigned ethnic labels used by British colonial administrators to sort out the South Indian multiethnic populations. No matter how anachronistic, when these labels are used by those in power to administrate and delineate peoples under their control, they often become fixed, taking on a meaningfulness and power of their own.

Hui in China, no matter where one travels, now refer to themselves as Hui. Sometimes, however, less-informed members of the community slip into old habits. I was amused when one of my Hui colleagues who was present at an interview would enter into a dialogue of state-defined discourse with the peasant, correcting his "politically incorrect" speech: "No you are not a Hui-religion disciple [Huijiao tu]," he would reprimand, "you are a Hui person [Hui min]. Hui believe in Islam [Yisilan jiao], not their own Hui religion." Even on Hainan Island, where Malay-Austronesian–speaking Muslims have difficulty communicating in Mandarin Chinese, when I visited them in 1985 they referred to themselves as Hui. In their local language they are known among themselves as Utsat. So also do the various peoples of the Tarim Basin refer to themselves by their locality oasis names, Kashgarlik, Aksulik, Turpanlik—only to outsiders or when visiting the city do they generally call themselves Uygur. Yet these terms are becoming more and more accepted by the people as inclusive ethnonyms, stimulating further communication and exchange between them.

This crystallization of ethnic identities based on state-assigned labels was emphasized to me recently by a Han scholar who went to Xinjiang in the early 1950s as a language student and teacher. After taking a one-month truck ride from Xian to Urumqi, she was assigned to a predominantly Uygur village that also had Kazakh and Hui residents. She noticed that there was not much division among them as Muslims: they worshiped in the same mosque and generally made little reference to their ethnic identities. On a recent return trip, however, she noted that they no longer prayed together and seemed to have much stronger ideas of their separateness from one another.

With the present benefits attached to ethnic identification in China, such as birth-planning exemptions, educational advancement, employment opportunities, tax reductions, and political mobility, this may sound like a return to a situationalist view of ethnicity—the Hui are Hui for utilitarian purposes. However, while I maintain that ethnic identity is an inherently political phenomenon, it is obvious that for the Hui there is an important dialogue involved between the state's preconceived notions of identity and the communities in question, who must respond in dialogical interaction with their own traditions. These traditions are drawn from their reservoir of ideas about ancestry, not manufactured in a vacuum; this is what separates an ethne, a people, from a mere social convention.

The Local Expression of Hui Identity

The dialogue between the state and the Hui communities can be seen in the nature of the response of the communities I described at the beginning of this chapter. For Hui communities in Northwest China, Islam is taken to be the fundamental marker of their identity—to be Hui is to be Muslim. An incredible variety of Islamic movements, which I have catalogued elsewhere (Gladney 1987: 518–25), have arisen through internal dialogues and debates in these communities as Hui reformers have sought to resolve the tensions created by adapting the ideals of Islam to the changing Chinese social world. Government policy that permits freer expression of Hui ethnic identity has also allowed the resurgence of Islam, since this is the primary marker of Hui identity in these communities, and Islam for them has taken on new, re-created meaning in the changed contexts. With the encouraged and improved relations between China and Muslim Middle Eastern governments, an increased number of people traveling on the hajj from China (three thousand last year) and further visits to Islamic holy sites in China by foreign Muslims have led to a heightened sense of Islamic identity—especially for the northwestern Hui.

Hui urban communities, such as that in Beijing, tend to express their identity in terms of cultural traditions: the pork tabu, entrepreneurship, and craft specializations. This leads to the growing importance of ethnic economic niches, such as the running of restaurants, in preserving and expressing Hui identity in the city, which Furnivall (1939) so clearly described regarding the rise of pluralism in Southeast Asia. The Hui's traditional occupations as small merchants, restaurateurs, butchers, and jewelry craftsmen have led to their being depicted as the "Jews of China" (Pillsbury 1973). Liberalized nationality and economic policies have contributed to the cultural and economic expansion of those specializations and small businesses that most reflect urban Hui descent from Hui ancestors—ethnic entrepreneurialism has become "symbolic capital" (Bourdieu 1977: 171) in Oxen Street and other urban Hui centers. This ethnic capital is being encouraged by the state as a marker of Hui identity. In a startling recognition of the importance of the business ethic among the Hui, Fei Xiaotong recently acknowledged that the Hui "had been blessed with this talent from their ancestors, who nurtured trading skills during centuries-long commercial dealings" (Fei Xiaotong, "Minorities Hold Key to Own Prosperity," interview in *China Daily*, Apr. 28, 1987, p. 4). Since they had no common language, locality, or other cultural markers of identity, Fei argued, Hui capitalism should be encouraged as their ethnic trait in the interests of modernization and development, and should not be criticized as feudal. Fei has perhaps unwittingly given credence to a very Weberian notion of economic rationality. Incredibly, in China the supposed Protestant ethic has been attributed to Muslims, who, because of their traditional proclivity for trade, were also described as the Jews of China.

In southeastern Hui lineages, genealogical descent is the most important aspect of Hui identity. To be Hui is to be a member of a lineage that traces its descent to foreign ancestors, who just happened to be Muslim. Recent state recognition of these lineages as members of the Hui nationality has led to ethnic resurgence among previously unrecognized Hui lineages throughout the southeast coast. In turn, contact with state-sponsored Hui and foreign Muslim delegations has led to a growing interest for many of these Hui in their ethnoreligious roots, and even in practicing Islam. Since the state follows a cultural definition of ethnic identity, the Hui in Quanzhou who have totally assimilated must manufacture generally Islam-associated cultural traits to ensure their continued acceptance by the state and the broader Hui community.

In line with this effort, the state in 1984 supported the bringing of four imams from the Ningxia Hui Autonomous Region to Fujian in order to train the local Hui in the ways of Islam, which only a few of them had remembered. Now other Hui who were not recognized by the state in the 1950s as Hui, since they no longer practiced Islam, are seeking to revive those Islamic cultural traditions thought to legitimate their claims to minority-nationality status. One lineage has built a mosque, has begun to train local imams, has initiated the Ramadan fast, and hopes to establish an autonomous Hui county. One delegation of applicants for Hui recognition asked me if their practice of opening the Quran (known as *kai jing*) at the head of largely Buddhist funeral processions qualified them as culturally Hui (see Gladney 1995). The salience of Hui identity and tradition, as culturally defined and encouraged by the Chinese state, is gradually being reinculcated in the daily habitus of their lives.

The Rise of Pan-Hui Ethnic Identity

There were, of course, many traditional contacts among disparate Muslim communities throughout Chinese history. It is significant that Muslim communities in Quanzhou, Hainan, and Yunnan often sent their neophytes to be trained in Islamic madrassahs at mosques in other Muslim centers in Beijing, Hezhou, and Ningxia, despite their not speaking the language or having a very different cultural background (see Gladney 1987: 495–532). Hui Sufi tarikats had extensive hierarchies of membership that included brotherhood communities from Yunnan to Harbin to Xinjiang (Yang M. U. H. forthcoming). But these itinerants traveled to these disparate communities as fellow Muslims, believers in the Hui religion (Hui jiao) of Islam, not as members of an ethnic group. Trade and caravan networks that brought wool from the Qinghai-Tibetan plateau all the way down the Yellow River to the northern port in Tianjin, in exchange for tea, guns, and luxury items, were often dominated by Hui Muslims (see Lipman 1988; Millward 1988). While important economic and socioreligious connections existed, there is little evidence of a transnational pan-Hui identity until the contemporary era.

The shift from "Hui religion" (Hui jiao) to "Hui people" (Hui min) is a crucial transition. Its importance is illustrated by the fact that in Taiwan the Nationalist government was reluctant to recognize the existence of any Hui people; it recognizes only the Hui religion (Hui jiao), which includes Hui, Uygur, and Kazakh people. There are lineages in Taiwan, directly related to the Hui in Quanzhou across the Taiwan Strait, who also do not follow Islamic dietary restrictions and who practice local Chinese folk religion. These Taiwanese lineages go a step farther, however: they no longer maintain any idea of their separate ancestry (see Gladney 1991: 279–84). They have completely lost their identity as Hui, which is not salient to them in the Taiwanese sociopolitical world, while for members of the same lineage on the mainland, Hui identity is once again becoming revitalized due to shifts in state policy and the new salience of their traditions.

Dialogic or Clashing "Civilizations" in China?

Understanding of majority/minority identity in China in the past has been hampered by models and policies that could not account for the wide diversity and present unity of the minority and majority groups. Models that relied on a cultural-trait analysis, such as the Stalinist and cultural approaches, foundered on the similarity between Hui and Han and on the diversity found within both groups. Although the Hui did not fit the Stalinist model, the government chose to recognize them on the basis of criteria developed before the revolution for the political goals of incorporation and state building, in a careful rewriting of history described by Richard Rubenstein (1978) in *The Cunning of History*. Inventing the Han, and by extension Chinese civilization, through contrasting them to internal and externally defined national groups became an effective means of building a national movement upon what Sun Yatsen described as a loose sheet of sand. This shifting sand coalesced into a national movement that not only ousted the Japanese and other foreign imperialists but dominated and defined internally perceived cultural differences as well, leading to the recognition of 55 minority nationalities. It was political expediency, not clashed civilizations, that led to the rise of the Han and invention of the Hui. Standing between Muslim and Chinese civilizations, the Hui become the perfect counterexample to Huntington's thesis that civilizations are fundamentally different and generally opposed. Quanzhou Hui, who comfortably worship their Muslim ancestors, raise pigs, and fully participate in southern Min Fujianese political culture, would object to the dichotomy of East/West, Muslim/Confucian, that Huntington finds so useful. Instead, their dialogical interaction with Islam, Confucian traditions, local southern Min popular religion, and Southeast Asian business connections have produced a vibrant cultural identity that cannot easily be placed in any category, though they continue to be labeled as Hui by the state.

More importantly, recent studies have suggested that Han identity, broadly represented as homogeneous and unified, is rapidly breaking apart along cultural and regional lines of local expression (see Friedman 1994; Gladney 1994a). It is now popular to be Cantonese and Shanghainese in China, and a resurgence of local power bases, often drawn along cultural fault lines, should give Huntington pause: not only was he wrong about Muslim homogeneity, but he is misinformed about Confucian continuity as well. Hong Kong–based triads are no respecters of their fellow Confucians in Beijing if they refuse to cooperate with their expanding operations. Huntington was correct about cultural fault lines, as power often flows along them. He was incorrect, however, to essentialize culture according to general categories of civilizations, without regard for cultural redefinition in dialogic interaction with significant others in the context of the modern nation-state.

Attention to power relations in the ongoing dialogue between the state and local ethnic groups, both externally and internally, is critical for our understanding of the current resurgence of cultural nationalisms, their meaningfulness and salience in the modern world. Foucault reminds us that the state is compelled to address a plethora of nonnegotiables:

> The state is superstructural in relation to a whole series of power networks that invest the body, sexuality, the family, kinship, knowledge, technology and so forth. True, these networks stand in a conditioning—conditioned relationship to a kind of "meta-power" which is structured essentially round a certain number of great prohibition functions; but this meta-power, with its prohibitions, can only take hold and secure its footing where it is rooted in a whole series of multiple and in-

definite power relations that supply the necessary basis for the great negative forms of power. (Foucault 1980)

Ethnicity and cultural identity is just one item of meta-power that is constantly negotiated between state and self: the dialogue is ongoing and regularly redefined in changing social contexts. At times, as in the assignment of the labels of ethnicity, it may take the form of protracted negotiation, argument, or one-sided mandate. Throughout the history of China's relations with its Muslim and minority peoples, there have been countless moments of resistance to state hegemony and incorporation. As recently as 1989, Hui rose up across China to protest a Chinese book they found as offensive as Salman Rushdie's *Satanic Verses* (see Gladney 1994b). In reponse, the state met all of their demands, confiscating the books, closing the publication house, and arresting the authors. This evidenced a marked change from the Cultural Revolution, when the state cracked down on a local Hui uprising in Yunnan, massacring 866 documented Hui and an estimated total of sixteen hundred people (Gladney 1991: 137–40). Perhaps the 1989 response was much more favorable toward the Hui because of the international dialogue the state is now engaging in with Middle Eastern Muslim governments, who would be reluctant to conduct military and construction trade with a state that represses its Muslim peoples.

The remarkable ethnogenesis of the Hui and the critical transition from Hui jiao to Hui min is generally absent from modern histories that attempt to emphasize the long history of the Hui living within the Chinese state, or the homogeneous nature of the Han. In this dialogical process of ethnogenesis, the Hui are not alone. Recent field studies of minorities in China have revealed a parallel process of movement from tribe to nation, particularly among the Yi (Harrell 1989), Uygur (Gladney 1991), Bai (Yokoyama 1988), and Tibetans (Goldstein 1990). In each case a dialogue took place in which local representatives of the Chinese state became convinced of claims to ethnic and cultural legitimacy, thereby leading to initial recognition. This protracted negotiation has continued to influence both sides over the course of the last thirty years, leading to the crystallization and in some cases revitalization of traditional ethnic identities. The population of the Tujia increased from 2.8 million in 1982 to an astonishing 5.7 million in 1990. The Manchu population has increased 128 percent between 1982 and 1990, from 4.3 to 9.8 million, though many sinologists had long assumed the Manchu to have vanished, inevitably assimilated into the homogenizing "Han" mainstream.

The state, holding to a Stalinist-cultural definition of ethnicity, must determine the legitimacy of cultural claims to ethnic status. Thus, it is the state that decides what constitutes language, economy, locality, and culture itself. Minorities and applicant groups must convince the state that their cultural traditions are legitimate enough to warrant political recognition, privilege, and further consideration. Thus the debate continues. For Bakhtin (1981: 84), this vitality is the essence of dialogue. It is also what engenders movement in ethnic change on both sides of the debate. As the dialogue evolves, hopefully new light will be shed on these emergent identities, the nature of the Han nationality itself, and the relevance of cultural nationalism in constructing majority/minority identity.

PART IV

MALAYNESS

7

Bureaucratic Management of Identity in a Modern State

"MALAYNESS" IN POSTWAR MALAYSIA

SHAMSUL A. B.

MALAYSIA has, if in imperfect form, all the features of a modern state similar to the East Asian countries it tries to imitate, such as Japan, Taiwan, and Korea (Yoshino 1994; Cho 1994; Hsieh 1994). It has a highly bureaucratized system of governance and a dependent capitalist economy inherited from British colonial rule, not unlike that of Fiji, also an ex-British colony (Kelly 1994; Kaplan 1994). It claims a monopoly of power within an internationally recognized territory and proclaims that all the people residing within the territory are citizens according to the rules provided in its constitution. It conducts democratic and fair elections regularly, once every four years. Its modern education system has provided not only workers, skilled and unskilled, but also intelligentsia. Together they contribute toward modernizing the state.

Modernization, which comprises the rise of capitalism and the emergence of the modern state and nation, is meant to be a leveling process, one that promotes universalism and destroys differences. As in other modern Western) and non-Western countries (Handler 1994; Okamura 1994; Kirişci 1994), however, replacing differences with universalism has been difficult, if not impossible. There are conceptual and historical-structural reasons for this difficulty.

Conceptually, the dismantling of local traditions by colonial rulers for purposes of domination affected the intelligentsia and the rest of the populace, in Malaysia as elsewhere (Andaya and Andaya 1982; Das 1986). In particular, the modernist outlook of the Malaysian intelligentsia has been constructed both by the experience of the modern education that they received during the colonial period and by the experience of being socialized within the modern-oriented colonial state that replaced the precolonial traditional *kerajaan* rule. These experiences have transformed their notion of time, which once was cosmological and cyclical and now is lineal or calendrical and evolutionary (Milner 1982, 1991). Anderson (1983: 30) has called such transformation "historicism."

During British colonial rule, the historicism factor was significant in engendering among the Malaysian intelligentsia a process of "invention of traditions" (Hobsbawm 1983: 13–14), that is, the invoking of symbols and idioms based on myths of ancestry and historical memories, as distinct from investigated historical inquiry. These invented traditions were necessarily culturally exclusive in nature and meant to emphasize a sense of distinctive identity. This was seen especially in the attempt to construct a nationalist discourse or notion of their "nation of intent." Such exclusive tendencies are the result of invidious comparisons with others (Smith 1981: 63–85; Miles 1989: 6–7). Therefore, although modernity in general emphasizes universalism, of which the historicist, modernist outlook is conceptually an integral component, the historicist tendency seemed to promote particularism.

In historical-structural terms, British colonialism also provided fertile ground for the development of a culturally exclusive outlook because the Malaysian intelligentsia were divided along ethnic lines. The origin of the ethnic constructs or the homogenized ethnic categories that now divide the population in Malaysia can be traced, as Hirschman (1986, 1987) has argued, to the decennial census taken by the colonial government beginning in 1871. Fijian society went through a similar experience around the same decade (Kelly 1994; Kaplan 1994). In principle, according to Said (1985: 322), "the notion that there are geographical spaces with indigenous, radically 'different' inhabitants who can be defined on the basis of some religion, culture, or racial essence proper to that geographical space is . . . a highly debatable idea." Nevertheless, to the British colonialists, conducting the population census and constructing ethnic categories for that purpose not only fulfilled a routine administrative need but was readily justified by an orientalist and racist colonial ideology, which, according to Kaplan (1994: 4–5), they carried out in Fiji, too. Such a discourse was amply evidenced in short stories and novels written by British authors, some of whom were colonial administrators in British Malaya (Zawiah 1994).

Sociologically speaking, therefore, what the British introduced, encouraged, and institutionalized through their population-census exercise in Malaysia was a process of signification. This process is representational in nature; through it "meanings are attributed to particular objects, features and processes, in such a way that the latter are given special significance, and carry or are embodied with a set of additional, second order features" (Potter and Wetherell 1987: 24–28). Signification therefore involves selection: from an available range of objects, features, and processes, only certain ones are chosen to convey additional meanings.

One therefore could argue that the emergence of "Malay," "Chinese," "Indian," and "others" as officially sanctioned ethnic categories under colonial governance led, for instance, to the designation of all sorts of imagined and real attributes, such as religion, language, indigenousness, and customary habits as Malay or Chinese or Indian. Prior to this, Malay identity and conciousness were based on subethnicities; people identified themselves as Javanese, Sumatran, Rawa, Achenese, Minangkabau, Bugis, and so on. The Chinese, too, identified themselves based on their dialect groups, and the Indians by caste and subethnic group.

The ethnic blocks or categories became an idiom of official and everyday discourse when a host of legal codes and enactments, both economic and political, were introduced by the colonial government based on the census-constructed ethnic categories. This resulted in the formalization, consolidation, and widespread use of these ethnic categories in social interaction at all levels. This usage prevailed not only between colonialists and other foreigners on one side and the ethnically categorized population on the other, but also among the different ethnic groups, who became increasingly conscious of their differences. In fact, the social construction of difference through the official census initiated and established a countrywide trend toward minority and majority discourse, especially at the official level. This was particularly true after the 1921 census, when the Malays came to realize that they were outnumbered by the immigrant Chinese and Indian population and hence were a minority in their own "motherland" (Mills 1942). One could argue that the politics of numbers, which so dominates modern electoral politics in Malaysia, had its origin in the 1921 census.

Demographic concern was not the only factor that led to the emergence of Malay nationalism, but it was a critical one (Roff 1967). More significantly, seen from the perspective of the subjectivist school within ethnic studies (Eriksen 1993: 10–12), the resultant minority-majority discourse during the 1920s led to countrywide acceptance of the existence of sociocultural boundaries separating the Malay, Chinese, and Indian communities and giving rise to communalism in the colonially constructed plural society of Malaysia.

Given this historical context, it could be said that the emergence of a nationalist discourse and movement in Malaysia inevitably has been shaped and given signification within an ethnic framework. So in order to configure the majority-minority discourse in Malaysia, it is useful to focus on the Malays as a case study. The Malay case is an excellent example of an ethnicized nationalist discourse and movement. More significantly, a dominant and British-favored faction within the movement came to power after winning the first general elections in July 1955 and later was entrusted by the British with the running of postcolonial Malaysia when it became independent on August 31, 1957. The nationalist paradigm of this particular group of Malay nationalists, sometimes called the administrator-aristocrat or "administocrat" faction (Chandra Muzaffar 1979), has become the dominant ideology articulated by the United Malays National Organisation (UMNO), the Malay-based main political party of the present ruling coalition, the National Front (NF).

To begin with, I will briefly examine what happened in postwar Malaysia vis-à-vis the Malays. During this period, the concept of Malay community, or *bangsa* Melayu, as an imagined community in the Andersonian sense and as a focus of identity was fully debated and developed. It was articulated and institutionalized in Malaysia's modern electoral politics and gained importance in the majority-minority discourse in Malaysia as the country approached independence in 1957. A brief survey of what happened between 1957 and 1970 will help us examine more fully the post-1970 period.

Bangsa Melayu as an Imagined Community in Postwar Malaysia

The Malay nationalist movement was not homogeneous. It was factionalized into three main strands, or *aliran*, often identified either by their ideological orientation or by their status-group background: the administocrats, the Malay left, and the Islamic group (Roff 1967). During the early part of the postwar period, each aliran had its own national organization, or political party, through which its ideological position was articulated: the Malay left had its Partai Kebangsaan Melayu Malaya (PKMM), or Malay Nationalist Party, and later Partai Sosialis Rakyat Malaysia (PSRM); the administocrats had UMNO; and the Islamic faction had Partai Islam SeMalaya, or PAS (later renamed Partai Islam).

A detailed study of party literature, such as texts of speeches and published manifestos, reveals that although the three aliran adopted different ideological positions, which could be easily identified through the type of "nation" or, more accurately, "nation of intent" that each proposed to establish, they had a common imagined community—namely, bangsa Melayu—as their point of reference of (communal) identity (Roff 1967; Ariffin Omar 1993; Shamsul 1996a). There were, however, furious debates within and between the aliran as to the composition of bangsa Melayu, who could and could not be called a Malay, and what the critical cultural markers should be to identify a Malay and to define Malayness (Milner 1994).

At one level, sociologically speaking, it was a classic example of an ethnic classification debate over who should be "us" and who "them." At another, it was also a debate over the kind of nation they wanted, because the Malay term "bangsa" can mean "people," "race," "community," "nationality," "state" (*negeri* or *negara*), or "nation" (*negara*). The multiple meanings of "bangsa," and its conjugation *kebangsaan*, provided the Malay elites, or at least the leaders of the nationalist factions, with meanings suitable for pursuing their culturally defined interests, some broad and inclusive and others parochial and exclusive. The PKMM-UMNO debate on "bangsa" and "kebangsaan," hence "Malayness," is instructive in this context.

The PKMM distinguished "bangsa," which it used to describe the Malay community, from "kebangsaan," a broader interpretation of "Malayness" with no precise territorial boundaries except the broad *kulturkreisse* of the Malay world. This was a crucial difference because it suggested that non-Malays could be part of kebangsaan Melayu, even though they were not from bangsa Melayu (Ariffin Omar 1993: 192–93). According to Burhanuddin, PKMM's leader, one could imbibe the meaning, purpose, and spirit of kebangsaan Melayu irrespective of one's communal origin (Kamaruddin Jaafar 1980: 110–11). He further emphasized that "a change in *kebangsaan* is not followed by a change in hereditary traits and racial descent of a particular group because these aspects are in the realm of feelings and characteristics of a person, but *kebangsaan* is within the ambit of law and politics" (Ariffin Omar 1993: 194). By implication it is possible, therefore, for a non-Malay to acquire and belong to kebangsaan Melayu if he or she severs ties with his or her original kebangsaan and adopts kebangsaan Melayu. It is also possible for a Malay to choose to opt out. PKMM was asserting that the focus of loyalty ought not to be the bangsa Melayu, or Malay community, but kebangsaan Melayu, or the Malay nation, and PKMM's nation of intent was the Melayu Raya (the Greater Malay nation). The loyalty that PKMM advocated was based on one's ability to adopt certain basic Malay characteristics, namely, custom, language, and political and social values. In a sense, acceptance into kebangsaan Melayu involved the necessity of becoming Melayu nonascriptively. Hence PKMM's concept of kebangsaan was not synonymous with "bangsa," and Malayness was based not on an assimilationist but on an enculturationist paradigm.

UMNO, however, denounced PKMM's concept of kebangsaan and adopted a far narrower, highly exclusive, territorially defined, and assimilationist-oriented one. UMNO even accused PKMM, in its use and definition of "kebangsaan," of "promoting internationalism under the guise of *kebangsaan Melayu* . . . [and] as a smokescreen for the destruction of *bangsa Melayu*" (Ariffin Omar 1993: 196). Many UMNO elites were alarmed that the acceptance of PKMM's kebangsaan concept would taint the purity of bangsa Melayu (Kamaruddin Jaafar 1980: 114). UMNO therefore claimed that it was more Malay than PKMM.

To UMNO, "bangsa Melayu" referred exclusively to the Malay community residing in the territory called Tanah Melayu (lit. "Malay land," geographically known then as the Malay Peninsula and now as Peninsula Malaysia), a community that speaks the Malay language, subscribes to the Islamic faith, is loyal to the raja (king), and has an Islamic-based culture and worldview. Therefore, UMNO did not consider the Indonesians, Filipinos, and Southern Thais to be subcomponents of bangsa Melayu, and it regarded the Chinese and Indians as *bangsa dagang* (foreigners) who were *menumpang* (lit. "on temporary stopover") in Tanah Melayu. The Malays were seen as the true *bumiputera* (lit. "sons of the soil") of Tanah Melayu.

The emergence of such a narrow perspective was the result of the anti-Malayan Union campaign that UMNO launched in 1946. In fact, the birth of UMNO as a political party could be seen as a negative reaction of the Malay administocrats toward the British Malayan Union plan. The Malayan Union policy offered citizenship and equal rights to the foreign bangsa, who would then have to consider Malaya, a unitary political entity supposed to be composed of the dissolved Malay states and the Straits Settlements, as their homeland (Lau 1991), hence the introduction of the *bangsa* Malayan. Both PKMM and UMNO strongly opposed the British-introduced concept of bangsa Malayan, with the "Malayan nation" as its nation of intent, because the new concept would potentially challenge the bangsa Melayu and kebangsaan Melayu concepts. However, PKMM's alternative to bangsa Malayan was a more broadly defined bangsa and kebangsaan *Melayu* compared to that of UMNO, which was clearly narrow and parochial.

Despite UMNO's concern for territoriality in its definition of bangsa Melayu, its nation of intent was not necessarily territorially grounded. UMNO still recognized the primacy of each of the Malay states (negeri Melayu) and acknowledged its raja as the ruler to whom all Malays in that state should be loyal. Hence it had no clear conception of its negara (nation). In some sense, UMNO still believed in the concept of kerajaan, which is not negara-based but negeri-based. UMNO's concept of negara was really formulated with the formation in 1948 of the Federation of Malaya, its alternative to the Malayan Union.

The adoption of the plural-society-based "Malayan federation" as

UMNO's nation was endorsed by the British. In the Federation of Malaya Agreement, and subsequently in the 1957 constitution of the independent Federation of Malaya, non-Malays were accepted as full-fledged citizens and, in return, Malay special position, rights, and privileges—in other words, *ketuanan* Melayu (Malay dominance)—were legally recognized and protected. The constitution, however, also guaranteed the right of freedom of speech for all citizens. Hence non-Malays, as rightful citizens, could question, and continuously have questioned, the special Malay rights—a contentious and highly sensitive political issue even in contemporary Malaysia (Milner 1994: 12–13).

UMNO, together with the elite-controlled Malaysian Chinese Association (MCA) and Malaysian Indian Congress (MIC), formed the Alliance, a coalition party, and won its first national election in 1955. It has continued to be successful, but now as part of a much-expanded coalition called the National Front. The Malayan federation concept, which legally recognized Malay dominance, remained the concept of nation that Malaysia upholds. It is within this ideological and political framework that bangsa and kebangsaan Melayu, as defined by UMNO, became the central and critical guiding concept of Malaysia's national ideology.

As generally understood, "national ideologies," irrespective of their origins and historical circumstances, usually claim some kind of constructed "national character" (Herzfeld 1993: 3). It is UMNO's concept of bangsa and kebangsaan Melayu that informed the construction of Malaysia's national character. The national bureaucracies then have the task of providing a guiding framework and a kind of operational social barometer, calibrated by legalistic and other measures, to gauge personal and social, local and national identities. I would call such efforts an exercise in top-down implementation of "official nationalism" (Shamsul 1996a). In Fiji, similar trends seem to have developed more clearly after the 1987 coup (Kelly 1994; Kaplan 1994), and it is no surprise that Fiji has been observing the "successful" Malaysian case very closely since then. It is also not a coincidence that the coalition party that won the 1987 Fijian election was also called the Alliance; like the one in Malaysia, it was established "as an alliance of races and communities" (Kaplan 1994: 7).

Of course, the Malay-controlled national government has made attempts to cater to the interests of non-Malays too, but because nationalism, in the Malaysian context, is highly Malayized, its everyday expression is also highly ethnicized. Because the Malayan administrative bureaucracy is a predominantly Malay institution, the implementation and articulation of, and the idiom used to explain, national policies at the grassroots and everyday level inevitably became highly ethnicized and deeply pro-Malay. Lower-ranking Malay civil servants have often been accused by the non-

Malay public of practicing racial discrimination in the way they discharge their duties vis-à-vis non-Malays (Kua 1987). Their usual response to the criticism is, "We are implementing national policies." I would call such an attitude an expression of everyday nationalism not dissimilar to some of the "sovereignty nationalism" in Hawaii mentioned by Okamura (1994). We shall now examine how the official nationalism found articulation in postcolonial Malaysia.

Articulation of Malay Dominance (1957–69)

It may be instructive to briefly examine some examples of the articulation of Malay dominance, and in some sense Malayness too (as understood in the context of UMNO's bangsa and kebangsaan Melayu), in early postcolonial Malaysia. Perhaps the best way to do this is to look at the government-initiated public policies relating to economic development during both the colonial and postcolonial periods, because there exists a close relationship between "ethnicity and the economy" in the Malaysian context (Jesudason 1989). The period since 1957 has seen tremendous change in Malaysia's economy and politics: economic growth at a pace unknown before, high population growth, and dramatic expansion of the educational system. These, in turn, have led to important, if unmeasurable, changes in the values, attitudes, ambitions, and expectations of Malaysians of all ethnic groups.

Through economic planning, Malaysia focused serious attention on "development," setting up the powerful Economic Planning Unit in 1961. This was the way the UMNO-dominated government of the day established its bona fides with the electorate. Development was an attractive political platform for the new Alliance-controlled government. On the one hand, it made possible the continuation, with very little change at first, of the colonial policies of liberal capitalism and monetary and fiscal conservatism. This was what powerful foreign and Chinese business interests wanted and what the World Bank recommended in its report of 1955, called the International Bank for Reconstruction and Development (IBRD) Report. On the other hand, the Alliance was impelled by political self-interest to launch a broad program of rural development, through which UMNO hoped to cement its support among rural Malays. The implementation of the rural development program did not directly challenge urban Chinese interests. On the contrary, without the support of Chinese businessmen, who controlled the supplies of machinery, raw material for construction, and food, the rural development program was doomed to fail. The only costs the Chinese had to bear were in the form of taxes and protection-inflated rice prices used to support the public expenditures for the much-expanded rural program.

The new rural development program was built around a government-funded body called the Rural Development and Industrial Authority (RIDA), which was given the task of stimulating the economy of the rural Malays. This concept had been introduced in 1950 by a pro-Malay, affirmative-action-oriented colonial government. One could say that the social origin of this concept and organization and the framework within which they were operationalized were directly related to UMNO's bangsa and kebangsaan Melayu concept, and particularly to the Malay special privileges and rights written into the Federation of Malaya Agreement of 1948. RIDA made loans for productive projects and carried out a variety of self-help schemes.

In 1956, the government established the Federal Land Development Authority (FLDA, later called FELDA), informed by the same concept that had underlain RIDA. FELDA at first coordinated and financed state (province or negeri) governments' land-development schemes. After independence, it became the central agency for the federal government's massive land-development projects. In 1959, a Ministry of Rural Development was set up, again within the framework and with the intention that had informed RIDA. This new program received an early test in the 1959 general elections, in which the Alliance government did not perform well compared with the 1955 elections. It lost miserably in the Malay-dominated states of Kelantan and Trengganu but did relatively well in the urban non-Malay-dominated states. In the next general election in 1964, the Alliance performed very well, mainly because the country was "under siege" as a result of the Konfrontasi with Indonesia, which protested the formation of Malaysia in 1963 (Sabah, Sarawak, and Singapore had become new member states of the Federation of Malaysia) and called Malaysia a neocolony. The vote for the Alliance was a vote of loyalty. With the fall of Sukarno and the rise of Suharto as the new leader of Indonesia, the Konfrontasi ended in 1966.

In that same year, the five-year First Malaysia Plan (FMP) of 1966–70 was launched. During the FMP period, a host of pro-Malay policies and strategies were introduced and implemented. All of them were based on the 1950 RIDA concept, necessarily modified and expanded to suit the day. Although the broad outline of the policy framework remained laissez-faire, special programs to benefit the Malays continued to expand as a result of the increasing political pressure brought to bear through the structure of UMNO, particularly after the UMNO-sponsored first Bumiputera Economic Congress of 1965. The congress provided opportunities for a wide cross-section of bumiputera to air their grievances and propose remedies, which were articulated mainly in the well-known UMNO framework of bangsa and kebangsaan Melayu (Shamsul 1986: 190–94). Most of these suggestions were later adopted by the Alliance government.

For instance, MARA (Majlis Amanah Rakyat Bumiputera, or the Council of Trust for the Indigenous People) was established in 1965 to replace RIDA with an expanded program, under which the Institut Teknologi MARA (ITM) was created in 1967. A Malay bank, called Bank Bumiputera, was set up in 1966 with the aim of breaking the foreign and Chinese monopoly of the banking industry. The Federal Agricultural and Marketing Authority (FAMA) was also established around the same period to attack the exploitive Chinese-controlled middleman network that was perceived as a major factor contributing to Malay economic backwardness. A host of other quasi-government institutions were set up from 1965 to 1970 in an effort to uplift the Malay economic position. The growth of such programs and bodies, though significant, did not change the general pattern of ownership and control of the country's economy, which was in the hands of foreigners and Chinese. Malays still remained predominantly rural peasants. Only a small proportion of them became urban dwellers, and these were mainly government employees.

The period also saw an increase in unemployment. Because the non-Malays were relatively more educated and urbanized than the Malays, they tended to be harder hit by unemployment. Malay unemployment was also high but was mostly disguised or involuntary in nature because of the subsistence economy practiced in the rural areas. The fall of rubber prices and low GNP growth between 1966 and 1968 increased unemployment further in both the rural and urban areas among both Malays and non-Malays. These circumstances may have contributed to or been the latent reasons behind the ethnic riot in Kuala Lumpur in May 1969, but the immediate cause was the antagonism stirred up during the late-1969 election campaign and the postelection celebration.

If by "ethnicity" we refer to a kind of bondedness as well as a particular form of social organization of communicated social difference, ethnicity appeared together with capitalism in many parts of the world, particularly through colonialism. In countries such as Malaysia and Fiji, colonialism constructed and introduced ethnic categories not only for administrative purposes—a "divide and rule" policy—but also for purposes of division of labor. The nationalist discourse ironically adopted similar idiom and structure but termed it "unity in diversity" (Chatterjee 1986). The postcolonial state in Malaysia existed within this ethnicity framework. In a situation not unlike that in Fiji, ethnicity has become Malaysia's major social preoccupation and a chief principle of organization and reallocation of the country's wealth. With a Malay-dominated government informed by a narrow and parochial concept of bangsa and kebangsaan Melayu, the planning and implementation of Malaysia's economic development have been highly selective and ethnically biased, as the public policies of the government between 1957 and 1969 have demonstrated. The consequences of such policies have been traumatic and unsettling. Nonetheless, attempts to redress the situation, however serious it may be, have been limited by historical-structural factors, as has been apparent in post-1970 Malaysia.

From Dominance to Hegemony: Malayness in Post-1970 Malaysia

From May 1969 to January 1971, about 21 months, Malaysia experienced its second Emergency. (The first had lasted for twelve years, from 1948 to 1960.) During the 21-month period there was much soul-searching as the Malaysian elites who were members of the National Consultative Council sought to restore "national unity." The country was ruled by a much smaller body called the National Operations Council. After considerable deliberation and bargaining among the elites and, to a limited extent, the Malaysian public, it was concluded that the breakdown of "national unity" was due mainly to economic factors. The economic backwardness of the Malays was seen as the main cause of Malay dissatisfaction, which triggered the ethnic riot. The government therefore decided to take remedial actions to address this economic problem, which, if unresolved, could again become a serious threat to national security and political stability, and hence to national unity.

The most significant outcome of the bargain was the launching of the New Economic Policy (NEP) in association with the Second Malaysia Plan of 1971–75 (Shamsul 1977). The NEP involved four five-year plans that were to be implemented over a period of twenty years, ending in 1990. Central to the NEP was the manyfold increase of public expenditure on special programs for the rural and urban Malays, aimed generally at urbanizing them. Under one of the two major objectives of the NEP, the most significant program was aimed at creating "a community of Malay entrepreneurs" within two decades. To achieve this aim many special schemes were introduced. Of particular importance were those involving education, such as the setting up of boarding schools for Malay pupils. These schools were to search for the best candidates to be sent abroad for further studies and to become the pool of potential Malay professionals and entrepreneurs. In its other objective, the NEP focused on the poor. Though poverty eradication programs were meant for all ethnic groups, the main recipients were the Malays, as they formed the largest number of poor in the country.

The NEP in a sense continued and made all-encompassing what the colonial government began in 1950 with RIDA and the postcolonial government expanded until 1969. It is important, therefore, to note that a pro-

Malay affirmative-action policy within the UMNO's bangsa and kebangsaan Melayu framework did not begin with the NEP, as many analysts have asserted.

The political and cultural implications of the NEP are also significant. In political terms, the NEP established some basic parameters, the most important of which was the transformation of Malay dominance into Malay hegemony within the nation concept of a Malaysian federation based on a plural society. Legislation was subsequently introduced to ensure that the bumiputera's interests were nonnegotiable, and "politicking" on bumiputera-related issues was deemed illegal. The Sedition Act of 1970 declared seditious and punishable any public discussion on Malay rights and privileges, on Islam, on Malay rulers or Malay language. Malay culture became the basis of the "national culture"—national dress, dance, theater, music, and so on. Malaysians were free to practice their own religions and cultures, but official functions, deemed national functions, exhibited a total Malay hegemony. For some years the Chinese lion dance could not be performed publicly. With the rise of Islamic revivalism (Shamsul 1994), Malayness was perceived, especially by non-Muslim non-Malays, as being asserted even more (Ackerman and Lee 1988).

The NEP had limited success. In the 1990s, the emergence of a Malay corporate class and the expansion of the Malay middle class not only redefined the economic position of the Malays in the domestic economy but also brought about significant changes among the Malays (Shamsul 1988). Partai Islam, which for a long time had seen itself as Malay first and Islamic second, changed its ideological position to one that was totally Islamic, subscribing to the universalistic principle of Islam. It claimed to be willing to accept as a member any Muslim of any ethnic origin. In fact, at one stage it formed an informal alliance with the Chinese-dominated opposition party, the Democratic Action Party (DAP). The change in Partai Islam was not unrelated to the rise of Islamic revivalism in Malaysia. The Islamic revival as a social phenomenon also affected UMNO and the ruling National Front coalition party.

Many observers have argued that UMNO, in its attempt to co-opt moderate Islamic revival activists, had subsequently adopted Partai Islam's earlier political position, thus giving Malayness and Islamic criteria equal importance. In fact, it prided itself on its ability to introduce Islamic banks, Islamic pawnshops, and Islamic insurance, to which many Partai Islam members subscribed (Shamsul 1995). The most important figure in UMNO today, and the one responsible for its Islamization, is the current deputy prime minister, Anwar Ibrahim, a former leader of an Islamic youth movement that played a critical role in Islamic revivalism in Malaysia.

The Islamization of UMNO has had an immediate impact upon Malays in the corporate and middle classes. Malay intellectual bureaucrats were given the task of creating a new moral paradigm for these Malays. In other words, Malay capitalists, unlike their non-Malay and Western counterparts, have to be "moral, trustworthy, responsible and honest" (Rustam A. Sani 1993). This effort could also be seen as an attempt by UMNO to redefine Malayness. It is within this context that the concept of Melayu Baru (lit. "New Malay") was recently introduced in a top-down manner.

It is also interesting to note, however, that since the introduction of UMNO in Sabah, a Malaysian state in Borneo, the term "bumiputera" has been somewhat relaxed to accommodate the Christian Kadazan/Dusun, a minority bumiputera group in the national context but a major one within Sabah. As a result, members of the Kazadan/Dusun group have been accepted as UMNO members in Sabah. This is the first time in UMNO's history that non-Muslims have been accepted within its framework of bangsa and kebangsaan Melayu. This came as no surprise to many, because UMNO needs to make political inroads into Sabah, which has been for at least a decade in the hands of the predominantly Kadazan/Dusun opposition party, Parti Bersatu Sabah (PBS). UMNO's cultural concession seems to have paid off; the UMNO-led national coalition party finally managed to wrest power from PBS in the state elections in January 1994 (Shamsul and Balasubramaniam 1994). This means that UMNO is no longer a Malay party as such; it has now technically become a truly bumiputera party, because the term "bumiputera" refers not only to Malays but also to other minor indigenous groups, such as the Orang Asli and Iban Penan, both in Peninsular Malaysia and in Sarawak and Sabah in Borneo.

Conclusion

Empirically, it is not true that the concept of bumiputera, UMNO's concept of bangsa and kebangsaan Melayu, the Malay-dominated "Malaysian federation" nation and its "national character" construct, and the pro-Malay, affirmative-action NEP have gone unchallenged. In other words, Malayness and Malay dominance and hegemony have been seriously questioned by non-Malays in various ways and at various times, especially after independence in 1957; the case is not unlike that of Fiji. Therefore, it could be argued that there has been a continuous majority and minority discourse in the Malaysian context despite UMNO's apparent political invincibility (Shamsul 1996b).

The Alliance's loss of its two-thirds majority in the 1969 general elections, which momentarily destabilized Malaysia politically during the 1969 ethnic riot, is a clear instance during which Malay dominance was put to a serious test. Subsequently UMNO, in a redefined political scenario, regained power, further increased Malay dominance, and institutionalized Malay hegemony. Prior to that, in 1964, the concept of "Malaysian Malaysia," which was similar in spirit to the colonial concept of bangsa Malayan that underpinned the aborted Malayan Union nation, was introduced and became popular among non-Malays because it promised them status equal to that of the Malays in the eyes of the law. It was mooted by Lee Kuan Yew, the leader of the People's Action Party (PAP) of Singapore, when that city-state was still in Malaysia. Of course, the creation of a Malaysian Malaysia would have had to be preceded by a total reform of the Malaysian constitution, which guarantees special Malay rights and privileges, and perhaps by the setting up of a unitary state as opposed to the federal state of post-colonial Malaysia. These changes, of course, did not take place, and the Malaysian federation remained as it was when it received independence.

The protracted controversy over the Education Act of 1961, which involved mainly Malays and Chinese, could also be seen as an example of a long-standing majority-minority discourse in the Malaysian context. After the Malay language was made the national language, it became the medium of instruction in fully government-sponsored "national" schools (both primary and secondary). The Chinese demanded that Mandarin be allowed in the partly government-sponsored "national-type" primary schools and that the schools remain as they were and not be converted to national school status. The Education Act of 1961 allowed the minister of education to make the decision unilaterally; this was a cause of grave concern to the Chinese community, who could lose their schools with the stroke of a pen (Kua 1985: 101–14), although in fact no such decision was made.

However, Mandarin continued to be the medium of instruction in Chinese private secondary schools all over the country. The continuous presence of such schools motivated the Chinese community, in 1967, to moot the idea of the formation of a Mandarin-based university, to be called the Merdeka University. This created a hot public debate for more than a decade in both the Malay and the Chinese presses, with the former opposing the university's establishment as being against the spirit of national unity and the latter supporting it. It took about fourteen years before the Merdeka University issue was finally settled, if unsatisfactorily, in 1981 when the Federal High Court rejected an appeal from its organizers for permission to set up and operate the university (Kua 1985: 151–80).

Conceptually, the majority-minority discourse in Malaysia has been mainly between the Malays and the Chinese. It has taken place within the framework of UMNO's concept of bangsa and kebangsaan Melayu because this concept has informed the construction of national identity and national character. Such a discourse has been possible and often articulated publicly, mainly through the media, because of an important demographic factor: the Malays and the non-Malays are almost equal in number. The Malays are actually in a limited majority position, unlike the Chinese in Singapore, who constitute about 75 percent of the population. Such a delicate demographic balance has enabled the Chinese and other non-Malays to articulate their discontent through the ballot box, at least in a limited way. This was also the experience of Fiji, as the 1987 election showed (Kaplan 1994; Kelly 1994). Since Malaysia runs relatively free democratic elections every four years, the elections have become a venue for majority-minority discourse, often conducted in a controlled manner.

At another level, particularly among the Malays and the bumiputera as a whole, there has been continuous debate around the concept of ketuanan Melayu (Malay dominance), the position of the sultan, Islam as a basis of Malayness, and the official position of the Malay language as the national language. For instance, when the constitutional crises of 1988 and 1993 occurred, Malays were polarized. The UMNO-controlled government was trying to curb the powers of the sultans as the final endorsers of any legislation introduced in the parliament. Some Malays felt this would reduce the political potency of the concept of Malayness, which has been based partly on the principle of loyalty to the sultans. Because the sultans are also the Islamic religious heads in the country, this group argued that a reduction in their power would also reduce the potency of Islam as another important pillar of Malayness. On another occasion, in early 1994, the prime minister suggested that English should be reintroduced as a medium of instruction for science and technical subjects in local universities. Self-proclaimed nationalist middle-class Malays strongly opposed this policy because they feared it would erode the national position of the Malay language, another pillar of Malayness.

Finally, it is interesting to note how the Malays coped, and the concept of Malayness fared, with Mahathir Mohamed's introduction in 1981 of the idea called "Vision 2020" according to which Malaysia must strive, by the year 2020, to become a modern society and a developed, industrialized nation (Mahathir 1991). The most visible signs of this new rhetoric were introduced in the early 1980s, especially after Mahathir Mohamed became the prime minister in 1981. Policies and slogans such as the "Look East Policy" and "Malaysia Incorporated" became household words. The new rhetoric, on the one hand, seems to indicate that Malaysia is ready to move in the direction of creating an international presence and responding to the so-called globalization process. On the other, it could be read as an attempt by Mahathir to initiate a new concept of national identity that is felt necessary for the future but would inevitably lead to the rupturing of continuity with the past. It could also be argued that the embracing of the international vocabulary by Mahathir and hence by UMNO and Malays in general, seems to suggest that a strong reorientation of the notion of subject and citizen within Malaysia has taken place. The need to participate in global culture has forced Malaysians, particularly Malays, to somehow sacrifice their traditions and ethnic identities.

Will the UMNO Malays, and hence the government, finally move to adopt the PKMM's concept of bangsa and kebangsaan Melayu? According to an astute and informed observer of the Malays in Malaysia, "the internationalisation of the Malaysian citizen cannot be accomplished without all the horrors that accompany the cultures of late capitalist societies" (Watson 1994). Since Malaysia, not unlike Korea (Cho 1994), is still deeply involved in its "modernist" project, "perhaps we will have to wait until it becomes "postmodern."

8

Ideological Work in Constructing the Malay Majority

ANTHONY MILNER

MALAYSIA is nearly always portrayed in terms of ethnicity—in terms of the struggle of "the Malays," who are barely a majority of the population, to dominate the nation. The Malays and their rivals, "the Chinese" and "the Indians," tend to be presented as homogeneous ethnic blocs, each possessing more or less consistent and predictable objectives. Ethnicity, it is implied, is a given in this quintessentially plural society.

Such an interpretation, however, is misleading. It denies the constructedness of the country's ethnic architecture. The so-called majority ethnicity, the Malay race or bangsa Melayu, is in fact a concept in motion. It is an invented concept, and one persistently subject to development and contest. It was promoted particularly in the colonial period by Malay and to some extent European ideologues who, at times displaying real ingenuity, defined, redefined, and bestowed dignity upon "Malayness." One author even wrote (in 1930) of lifting the Malay bangsa "up onto a throne" (Abdul Latiff Abu Bakar 1987: 22)—an idea that suggests, among other things, a dynamic relation between race and monarchy. Today, in the context of Malaysia's political and economic dynamism, the concept of bangsa Melayu continues to be redefined and argued about.

A Plural Society

In one study after another (Ratnam 1965; Vasil 1971; Wan Hashim 1983; Lee 1986) Malaysia is portrayed as the plural society par excellence, with its three large ethnic blocs—Malay, Chinese, and Indian—each possessing its own social and economic role and its own cultural perspectives. The fault lines dividing these blocs are presented in a way that implies they are no less rigid than those defining the "civilizations" that Samuel Huntington has identified as the most significant human groupings in the post–cold war period (Huntington 1993). None of Malaysia's ethnic blocs, including the Malay one, comprises a large majority of the population, and the political situation, it is argued, is a product of this ethnic structure and ethnic rivalry. The "central issues of Malayan politics," writes one prominent commentator, have been of a communal character (Means 1976: 12). Seen in plural-society terms, each ethnic community possesses its own interests, and it is the job of government to reconcile the differences by achieving some form of balance.

When divisions are identified within a single ethnic community, they are understood (according to the plural-society approach) to be about how far and how hard to press that community's claims in the wider state. So-called ultras or extremists are portrayed as arguing with moderates about how vigorous and even aggressive their ethnic community ought to be in advocating its case. Even the Islamic fundamentalist movement, which has split the Malay community in recent decades, has been interpreted in this manner. It is argued that those Malays who demand what they consider to be a more orthodox implementation of Islamic law and doctrine are in reality driven by a desire to strengthen the ethnic identity of their group. Islam, that is to say, is given "a symbolic role in differentiating Malays . . . from others, predictably of course the Chinese" (Nagata 1981: 110).

Ethnicity in such constructions of modern Malaysia is presented as mere given fact. Malayness, Chineseness, and Indianness are seen as natural categories, the solid building blocks upon which the analysis of the contest and mechanisms of the plural society is founded. Even those studies that focus on a single ethnic group tend to give little consideration to the artificiality, the inventedness, of race (Comaroff 1987; Reynolds 1991; Gladney 1994). In the case of "the Malays" (to employ the usual terminology), specialists write monographs on Malay nationalism, Malay leadership, Malay ideas of development, and so forth, and only rarely is the concept of "the Malay" treated as problematic (Kahn 1992; Hirschman 1987; Anderson 1991).

To appreciate the way Malayness is a product of historical process entails focusing on different types of dialogue—dialogues, for instance, that occurred not only with the Chinese and other minorities in the country but also with British colonialism. The development of the Malay "race," or bangsa, moreover, is in one sense driven by internal Malay dynamics. Within the Malay community Malayness has persistently been advocated in competition with other concepts of community or collective identity.[1]

A further point concerns the relationship between the Malay bangsa of today and Malay social thinking in the past. The stress on the novelty of the modern Malay ethnicity, on its invented or imagined character, needs to be tempered by a sense of its historical antecedents. As Bruce Kapferer has insisted, "No tradition is constructed or invented and discontinuous with history" (1988: 211). Those constituting themselves as Malays have done so partly in a dialectical reaction against certain assumptions about community and identity inherited from earlier generations.

The present chapter focuses on the process of constituting Malayness, or, perhaps more precisely, the ideological labor involved in that process. The chapter by Shamsul in this volume is a more general survey of ethnicity and its management in modern Malaysia, though it opens up the issue of the appropriation by Malays of Western ideas of race. In discussing the contest and creativity operating among Malay intellectuals engaged in the business of constructing the Malay majority, this chapter suggests that the constituting of Malayness, even allowing for the influence of colonial ideas of race, may in fact be seen as an autonomous process.

The modern study of Malay history and other Southeast Asian histories has been much influenced by a concern with identifying autonomous processes and perspectives (Van Leur 1955; Smail 1961; Ileto 1979). The current historiographical focus on the "fragmentary, the local and the subjugated" (Chatterjee 1993) reinforces the significance of autonomous history, but it must be stressed that autonomies and continuities are not the same thing. In the case of the Malay bangsa, one encounters autonomies of a dialectical character: certain Malay ideologues play a creative role in a process that involves achieving a dialectical synthesis of the local and the new.

Melayu in Early Writings

In the earliest Malay writings, "Malay," or rather "Melayu," referred specifically to representatives and close associates of a single dynasty that, until the Portuguese conquest of 1511, ruled the polity of Malacca, based on the west coast of the Malay Peninsula. In this early period there seems to have been no clear concept of race. The term "bangsa," which was given that meaning in later centuries, still referred primarily to lineage or status. As will be explained below, race or ethnicity was also something a person could change rather easily. In the centuries before the British colonial period, most of the people who were later referred to as Malays appear to have perceived themselves to be subjects of sultans (kerajaan) and members of local communities (Milner 1982).

It was in writings of the eighteenth and nineteenth centuries that

"Malay" began to be used to describe people located in not one but many of the little kingdoms on the peninsula, kingdoms that were later joined together in the Federation of Malaya (Matheson 1979). The Chinese and Europeans who wrote accounts of the region in these centuries used the term "Melayu" when referring to such polities and districts as Chaiya, Ligor, Songkhla, Patani, Kelantan, Trengganu, Pahang, and Johore (Cushman and Milner 1979: 8). It may be asked whether the perceptions and categories of such outsiders helped to shape the consciousness of the Malays themselves. The presence of outsiders, particularly in the large numbers arriving in the nineteenth century (including hundreds of thousands of Chinese), can hardly have been irrelevant to the development of the Malay bangsa. Matheson suggests that this migration "may have resulted in the formulation of popular expressions of group identity by the long-established peasant Malays" (1979: 369).

In Malay writings themselves, at least until the early nineteenth century, there remains a certain vagueness about whether "Melayu" refers to the people of Malacca and its successor states or more generally to the subjects of the peninsular sultanates. The situation alters with the appearance of a number of books by Munshi Abdullah (1797–1854). A translator and language teacher of Arab/Indian background, Abdullah lived in the British settlements of Malacca and Singapore, where he worked largely for the British community. With Abdullah we begin to get an inside view of the process of constituting Malayness. It is not that he was precise about exactly who might be classified as a Malay. Like the Chinese and Indian authors, he listed numerous polities on the Malay Peninsula as Malay, but he was contradictory even about whether or not he himself might be classified as Malay. In his last works he wrote of "us Malays"; earlier he had presented himself more as an outsider to the Malay community.

For Abdullah (see Datoek Besar and Roolvink 1953; Kassim Ahmad 1964), race, or bangsa, was the primary community or collective identity, the most important of the communities into which humankind might be classified. He divided the world up into bangsa rather than kingdoms or religious groupings, and his particular concern was the Malay bangsa. Abdullah warned that this bangsa ran the risk of always being governed by other races, and in order to avoid that fate he proceeded to make many suggestions about how to reform the Malays. Like another author and traveler of the 1830s, Alexis de Tocqueville (Dumont 1972: 52–53), Abdullah also made a connection between race and egalitarianism. His discussion of the bangsa Melayu consistently conveys a concern for the common people and a strong suspicion of the royal elites in the intensely hierarchical sultanates located a short distance away on the peninsula.

The fact that Abdullah placed so much stress on the bangsa rather than some other form of social grouping—for instance, the sultanate (he tended to ridicule Malay royalty) or the community (*umat*) of Islam (which contained members of many other groups as well as the Malays)—is likely to have been in one sense a result of British influence. Dealing with a later period in the nineteenth century, Charles Hirschman has written of the influence of British colonial ideology on the constituting of racial categories, and thus of the plural society, in Malaysia. When the British used the category "race" in their population censuses, for example, their choice of term was not "the inevitable solution to a complex ethnographic maze but rather a particular contribution of European taste." In this way, Hirschman argues, the British helped to create the "racial ideology which continues to haunt contemporary Malaysia" (1987: 567, 570).[2]

Although Hirschman focuses on a later period, even in the 1830s and 1840s, when Abdullah was writing, it was increasingly common in Europe to discuss humankind in terms of its division into races, though not at that stage in a biological sense (Banton 1988: 20, 21). Abdullah, working closely with members of the European community in Singapore and Malacca, was in touch with these trends. For instance, he knew well the conceptually innovative author of the three-volume *History of the Indian Archipelago*, John Crawfurd, who was Resident (or administrator) of Singapore from 1823 to 1826. Race was certainly a central category for Crawfurd; he divided the archipelago's population into races, taking pains to point out "the most abject races" and to make a general observation about the lack of a "great or civilized race" (Crawfurd 1967, 1: 1–17).

By midcentury, an example of this new racial thinking was available in the Malay language. The missionary press, for which Abdullah sometimes worked, published a geography text (*Hikayat Dunia* [1855]) that examined human society in terms of races, noting their locations and their origins. Unlike most traditional Malay writings, this geography is concerned with the origins not of a royal dynasty but of the Malay bangsa. Furthermore, it gives races particular characteristics and qualities—some are lazy, others industrious, for example. Race, the text implies, is something one might be proud of, and the geography certainly expresses pride in the achievements of the English bangsa.

Abdullah's writings can be read in dialogue with this geography. In this way Abdullah might be seen as responding to a British challenge, taking up a European concept and encouraging Malays to perceive themselves as a single race locked in competition with other races. He holds up the English as an example of a race that has reformed itself and urges Malays to adopt many changes, including a more diligent study of their own language. Influenced by his British employers, therefore, Abdullah urges Malays to think of themselves as belonging not primarily to local communities but to a wider racial unity. He ignores the claims of the sultans and also of the Islamic umat. In his writing we can detect an indigenous response to the type of colonial implementation of ideology to which Hirschman has drawn attention.

The Colonial Period: "Fixing" Malayness

The stress on bangsa Melayu as a classification and as a focus of identity and loyalty was taken up and developed by later Malay authors. Like Abdullah, they wrote in the context of British colonialism, with its increasingly "scientific" perception of race. One Malay ideologue who contributed to the developing discourse of race in early-twentieth-century British Malaya (as it came to be called) was Mohd. Eunos Abdullah. Editor of the *Utusan Melayu* (a Malay newspaper that commenced in 1907), and later Malay representative on the colonial legislative council, Eunos was well acquainted with Abdullah's works.

Eunos added new content—new signification—to the term "bangsa" (Milner 1995: chaps. 4, 5). Some of this new content, it is important to note, was drawn from the earlier Malay political tradition focused on the royal courts. At first glance, however, Eunos's doctrines seem designed precisely to displace that earlier tradition.

From the first editorial of his newspaper, Eunos focused on the Malay race rather than any other form of community. Implicitly he, like Abdullah, was in competition with other ideologies. In advocating the racial community, however, Eunos went beyond Abdullah. Although Abdullah warned, admonished, and tried to inspire the Malays, he did not directly advocate the type of emotionalism, the love of race, that emerges in Eunos's editorials. The latter writes of the Malays "with great affection"; he praises "love of race" in other peoples, and he urges Malays to make their race "great" and "powerful." Malays, he says, should enhance the *nama*, or reputation, of their race; they should try to "lift its rank."

Eunos's emotional investment in the concept of the bangsa can be explained partly in terms of the influence of a growing British commitment to race as a social category, but the actual rhetoric he employed suggests a further consideration. This "love," this "enhancing of nama" and "lifting of rank," is resonant of royal, or kerajaan, culture. It is the specific object of loyalty and devotion that has changed. In applying these sentiments to race rather than ruler, Eunos was by no means the last Malay ideologue to appropriate the vocabulary of the sultanates in the service of new political doctrines. The use of this vocabulary might also provide a clue as to why bangsa began to be perceived with such emotion.

The second way in which Eunos's handling of "Malay bangsa" may be distinguished from that of Abdullah arises from the newspaper editor's deliberate emphasis on the problematic character of Malay ethnicity. The *Utusan* does not treat bangsa as a given. Abdullah's writing constantly foregrounded the Malay bangsa and so contributed to the growing power of the concept, but the *Utusan* differs in explicitly treating bangsa Melayu as a concept open to discussion.

The problematic character of bangsa is suggested partly by an apparent apprehension about its future survival. Thus, the *Utusan* explains to its readers that people who do not work diligently might be unable to make their race "permanent in this world" (*Utusan*, Dec. 17, 1917). This anxiety about permanence raises an issue that had long concerned Malay thinkers. Life itself was considered transitory: dying rulers and other leaders are described in Malay royal chronicles as warning their followers that "this world will not endure . . . all that liveth here upon earth cannot but die in the end" (Brown 1952: 124). Polities, too, were capable of disappearing from view—Aru in Sumatra, for instance, dissolved sometime in the sixteenth century—and even the wooden physical remains of such polities were unlikely to be able to withstand the moisture of the tropics. Written chronicles—manuscripts carefully preserved—give the impression of attempting to capture a kingdom, to fix it in time as an heirloom for future generations. In these circumstances, the aspiration recorded in some texts to make a sultanate "permanent" was understandable. When the *Utusan* speaks of the need to give permanence to the bangsa, therefore, it seems to invoke a long-standing Malay anxiety.

To "fix" the Malay bangsa, Mohd. Eunos argues for the need to understand it in a specific way and to commit oneself to that understanding. The manner in which he educates his readers about the race, however, is often indirect. Discussions of developments in Egypt or Japan, for instance, provide opportunities to make general observations that might otherwise have provoked official antagonism in the colonial situation. When an editorial on Egypt refers to the people of that country wishing to "raise themselves up and become one bangsa" (*Utusan*, Apr. 14, 1908), the message for Malays is not difficult to determine.

A number of more express messages. For instance, they are warned not to become like those communities of people "who are so confused that they do not know their own race" (*Utusan*, Nov. 26, 1907). Certain Malays, members of what might be called the new middle class, are warned that they could "lose" their race. One editorial explains that with the success of the rubber industry—by the early nineteenth century there was a boom in Malay planting and a good deal of lively land selling—it would be possible for an increasing number of Malays to go to Europe for schooling. The

Utusan argues that just as many Indians had "become European" through European education, so Malays might also "forget their race in their intention to become Europeans" (*Utusan*, Apr. 9, 1908).

The *Utusan* attempts to assist Malays to "remember" their race. Readers are reminded that in training their children they must never neglect to teach the type of "courteous" and "soft and gentle" manners long associated with the Malays (*Utusan*, Dec. 24, 1907). In a discussion of the Malays of Ceylon and South Africa, the *Utusan* delineates what it considers a further characteristic of Malayness. A brief account is given of the origins of these Malay groups, and then it is related that in 1885 the sultan of Johore met Malays in Colombo on his way to Europe. In this meeting, the editorial explains, he encountered the same "love and affection" and "submission" that were normally offered by Malays to Malay rulers. The editorial continues: "They are bangsa Melayu and because of that it is appropriate for people here to take notice of them and seek ways to bring about a unity with them" (*Utusan*, Nov. 26, 1907).

In one important respect the statement differs substantially from the views expressed half a century earlier by Abdullah. The "Raja Melayu" is not treated with the same ridicule and disdain that generally characterize Abdullah's comments on Malay rulers. The criticism is more subtle than this, yet, from the perspective of the royal courts, no less dangerous. The Malays of Ceylon are considered to be expressing their Malayness by greeting the Malay ruler in a traditional fashion. That is, in the *Utusan* the significance of rajaship is grounded not so much in the potency of the institution itself as in its potential usefulness to the bangsa. It is introduced specifically in the course of enumerating the characteristics of Malayness.

Kerajaan culture is used again to define Malayness in a special series of articles about another Malay sultanate (commencing with *Utusan*, May 12, 1908). These articles come as a further surprise after reading Abdullah. Far from ridiculing royal ceremony, they provide detailed and lengthy descriptions of the wedding of the sultan of Perak, including information about titles, ceremony, and music. In this way, they draw upon a readily accessible tradition. Once more, however, the concern appears to be not to pay homage to the raja but to record, and remind readers of, the ancient customs of the Malays. Such a bangsa-minded concern for royalty arises again in a later issue of the *Utusan* (Nov. 16, 1907), which contains the demand that the dignity of the rulers under British "protection" should be maintained. The precise wording of this editorial is significant. It insists that the raja's dignity be protected in accordance with "the customs [*adat*] of the race [bangsa]." Texts written by ideologues of the royal courts, it is important to note, had presented the reverse position. "Custom" was said to be "in the hands" of the ruler (Milner 1982: 97), and Munshi Abdullah observed that the subjects of Malay rajas were reluctant to alter the adat for fear of invoking the wrath of "rulers of old" (Kassim Ahmad 1964: 40). By contrast, when the *Utusan* states that the ruler must be treated in accordance with the customs of his bangsa, it is insisting in effect that the bangsa be given precedence over him. In this way, the impression is given that rulers and their ceremonies are dimensions of Malayness and that they are to be preserved in the service of the race.

Such attempts to define and fix Malayness, together with anxiety about whether Malays might actually forget their race, give the editorials a tone of defensiveness. A further reason for anxiety on the part of the editor of the *Utusan* might have been that in developing race as a social vision to replace the old kingdom, or kerajaan, he was dependent on what he may have perceived to be a particularly fragile social category. As already indicated, there was little conceptual basis in Malay court writing for developing a strong, genetic view of race. In the precolonial world, royal texts suggest, people could change their ethnic orientation with considerable ease, losing or acquiring what was increasingly described as "Malayness." One chronicle even explains that certain people who altered their customs, language, and attire were able to become Jakun or Aborigines (Milner 1982: 89).

During the nineteenth century in Sumatra and Borneo, as well as on the Malay Peninsula, European observers also commented on this type of ethnic fluidity. They claimed to encounter a phenomenon of ethnic change in which peoples on the periphery of a sultanate were gradually absorbed into the kerajaan, adopting its language and culture. The reverse movement, away from the kerajaan, might also occur (Milner 1982: chap. 5). Eunos would have perceived the issue of race in the context of this inheritance. Such a perception of ethnicity would have influenced him in recognizing the possibility that the bangsa Melayu, still in the process of being constructed, could also decline and perhaps disappear.

A further factor certain to have inspired a defensive tone in the *Utusan*'s discussion of bangsa arose from the momentous social developments taking place in Malaya at the turn of the century. By this time the dimensions of Asian immigration into Malaya and the Straits Settlements were dramatic. Eunos himself, when he surveyed the progress of "British Malaya" in 1907 (*Utusan*, Dec. 5, 1907), reported that from 1901 to 1905 the population of the four states of Perak, Selangor, Negri Sembilan, and Pahang had increased by 20 percent and that the majority of the increase was made up of Chinese and Indians. If the Malays, he warned, did not wish to be "driven away from their own states by other races," then it was necessary that they "work hard day by day for themselves and their race."

Although five decades earlier Abdullah had referred to the competition that the Malays would have to face from other races, he did not specify the precise nature of the threat. To some extent his Indian and Arab background may have discouraged Abdullah from discussing racial threat in the manner of Eunos, but in 1850 the potential immigrant danger was also less apparent. Large-scale immigration, particularly of people displaying what the *Utusan* perceived to be great energy (*Utusan*, Dec. 5, 1907), must have sharpened Malay concern about the future prospects of their own bangsa. Such apprehensions, of course, would also have tended to strengthen the bonds of Malay ethnicity.

Bangsa: Kerajaan Dialectics

Defensiveness and anxiety about the Malay bangsa—as a concept as well as a social group—form only a part of the reason for the fervor with which Eunos and others wrote. The sentiment embedded in the idea of bangsa Melayu was also inspired by earlier Malay thinking about collective identity. As noted above, the precise terminology used to convey loyalty to race is worth examining. When Eunos and later Malay writers used the language of the old royal courts to describe devotion to *bangsa*—when they wrote of "loving the bangsa," of "raising its rank," and of "enhancing its nama"—they engaged in more than skillful appropriation of a potent vocabulary. The use of such language suggests the possibility that the *Utusan* was presenting bangsa as a category of social unity possessing some of the qualities of the old Malay kingdom or kerajaan.

The participation of the Malay subject in the royal polities of the peninsula had a strong psychological and religious significance. What might today be termed the subject's personal identity and prospects for the afterlife—the subject's reputation, or nama—were defined in relation to the ruler-centered kerajaan. Ceremony, sumptuary laws, and costume played a critical role in this definition. The Malay subject from a modern perspective was a "public man" (Sennett 1976). In the royal ideology there was no room for private identity, private ambition, or private property. The subject was immersed—so the royal texts suggest—in the royal polity, the kerajaan (Milner 1982).

Mohd. Eunos Abdullah's *Utusan* implies that the bangsa might be expected to define and recognize the Malay subject and his achievements, which royal texts had also done. The substitution would not always have been complete. Advocates of bangsa such as Munshi Abdullah and Eunos were, at the same time, enthusiasts for the new individualistic way of thinking that was so influential in Europe. They spoke of the rights and opportunities that the individual might enjoy and of the importance of individualism and economic progress. Nevertheless, there is evidence that many Malays continued to be anxious about such full-blown individualism (Milner 1995). The strong communitarian assumptions that underpinned the old kerajaan continued to be influential, and it can be conjectured that some Malays would have been reassured by the use of royal terminology to describe loyalty to race. Such terminology might seem to offer the opportunity for the type of personal immersion in bangsa that had once been experienced in the kerajaan. In this sense the bangsa can be seen as having developed in a dialectical relation to the earlier kerajaan.

The Scope of Malayness

The constituting of the Malay bangsa continued into the high colonial period and beyond independence in 1957. The challenge of the Chinese immigrant community has been persistently commented upon. The census of 1931 showed that the Chinese had become a larger community than the Malays in British Malaya (which included Singapore), and the English historian A. J. Toynbee, after a tour of the region, predicted that eventually the country would ("by peaceful penetration") become a Chinese province (Khoo 1981: 101). Faced with this prospect, the leading Malay journalist, Abdul Rahim Kajai, seeking to promote Malay unity, spoke in hostile terms of "the yellow race" that had "successfully sucked our blood" (Khoo 1981: 105).

Further changes in colonial ideology also shaped the way Malay unity was promoted. The growing biological element in European racial thinking (Williams 1983: 248–50) is probably partly responsible for the way Kajai stressed descent in his construction of Malayness. He attempted to discredit the Malay credentials of Muslims of Arab or Indian "blood" as DKA (Darah Keturunan Arab, possessors of Arab blood) and DKK (Darah Keturunan Kling, possessors of Indian blood) (Abdul Latiff Abu Bakar 1987: 373–74; Roff 1967: 220; Zabedah 1964: 157). The exclusivist perception of Malay ethnicity advocated here—one that also asserted the primacy of bangsa over the wider Islamic community—could not be more different from the perceptions prevalent in the nineteenth century. Abdullah, it will be recalled, virtually changed his own ethnicity, and a traditional chronicle argued that merely by altering one's customs, language, and attire it was possible to assume a new ethnicity.

The scope of Malay ethnicity was also the subject of deliberation both during and after the colonial period. In 1941 Ibrahim Yaacob, another prominent journalist and one with socialist leanings, described the whole archipelago as being "Malay." The term, he said, did not refer merely to

2.5 million people in Malaya but also to 65 million in Dutch-ruled Indonesia (Ibrahim 1941: 12). In the 1940s and 1950s such a view encouraged Ibrahim and others to advocate a Greater Indonesia incorporating both the former Dutch and former British territories.

Against this view, the elite Malays who inherited the government of Malaya from the British sought to restrict the scope of "Melayu" largely to the "Malay" people on the peninsula. The national constitution of the independent state of Malaya was consistent with this view in defining a "Malay" as a "person who professes the Muslim religion, habitually speaks Malay, conforms to Malay custom," and either was born in Malaya or Singapore before independence or is the child of someone born there at that time (Mohd. Suffian 1972: 247). Kajai's blood qualification, it should be noted, is not mentioned. The emphasis on the peninsula as a birthplace, however, implies a narrower interpretation of the bangsa than Ibrahim's.

The issue of scope arose in earnest in the early 1960s when President Sukarno's Indonesia opposed the expansion of Malaya to incorporate certain Borneo territories. At this time, the Malayan—or Malaysian, as they were now known—leaders were in contest with Ibrahim and his followers within Malaysia as much as with President Sukarno. The Malaysian leaders stressed the link between Malayness and the Malay Peninsula, using the phrase "Malay homeland," and celebrated the history of such renowned peninsular polities as Malacca. They invoked the idea of a "Melayu Raya" (a "Greater Malaydom"), a phrase sometimes used by Ibrahim to convey the "Greater Indonesia" idea. But in hijacking this phrase the Malaysian Malay leaders implied the narrower Malayness, one focused on Kuala Lumpur. In the cultural sphere, this narrower vision led, for instance, to the insistence that Malay literature was separate from Indonesian literature, a view that would have been strongly contested by many Malay commentators in earlier years (Milner 1992).

In the independence period the scope of the bangsa Melayu has been the subject of other equally important types of disagreement. The fact that the national constitution and much government policy have given special political and economic privileges to the Malays is an obvious incentive for those currently defined as "Malays" to tighten that definition. The open ethnicity of the past—challenged so strongly by Kajai's insistence on blood relationships but still implied by the definition of "Malay" in the national constitution—could easily be exploited. Jealous of their special rights, Malays have been wary of Chinese and Indians who might change their religion, language, and customs to obtain the accompanying material benefits. As noted already, the intensification of Islamic piety in certain sections of the Malay community has also been portrayed as a strategy for sharpening Malay ethnic definition. It is not the only possible way of interpreting Islamic fundamentalism in Malaysia, but such a strategy certainly possesses immediate advantages for those concerned about the potential practical implications of a loose Malay ethnicity. The recent burgeoning of interest in "traditional culture" in Malaysia—one observer describes the country today as being "awash with the symbolism of 'traditional Malay culture' "—has also been explained partly in terms of a desire to strengthen Malay identity. There is said to be a fear that "ethnically blind market forces" might challenge the Malay special privileges (J. S. Kahn, quoted in Kessler 1992: 146).

Majority/Minority

How then are Malays to relate to other communities in the building of a national society in Malaysia? On the eve of independence, Burhanuddin Al-Helmy, a leader of a prominent leftist Malay party, suggested that members of every race (bangsa) in Malaya might be brought together into a single Malay nationality (kebangsaan). That is, he was distinguishing nationality from bangsa. Kebangsaan evidently would be as open to newcomers as the ethnic (bangsa) community had been in the past, before Abdul Rahim Kajai and others introduced the insistence on descent. In this formulation, Chinese or Indians who adopted Malay language, values, and culture would become members of the *kebangsaan Melayu* (Ariffin Omar 1993: 192–95; Tan 1988: 18–20).

In opposition to this view, the conservative elite of UMNO—those who also opposed the "Greater Indonesia" scope for Malayness—argued that the kebangsaan Melayu idea was a threat to Malay identity. They insisted that adherence to Islam be a key requirement of Malayness and successfully urged that this be incorporated in the definition of "Malay" in the national constitution (Ariffin Omar 1993: 201).

Conservatives and radicals appear to have combined in opposing a further concept, the idea of a bangsa Malaya (a Malayan race or people), though Sukarno had summoned up the image of a bangsa Indonesia back in 1945. In colonial Malaya, the term "Malaya" had come to be associated with the special interests of the Chinese and other non-Malays. Malays in general never referred to their country by that name but rather used the Malay name "Tanah Melayu" (lit. "the Malay land"). In these circumstances, it would appear that if the Chinese and others were not to be joined with Malays in a Malay-based kebangsaan (as Burhanuddin desired), they would simply have to remain separate bangsa in the plural society of the new independent state (Tan 1988: 17; Ariffin Omar 1993: 215).

The name given in 1963 to the enlarged state, Malaysia, never possessed such negative connotations for Malays. In this respect it is intriguing to note that in the 1980s the ruling Malay party, UMNO, introduced into its constitution the idea of promoting a "bangsa Malaysia." This is an important departure. The idea seems to hark back to the Burhanuddin notion of a "kebangsaan Melayu," of building a nationality in the country of Malaysia that, although based on Malay principles and culture, could incorporate people of all races. It also suggests a more open-ended interpretation of "bangsa," one similar to that employed forty years earlier by President Sukarno when he spoke of a single "bangsa Indonesia." The question one might ask of the use of "bangsa Malaysia" is, what relation would exist between it and the bangsa Melayu? Even to contemplate the possibility of such a departure as the introduction of bangsa Malaysia, however, suggests a new confidence among members of the Malay elite about the strength of their own ethnicity.

A further way in which the presence of a large Chinese community in the country has helped shape Malayness (and continues to do so) concerns the qualities attributed to the Malay bangsa. In the colonial period, members of the Chinese community (itself only in the process of formation as a homogeneous entity; Milner 1996) helped to determine the characteristics—negative as well as positive—of the Malay bangsa. Abdullah had presented the Malays as idle compared to their competitors, those races that he had described as "being on the move" (Datoek Besar and Roolvink 1953: 426). At the end of the nineteenth century, certain Chinese writers also portrayed the Malays in such terms, and in a Malay-language newspaper. They asked why "the Malays" were "inert" and suggested they were bound by age-old custom and lacking in ambition (Roff 1967: 54–55). Malay spokesmen replied angrily to these accusations, but some saw truth in the Malay-Chinese contrasts and (as Abdullah had done long before) urged their own community to undertake radical reform (Khoo 1981: 97).

Not all the contrasts between Malays and Chinese were so explicitly value laden. A major Malay-authored history text of the 1920s, for instance, makes the revealing observation that "while Chinese devote their lives to industry Malays are engaged in a quest for reputation [nama]" (Abdul Hadi 1948: 6). Negative comparisons, however, have continued to be most common. Indeed, in the postindependence period, in the aftermath of the severe communal rioting of 1969, the Malay-dominated government itself sponsored a major study exploring Malay-Chinese differences. The aim was to bring about a mental revolution among the Malays (the title of the book was *Revolusi mental*), and to this end the authors compared the national character of "the Malays" to that of "the Chinese." Significant Malay and Chinese proverbs are identified in the book, and it is noted, for instance, that the Malay proverbs do not generally hold out hope that man can influence his fate. The Malays are also seen to give far less attention to the accumulation of money. Not unexpectedly, the examination of proverbs indicates that Malays place more value on the afterlife, Chinese on worldly existence (Senu Abdul Rahman 1973). The object of such contrasts was to bring about change in Malay thinking—the ambition to do so continues today under the prime ministership of Mahathir Mohamed (Rustam Sani 1994)—but, in attempting to achieve this end, such comparative exercises also tend to elaborate the character of the Malay community, thereby assisting in the promotion of its unity. Here we see one way in which the politics of minority/majority representation help to shape the "relational identity" of the majority community (Gladney 1994: 93).

Ideological Work: Ideological Contest

It is the process of providing unity within the Malay community that I wish to consider in concluding this chapter. In retrospect we can see such authors as Abdullah and Eunos as engaged in the construction of a powerful Malayness. But their writing was never explicit in declaring an intention to work ideologically to such an end. Ibrahim, in one of his earliest books, *Surveying the Homeland* (1941), throws light on the character of the ideological task undertaken by such Malay leaders.

In *Surveying the Homeland*, Ibrahim reports on the condition of the Malay community and tells of his own work lecturing around the country, urging his people to think proudly of themselves as members of the bangsa Melayu. In his book the bangsa is revealed with clarity as a community that requires to be actively constructed or conceptualized. Ibrahim explains that after the fall of Malacca to the Portuguese, in the period when the Malay world was divided by all sorts of squabbling and warfare, the people did not even "know their bangsa" (p. 19). During the time he was writing, he says, many Malays continued to give priority to local or factional identities. In Perak, for instance, he encountered immigrant peoples from Minangkabau (Sumatra), Banjar (Borneo), and Baweyan (near Java) who did not consider themselves Malays (pp. 59–60). In Perlis many of the Malays did not "understand how to love their bangsa." In commenting on this inability some years later, he added that the Perlis people were "loyal only to their raja" (1975: 81).

This opposition between court and bangsa is a persistent theme in the book. The contest over the preferred foundations of collective identity is evident throughout. The sultans are portrayed not just as alternative foci of loyalty but also as active enemies of bangsa-mindedness. The royal courts, Ibrahim asserts, "still hold firmly to the old feeling and strongly oppose the new desire to unify the Malay people" (1041: 11–12). In Kedah, for instance, a certain section of the ruling elite opposed the formation of a Malay association on the ground that Kedah "possesses a raja" (p. 72).

The apparent ability of the sultans to frustrate the bangsa movement, as suggested above and in other accounts of the interwar period (Roff 1967: 230), illustrates their continued potency under colonialism. It is a reminder that much of the old ideology, as well as the old establishment, remained powerful in the Malay community. But Ibrahim's account conveys just as distinctly the dynamic character of the movement to create a Malay identity and a community. In the west coast states—in Pahang, in Kedah, indeed in "every state of Malaya"—he records the rise of a "spirit of unity" among the people (1941: 13). It is well known that in the late 1930s newspapers had done much to promote this spirit (Milner 1995: chap. 10). Associations had also been formed to struggle for the Malays and in some states, such as Selangor, they were known as "Malay associations" (Ibrahim 1941: 62). (In Perak as in Kedah, Ibrahim explains, royal opposition seems to have discouraged the use of the term "Malay" [pp. 62, 71].) Young people in particular were acquiring a consciousness of bangsa, some at Ibrahim's instigation. On his visit to Selangor, for instance, Ibrahim stresses this aspect of his lecture to an audience of Baweyan youths. He tells them to be aware that Baweyan is only a small island north of Java and urges them to remember above all that their bangsa is Malay (p. 60).

Although no text of a lecture is given, it is clear from Ibrahim's comments in *Surveying the Homeland* that he was passionately concerned both with making his listeners conscious of political matters and of instilling among them "a feeling of bangsa identity" (p. 11). As he declares at one point, he hoped to "erase" the divisions within the Malay community (p. 60). Ibrahim traveled widely, in almost electioneering style, to achieve these aims, wherever he could arousing a Malay sentiment and inculcating a vision of a united Malay race, struggling against what he saw as the forces of colonial capitalism. Such electioneering offers us a glimpse of the spirit of the contest of ideologies. Ibrahim's account of the bangsa campaign brings the operations of both his Islamic and his royal rivals into sharp focus. He is entirely open about the fact that he advocates bangsa-mindedness in the face of competition from advocates of other types of social vision. In his presentation, the bangsa contends not only against local loyalties—the small Baweyan community is an example—but also against the "feudal" elites that defend that other social construct, the kerajaan. In the case of Islam, he does not debate his religious-scholar (*ulama*) rivals head on. He argues more by emphasis, answering their demands merely by neglecting the umat of Islam in favor of the bangsa Melayu. Islam, as Ibrahim plainly implies in a later writing, was in one sense to serve the purposes of the bangsa (1975: 86).

Another period in which one can observe vigorous contest concerning the promotion of the bangsa Melayu is immediately following the Second World War, when the British attempted to create a new Malayan state in which the Malay rulers and their Malay subjects would no longer hold precedence. A massive movement developed to oppose the implementation of this policy, and one of its objectives was to shift Malay loyalty away from the old kerajaan toward the bangsa. The proper role for the rajas, in the view of Dato Onn, the conservative leader of the movement, was to become "a bond or cement to unite and strengthen" the Malay community (Ariffin Omar 1993: 199). In this formulation (as anticipated above in the discussion of Mohd. Eunos Abdullah), the precedence of the bangsa over the kerajaan is obvious. Other formulations dealt with Islam in a similar fashion. Just as in the writings of Ibrahim, Islam was virtually demoted to the role of helping to provide the bonds of loyalty for the Malay community. Again, however, Islamic leaders, like royal court ideologues, reacted strongly to such demands. Bangsa consciousness, in their view, should not be something that (in the words of an Islamic newspaper) competed with the "aims and obligations of the religion" (*Saudara*, Nov. 24, 1928). The ulama took the view that the umat ought to be the primary community for Malays and that people like themselves, learned in the doctrines of the religion, ought to lead that community.

The Islamic critique of bangsa, and of the concept of nationalism, continues today. The fundamentalist movement, which has become so powerful in the Malay community over the last two decades, may be partly understood (as suggested above) in terms of a strengthening of Malay ethnicity (Chandra Muzaffar 1987). But the "plural society" analysis tends to disguise the fact that the movement has also divided the Malay community. Malay nationalism, which is so deeply embedded in Malay bangsa feeling, is perceived by the fundamentalists to be an artificial, man-made phenomenon, illegitimate in strictly Islamic terms. The fundamentalists—who seek a return to what they consider to be the "fundamentals" of Islam—are inspired by scholars such as Abu Ala Maududi of Pakistan, who declares that "Islam cannot flourish in the lap of nationalism, and nationalism, too, cannot find a place in the fold of Islam" (Mohamad Abu Bakar 1988: 163).

To counter this growing movement, the governing Malay party, UMNO—more bangsa- than umat-minded in its orientation—has adopted a number of new and well-publicized Islamic measures, such as the establishing of an Islamic bank and an Islamic university. The current promotion of "traditional Malay culture," it can be argued, can also be understood in the context of this struggle against radical Islam. It is possible, of course, that cultural revivalism, like fundamentalism, has been driven partly by the desire to sharpen Malay ethnic definition in the face of a threat from the Chinese and other non-Malay communities. Such revivalism may spring also from a middle-class commitment to "debate with 'the west' on the one hand and notions of modernity on the other" (Kahn 1992: 174). Nevertheless, a further perspective would examine the propagation (or even reconstruction or invention) of traditional culture in terms of a perceived need to strengthen Malay resistance to the incorporation of Malaydom into a wider Islamic community (Mohamad Abu Bakar 1988; Milner 1986, 1991).

The constituting of the bangsa Melayu, it is clear, was carried out not only in the face of the British and Chinese challenges but also in contest with other forms of community and identity within "Malay" society. In reflecting on this contest, we return once again to the royal language by means of which emotion was embedded in the concept of bangsa. The employing of this language is a reminder that the debate within the Malay community entailed more than the assertion and repetition of contrary philosophies. A dialogue took place, and new ideas were constructed in this dialogic—or perhaps, a term I would consider more accurate, dialectical—context (Bakhtin 1984; Gladney, this volume).

The appropriation of such royal language continued well after the time when it was used by Mohd. Eunos Abdullah. "Love your bangsa until eternity," wrote one 1930 Malay author; "lift it up onto a throne." This author also wrote of "service" to the bangsa, again using a term with strong courtly connotations (Abdul Latiff Abu Bakar 1987: 22, 29). When Ibrahim—quasi socialist as he was—declared that he was offering his book, *Surveying the Homeland*, as "a gift" to the Malay people, the word he used for gift, *persembahan*, carried the notion of obeisance to a raja (1941: 4). It was even thought possible to speak of "treason" to the bangsa, employing the potent term *derhaka*, which had once been strictly reserved for disloyalty to a ruler (Tan 1988: 16–17).

In this later colonial period, as in Eunos's time, the urging of such an emotive concept of bangsa can be seen, at least in part, as emerging from a dialogue with the claims of the kerajaan, the older royal ideology. In this sense "race" is not to be seen entirely as part of a "derivative discourse" (Chatterjee 1986), the mere product of British colonial ideology. The bangsa was being designed by Malay ideologues to replace the kerajaan, and in the process it was injected with some of the latter's vital qualities.

Conclusion

The majority community in Malaysia, therefore, is to be seen, at least in part, as the product of ideological work. The innovative Malay ideologues, who showed considerable virtuosity in constituting the Malay bangsa, operated in the context of the challenge of the dynamic Chinese minority, and in some situations they actually defined Malayness with reference to Chineseness. They were much influenced, in addition, by British ideas and epistemology. The process in which the ideologues engaged, however, possessed one further and special feature. The ideologues took part in an autonomous dialectic, one that drew upon earlier, local thinking about community and, in the long run, generated a distinctive concept of race and commitment to race.

PART V

FIJIANNESS

9

Aspiring to Minority and Other Tactics Against Violence

JOHN D. KELLY

THE center has not held, but things have not fallen apart in Fiji. The British Commonwealth vision—the vision of an alliance of geographically dispersed, culturally backward pockets all striving to become like the British, once aided by British colonial investment and inspiration, now partners in a network of economic mutual aid (a common wealth)—was rejected in Fiji by two military coups in 1987. The constitution written in London was abandoned, the Commonwealth ruptured, a republic declared. The Commonwealth ideal was rejected in Fiji by the closest allies the British had thought that they had there, the chiefs and the indigenous Fijian military elite. In place of the Commonwealth vision of benign Westernization, the indigenous elite has promoted a goal that the British themselves had often used tactically to rule in Fiji: perpetual firstness, vaguely defined, for the indigenous Fijians and therefore especially for their guardians. Denied any right to equal priority, yet again, is the other half of Fiji's population, the descendants of South Asians, descendants largely of the people brought to labor on British plantations: the descendants of the people the British once called "coolies."

Guardians for indigenous Fijians (or "ethnic Fijians"), self-appointed and otherwise, have always had their roles in Fiji's politics because metaphors of childhood and adolescence have been used quite freely, especially by British policymakers, to describe indigenous Fijians. (The descendants of the plantation labor, the "Fiji Indians" or "Indo-Fijians," on the other hand, were never again seen as childlike in the British Empire after the 1857 "mutiny" in India; in Fiji their difference has always been typed by others more as sinister than as pediatric or exotic.) The appointed guardians of the ethnic Fijians were once the British and the indigenous chiefs; now they are chiefs and more nouveau claimants (army officers, the Methodist church elite, etc.). What was once an expedient to lead people regarded as very backward through a cultural adolescence became the hammer that shattered the Commonwealth goal and plan.

Since the coups, the constitution breakers have been unable to found stable new governments. Contradictions in their plans for the new nation-state and its purposes have not been resolved. But despite these failures, and despite multiple new regimes based on severe formal discrimination against nonethnic Fijians, especially Indo-Fijians, Fiji has not (and of course in fairness we must admit, not yet) come in any real way to resemble a Sri Lanka, a Rwanda, a Bosnia. Repeated, deliberately provocative efforts of new national leaders to devise schemes of permanent discrimination have not led to ratcheting ethnic violence. The center does not hold, but things do not fall apart. How can we explain this extraordinary absence, this limit to violence?

We might look into the literature on the politics of culture for some help here. One might even imagine that current metropolitan, North Atlantic debates on multiculturalism might provide a frame of reference from which to pose questions about ethnic self-assertion and its consequences. But this quest quickly explodes in ironies. The earnest efforts of reigning theorists of "liberal democracy," such as Charles Taylor's "The Politics of Recognition" and its companion commentaries (Taylor et al. 1992), see universalistic values in liberal democracy, see culture as particularistic in contrast, and worry over types and modes of compromise or even pollution as the latter expresses itself in the former.[1] After a fashion, one could try to present Fiji in this mode as the failure of the general form when a particularistic group hijacks the state. But there is a deeper problem with the model, and it is visible right in the title of Taylor's paper. To the doctors of liberal democracy, culture is intrinsically a matter of identity formation, group assertion, and recognition or misrecognition by others. Surely, they assume, what minorities want is respect and recognition, and the issue, as Taylor et al. pose it, is how much respect and recognition for authentic cultural differences the liberal democracy can afford. However, if we look more closely at real cases, here Fiji, we find imputed ethnic homogeneities—groups represented by others as homogenous and self-assertive—as well as groups feeling and representing themselves as such. We find people, such as many among the Indo-Fijians, aspiring to make their demographically large group appear smaller, more various, and more minor in its presence and interests in the nation as a whole. We find not only aggressive self-assertion of cultural identity, but very principled as well as interested denial of it. There is more to the politics of culture than liberal democracy seeking to accommodate ethnic self-assertion.

A more promising point of connection for reflections on the situation in Fiji is scholarship less anxious to suppose that minorities are intrinsically the problem, scholarship that does not start from the premises that minority groups have intrinsically separate (to Taylor, "authentic") cultures and that they are less central to the social and cultural history of larger polities than are majority groups. Along such lines one might consider the works of the subaltern studies school of historians, the multidisciplinary work following Anderson (1991) or Corrigan and Sayer (1985) on nationalism, and much recent anthropology.

As an example, Dru Gladney (1994) has recently argued that for a century nationalists in China, both capitalist and communist, have stigmatized China's minorities as primitive, exotic, and erotic, creating by contrast an image of a civilized, rational, and homogenous Han majority. They have thus found in a minority problem both an outlet for social and sexual imagination and a means, by play of contrast, to constitute a useful national homogeneity and modernity in the majority. Gladney scrutinizes the majority claims to universalism as carefully as the representations of minority culture and finds the latter often to be literally authored by members of the majority elite, as when a new art school's Gauguin- and Picasso-influenced paintings of minority peoples are taken by the art world to be paintings by China's close-to-nature minorities. Gladney argues that this modality of contrast—rational, civilized majority self; cultural, exotic minority other—not only is characteristic of Chinese and other East Asian national majorities, but can be paralleled with European colonial imagining of colonizer and native and continuing Euro-American imagining of white and colored races. "It is only the so-called 'ethnics' . . . who are marked by 'culture.' Majorities by extension, become denaturalized, homogenized, essentialized as 'same'" (Gladney 1994: 103). The tables have been thoroughly turned on the theorists of liberal democracy; the representations of minority authenticity and difference are found to be the machinery constructing the faux universal majority self.

In discourse, however, there is never a pure antithesis. Clear reversals must reproduce many premises of the original argument. To again essay reconsideration of the premises of the multiculturalism theorists, I suggest new questions: When do majorities matter? When do culture and, especially, identity itself matter in political discourse? I suggest that we might seek the conditions that make it possible for majorities and minorities, and for cultural identities, to exist. Thus we might denaturalize not only the majority identities so foundational to many nation-states, but also the identity fetishism increasingly foundational in contemporary theory and politics.

I offer three theoretical arguments. First, we should reconsider what we might call the democracy premise in the correlation of majority/minority with center/periphery in the delineation of discourses (see also Kaplan's and Handler's chapters in this volume). Second, it is only sometimes that people have a cultural identity, in the double sense of affiliation and possession. We can investigate specific and delineable situations in which some people do not have such cultural identities, or do not want them, or even resist having them imposed, and it will not simply be the case that minorities or weak people have them and majorities or dominant people do not. Third, identity assertion itself, far from being intrinsic to all discourse or even all political discourse, is a family of political strategies that are often—perhaps even generally—employed unevenly. Again, assertions about the identity of the self or others are not always deployed by majority against minority, center against periphery, high against low, patron against client, or vice versa. More important, I strongly suspect that they are rarely deployed the same way by two or more sides. A dialogics capable of rendering identity politics intelligible will have to map not only claim and counterclaim dialectics but also refusals, deflections, and alternative assertions, rendering identity representations as a group of tactics among others in a larger set. In short, to bring representations of majority and minority cultural identities into better focus, I seek to understand more about conditions of possibility that make majority and minority identities relevant. Relevant to what? Nation-states? Only democratic nation-states? Only peaceful, democratic nation-states? Or how about only civil societies? Is it universes of discourse framed and bounded by standards of civility that are crucial?

Fiji might seem a privileged place to study majority-minority relations: by census classification its majority population has shifted twice this century. First, the majority was said to be the indigenous Fijians, that is, the descendants of the Pacific Islanders already resident when the colonial Europeans arrived. Then, roughly from 1945 to 1988, the largest group was said to be the Fiji Indians or Indo-Fijians (from approximately 1960 to 1985, this categorization actually encompassed more than 50 percent of the population). Then, perhaps in 1988, the indigenous Fijian population again superseded the Indo-Fijian and is now very close to 50 percent of the population as counted in the census. As Kaplan (this volume) shows, however, this pendulum is more irrelevant than it is determinative of group relations, standing, tactics, and even existence in the history of the islands. When we pay closer attention, the demographic movements, especially the more recent ones, stand more as effects than as causes of political movements. Fiji's political movements find their mainspring less in discourses on identity than in those on sovereignty, especially assertions of the necessity of indigenous Fijian chiefly hegemony that are threatened by the discourse of democracy itself. The principal argument for this chapter, then, will be not theoretical but ethnographic: that curiously enough, there are sensible Indo-Fijians who aspire to minority status, and a minority status as featureless as possible, precisely in order to allay others' fears of democracy and thereby combat a rising tide of violence, both real and threatened.

In polities with self-assertive, dominant ethnic groups, where others are dominated—whether they are "minorities" or otherwise militarily weak ethnicities, imputed ethnicities, or otherwise categorized peoples—what options do the dominated people have to preempt, forestall, or combat forms of violence directed against them? Particularly, what options are there apart from vigorous group self-assertion, in situations where such counterassertiveness might be unwise? Analyses of violent ethnic schismogenesis frequently trace spirals of increasingly grotesque hate crime. We all can think of things in surplus of mere death visited upon ethnic enemies in parts of the world far more violent than Fiji. The retrospective clarity of the hate inscriptions can make the acceleration of hate and violence seem inevitable. The energy of violence, in narrative and all the more in its physical presence, can make it appear almost irresistible. But in Fiji, it is resisted, and especially by Indo-Fijians, who have been victims of a variety of forms of violence for more than a century. There is no spiral; the grotesque gifts are not returned with a surplus. But this does not exactly make Fiji peaceful, or make the lives of various sorts of Indo-Fijians settled or happy, either.

We shall return to the specific modality of alterity mapping—rational, civilized self versus culturally marked, exotic others—that was pirated by the Chinese, Gladney argues, from Europe. I will try to trace some existing transformations as well as extensions of this colonial alterity paradigm. We also have some more basic matters to ponder concerning violence and discourse. But theoretical questions are best engaged with purpose, and we are better served if we turn to paradoxes of contemporary political reality in Fiji.

Paradoxes of Preemptive Nonviolence

Is a boycott discourse? When does a dialogue end?

On June 16, 1994, a large group of parliamentarians in the Fiji Islands refused to return to parliamentary sessions in the wake of a speech made by prime minister, and ex-brigadier general, Sitiveni Rabuka during debate over a crime bill.[2] Their boycott ended on June 20. "Opposition members felt we'd made our point," said Jai Ram Reddy, leader of the National Federation Party, of the parliamentary opposition, and of the boycott. "It was our duty to stage a protest," said Mahendra Chaudhry, leader of the Fiji Labour Party, also part of the opposition and boycott.

Clearly, the opposition leaders sought to portray their boycott, their temporary refusal to engage in parliamentary dialogue, as a communicative act, an act that communicated a point, made visible ("staged") a point of view. Communication by boycott has a long history in colonial and postcolonial Fiji. It offers a chance for ethnographic observations to contribute to efforts to theorize about discourse, dialogue, and civility, a chance for ethnography with attention both to theoretical and political complexity.

Aren't all coups intrinsically acts of violence? When does violence interrupt dialogue, and how can it become part of it?

Though Rabuka later denied it, his remarks that caused the boycott were understood as an effort to chill opposition resistance to his crime bill, indeed to threaten Fiji's Indian or Indo-Fijian residents with violence if they did not support his government's policies. Rabuka, the leader of Fiji's two 1987 coups, said on June 16, "I cannot guarantee nor can anyone guarantee that there will not be another coup in this land." He said, "When that happens, I cannot guarantee that it will be bloodless like mine." Said Krishna Datt, deputy leader of the Fiji Labour Party, "It was a threat—he was telling everybody 'shut up' or this is what we will do again."

Two preliminary points here: first, the boycott was thus presented as a best alternative to "shutting up." The refusal to engage in parliamentary exchange, which caused proceedings in the House of Representatives to be abandoned, was a silence intended to be a sharp comment on silencing. Second, in this debate within, outside of, and especially about parliamentary normality, one of the issues to be tracked is the meaning and measure of the 1987 coups themselves. Datt's quoted comment recounts mainly a threat to repeat, an interpretation justified by other Rabuka statements from the same speech: "I will not and will never apologise for the coup of 1987," and "I will not even say that it will not happen again." But Rabuka also, in his "guarantee" comment quoted above, sought to position himself not merely as unapologetic but as the good coup maker, the maker of the good, bloodless coups, with unique powers also to forestall a terrible alternative, a bloody coup led by others. Rabuka at least seeks to distinguish his coups from violence and enter them into a political history of acceptable, even heroic, nationalist peacemaking. Like the rest of the postcoup "interim" governments of which he was intermittently a leader, he seeks a way to rediscover his authority, taken originally by military force, within some nexus of civil relations and needs, and to recast his foundations in civil society. But what civil society?

The Center Does Not Hold, but Things Don't Fall Apart

We proceed toward a brief history of violence in Fiji, and of boycotts there. A useful step will be an outline of the breaks in sovereignty over the islands, especially the latest, the coups of 1987. The first assertion of sovereignty over all of Fiji was that of a chief named Cakobau in the latter nineteenth century; European settlers joined with him to constitute a short-lived kingdom with a parliament, strongest in its control of the eastern half of the islands, in the early 1870s. American gunships prosecuting alleged debts, and other debt catastrophes, drove Cakobau and other chiefs assembled for the purpose to cede sovereignty to the British in 1874. Thereafter the British ruled a colony for almost a century, until independence and Commonwealth membership in 1970. Under a constitution installed by the British for the new nation-state, an Alliance Party managed to form an unbroken series of stable governments until the 1987 election. In 1987 the Alliance Party, self-described as an alliance of races or communities, but increasingly baldly acting as the party of indigenous Fijian chiefly interests, lost the election to a coalition of rival parties, and for about a month Fiji was governed by the coalition. The coups followed, by all accounts intended to restore the chiefs to power, and after the second coup, Fiji was forced out of the British Commonwealth and declared itself a republic.[3] In the wake of the coups there has not been a coherent polity or clearly organized politics, however, but instead a rapid succession of movements, parties, and chiefly factions competing for rank and office, variously insisting upon prowess based on military, lineage, or regional rank or Christian religious mission.

Is Fiji now and was it ever a nation? If we operate with Anderson's now ubiquitous formulation of the nation as an "imagined community," Fiji's problem could be described as either a deficit of consensus or a surplus of imaginations (which is not simply to assert Fiji exceptionalism).[4] The situation is often described the way one Fiji-born Fiji citizen of European descent described it to me: "separate nations living in each other's backyards." But as I will make clear, in crucial ways this depiction of ethnic groups constituting their own communities, their own nations, though mixed in one territory, is unfortunately oversimplifying. A topic of major local controversy is whether "race," as the British taught everyone to call it, is ineluctably the same thing as identity and "community," another thing the British liked to call it. In recent politics, the succession of parties and governments committed to perpetual rule by indigenous chiefs has competed with a coalition of rival parties not only over whether the nation should be ruled exclusively by chiefly indigenous Fijians (or, as they would likely put it, whether Fiji should be ruled by Fijians or Indians), but also over the boundaries of the real nation itself. The dialogics of this confrontation are best conveyed by a detailed example.

On the night of October 14, 1989, an indigenous Fijian Methodist Youth Fellowship group prayed until 4:00 A.M. Then ten men and eight women left church, bought benzine at a gas station, and set out to burn down all the Indo-Fijian houses of worship in Lautoka, Fiji's second-largest city. They got the four largest and then were arrested while regrouping. They told police that they acted because the Bible said to burn idols; they did not quibble over setting fire to a mosque along with two Hindu temples and a Sikh *gurudwara*. Four days later, the interim government issued a press release deploring the "fire incidents." Much controversy followed over whether and how to punish the youths, in a country that, after the second coup, had passed Sunday observance regulations requiring all citizens to restrict not only business but also leisure activities (no buses or taxis, no picnics) on the Christian Sabbath. By 1989, the government had relaxed these bans, and this relaxation itself was taken up as an issue by Christian extremists in the wake of the "fire incidents." The interim government's minister for women, culture, and social welfare criticized the Methodist Church for condemning the attacks, arguing that "the Methodist Church should have acted more responsibly by preparing something that was more remedial rather than outright condemnation of the act." This minister was petitioned by the Ba Province Women's Council and the Methodist Youth Fellowship to seek pardons for the arsonists; the petitioners argued that the arsonists "should not be condemned for the act but should be loved and cared for in accordance with Christian belief" (*Daily Post*, Oct. 28, 1989).

Meanwhile a one-day stop-work protest was respected by most Indo-Fijians and many others. Hindu religious organizations led Fiji's Hindus (close to 80 percent of the Indo-Fijians) to cancel all public celebrations of Diwali, a holiday that since independence in 1970 had come to celebrate the advent of righteous rule.[5] Pardon for the arsonists receded as an issue when all but their leader received absolute discharges (in the interests of harmony, the Lautoka High Court judge explained) after pleading guilty. And in the aftermath of these events, informal attacks on Indo-Fijian (but almost never indigenous Fijian or Christian) places of worship have become common. So-called idols and religious texts are sometimes damaged or destroyed, and defecation is sometimes involved, but, according to working-class Indo-Fijians I know, the break-ins usually seem to be in search of money.

So, against this backdrop, to the promised dialogics in search of the terms of reference for the "nation," an "imagined community." After deciding to deplore the incidents, the interim government sent a team including the acting prime minister to visit the sites and the victimized religious organizations.[6] The acting prime minister's remarks to the groups were released to the press (in English) on October 19. Watch the uses of "us," "we," "you," and "your":

> All of us in government are deeply saddened and shocked by the fire incidents of last Sunday. . . . We have come here today to let you know that we are deeply concerned about the welfare of people of all religions. We want to assure you that your individual religious freedom will be protected and you will continue to have the freedom of religious worship and association which everyone has enjoyed in Fiji.
>
> We ourselves deeply value our religious beliefs and therefore we understand and share your feelings of grief and shock at the desecration of your holy sites. . . . We know and accept that there are many paths to God and we fully respect your path. We will always ensure that in Fiji every man, woman, and child is given the right to follow the path of his or her choice.
>
> The unpleasant actions which bring us here today are those of a few isolated fanatics and extremists. They do not in any way represent the behaviour of the majority of the people. The majority in this country have always practised religious tolerance, respect and goodwill towards one another, that too is the Fijian way—the way of Fiji.

Here is our key word, *majority*. To what majority, of what nation, does it refer? From an ecumenical point of view, it is at best ambiguous. Clearly the government officers' "we" with "our religious beliefs" are separated from "you" with "your holy sites." The "majority of the people" might include more than the indigenous Fijians, 99 percent of whom are Christian, but "the Fijian way" is laden with connotations of islander ethos. At the very least, the nation represented by this official "we" is indigenous Fijian at its core; by another reading, the distanced "you" are placed outside it altogether, as resident foreigners.

Days later, a message was sent from a hospital bed in New Zealand to "the people of Fiji" on the occasion of Diwali, by the onetime leader of the Labour Party and onetime coalition prime minister, indigenous Fijian Dr. Timoci Bavadra. His uses of "our," "we," and "you" contrast radically with the discourse of his postcoup successors:

> Our religions should not be used to divide us. Even if our places of worship are burned, no one can take away the religious beliefs and standards of goodness we set ourselves in our daily life.
>
> Our different religious faiths are beacons which light up our understanding of the ideals we all commonly share as human beings.
>
> Even if the ceremonial Diwali lights do not shine this year, I hope we will all remember their significance—with a prayer that the lighted candle of democracy will one day be rekindled. We hope its warm rays will nurture the tolerance of Fiji's people, in their different religions, beliefs, ethnic groups and social classes.

> I continue to work and pray for a new dawn of peace and goodwill in our country. God's light, at the beginning of every day, is among his greatest gifts. Our faith in him—and in Fiji—must remain unshakable. I ask you to join me in working and praying for the light to return to our country, not only during Diwali, but at all times. (Bavadra 1990: 357)

Bavadra died four days later, the day after the Indian ambassador was expelled from Fiji. This note provides an entry into the Fiji Labour Party and coalition government's vision of a nation in Fiji: a nation not founded on a core culture or religion, but illuminated by democracy, made up of differing, civil, tolerant "human beings."

Let us be clear here that the Labour Party does not aspire to constitute a minority status for its members. Labour broke open Fiji's electoral politics and enabled coalition victory over the Alliance Party before the coups by denying racial and cultural foundations to political affiliation, by promoting not so much a class-based as simply a political-economy-based definition of agency and interests. And Labour succeeded, briefly, in substituting a human for a racial definition of being in Fiji citizenship and politics, but only for as long as it took the army to overturn a democratic constitution that had not absolutely guaranteed which race would rule. When the British gave up rule over Fiji in 1970, they wrote a constitution that enshrined racial divisions among the voters, restricting some parliamentary seats to members of a "race," either indigenous Fijian, Indian, or "general elector" (all others), and restricting the electorate for the other seats to voters of one race. Furthermore, they gave Indians, then 51 percent of Fiji's population, only 40 percent of the seats, not a small shift in a putative democracy. As long as the general electors and indigenous Fijians voted together, as they always had and generally did until 1987, the racial hierarchy (whites on top) and the hierarchy within indigenous Fijian society (chiefs on top) that had defined civil order in Fiji could continue. Under Indo-Fijian and international pressure to decolonize Fiji, the British also took further steps to secure indigenous Fijian privileges and thus convince reluctant indigenous chiefs to accept the withdrawal of their colonial patrons.[7] The colonial British had not imagined a Fiji running on egalitarian democratic principles, but Labour did, and it won enough of the urban seats to be able to combine with the National Federation Party (seen as "the Indian party," though it also was founded by labor unions) to create the coalition parliamentary majority.

As Kaplan (this volume) shows, assertions of indigenous Fijian paramountcy are rarely based on a notion of indigenous Fijians as Fiji's majority. The acting prime minister's vague depiction in the "fire incidents" speech of a majority in Fiji who were tolerant was challenged by Fijian nationalist Sakeasi Butadroka, who declared that there was a "Fijian silent majority" who supported the "temple burnings" (*Daily Post*, Oct. 25, 1989). The shift here to concern for majority sentiment within the indigenous Fijian community is telling—and unusual less for its exclusive concern with indigenous Fijian sentiments than for its concern with locating majority indigene sentiments. Commoner Butadroka's brand of Fijian nationalism has always tended toward an antichiefly, commoner Fijian populism. In the tumult of postcoup indigenous Fijian political confrontations, such self-promotions as indigenous commoner popular protest voices have vied with several other vehicles—especially military achievement and Christian commitment—in multiple challenges to sheer chiefly rank as a basis for political authority in Fiji. And to all this the Indo-Fijians, like others in Fiji, would remain largely spectators, if not for the fact that they are continually invoked as the bogey and scapegoat.

When announcing to the Methodist Youth Group arsonists their "noncustodial sentences," the Lautoka High Court judge, Mr. Justice Saunders, did condemn the arson. He told them that their leader was "acting in the name of the devil more than in the name of the Lord." But if he thereby presumed a Christian set of options in a religiously plural polity, he did not neglect the victims altogether. He noted that the attacks would have led to "anarchy if the victims were not tolerant" (*Fiji Times*, May 19, 1991). We now branch off in pursuit of this tolerance, and its political dramas.

Pursuit of Śānti in the Realm of Mana

The climactic moment of the well-attended *bhajans* (prayer songs) nights in Fiji's Sai Baba temples and centers is almost always the same: a high-tech or, if necessary, low-tech manipulation of the cadence of the singing, first quickening, then sharply slowing, as the lighting is suddenly reduced to a single central flame. A triple, slowing intonation of the word for peace—*śānti, śānti, śāānti . . . i*—is followed by silence. Outside Sai Baba circles one hears many other devotional Hindu accounts of attainment of peace, śānti, as one of the highly desirable results of clean living, hard work, and closeness to god.

In ethnic Fijian Christianity the concept of *loloma*, kindly love, might in some ways bear comparison to the Hindu ideal of inner and worldly peace; the topic is of interest to many practical theologians in the ecumenically oriented portion of Fiji's religious leadership. But the theological mantra that bears most weight in most of the ubiquitous and often quite consequential indigenous Fijian rituals is not *loloma e dina*, "truth is love," but *mana e dina*, "truth is power." (The literature is vast on whether "power" is an adequate gloss for "mana"; of course, it is so only in a limited way.)

Even though the relation between people and chiefs is often claimed to be characterized by loloma, kindly love, it is not loloma but mana that securely distinguishes chiefs from other people and enables them to speak with the force and adequacy that entitles them to respect and sway.

I have no intention of assembling a cultural-template argument here. I will not argue that devotional Hindu constructions of divinity impel one kind of politics, indigenous cosmology another. A partial parallel for mana could be found in conceptions of divine and humanly attained *śakti*, power, in Hindu religious discourse. It would be possible to imagine a consequential confrontation between invocations of Fijian Christian loloma and Hindu śakti; I could even cite small-scale examples of such. It did not have to be a search for śānti confronting an advancing mana. My point is merely that for ten years or so, it has been. (And though it is not our topic, politics have probably influenced the quests in worship.)

As indigenous Fijians and others in Fiji will often note with some exasperation, Indo-Fijians resort often to strikes, boycotts, one-day work stoppages, and other tactics of withdrawal and simple refusal to accept asserted rules. Both the National Federation Party and the Fiji Labour Party strongly considered boycotting elections under the new, discriminatory, "promulgated" postcoup constitution; the former was the first to decide not to boycott, after being advised to participate by Lal Krishna Advani of the Bharatiya Janata Party in India (who cited the British political chestnut "Politics is the art of the possible"). Between the 1989 national stop-work protest over the "fire incidents" and the parliamentary crime-bill boycott of June 1994, there was another national crisis in 1991, when labor unions and cane growers led by Labour Party head Mahendra Chaudhry threatened and organized for a national strike. Facing death threats and angry pro-Fijian and pro-Christian marches whose leadership articulated their causes directly against that of the laborers, the union leadership forced the interim government to withdraw harsh decrees that would have made strikes in general and any actions interfering in the sugar harvest (a perennial point of possible boycott) into matters of treason.

In Fiji since independence, the formalities of political-economic theory and the liberal, democratic state have had their advocates. Ironically, it has been the Labour Party that has worked most consistently for the realization of a nation of economic individuals. But generally, debates over the forms of law and the order of the state have been pushed and pulled by the tidal forces of a larger confrontation over indigenous mana and its limits, as in 1984, the occasion of another boycott: the opposition National Federation Party boycotted Parliament for months after its leader, Jai Ram Reddy, was expelled from the chamber of Parliament by force because his sitting posture and demeanor were found by the Speaker of the House not to express enough respect for chiefly and official stature.

The boycott strategy has multiple historic inspirations, easily traceable into both British and South Asian history. European labor leaders and Christian missionaries and other churchmen had an enormous influence on Gandhi and other leaders in the Indian National Congress and other anticolonial movements, which quickly found strikes, boycotts, and other forms of organized refusal to be their most effective tactics against the British. But we would be rash to trace the strategy simply through India to England; the resonances with purifying refusal to deal with evil can easily be traced also to *bhakti* devotional insistence on the importance of *satsang* (wise, good company) and, in addition, should surely be compared to the logics of outcasting and of world renunciation, complex practices long antedating European and even bhakti influence.

Thus, the tactical repertoire of strikes, stoppages, and boycotts has a deep dialogic history, not always under any one sign, śānti included. And in Fiji, in turn, the history of strikes and boycotts is not simple. Jaikumari, a woman trained at Gandhi's ashram, was perhaps the central organizer of the first major strike in Fiji in 1920 (though the man who was formally her husband, the barrister Manilal, was widely blamed, and both were forced out of Fiji for it). A visiting mendicant, Sadhu Basist Muni, claimed Gandhian inspiration as he led the second, a major cane strike in 1921. (He too was exiled.) Even before this time, informal *pancayats* sought to impose forms of outcasting as social controls within Fiji Indian society. From 1929 into the 1930s came perhaps the most consequential failed boycott of Fiji's history, the effort of a Fiji Indian National Congress led by S. B. Patel, A. D. Patel, barristers sent by Gandhi, and especially local-born Vishnu Deo to boycott the first elected seats for Indians on Fiji's Legislative Council. Its goal was to force Fiji elections to be held on a principle of common roll rather than racial or communal roll. As the Indians sought to articulate carefully, they sought only "a fair field and no favour," in Vishnu Deo's words; if the government established property and literacy requirements that qualified far more European (as they called themselves in 1920s Fiji) than Indian voters, this was acceptable, as long as the principle of imperial citizenship for all the queen's subjects was adhered to. This boycott failed, actually, in an empirewide contest; Churchill, among others, was an advocate for common rolls with stringent tests and "equal rights for Civilised Men" (as he put it), but Kenya was the key domino, where threatened South Africa–style white breakaway led London to concede to local racialism. I have written about these strikes and boycotts extensively elsewhere (Kelly 1991; Kaplan and Kelly 1994); many others followed them. But rather than continuing the list, I will finish this account by offering a more extensive look inside a particular set of controversies, an occasion in the 1930s in which, under the shadow of the continuing Legislative Council boycott, groups of Indo-Fijians organized boycotts against each other.

Despite my argument here for a general confrontation between śānti and mana in Fiji's recent cultural politics, I have tried to avoid settling into a language that presumes that a unitary "Indo-Fijian community" (this itself a pernicious mask for "Indian race") exists in Fiji. The Muslims are not Hindus. The Indian Christians, who have recently come to constitute more than 5 percent of the Indo-Fijians, are neither of these. And there are many kinds of Hindus, and some say (though some deny it) more than one kind of Muslim, in Fiji. The vast numbers of Indo-Fijian poor are not rich and are largely invisible to non-Indians. The Gujaratis and the Punjabis distinguish themselves and are distinguished. South Indians, at least sometimes, also insist on distinction.

This last difference, between South Indians and others, became a major issue in boycott controversies in rural Rewa in the 1930s. Vishnu Deo led not only the Legislative Council boycott of the Fiji Indian National Congress, but also a religious reform movement called the Arya Samaj, a group inspired by multiple sources, Indian and European (see Kelly 1991), to seek a Great Awakening of Vedic Hinduism and Aryan society. Among its many goals in India and in Fiji was to counter the Christian influence through schools. In Fiji as in India, the Arya Samaj led the way in building schools that combined Indian and Western curricula to create an elite alternative to a colonial education. In India, some Arya Samaj leaders observed with interest the successes of fascists in Europe and sought to build organizational strength by constituting a network of clubs or social cells that would strictly regulate their social boundaries, that would in effect socially and religiously outcast all those who did not join in their activities. In Rewa, with tacit support from the Fijiwide Samaj leadership, aggressive efforts were made to organize *sangathan sabha* (cooperative societies) and to boycott/outcast those who sullied their Aryan identity by continuing social relations with Muslims. Among its many goals, the Samaj leadership sought not only a Hinduism freed of corrupt and vulgar mythology, but also a nation capable of standing up to the British. I have detailed (Kelly 1991) all the ways their project ran aground. What happened in Rewa was both key and relatively simple.

Addressing South Indian "Hindus" as, first of all, Aryans, the Arya Samaj organizers were, in effect, asking South Indian "Hindus" to break off social relations with South Indian Muslims. And even here we only scratch the surface. As recruiting of indentured labor grew more politically and economically difficult in North India in the 1900s, the Fiji colonial government had switched depots from Calcutta to Madras; the last quarter of the indentured laborers to come to Fiji came from various points in South India. "Various points" is important here. Some spoke Tamil, some Telagu, some Malayalam, and so forth. All had to adjust not only to Fiji's plantations but to the pidgin North Indian language, since called Fiji Hindi, that developed there (see Siegel 1987). (And all of this is in addition to anti-Brahman and anti-Aryan "Dravidian" political movements in South India itself.) In Rewa, the Arya Samaj sought to make Muslim conversion to Vedic religion (they saw it as *suddhi*, repurification of Aryan descendants to their Aryan identity) the condition of continuing association of people sharing language and region of birth. The result was trouble. Some South Indians sponsored sangathan sabhas and called for boycotts of Muslims; others resisted, and violent incidents led to police antagonism to the Arya Samaj. Newspapers debated. A South Indian community organizing project, the Madras Maha-Sangam, was already in existence, and it led the counterprotest and convinced the bulk of the Rewa South Indian Hindus to refuse to participate in the sangathan boycotts, in effect to boycott the boycotts. The leading Indo-Fijian newspaper of the time, the *Fiji Samachar* (at one time edited by Vishnu Deo), called those resisting the sangathan project traitors, but the Sangam survived the controversy strengthened, especially when a new brand of Hindu missionaries from India, those known as Sanatan Dharm and advocating a Tulsi Das–guided bhakti Hinduism, arrived in Fiji and soon weighed in against the sangathan project. Upon South Indian insistence upon their own social rights and Sanatan Dharm insistence on the value of śānti and harmony, the Indo-Fijians lost their best chance to be constituted as an Aryan nation. Eventually, the majority of Fiji Hindus, especially those of North Indian descent, became affiliated with the Sanatan Dharm movement; the Sangam next turned to the Ramakrishna Mission, an originally Bengali religious reform group, to send missionaries and build schools, perhaps mainly because that mission had successfully sponsored the best non-Christian educational program in Madras.

There are thus at least two kinds of boycotts, those insisting on transformation of the status quo (for example, many of Gandhi's boycott campaigns) and those resisting efforts to change it. The latter especially has become a major modality of political action in independent Fiji, as that state's fragile parody of liberal democracy has descended into something more ominous, but also more changeable, than farce.

A Note on Comparative Methods

Like many recent scholars, Dru Gladney (1994) locates his account of nationalism in the framework of Anderson's "imagined communities" argument. Above, I began with Anderson also; now I want to reconsider a bit. First of all, we might pose new questions noticing the colonial admiration for the category of "community." Acknowledging "communities" and their differences was useful to colonial officials. Natural contours found in the social fabric made for moral as well as natural boundaries and, as in Fiji, could justify and even seem to necessitate illiberal voting systems. Communities in colonies were a useful alternative to nations there. Second, we have to address the entwining of what are typed as religious identities, claims, and projects into the politics of community, nation, and state.

Let us recall Anderson's argument. Beginning with Renan's location of the nation not in race, language, territory, and so on but in memory and will, Anderson locates the birth of such national consciousness, memory, and will in the genres of print capitalism (especially newspaper and novel) in the European New World, in its new societies self-conscious of parallel difference from the old. A new kind of secular society is born, conscious of deep horizontal comradeship and difference between nations in a Benjaminian empty, even world of space and time without sacred centers. This general idea of a kind of society, a nation, is then transmitted back to the European metropole, where nations experience themselves awakening, and is pirated by the colonized others. In both cases the form is filled with local content.

Apart from a chapter on colonial censuses, maps, and museums that was added to the second edition, *Imagined Communities* includes little discussion of colonial constructions of community or social difference. Indonesia, the key case for Anderson, comes into focus for him principally in precolonial and postcolonial crystallizations, jumping from Indic and Islamic sacred centers to anticolonial nationalism and postcolonial nation-state. The colonial period seems something like an interregnum in his account, a vague period of foreign rule of interest mainly for how it generated the print capitalism and intelligentsia necessary for the nation in the making. On the second problem, religious content of identity, Anderson is very clear. He thinks there is something impossible about the religious nation—about the goal, for example, of Hindu nationalists in present-day India—on cosmological/typological (Anderson calls them "cultural") grounds:

> Essentially, I have been arguing that the very possibility of imagining the nation only arose historically when, and where, three fundamental cultural conceptions, all of great antiquity, lost their axiomatic grip on men's minds. The first of these was the idea that a particular script-language offered privileged access to ontological truth. . . . Second was the belief that society was naturally organized around and under high centres. . . . Third was a conception of temporality in which cosmology and history were indistinguishable, the origins of the world and of men essentially identical. . . . The slow, uneven decline of these interlinked certainties, first in Western Europe, later elsewhere . . . [meant that] the search was on, so to speak, for a new way of linking fraternity, power and time meaningfully together. Nothing perhaps more precipitated this search, nor made it more fruitful, than print-capitalism. (1991: 36)

A template theory of culture is unabashed here: cultural conceptions have axiomatic grips and have to be made to let go, perhaps by the rain of print capitalism, before new links can be thought. Is the new form of imagination also a culture of axiomatic grips? This possibility makes Anderson useful to deploy against the earnest bromides of self-commitment to universalism we heard earlier from Taylor and his colleagues. But is not the cost too high here, especially when reality includes things not dreamed of in our philosophies? Gladney traces the social evolutionism intrinsic to Chinese self-other distinctions into nineteenth-century Marxism and anthropology, especially Lewis Henry Morgan. Surely we could trace the evolutionary civilization schemes into European comparative methods and colonial enterprises well before the nineteenth century (see, e.g., Stocking 1987)—and don't we also find a descendant here in Anderson's own model? If Anderson, or Taylor for that matter, finds his core targets for contemplation in vaguely adduced historical relationships (as Taylor puts it, "This new ideal of authenticity was, like the ideal of dignity, also in part an offshoot of the decline of hierarchical society. In those earlier societies, what we would now call identity was largely fixed by one's social position" [Taylor et al. 1992: 31]), do we have any better options?

One option—and the only one I will offer here—I will simply call more specifically adduced historical relationships. There is of course a utility to noting the commonalities in functioning discriminatory schemes of alterity, as when gender hierarchies are compared with colonial hierarchies or majority/minority hierarchies, or when China is compared with the United States or with colonial India. But old Boasian critiques still stand here. It does not necessarily help, to put it mildly, to fashion general types or stages out of perceived similarities, especially when more specific delineations of relationship are possible. So I am one of the scholars who do not seek to locate an essential nationalism or print capitalism as a station in the human career, or, in the coordinate masculinist usage, a stage in the life of man.

What then to do with the perceived similarities? If the point is not to find the simplest units and their generative properties, but rather (as Gaston Bachelard typed the change he perceived in early-twentieth-century physics) to make complexity intelligible, we can seek to work out the dialogical relations, not just the essential sameness, or pirating (or diffusion) between histories such as that of newly nationalist China and late colonial Europe. Specifically, let us return a final time to the problem of the conditions of relevance of "majority."

There is a similarity between Gladney's observation that the minority others have ethnicity and culture, while the majority self does not, and Brackette Williams's work in critique of concepts of ethnicity (1989, 1990). Williams observes,

> Not all individuals have equal power to fix the coordinates of self-other identity formation. Nor are individuals equally empowered to opt out of the labeling process, to become the invisible against which others' visibility is measured. The illusion that self and other ascriptions among groups are made on equal terms fades when we ask whether those who identify themselves with a particular ethnic identity could also successfully claim *no* ethnic identification. (Williams 1989: 420)

Williams has argued that unified national cultures did not emerge in Caribbean plantation colonies especially because the colonial Europeans reserved top rank (and cultural invisibility) for themselves and virtually sponsored ethnic competitions for second rank among the other groups present, especially African-descendant ex-slaves and South Asian–descendant ex-coolies. Williams's model in some ways resembles and in some ways diverges from Gladney's depiction of majority/minority discourse in China. The two models both depict a central and top-ranking group that regards itself as most civilized and views others as less rational, more animal, and less culturally advanced. In this dimension both would apply to colonial Fiji, where the British of course viewed themselves in such terms. But where Gladney describes nations in which this central group, once self-homogenized, can act as a majority, in the colonies Williams describes, the priority of the colonials has more to do with class power, ownership, and world connections—general capacity to run the show—than with any past, present, or future reality of demographic domination. Of course, and this is crucial here, Guyana is not China. Homogenizing the models would be entirely beside the point.

Fiji realities contrast clearly with what Williams delineates for the Caribbean colonies in that, in Fiji, the non-European others set below the British in racial hierarchy were not all brought into the colonies by British money and power to serve British interests. But the indigenous Fijians still accepted British priority on other grounds, acceding to the mana of the new strangers from the sea. In Fiji, as Kaplan (this volume) shows, neither the British nor the chiefly indigenous Fijians saw any need for a majoritarian definition of their height in rank; what indigenous conceptions of mana did not cover, the British conceptions of aristocracy did, and vice versa. Then, in a second distinction between the Pacific reality and Williams's Caribbean, the British in Fiji never really arranged a competition between the Indians and the Fijians for second rank. The priority of the Fijians, as against the Indians, was a theme from early days (see Kelly 1988) and gained increasing stress as an emerging Indo-Fijian bourgeoisie (with little interest in ranking second) challenged British firstness on many levels, against the backdrop of the collapsing Raj and empire. Fiji, like Guyana, faced the challenge at independence of uncapped sovereignty in a social field of deliberately cultivated "racial" and "communal" difference. In both the balance and the configuration of power, however, the cases are very different. Fiji, more like Malaysia than Guyana (see Shamsul's and Milner's chapters in this volume), pitted colonially privileged sons of the soil (as Hugh Tinker might put it) against diaspora descendants, a minority of whom had become powerful local capitalists.

I am arguing for a scheme where we can identify clear transformations on themes—a British empire where some people of the soil were privileged more than others, some colonies more repopulated by labor diaspora than others, and so on—but not equally simple causal explanations, because dialogical relations are irreducible. What I am suggesting, most simply, is as follows: that we can most fruitfully compare the politics of cultural identity between, say, Fiji and China by realizing the chains of actual connection, not only formally and textually-genetically between a Morgan, a Marx, and a Sir Arthur Gordon rewriting versions of an evolutionary story of European universalist uniqueness, but also in political discourse in situations, in use. We can locate when, where, and why majority only sometimes matters by tracing its place in the history of the nation, here especially in England and its empire, following Corrigan and Sayer rather than Anderson. The nation did not need majoritarian logic to justify its control over the whole human society it ruled when it was understood, as it once was, to be the aristocratic class. From the days of the Magna Carta, it used a majority of itself for certain purposes, and as it always reconsolidated its domination by including the most powerful outsiders, it found great utility in representation schemes where representatives of majorities of itself spoke for itself, especially with internal checks, such as the restrictions posed by the House of Lords on those admitted to a House of Commons. Majoritarian logic is first appropriate only within the nation.

From such a point of view there was no problem, then, with an India ruled by a demographically minuscule company, if the company was run on the best civil, political, and commercial principles; the company's board and court were strictly democratic in procedure. No problem, that is, until simultaneous pressures emerged from political economists against monopoly; from a European-literate, largely employee audience for inclusion in the deliberations; and from the sorts of other social classes whose politics would generally, at home as well as abroad, be typed as rebellious rather than deliberate. Without a whole history of not only the British but all European empires, the point remains simply an assertion, but I doubt we will find a single point of transhistoric break, where suddenly majorities absolutely matter, hierarchy is relegated to the evil past, and deep horizontal comradeship is the norm. For all that there are intrinsically universalistic and formally egalitarian norms within the political-economic imagination of human agency and motives, and for all the influence of political economy (here I mean the discourse, not some underlying reality) in the affairs of so many places of our times, notice still how irrelevant some easily imagined voting pools are: that of children counted together with adults, anywhere (when children don't eat vegetables, is it resistance?), and those extending beyond nation-state boundaries. How many U.S. citizens could be said even to have noticed that the United Nations still organizes itself by indirect representation, an idea they firmly rejected, after several bad elections, more than a century ago? Majorities and their dynamics become visible only when the crucial inclusions and exclusions are already settled.

If China is pirating and redeploying European models, then, I submit that it is not *the* European nation but very particular editions of European alterity theory that should be traced crossing the borders. From an "imagined communities" point of view, the central problem for an empire becoming a nation would be the constitution of a sense of deep, horizontal comradeship among a majority citizenry, the teaching of a national culture. But in light of the close resemblance of the minority representations in China to British imperial representations of the colonized, representations constituting license to own, "develop," and rule regardless of demographics, I suggest we not abandon the more prosaic explanation of their utility: not the means to cross a collective cognitive threshold from empire to nation-state, but the means to constitute license, as a Chinese empire found its place and boundaries as a nation-state, to benevolently hang onto its possessions.

Discourse and Violence

I hope it is clear, by now, first that in Fiji since the coups, the contests waged between organized political parties have been about how to organize the electoral units in which important majorities will reside, and second that another, larger political tide is pushing and pulling at this deadlock over constitutional formalities. After the coups, forces intending to secure indigenous Fijian chiefly paramountcy debated multiple constitutions, some not even including indigenous Fijian voting, and finally determined and promulgated the current scheme of racially specific voting and an absolute indigenous majority. To their surprise they have made majority indigenous sentiment matter and have let the Indo-Fijians back into influence whenever indigenous Fijian sentiment is not near to homogenous. Meanwhile, the Labour Party especially still seeks to represent those most committed to a constitutional reform that would move Fiji again toward a common-roll system of adult representation, a deep horizontal comradeship in the nation based on humanity rather than race.

One might expect that Indo-Fijians would push avidly for constitutional reform, demand common-roll voting as they did with their boycott in the 1920s and 1930s. I have not taken a poll and cannot assure you that a majority of Indo-Fijians would not declare themselves extremists in favor of constitutional reform. But my sense is that many would say first, not that they seek equal political voice, let alone Indian rule, but rather that they want an end to violence. And I have certainly heard some argue, with real conviction, that the best path for this is not constitutional reform to increase Indo-Fijian power, but rather the securing of a permanent minority status for Indians in Fiji. In my scholarship to date, I have always favored those who took initiative to challenge the status quo, past and present, and here I want to finish with recognition of those seeking minority safety, some of them supporters, in the cases I know, of the recent boycotts and planned strikes, others not.

I have promised some general comments on discourse and violence, and these will lead into a last ethnographic return, the current crime bill. I am not sure whether scholars need a better general theory of the relationship between discourse and violence. But the question keeps coming up, and in remarkably varied contexts. A major anthropologist announced writing against terror to be the purpose of a recent book (Taussig 1987); many others have declared this purpose unmet because the text requires elite skills to read. We are awash in sociological and literary theories that find no bounds to discourse, nor any preserve within it where acts of violence are not intrinsic. But others insist that we have to learn again to contextualize discourse and to distinguish between ink and blood.

The situation calls for reconsideration of basic principles, and an entry point I like is a very old argument by one of my favorite semioticians. Sometime around the fifth century A.D., Sanskrit grammarian Bhartṛhari commented on another grammarian's proposal to constitute a list, a totality of possible forms in Sanskrit, as a supplement to complete the existing compendium of grammatical rules for generation, transformation, and aggregation of word forms. (Anyone with a background in philology will probably recognize that generations of scholars have tried to complete such a list.) Bhartṛhari was against the list in principle, on the grounds that it could not be complete. How then, he posed the question in a dialogical genre of text, can one be sure whether a form is a sign? You know it is a sign, he argued, you know it as a sign, if it has a meaning.

The epistemic murk of terror, the terrain for which Taussig has provided extravagant, masterful ethnography, is a space of ascription of meaning to violence, not only clear, obvious meanings, but both private horrors and contagious surpluses, ascribed to violence not only received or imagined but also produced. But does all violence intrinsically have meaning? Is an act of violence always a sign? Is an experience of violence always an act? If the answer to any of the three is negative, we have some basic definitional problems on hand. With the putative collapse of Marxism, varieties of Weberian definition of social fact are in new flower in theories of social field from Habermas through Bourdieu and Lyotard into "the new social sciences" (Latour, Boltanski, et al.; for an overview, see Wagner 1994) in France. The anti-Hegelian openness that follows from Weber rather than Marx I of course applaud, and the positions of these more recent theorists vary in their emphases on emergent rationality, on competition, and on uncertainty, interpretive effort, and tests of strength in communication. But they share with Weber a bounding of the social with the meaningful.[8]

I am suspicious of the tendency of so much of this recent theory to make all communication competitive; Deborah Tannen would surely see this emphasis on agonistics as amusingly masculine theorizing. But even if we focus on real and consequential tests of strength in making interpretations real, I think we need social fields with disruptive things like death in them, things difficult to stick with an adequate identity or point, and need also to include the possibility that some agents in some social situations seek to do otherwise than compel interpretive agreement from others whom they actively address (a version of Taussig's point). Violent acts and events can be made and contested signs in social dialogues—consider the "fire incidents" in Fiji in 1989—and in extremity they can seek to end dialogue with purpose (war, murder, genocide). Or they can arrive as "noise," as the communication channel theorists might term it, with no particular meaning or purpose in relation to the victim, or the victim's social identity, as is often the case with crime. Sometimes, with crime especially, whether there is meaning in the targeting can be highly controversial: consider, for example, the question of whether rape is tolerated or even promoted in order to keep women in terror. Similar is the latest issue in the tidal push and pull in Fiji.

Ascribing Meanings to Crime in Fiji

I have been warned to be sure to note that by emphasizing the multiply tiered goal of śānti, peace, especially among Fiji Hindus, I am not representating Hindu fatalism, nonviolence, or quiescence as a cultural given (one of Anderson's mind-gripping cultural things). The goal of śānti is not inextricably connected to commitment to the practice of *ahimsa*, nonviolence, the Buddhist and Jainist commitment revitalized and made famous by Gandhi. Put another way, some Indo-Fijians are committed to ahimsa as an absolute value, and probably a substantially larger number to it as a tactic, but many would disclaim it altogether and would seek peace (as it is said in the United States) through strength. Another way, again: the Fiji Indians are quite capable of violence. In indenture days, the rates of violent crime in what was then called "the Indian community" were awesome, swamping the Fiji court system and generating quite different stereotypes of Indian pride and temper. Most of the violence centered on what we now call domestic relationships. Almost all of the criminals were men, and many of the victims were women (see Kelly 1991, 1997).

Violence directly connected to labor relations was also common in indenture days, routine violence directed against laborers, and both spontaneous and organized retaliations. At the end of indenture, the crime and violence rates dropped dramatically. To generalize too briefly, except for the occasional excursion into the organized violence of war—indigenous Fijians have rushed to join the fight at each opportunity with great avidity, loyalty, and pride, while the Indo-Fijians have generally been both uninvited and averse to participation—Fiji knew very little violence from 1920 into recent decades. And it is not only coups that constitute the most important violence of recent days in Fiji. Since independence—actually, since the relaxation of the pass laws that restricted unemployed indigenous Fijians to their villages—Fiji has had a new, growing violence problem: very high rates of crime from burglary to robbery, rape, and assault (and more rarely, murder). By all accounts, this crime follows one major vector: poor, unemployed indigenous Fijian youth, mostly male, victimizing the rich and middle class.[9] House compounds in urban Fiji have tended toward larger fences and barriers.

In this light, let us return to the crime-bill debate we began with. At stake in the parliamentary dialogue, with its resort to threats and boycott as well as ordinary means of disputation, is how to assign meaning to this violence and therefore what to do about it. A good case could be made that the crime in Fiji bears a clear family resemblance to the crime endemic in other Pacific Island nations in recent years, notably the notorious "rascal" problem (as pidgin types the perpetrators) in Papua New Guinea. Violent crime is more commonplace in Papua New Guinea than it is in Fiji, and police are far more overwhelmed. On April 30, 1993, while the prime minister of New Guinea was upstairs announcing new measures to fight crime, armed men robbed pay officers on the threshold of his building and stole his staff's wages (*Pacific Islands Monthly*, June 1993, pp. 14–15). Whatever one thinks of the absoluteness of the distinction between gift- and commodity-oriented economies (see, e.g., Parry and Bloch 1989; Thomas 1991; Sahlins 1993), in both Fiji and New Guinea, at least, many Islander youths more or less new to the urban world have decided that crime pays. In Fiji at present, however, the explanation has not been left there; in any case, the issue is how the state should intervene.

Rabuka brought to Fiji's Parliament a bill that would eliminate the need to jail all of Fiji's criminals, a bill to provide for community work as a sufficient alternative to prison. He spoke against those who blamed lawlessness on his coups; this is apparently when he announced that he would "never apologize." He offered a different account of the cause of crime: "Is it the constitution or is it the distribution of wealth in this nation?" Writes *Pacific Islands Monthly*,

> Rabuka pointed to a recent speech by Fiji President Ratu Sir Kamisese Mara, who warned poor, urban Fijians could become a destabilizing force in Fiji if their situation was not improved.
>
> Fiji's Indians, while politically disadvantaged, represent the bulk of the business class in Fiji and make up 45% of its population. "Let us look at the distribution of wealth in this country," Rabuka told parliament. "Why are others coming up and rebelling against society and against the laws of this country?
>
> "They (Fijians) feel disadvantaged. They feel they are starving. They may look well but their very soul is starving. As long as that happens, I cannot guarantee nor can anyone guarantee that there will not be another coup in this land." (This and all quotes from *PIM*, July 1994)

This is the speech that caused the short parliamentary boycott, the speech in which Rabuka portrayed his coups as peacemaking and threatened worse. In the aftermath of the boycott, Parliament decided to launch further official inquiry into the causes of crime rather than to pass legislation. I do not know what is now being said. In any case, insofar as the state is contemplating softening its barriers to violence along specific social vectors, it is not only the coup rhetoric but also the new apologetics for crime that are fraught with peril for Fiji. Upon return to Parliament, Jai Ram Reddy told the press, "The issue was not fundamental enough to justify an indefinite boycott. We'll just carefully have to watch developments."

Ruth Benedict, accused by many of being a template theorist of culture, would not have liked the argument that a "deep, horizontal comradeship" was intrinsic to the "modern nation." Not only would she have expected differences between national structures and sentiments in different nations, but she located the deepest impulse to equal treatment and social horizontality in the West not in the mental axioms of a civilization, but in the operational workings of state institutions. Benedict was acutely aware that Americans who saw themselves as generally egalitarian, individualistic, and fair-minded could justify large numbers of discriminatory impulses in the name of science, religion, or common sense. She wrote in 1947, amid struggles against racism,

> The greatest asset we have in the United States is the public policy of the state. This is not to say that our Federal government, our states, our police forces, and

> our courts have been blameless; of course they have not. But as compared with the grass-roots discriminations and segregations current in the United States, public policy has been a brake, not an incentive. . . . Of course it [law against discrimination] cannot be fully implemented in a democracy where there is so much free-floating racial and ethnic prejudice. But the fact that public authorities take such stands, often in the face of public sentiment, is a remarkable fact. For the great crises of racial and ethnic persecution have occurred in all countries precisely when the government gave the green light. From the pogroms of Czarist Russia to the mass murder of Jews in Hitler Germany, the constant precondition was favorable state policy. (Quoted in Mintz 1981: 148–49)

If Benedict is right, Fiji's citizens all have much to watch carefully. But to date, the remarkable feature of civil strife in Fiji has been the extraordinary ability of those without obvious political power (though I would not, in the final analysis, call them or their weapons weak) to turn public policy away from a succession of dangerous courses without resorting to acts that would ratchet up the violence.

10

When 8,870 − 850 = 1

DISCOURSES AGAINST DEMOCRACY IN FIJI, PAST AND PRESENT

MARTHA KAPLAN

MUCH has been written about colonial discourse in Fiji, about how a powerful coalition of British colonizers and eastern coastal Fijian chiefs constructed themselves as legitimate, aristocratic, ordering, chiefly (for Fijians), and white and aristocratic (for colonizers) through imaging others in Fiji, notably hinterland Fijians, as illegitimate, common, dark-souled, and disorderly. (For critical analyses of the British colonial project in Fiji, see, e.g., Clammer 1975; France 1969; Kaplan 1989a, 1989b, n.d., 1995; Kelly 1988; Lawson 1990; Thomas 1990.) The relation of British colonial discourse about orderly selves and disorderly Fijians to scholarly reification of "cargo cults" has also been noted (Kaplan 1989a, 1995; see also Lattas 1992). Others have addressed the colonial British imagination of an Indo-Fijian "racial" nature as both violent and sensual (e.g., Lal 1985; Kelly 1991). Pondering Fiji's colonial past and postcolonial national crises, I feel that "majority" and "minority" as terms sit oddly within Fiji's political discourse and are often notable by their absence. They therefore also fit oddly as a basis for analyzing Fiji. Clearly relevant elsewhere, perhaps even crucial for understanding debates in the United States, are they not nonetheless terms from a democratic/political-economic discourse that is historically and culturally specific?

This chapter has two parts. The first is about social categories in Fiji. Since the late nineteenth century Fiji has been a heterogenous colonial and postcolonial society, with three or perhaps four major ethnic groups: "indigenous Fijians," who see themselves as descendants of Pacific Islanders;

"Indo-Fijians," who see themselves as descendants of South Asian indentured laborers who came to work the plantations of the British colony; and the colonial British (administrators, missionaries, settlers, businesspeople, some of whom came via New Zealand and Australia). Since independence in 1970 the colonial British are no more, and official electoral categories distinguish "Fijians," "Indians," and "general electors." The final category includes people of a range of self-descriptions and identities, including colonial descendants, "part-Europeans," Chinese, Japanese, Rotumans, and other islanders. These "ethnic" identities/divisions are of course constructed. The European, Fijian, and Indian categories are known locally as "races," a legacy of nineteenth-century colonial social-evolutionary racial theory. In this chapter I will discuss the origins of these categories in Fiji's complex English-colonial and Fijian-chiefly project at the inception of the colony. Turning to Fiji's twentieth-century postcolonial electoral history, especially its constitutional institutionalization of "race" at independence in 1970, I will discuss some of the more recent ways in which ethnic/racial othering has been used to create powerful selves.

The second part of the chapter is about the ways in which the terms "majority" and "minority," and the demographic/democratic/political-economic discourse in which they arise, have and have not become important in discourse in Fiji. For, while arguments about the nature and rights of these ethnic groups and subdivisions of them have been crucial in Fiji, arguments about the nature and rights of "minorities" and "majorities" are not always central to political discourse there. This is not because Fiji was a homogeneous or placid colony, nor that it is a paradise in which there is no self-other objectification (far from it, in fact, as the 1987 military coups attest). But political discourse in Fiji invokes categories other than, or at least in addition to, those of majority and minority, so familiar to us from our democratic/political-economic discourse. And those who invoke and impose are not necessarily the majority population. Principles of hierarchy (rank) and belief in the distinctive natures of groups ("races"), irrespective of demographic calculations, have been as important, even electorally, as "majority/minority" calculations and constructions. In this chapter, I am interested in ways in which "majority" and "minority" have been used in Fiji. But I am also interested in the extent to which they have not been used, and I am concerned with tracing the other constructions of identity and rights that have emerged during Fiji's complex colonial history. Crucial to Fiji's political discourse are terms like "rank" and "race." These ways of conceiving of the nature and rights of people overshadow, for the present at least, discourses invoking majority and minority.

The chapter begins with a brief story and a discussion of the nineteenth-century colonial construction of racial categories in Fiji. It then turns to twentieth-century challenges to the colonial categories, focusing on key political debates over representation. In these debates terms like "majority" and "democratic representation" have been invoked but have not shaped the terms and practices of national Fiji.

"Our Relatives the Indians"

This is the story: In 1985 I was living in the village of Drauniivi, in the north of Fiji's biggest island, Viti Levu. One evening at a village meeting I listened to a discussion of the needs of the local public school. Drauniivi Public School is a "mixed" school for both Fijian and Indo-Fijian children. One parent complained, "We Fijians have to do everything; why don't the Indian families do more?" Discussion proceeded this way for quite a while. I grew anxious, wondering if someone would point out that there were very few "Indian" children at the school (less than 10 percent), and therefore that their parents should owe less, and the Fijians should do the majority of the work. Finally (as I experienced it), the Methodist pastor did mention this. His comments were atypical of the discussion, first because he made this kind of argument, and second because, in speaking of the Indo-Fijian families, he used the phrase *na wekada na Idia* (our relatives the Indians). I never heard anyone else in the village use this form. In retrospect I think that my anxiety came from an unexamined sense that the argument should have relied on demographic calculation of rights and responsibilities; I was baffled because my Fijian friends did not calculate in the same way. To this day I am sad that the phrase "na wekada na Idia" was so atypical in Fijian daily life. It is not surprising, however, since colonial practice from the very beginning insisted on the separate racial natures of Europeans, Fijians, and Fiji Indians, and in this century England kept Fiji as a colony for many years by institutionalizing at many levels a policy of "divide and rule."

Common Roll Versus Race

Fiji's government works on the Westminster model, with the majority party's (or coalition's) leader becoming the prime minister. The constitution at independence in 1970 had been negotiated between the departing British and two political parties (one led by high chiefs and primarily supported by Fijians, one having its origins in farmers' unions and primarily supported by Indo-Fijians). While Indo-Fijian political leaders had worked for a common-roll electoral system, in the compromises leading to independence the constitution was written to distinguish among voters. Rather than a single common roll of voters, there were three "communal" voters' rolls: Fijians, Indians, and "others" (general electors). There was also a so-called national roll on which all voters were listed.

Voters elected candidates to the House of Representatives, which had 52 members. Twenty-two of these were "Fijians," twelve elected by Fijians and ten elected by all of the voters (on the national roll) in their districts. Twenty-two members were "Indians," twelve similarly elected by Indo-Fijians and ten by all of the voters in their districts. Eight were "general electors," three elected by general electors and five by all of the voters in their districts. (These numbers were not proportionate. In 1980 Fijians, who were 44 percent of the population, elected 42 percent of the representatives. Indo-Fijians, who were 50 percent of the population, also elected 42 percent, while general electors, at 4 percent of the population, had 15 percent of the seats [Lal 1986: 76]. The overrepresentation [as some would see it] of general electors worked largely to Fijian advantage, since general electors tended to form coalitions with the predominantly Fijian party.) There was also a second house, the Senate, whose members were appointed: eight by the Fijian Great Council of Chiefs, seven by the prime minister (head of the party in power), six by the opposition party, and one representing Rotumans.

The constitution implemented after the military coups simultaneously simplifies and amplifies principles already at work in Fiji's constitution at independence in 1970.[1] Like the 1970 constitution, the 1990 one seeks to ensure that Fijians will always dominate government, irrespective of demographics. It is simply more direct about it. The office of prime minister must be filled by a Fijian. There is a single-house legislature of 70 representatives, of whom Fijians elect 37.

In both systems, two points are important. First, individuals have been required to register as belonging to one or another racial/political group. The electoral system concretizes and perpetuates a system of categorization of persons developed in the colonial era. In essence, it enshrines constitutionally the claim that it is impossible for a Fijian to say "na wekada na Idia" (our relatives the Indians) because Fiji's people are to be separate, bounded "races," with different natures, interests, and political and property rights. And second, the racial/political divisions are hierarchically ordered, with a presumption of Fijian political paramountcy.

Origins of Racial Discourse in Fiji

Now it is the case that indigenously, Fijians internally classified themselves and others according to *itutu vakavanua*, "standings in the way of the land" (hereditary, ranked ritual-occupational categories, such as chief, priest, warrior, and farmer). And South Asian caste classifications (*pace* recent arguments that they are a colonial invention) also designate ritual-political and occupational natures, and rank them. But most important for the construction of "race" and racism in the colony of Fiji were nineteenth-century British social-evolutionary racial hierarchies. In this section, I first discuss indigenous Fijian hierarchy, then colonial social-evolutionary schemes.

When 8,870 – 850 = 1

My chapter title and this subsection title are borrowed from Marshall Sahlins's argument about hierarchy and history making in Fiji. Sahlins proposes that different societies can make history differently. In Fiji, he argues, the projects of chiefs, their decisions, their very being, ordered and reordered social lives. In "The Anthropology of History" he recounts the effect of Cakobau (pronounced and sometimes spelled Thakombau) of Bau's conversion to Methodism.

> Thakombau was the ruling chief of the great Mbau confederacy, the dominant power in the nineteenth-century Fiji. On 30 April 1854, he finally declared for Jehovah, after more than fifteen years of missionary hectoring. Earlier, in mid-1852, the missionaries had counted only 850 "regular worshippers" in the Mbau area (Meth. Miss. Soc.: Fiji Dist. 1852). But directly on Thakombau's conversion, together with certain military successes, "the Holy Ghost was poured out plentifully" in the Mbau dominions, so that by mid-1855 church attendance had increased to 8,870 (Williams and Calvert 1859: 484). This proves that in the mathematics of Fijian history, 8,870 – 850 = 1. The statistical difference was Thakombau. (1985: 37)

Sahlins's argument is that in Fiji, chiefs were (and are) considered to be living instantiations of ancestor gods, and that in making history in the islands they "count" (to use our demographic/democratic discourse) for more than commoners. Here chiefly "example" in fact decreed a major transformation in ritual-political practice.

Nineteenth-century Fijian *matanitu*, great eastern coastal kingdoms, were ordered by rank, with chiefs hegemonically devising the social order. Contestation over rights and truth did not hinge on arguments about demography, but rather was carried out over genealogy, through ritual, through searches for truth from gods (via priests and sacrifice), and in armed contests. (Much more could and should be said about variations in chiefly practice, and multiple interpretations of the powers and limits of chiefs, in the nineteenth century and the present. I return to some of these issues at the end of this chapter.)

Now of course I don't want to suggest that Fijian chiefship of the nineteenth century moved untransformed into the politics of the postcolonial nation (though since independence, a number of national leaders have been the grandsons and -daughters of high chiefs of the nineteenth century). There was an interesting complementary conjuncture between Fijian and British hierarchy in the colonial era, resulting in a distinctive chiefly and Christian colonial polity.

"No One Would Dream of Placing on One level . . ."

Sir Arthur Gordon, Fiji's first colonial governor, musing on strategies for governance (he eventually settled on a form of what later, in Africa, was called indirect rule), wrote in 1879,

> No one would dream of placing on one level the acute and cultivated Hindoo or Cingalese and the wandering and naked savage of the Australian bush. The Fijian resembles neither but he has more affinity with the former than the latter. . . .
>
> The people are not nomadic; they live a settled life in towns of good and comfortable houses; they respect and follow agriculture; their social and political organization is complex; they amass property and have laws for its descent; their land tenures are elaborate; they read, they write and cypher. Women are respected, hold a high social position and are exempt from agricultural labour. There is a [Methodist] school in almost every village. The chiefs possess accounts at the bank, conduct correspondence, and generally exhibit capacities for a higher grade of civilization. . . . The Fijians all profess an at least nominal allegiance to Christianity. . . . They have shown a gradual progress. . . .
>
> It should always be borne in mind that the state of society for which they are intended is not that of England in the present day, but more nearly resembles that of the Highlands of Scotland some three or four hundred years ago, or that of the remote parts of Ireland in the days of Queen Elizabeth. (1879: 12–14)

Implicit here, and explicit in many another colonial author's social-evolutionary scheme, is the authority of the English aristocrat, who positions himself and his civilization at the end of a historical and civilizational time line. Not all nineteenth-century social-evolutionary schemes were explicitly racist. Some proposed the "psychic unity of mankind," which, while assuming that "races" exist, held that any group might achieve any level of civilization along the unilineal evolutionary ladder. (When examples were given, however, only European societies were ranked at higher levels of achievement.) Other schemes, like that of Gordon, were more explicitly racially premised, in theory and practice.

Based on his social-evolutionary assessments and his unusual degree of freedom in organizing a new colony (he was the son of a former prime minister and had real influence in London), Gordon set in place an elaborate system of "indirect rule" for Fijians and, side by side with it, a brutal plantation system worked by Indian indentured laborers. Gordon's peculiar arrangements had an enduring effect. An aristocrat himself, he had little sympathy for white planters (one could argue that he saw them as off-white whites) and wanted no New Zealand in Fiji. Instead, beginning in 1875, he imagined Fijian chiefs in an aristocratic British image, institutionalized regulations and a bureaucracy that composed what later in colonial history was called "indirect rule," sought to protect Fijians from the depredations of the market and white settlers by reserving 83 percent of Fiji's land for Fijians inalienably, and brought the first indentured laborers from India to work the sugar plantations that would support the colony. Ironically, he saw these "Hindoos" as advanced enough to face the market, while low enough to be coolies.

Essentially Gordon set in place a Fijian polity within the colonial polity.[2] The Native Administration (postcolonially the Fijian Administration) constituted Fijians as separate, politically autonomous, and special. It insisted on hierarchy, communalism, and noncapitalism as defining traits of Fijian society. It insisted on the necessity of Fijian chiefly leadership to preserve Fijian culture and continuity. Of crucial significance for Fiji's political discourse and practical politics from the 1870s through the 1990s was the formation of the Great Council of Chiefs. Without precedent in pre-1860s Fiji, this group of Fijian chiefs was first gathered yearly by Gordon as an advisory board and was later institutionalized as the vehicle for Fijian representation and policy making in the colony. It was composed of colonially selected "traditional high chiefs" and Fijian officials of the indirect-rule hierarchy.

Gordon's colonial strategy is far from atypical of British polity forms, if we follow Philip Corrigan and Derek Sayer (1985), who insist on the continuities in the English state form from medieval days to the capitalist present. They are most fascinated by the hierarchical presuppositions of the English state, which endure despite all manner of seeming emancipation and democratization, and the way in which, over time, a center has continually defined itself as legitimate and made itself powerful, from the top down.

In contrast to Fijian chiefs, whom the British installed as officials, Fiji Indians were treated by the British as "labor units," their social systems denigrated, their leaders denigrated and denied any forum. Religious organization and strikes were perhaps the first forms of Fiji Indian protest (for more on this, see John Kelly's chapter in this volume).

Routinization of Race

In a complex project, English aristocrats (and would-be aristocrats, as many of the colonial officials were) idealized Fijian chiefly hierarchy to create and maintain a hierarchy of colonial racial categories, with all of their practical (legal, bureaucratic, landowning) concomitants. Of course, there have always been actual and potential challenges to this constructed, asymmetric, "racial" system. One potential challenge is in daily experience. Race as a social category silences histories of intermixture, past and present. "Genetically" it can be said, for example, that Fijians and Indians are *na wekada* (related).[3] In the village of Drauniivi, there are several children whose mothers are Fijian and whose fathers are Indo-Fijian. (In each case the parents are not married.) Yet the insistence on separation persists, demonstrating, at the very least, the social construction of "race," and particularly, in this social field, the specific ways in which boundaries are created.[4]

Serious political and legal challenges to categories of "race" came in the 1920s, in the negotiations for Fiji's 1970s independence, and in 1984 with the founding of the Fiji Labour Party. Before turning to this history, let me note an interesting case, about which I read in the Fiji Archives, that underlines the way "race" was made the organizing concept of group identity and difference in colonial Fiji.

In 1912, close to the end of the indenture system, a formerly indentured Indian man tested the bounds of racial categories when he applied to be "treated as a Fijian." The man, who called himself Jiale [Charlie] Taragi (a Fijian form), had married a Fijian woman and had lived in her village for many years. He applied through the local *buli* (indigenous district official) to be "treated as a native." He was willing to assume all tax and communal work duties and in fact was performing them already as a member of his village community.

The local officials of the indigenous Fijian administrative system of Ra Province approved Jiale Taragi's request. The *roko tui ra*, highest provincial officer and himself an indigenous Fijian, was asked his views, and he, like the buli, was in favor of granting the request. He minuted that the man was "energetic concerning the work of the land." The (English) secretary for native affairs, William Sutherland, also minuted in favor of the request:

> I have only known of one case similar to this one and that was many years ago at Nadroga. I see no objection to the Indian being recognized as a native and a taxpayer. They will doubtless allot him some land or rather the use of some land as there is no provision for the N.L.C. [Native Lands Commission] registering him as a member of a mataqali.

A number of Polynesians have joined native communities and been recognized as natives.

The colonial secretary minuted next and was concerned:

It seems to me that by acceding to [the] request we would be creating or recognizing an undesirable precedent and opening the door to E. Indians securing by marriage with Fijians the use of native land without paying rent.

Would his children have the right to be registered as member of mataqali?

As John Kelly has written,

At stake, then, was the boundaries of the mataqali, the "clan" made into the land-owning unit in the native lands scheme. It was one thing for a few "other Islanders" to enter the villages. But "opening the door" to the Indians could be dangerous. The matter was referred to Executive Council, who had it announced that "It was considered and advised that it was not competent for the Governor in Council to sanction the formal recognition of an Indian as a Fijian." The problem of legal rights could have gotten complicated. Much better for it to melt away in the face of facts of heredity. Much better for the governor to be incompetent to change such facts, and rights, than to refuse to. Thus, while the "native" lands system itself was regarded as a codification of a customary legal system, a matter of "customs," its foundation was now found to be a bedrock of "race." (Kelly 1995)

Administrators saw property as what was at stake, yet clearly this case illustrates as well their dependence on their construction of "race." An implicit key to European "whiteness" and a European position on a racial social-evolutionary ladder was the authority of the European colonizers to determine the "races" and racial natures of others.

Since the days of Jiale Taragi, explicit and powerful challenges to these "race" categories have come at the level of political debate over electoral systems of representation. Here we turn to a very brief history of the debates over representation and common roll and the arguments of the Fiji Labour Party from 1984 to the present.

Challenges to Race and Discourses of Democracy in Fiji

In 1904 Fiji's colonial governor "gave" the franchise to about 2,440 Fiji Europeans, who could elect six representatives to a Legislative Council. (Through most of the colonial era the majority of members of the Legislative Council were government officials, not the elected representatives.) Not all Europeans could vote: age, income, and property clauses restricted this electoral roll (as did gender, which was not even a clause but an assumption). Fijians, numbering 92,000, were represented by two members, selected by the Great Council of Chiefs and the governor. The Native Administration, with its Fijian-colonial-chiefly bureaucracy, remained the primary locus of administration and policy for Fijians. Indians, then 22,790 in number, had no representation. In 1916, with a population of around 3,707 Europeans, 87,096 Fijians, and 40,286 Indians (1911 census figures), the Indians gained their first political representation when the governor "gave" them a nominated representative to the Legislative Council. With the end of plantation indenture, Fiji Indians were no longer subject to the Colonial Sugar Refinery. In close touch with the Indian nationalist struggle, they began a struggle for Legislative Council representation equivalent to that of Europeans. In 1929 they received three seats on the council; those members were elected by Indians, with gender, income, and property restrictions on the franchise. The European seats were reduced from seven to six, and the Fijian seats increased from two to three. (Fijians did not elect their representatives to the Legislative Council until 1963. Throughout this time two elected Europeans and no Indians or Fijians served on the Executive Council [again, composed mainly of appointed officials], the governor's real policy-making council.) In 1929 the three newly elected Fiji Indian Legislative Council members resigned their seats in protest, demanding a common roll. Unsuccessful in this boycott, Indian representatives returned in 1933.

Thus began a discourse on democracy, phrased by Fiji Indians as a demand for equality, for respect for their contribution of labor and suffering to the colony. Colonial whites and Fijians responded with an invocation of the "racial" perils of democracy. Indian population growth was portrayed as a wave of threatening, sinister disorder, especially by 1936, when Indians became 43 percent of the colony's population and Fijians 49 percent, no longer a "majority" in their native land. In colonial and Fijian chiefly discourse, the very term "majority" turned into a slur, evoking a picture of a teeming foreign population (which was subtly and racially distinguished in colonial discourse from the foreignness of the colonizers).

Sometimes Europeans were explicit about their own interests in maintaining electoral power, despite demographics. In 1917 European candidate Henry Scott warned that Europeans "were outnumbered 30: 1 by the coloured population and under these circumstances democracy would mean that whites would be ruled by non-whites" (Ali 1986: 5). And in 1934 Governor Murchison Fletcher told the Legislative Council, "I have been afraid—I am afraid—for the very small white minority, lest overwhelming weight of numbers should crush them to the wall. If, when I say farewell to Fiji, I leave that minority more firmly established—more safe, I shall not have spent myself in vain" (ibid.: 12). But far more common, and with crucial implications for the present, were colonial claims that Indian demographics and demands for democracy threatened the interests of Fijians.

Colonizers projected onto Fijians a special, vulnerable nature requiring European domination and protection.

Fijian chiefs in particular participated in this discourse against democracy. Most famous perhaps is the analysis of Ratu Sir Lala Sukuna, the first Fijian secretary of the Native Administration, written in 1935 on behalf of Fijian members of the Great Council of Chiefs and of other "senior chiefs of Fiji." Asked to comment on an electoral or nominative system of representation, he argued for Fijian social evolutionary difference as grounds for nomination rather than election of representatives. (Later, when election replaced nomination, the same arguments would be used to counter arguments for a common roll and to insist instead on separate racial rolls in electoral politics.) Sukuna and his fellow chiefs wrote:

> In November 1933 after a debate on the opposing principles of election and nomination, the Great Council of Chiefs, (of which we are members) passed the following resolution: "That this Council records its strong and unanimous opinion that Fiji, having been ceded to Her Majesty the Queen of Great Britain and Ireland, Her Heirs and successors, the immigrant Indian population should neither directly nor indirectly have any part in the control or direction of matters affecting the interests of Fijians." To form some conception of the native idea of government, as we ourselves experience it, and be in the position to see and judge democratic institutions from its angle of view, it is necessary to bear in mind that, until towards the close of the eighteenth century, the only form of society known to us and handed down in tradition was the tribal, at the head of which stood the ablest and most senior agnate whose counselors were the clan patriarchs, that early in the nineteenth century there emerged a number of chieftains who by conquest and amalgamation began the formation of states. . . . As in tribalism, so in the local form of feudalism, it was the ablest and wisest that ruled.
>
> Reared for ages in this atmosphere, the native possesses a strong sense of obligation towards the state. Rights he does not press, the tribal structure of society affording him sufficient protection. For instance, he could never regard the possession of the vote as a personal right but rather as an obligation to serve the best interests of the state. He visualizes government as commands issued in the general interest by a hierarchy composed of chiefs, priest and elders. Authority he regards as something chiefs alone are qualified to wield. . . .
>
> D. Toganivalu
> P. E. Cakobau
> J. L. V. Sukuna
> *Native Members of the Legislative Council*
> *(Sukuna 1983: 173–77)*

At the so-called Deed of Cession debate in the Legislative Council in 1946, European members argued that the original Deed of Cession, "giving" Fiji to Queen Victoria and her heirs in 1874, provided that the British would preserve and protect Fijian interests. Fiji Indian legislative council member A. D. Patel pointed out the irony of colonial claims of protecting Fijians against foreigners and made powerful humanistic and political-economic arguments against the colonial position.

> It should be well understood and well appreciated that we came here to play our part in turning this country into a paradise. Indians came here and worked here for those people who gobbled up half a million acres of free-hold land from the Fijian owners. We came and worked, under a semi-servile state, and thank God, saved the Fijian race from the infamy of coming under the same system. As a matter of fact, if anything the coming of my people to this country gave the Fijians their honor, their prestige, nay indeed their very soul. Otherwise I have no hesitation in saying that the Fijians of this colony would have met with the same fate that some other indigenous races in parts of Africa met with. (Legislative Council of Fiji 1946: 48)

But Patel's arguments for a common roll and the Indian contribution to Fiji failed to prevail against the colonial–Fijian chiefly position.

Throughout this debate over rights, representation, and the nature of peoples in Fiji, an interesting thing happened to terms like "democracy," "demographics," "population," and "representation." They came to be associated with either an antiracist, anticolonial stance (in the Indo-Fijian historical construction) or with a foreign discourse that denies cultural self-determination to an endangered, yet ultimately superior, minority. Given this discourse, Fiji's independence was a contested matter. On the one hand, Indo-Fijians had long sought equality with the colonial British and equivalent forms of political representation. They argued for a democracy with a common electoral roll. Fijians and colonial whites wished to preserve their own special rights through separate voting rolls, constitutionally mandated proportions of representation, and, especially, nominated representation by the Great Council of Chiefs. As I have described above, the colonial and chiefly plan prevailed in independent Fiji's 1970 constitution.

The same issues arose in 1984. Timoci Bavadra's Labour Party proposed an inclusive language in which all would be called "Fiji citizens." The Labour Party analyzed divisions in Fijian society, but argued that these were divisions of class that subsumed "race/ethnicity." Its platform sought a minimum wage, health care, and privileges (such as reduced bus fares) for schoolchildren, old-age pensioners, and veterans. It is no exaggeration to say that, ironically, the Labour party sought to insist on use of political-economic categories to describe fundamental identities in Fiji.

Considering the discourse against "race" used by the Labour Party, it is particularly interesting that democratic/political-economic arguments had to be made explicitly in an attempt to (re)define the very terms by which political leadership could be shaped. Dr. Bavadra explicitly addressed issues of legitimacy, representation, and the power of chiefs:

> In the contest that democracy provides us, one person's vote is exactly the same as another's. A chief, be he ever so high in the traditional system, does not have five votes where his people have four. . . . In previous elections, the Alliance fear tactic used to include asking people whether they wanted an Indian Prime Minister; now the [opposition Labour/National Federation Party] leader is a Fijian, so the question is whether a non-chief should be Prime Minister. (*Fiji Times*, Mar. 31, 1987, quoted in Lawson 1990: 818)

Labour's victory in 1987, in coalition with the primarily Indo-Fijian National Federation Party, was a brief and extraordinary blow to those who depended on the categories of "race" to remain in power. Fiji's current prime minister responded by leading the military coups. To Rabuka the inherent rights of Fijians are paramount. He rejects the discourse of democracy, demographics, and the like. Instead, he first proposed that the rights of Fijians are based on aristocracy and reinstated the high chiefly government leaders who had lost the elections. More recently he has broken with those high chiefs and has himself taken on political leadership. The bridge between the two positions has been his insistence on the danger Indians pose to Fijians and the special nature of Fijians as indigenes and Christians. His first, prochiefly arguments focused on chiefs as the vehicles of conversion in the nineteenth century; more recently he has simply invoked the image of Fijians as special and godly. The connection here between Christianity and a special Fijian nature, hierarchy, noncapitalism, and indigenousness has been explored by Toren (1988; see also Kaplan 1990).

Conclusions

Thus far, I have sought to show the ways in which "majority/minority" discourse itself has been rejected by colonizers and certain Fijians in Fiji's political and electoral history. My goal has thus been to problematize the terms for use in any more general analytic framework. Now let me pause to consider several questions for my argument so far.

First, have I overreified Fijians or the British? Of course I have, in a chapter this short. Let me quickly point out some ways in which both have internal, debating, even contradictory discourses. Among the British, for example, there were many powerful counterdiscourses, some of which were demographic/democratic. For example, the missionaries writing about Cakobau's 1854 conversion were Wesleyans. Themselves of lower-class English background, they represented a sector of British society antithetical to the established monarchy/church/state. (Some missionary ruminations on the problem of chiefly and subsequent popular conversion saw a profound contradiction between conversion following a leader and individual conviction of sin and redemption. Others were not so philosophically inclined.) On the other hand, I have written elsewhere of the ways in which European "others" sought to become colonial, white, and legitimate by objectifying Fijians as other. One such story is that of A. B. Joske, German-named, off-white white settler, who became a colonial commissioner and in his retirement in England changed his name to Brewster. His self-transformation depended, I have argued, on the objectification and exoticization of Fijians, notably hinterland peoples.

And as to Fijian society, most of my research in Fiji has been about internal Fijian differences, ritual, political, regional, and historical. Much of my field research there has been with a group of hinterland people, the Vatukaloko, who from the 1870s on followed an oracle-priest, Navosavakadua, leader of the Tuka movement (Kaplan 1995). Tuka is used as a flagship example of the cargo cult by Peter Worsley (1969) and of the millenarian movement by Kenelm Burridge (1980). The Vatukaloko live in the north of Fiji's largest island, in an area stretching from the coast into the hills where Fiji's ancestor-gods reside. Like those of other northern and hill people, their polities were smaller and less stratified than Fiji's great coastal and island kingdoms. (These are the sorts of people whom a colonial administrator named Carew, who saw highly stratified Fijian kingdoms as both natural and desirable, called "petty republics.") From the 1840s at least, the Vatukaloko resisted encroachment from the kingdoms, including Bau, and from the 1870s well into this century they contested colonial claims to sovereignty, most notably under Navosavakadua's leadership. Their land lies on the edge of the western region of Viti Levu Island, which was an important basis of Fijian support for the Fiji Labour Party, led by a commoner.

Elsewhere I have described at length the ways in which Fijian chiefs (often colonial officials) and British officials created themselves as aristocratic, legitimate, Christian, and orderly through the subjugation of the northern and interior peoples of Fiji. Carew's disdain for the petty republics of the north and the interior led him to "demonize" a local chief who refused British sovereignty. This man, Na Bisiki, became an obsession to the British official, who ordered special handcuffs with which to restrain him when captured (Kaplan 1989a).

In short, on the one hand, by raising the example of the Vatukaloko, let me stress the nonhomogeneity of Fiji, indigenously and into the present. On the other hand, let me also note the ways in which even nonchiefly Fijians, in hinterland areas such as this, share cultural assumptions about rank and precedence and do not make use of a liberal democratic/demographic discourse. Above I told the story of a discussion in which the villagers in general did not calculate obligation in relation to numerical percentages of participation. On a much broader scale, let me note something interesting about the nature of leadership in this village and its history. Drauniivi is the home of descendants of Navosavakadua, who led the anticolonial political-religious Tuka movement I mentioned above. Thus these people, the Vatukaloko, have a very long history of opposition, armed and otherwise, to encroaching Fijian kingdoms, including the kingdom of Bau that Sahlins writes about. And they are from an area where polities are much smaller and less stratified than the eastern coastal kingdoms (hence colonial disdain for them as members of a "petty republic"). Navosavakadua is said to have prophesied that whites and chiefs would be driven from the land, and the people would rule. Nevertheless, the form of power generally asserted in the area always involved single, focal, powerful leaders, often to this day described in terms of rank or special hereditary nature. Navosavakadua himself is the focus of Fijian depiction of the power of his movement.

With regret, I am going to leave aside the intricate cultural and historical complexities of Navosavakadua, Tuka, colonial constructions of selves and of dangerous and disaffected natives, and the like (see Kaplan 1995). Instead, I want to point out a disappointment to Peter Worsley (for whom I have much respect). A good Marxist, in *The Trumpet Shall Sound* (1969), he proposes that Tuka and other cargo cults are protonationalist populist movements. He also urges scholars to pay less attention to cargo-cult leaders. (Here I think he perceptively felt that colonial officials sought to identify seats of corruption, "outside agitators," if you will—I would say the colonizers assumed a sinister mirror image to the orderly hierarchy they felt themselves to have established.) But Worsley is wrong about Tuka, at least, and the form of other such movements in Fiji. Over and over they do center on individual leaders, who, even when patently not chiefs (Navosavakadua was an oracle-priest), become chiefs in the telling. In current accounts, for example, some term him Sir (Ratu, a chiefly title) Navosavakadua. Considerations of rank, and more importantly of the special nature of certain peoples, are paramount in Drauniivi.

So here an oppositional movement that we might long to see as protonationalist and populist probably was not. If the Fijian insistence on the specialness of Fijian culture and identity owes much to the British, it also innovates. In Drauniivi arguments for Fijian distinctiveness sometimes depend less on hierarchy and more on Christianity. (Of course, Fijian hierarchy depended on the godliness of chiefs. As Christina Toren has shown [1988], in many places in Fiji Christianity and chiefship depended on each other.) But the potential is flexible, for now all Fijians can be godly (and chiefly?) because they are Christian, in opposition to "heathen" Indians.

A second query suggested by this chapter involves an "invention of tradition" argument. One could say that Fijians insisting on chiefly leadership and seizing political rights in the name of a distinctive culture are simply playing out a majority's discourse about a minority (or that Fijians have been hegemonized by colonizers, their chiefs, or both). Again, let us remember that throughout Fiji's colonial history, the constructions of Fijians with which Europeans and Americans are familiar have been British constructions, not those of "majority" Indians. And British colonizers were never a majority in Fiji. At another level, however, all Western, including scholarly, understandings of Fijians are always in complex relation with the explicit and overt representations of colonizers in practice, let alone Western "orientalist" discourse in Said's widest sense. But to deny cultural difference because stereotyping is a potential seems equally colonial. And it seems to me that Fijian practice, recent military coups included, demonstrates fairly clearly the reality of this Fijian commitment to hierarchical premises.

It is really only very recently, in the wake of Colonel Rabuka's coups and the 1990 constitution with its permanent majority for Fijians in Parliament, that elections have presented Fijians with multiple Fijian parties and entertainable options. Under the 1970 constitution, where Fijian solidarity was necessary to keep the Alliance Party in office, most Fijians voted unswervingly for the dominant chiefly Fijian party, the Alliance Party. In the late 1970s and early 1980s a right-wing nationalist Fijian party took some Fijian seats from this chiefly party. But since the 1987 coups, Fijian voters have received and created myriad new options: factions within the new party sponsored by the chiefs, the Labour Party, and new alternative Fijian parties. For the first time, the idea of a majority voice within the Fijian community as more than an endorsement of given hierarchy has become a powerful reality in Fijian life, and the controversy and upheaval it entails are still just beginning.

If we want to discern a stable shape of a majoritarian Fijian discourse, we will need the vantage of another election, at least. And we should not assume that democratic/political-economic terms will inevitably be the only ones that shape this discourse. Options for Fijian leadership discussed in the postcoups era have included having all leaders appointed by the Great Council of Chiefs and apportioning electoral districts along the lines of "ancient" (nineteenth-century) chiefly-led confederacies. This second option provoked massive discussion of the rights (or lack of rights) of urban Fijians to representation. It also provoked claims of kingdom/confederacy status by peoples of the less hierarchically organized northern and western areas of Fiji's biggest island, as they sought to be constructed as a "Fourth Confederacy" that would merit an equal share of electoral power. Ironically, as I have noted elsewhere, Indo-Fijians can make no electoral claims based on belonging to ancient Fijian confederacies.

Finally, I would like to close with a caution. It would be all too easy to read Fiji's history as one in which hierarchy will turn to democracy and considerations of "race" be replaced with political-economic discourse, because, we might assume, such is the trajectory into modernity that all nations follow. We could imagine nineteenth-century aristocratic English colonizers and even present-day Fijian chiefs and their discourses as figures from a past destined to be transformed. Of course, this would be to equate cultural others with Europe's past, and to assume that all are headed in the direction in which Europe seems to have gone. Would this not be to slip into Sir Arthur Gordon's social-evolutionary discourse?

PART VI

TURKISHNESS

11

From Ottoman to Turk

SELF-IMAGE AND SOCIAL ENGINEERING IN TURKEY

SELIM DERINGIL

THE aim of this chapter is to trace a general outline of the story of how the Ottomans became "Turks" and to situate this development in a majority-minority discourse. The term "minority" (*ekalliyet*) would have meant nothing to the Ottomans of the sixteenth to the eighteenth century. It was only after the Lausanne Treaty of 1923 that the term acquired the meaning it has today (Sonyel 1975: 67–68, 97–98).

First, I will trace the development of Ottoman/Turkish "protonationalist" themes in a small sampling of primary sources and contemporary accounts.[1] Second, as a case study, I will focus on the attempts to incorporate the Kurds into the population on whom the Ottoman Empire could rely through their inclusion in the Hamidiye irregular cavalry in the 1890s.

From Ottomanism to Turkism

The standard jargon of Turkish official historiography is that Turks were always seen as inferior, churlish types by the practitioners of the Ottoman high culture (Berkes 1964). According to Bernard Lewis (1961: 1), "the ethnic term Turk was little used, and then chiefly in a derogatory sense to designate . . . ignorant peasants." The new nationalist elite felt that they needed to distance themselves from their "dissolute and degenerate past" and from their predecessors, the Ottoman ruling elite. If the old elite could be shown to have looked down on the "true Turks," the new elite's credibility would be proportionately increased. This value judgment was then transmitted to subsequent generations via the work of leading Turkish and foreign scholars (see Deringil 1993). Recent research is beginning to show quite convincingly, however, that even in the "Golden Age" of the empire in the sixteenth and seventeenth centuries, the ruling elite had a clear notion of their Turco-Central Asian heritage and were very proud of it (Fleischer 1986: 286–90).

As the empire shrank, particularly after the loss of the Balkans in the last quarter of the nineteenth century, Anatolia began to receive emphasis as the "heartland of the Turks." This went hand in hand with efforts to legitimize the rule of the Ottoman dynasty and reinforced the universal Islamic legitimation of the sultan as the caliph of all Muslims (Deringil 1991). A geographical encyclopedia published in 1889 stated under the title "Anatolia":

> It can be said that Anatolia is entirely a land of Turks, and the majority of its population are Muslims. Even most of the Christians are ethnic Turks [Hiristiyanlarìn kìsm-ì azamì dahi yine Türk cinsine mensubdurlar]. In the aforesaid Anatolian peninsula, with the exception of a few Christians in the ports, the only difference between the Muslim Turks and their Christian compatriots [*vatandasları*] is religion. It would therefore be quite correct to call these latter "Christian Turks." (Sami A.H. 1306 [A.D. 1896]: 396–97)

It was an additional irony that the writer of these lines was an Albanian by the name of Şemseddin Sami. Sami was also well known in late Ottoman cultural circles as a distinguished lexicographer of the Turkish language. His *Kamus-u Türki* is still the standard reference work for students of Ottoman Turkish.

Sami's *Kamus-u Alam* is interesting testimony to the intellectual atmosphere of the time. Evidently a translation of a French encyclopedic dictionary, with additional materials for the Ottoman domains, it remains mostly a rather stolid publication. Even on subjects on which we might expect a more personal approach, such as Sami's native land of Albania, the tone is very anodyne. The extremely polemical tone of the Anatolian section is therefore all the more striking. For instance, Sami's views on how the Greek and Armenian "Turks" had "betrayed their origins" is very interesting: "It is therefore deplorable that [these Christian Turks] have become subject to the Christian and Armenian churches, forgetting that they had no previous connection with these whatever. They have thus taken up the unfortunate cause of the Greeks and Armenians, writing their mother tongue, which is Turkish, in the Greek and Armenian alphabets." Sami heavily hinted at foreign provocation in these matters: "Recently in these past few years, with the encouragement of so-called scientific societies they [the Christians] have been abandoning the official language of state, and have begun learning Greek and Armenian. This has led to the strange spectacle of fathers who do not speak a word of Greek or Armenian but who have sons who do not understand a word of Turkish!" (Sami 1306/1896).

A British publication that appeared at almost the same time noted that the reign of Abdülhamid II (1876–1909) was a particular landmark in the achievement of a relatively integrated population in the empire: "He deliberately and consciously worked toward the end of creating a uniform empire, peopled by Muslims, who should as far as possible be similar in character and aims, and united in their loyalty to the Sultan as Khalif" (Ramsay 1890: 51).

The answer of the Hamidian Empire to this dilemma was to lay increasing stress on the official religion of the state, which was the Hanefi school of Islamic jurisprudence (*mezheb*). Whereas other, more heterodox branches of Islam had received relatively more tolerant treatment in earlier centuries, the shrinking of the empire's resources in the late 1880s meant the enforcement of a new orthodoxy.

Süleyman Hüsnü Paşa, a major figure in Ottoman politics in the 1870s, had interesting views on the subject. He is a good example of the type of bureaucrat/soldier/intellectual who ran the empire. Something of an illustrious exile, he was banished to Baghdad by a suspicious Abdülhamid for his central role in the deposition of Sultan Abdülaziz in May 1876 (see *Türk Meshurlarì Ansiklopedisi*). From his political exile in Iraq he penned an extremely detailed memorandum, dated April 8, 1892, relating to measures to be undertaken by the state to ensure the integration of heterodox and heretical elements into the official beliefs.

Displaying an intricate knowledge of what would today be called ethnography, the pasha gave a rather sophisticated and detailed breakdown of the ethnic mosaic of Iraq, covering Turks, Kurds, Arabs, Chaldeans, Nestorians, and Armenians, distributed across various sects and subsects of Islam and Christianity, as well as Jews. He commented, "As can be seen from the above the elements belonging to the official faith and language of the state are in a clear minority whereas the majority falls to the hordes of the opposition" (BBA YEE 14/1188/126/9).[2] This situation was to be remedied by systematic propaganda and the "correction of the beliefs" (*tashih-i akaid*) of the "heretics" or "deviants" (*fìrak-ì dalle*). In order to accomplish this, the Ottoman state should sponsor the writing of a "book of beliefs" (*Kitab-ul Akaid*), which should consist of some fifteen chapters, each dealing with one unorthodox element. The correction of the beliefs was to be accomplished largely through the efforts of Ottoman missionaries, who were to be modeled on their Protestant contemporaries. The pasha was quite generous in his wisdom, and the projected chapters to be included ranged from obvious targets such as Shiism through Christianity and Judaism to "the pagan practices of Indo-China."[3] It is also significant that one of the heretical beliefs he mentioned was positivism, referred to as "the new philosophy" (*felsefe-i cedide*); hence he maintained that the book should also be translated into French. This is a clear reference to what some among the Hamidian Islamic-conservative Ottoman elite saw as the secularizing, subversive influence of positivism (Taneri 1963).[4] This trend was to be reversed in the Young Turk period, when a younger generation of relative upstarts was to stress French positivism. Leading Young Turks such as Ahmet Riza and Abdullah Cevdet, having come under the influence of thinkers such as Auguste Compe and Gustav Lebon, were to lead the field in this regard (Hanioglu 1986).

Another example of the genre of what can be called "intellectual mobilization literature" was a long memorandum by Osman Nuri Paşa, one of the most controversial *vali* (governors) of the Hicaz in Abdülhamid's reign and something of an unknown soldier in late Ottoman history. A good example of the diligent provincial administrator, he expressed views representative of the late Ottoman worldview. His July 18, 1885, memorandum dwelled at length on reform measures to be taken in the Hicaz and other Arab provinces. The pasha stated that the majority of the armies stationed in the Hicaz, Bingazi, and Yemen were made up of "the fundamental elements" (*unsur-u asli*) of the empire, namely, who were "the Turks and Anatolian peoples"; it was they who paid "the blood tax," that is, fought in the armies. It was therefore imperative that the Hicaz be annexed as a regular province of the empire and its population be made to contribute to its defense[5] Osman Nuri Paşa was clearly imbued with the "mobilizational" ethic of the nineteenth century that informed so much of late Ottoman statecraft:

> Although it is possible to transform all of the Muslim population into a fundamental element, events have shown that the time is not yet ripe. Even if it were possible today to blend all the Muslim tribes and nations together by causing them to lose their special characteristics through the application of rigorous policies, they would still be no more than the boughs and branches of the tree whose trunk would still be constituted by the Turks. (BBA YEE 14/292/126/8)

Thus, to Osman Nuri Paşa, the Turks were to be the foundation of the Muslim Ottoman nation, while the "other Muslims," that is, Arabs, Kurds, Albanians, and so forth, were to be supporting, auxiliary elements.

The major aim of the late Ottoman center was therefore the creation of a reliable core population who would be duly imbued with the "correct" ideology. This was to be done primarily through education. The emphasis on mass primary education dates from the Hamidian period. Although literacy levels in the late Ottoman Empire remained very low by European standards, by the turn of the century there had been a significant increase (Findley 1989: 52, 86, 139). A report on educational reform dated May 6,

1899, pointed out that the aim of establishing "primary schools in each village" was "the preservation of the morals and language of our people," particularly against the threat of missionary schools. It specified that by competing with the missionary schools in improving the quality of education, and making sure that the language of instruction would be Turkish, the aims of a national education policy would be served. One of its main points was "It is of the utmost importance that no foreign teachers be employed in these schools; particularly, the employment of Rumanian, Serbian, or Greek teachers is to be strictly avoided." In terms of the "national character" of the educational program, the report was very outspoken:

> The fact that states are spending a great deal of money on education, and even small states such as Rumania, Serbia, and Greece spend as much as 10 percent of their revenue on education, should be instructive for us. Particularly the fact that even Bulgaria is spending 6 percent of its revenue on education, while the Ottoman State spends only one and a half percent, should show the need for educational reform. (BBA Y.A. Res. 101/39, 25 Zilhicce 1316/6 May 1899, Report by Special Commission on Educational Reforms)

This last point suggests a perception of competition with countries that had formerly been Ottoman domains.

Together with education, military service was seen as a formative process for the creation of the reliable majority. It is to this that we now turn.

The Kurdish Issue

In a panel discussion on Turkish television in November 1993, a group of "loyal" Kurdish tribal leaders were invited to comment on the Kurdistan Workers Party (PKK). They were extremely virulent in their attacks on the PKK, referring to its members as "not Kurds but Armenians." They actually told an audience of millions that many of the PKK killed had been found to be uncircumcised. The tragic irony of this situation only becomes apparent when one goes back to the Ottoman Empire in the 1890s. The chances are that the Kurdish chiefs on television are the descendants of the Hamidiye irregular cavalry forces formed during the reign of Abdülhamid II. These regiments, consisting of Kurdish light cavalry commanded by Turkish officers, were primarily involved in the Armenian massacres of the 1890s and the mass deportations of 1915, in which hundreds of thousands of Armenians perished. The original idea of the Hamidiye included not only the Kurds but also the Arab tribesmen of Ottoman Libya and the Turcoman nomads, Turkic peoples whose nomadic lifestyle had retained many of their early central Asian practices.

The Kurds themselves had traditionally been a volatile element in eastern Anatolia. The last major Kurdish sheikh, Şeyh Ubaydallah, has been seen by some historians as the leader of an independence movement under the guise of his short-lived Kurdish League in the early 1880s (Olson 1989: 5–7). The creation of the Hamidiye irregular cavalry regiments out of the Kurdish tribes was a double-ended policy, intended both to pacify the Kurds and assimilate them into the reliable Islamic population, and to use them as a weapon against the Armenian independence movement. The choices open to the Ottoman government were much the same ones that are available to the Turkish government today: "The Kurds were a potentially dangerous element in the region which needed to be either totally suppressed—an unreasonable policy given the character of the times and the government—or pampered and appeased while kept under loose supervision" (Duguid 1973: 146).

The Hamidiye regiments were conceived of as an irregular force on the Russian cossack model. Ottoman officers were actually sent to St. Petersburg in order to "learn cossack style drill," which they would then practice in training the Hamidiye (BBA Y. Mtv. 57/38, 15 Cemaziyelevvel 1309/17 Dec. 1891, Ottoman Chief of General Staff Rìza Paşa to Sublime Porte). Several cavalry captains returned in 1896, "having completed their training in Petersburg in cossack style tactics," which they were now to impart to the Hamidiye units in the Ottoman Fourth and Fifth Armies (BBA Y. Mtv. 138/92, 7 Şevval 1313/23 Mar. 1896., Imperial General Staff, General in Charge of Cavalry Forces Osman Ferid Paşa).[6] It was specifically stated that these units would be deployed "against Armenian brigands" (BBA Y. Mtv. 186/82, 30 Kanun-u Sani 1314/11 Feb. 1898, Chief of Staff Rìza Paşa to Sublime Porte). Therefore, Armenian historians have been right in pointing out the anti-Armenian priority of the Hamidiye regiments: "Though the Kurds had been much more a threat to Ottoman unity than the Armenians in the years past, the sultan backed these fellow Muslims against Christian Armenians whom he saw as a disruptive element linked to his enemies abroad" (Suny 1993: 105).

The Hamidiye regiments were also designed as a vehicle for social engineering; the tribes selected would have special primary schools established in their regions (BBA Y. Mtv. 87/133, 19 Cemaziyelevvel 1311/28 Nov. 1893). The leading chiefs' sons would also be brought to Istanbul, where they would be trained in Turkish language and manners in the famous "Tribal School" (Mekteb-i Aşiret). This school was intended to have a long-term "civilizing influence" on the Kurds, and it particularly aimed to socialize the children of the Kurdish elite as good Ottomans. It also admitted the sons of leading Arab sheikhs as well as those of Albanian notables. In this sense, the logic behind this experiment was very like Thomas Babington Macaulay's aim in British India to "create a class of persons, Indian in blood and colour, but English in taste, morals and intellect" (Kodaman 1983: 110–19; Anderson 1991: 91). In this respect, the raj was much more successful than the Ottomans.

Another privilege of the Hamidiye was tax exemption. For the duration of their service, Hamidiye tribesmen and their families were exempted from taxation on their herds and other resources (BBA Meclis-i Vükela Mazbatalarì [Minutes of the Ottoman Cabinet] 72/82, 6 Kanun-u Evvel 1308/19 Dec. 1892). These privileges are similar to the present-day advantages granted to Kurdish elements in eastern Anatolia, which are armed by the state and expected to contribute to the fight against the PKK as "local defense units" (*kolcu*).

Very soon after the formation of the first Hamidiye regiments, it became apparent that the degree of state control over them was to be problematic. As early as 1887, reports began to come in of unruly behavior among the tribes armed by the state (BBA Y. Mtv. 165/2, 3 Agustos 1313/16 Aug. 1887, telegram from the governor of Erzurum). Yet the scheme went forward. By 1892 tribes were being recruited in the areas of the Fourth, Fifth, and Sixth Ottoman Armies—northeastern Anatolia, northern Syria, and north-central Iraq, respectively (BBA Y. Mtv. 67/1, telegram from Mehmed Zeki Paşa, imperial commissioner for the constitution of the Hamidiye regiments). It is important to realize that these regiments were to comprise not only Kurds, but also Arab bedouin and Turcoman nomads (BBA Y. Mtv. 68/21, telegram from imperial ADC Şakir Paşa, commissioner in charge of reform in the eastern provinces).

The Commission for the Establishment of the Hamidiye Regiments reported regularly during this period that the "bold warriors who have never seen a city or a town and remain in a state of savagery" had given elaborate feasts to honor the envoys of the sultan and to celebrate their inclusion "in this singular honor" (BBA Y. Mtv. 68/28, telegram from Hakkì Paşa, chief of the Commission for the Establishment of Hamidiye Regiments in Urfa). By mid-1892 it had been established that the number of regiments should be increased to one hundred and that these should include the desert-dwelling bedouin (BBA Y. Mtv. 67/1, 25 Agustos /25 Aug. 1892, Şakir Paşa to Yıldız Palace). Another aspect of what would today be called the socialization of these tribes was their periodic rotation to Istanbul to serve as the sultan's imperial guard for one year. It was hoped that this period of service would "improve the demeanor and general conduct" of the tribes (BBA Y. Mtv. 73/46, 13 Kanun-u Evvel/26 Dec. 1892. General Directives on the Rotation of the Hamidiye Regiments to Istanbul). The tribesmen in Istanbul would be given special dress uniforms, and each regiment would be given an elaborately embroidered banner to symbolize its attachment to the state. By the end of 1892 it was reported that 52 regiments had been formed and 21 were in the process of formation (BBA Y. Mtv. 73/69, 17 Kanun-u Evvel/30 Dec. 1892, imperial ADC Şakir Paşa to Yıldız Palace).

Although Istanbul thought that it could ultimately control these units, as the century drew to a close it became painfully apparent that this was not the case. Not only did the Hamidiye prey on defenseless Armenian villagers, they also ceaselessly fought other Kurds, particularly the Alewis, who were mostly Shiite, whereas most Hamidiye units were Sunni (Suny 1993: 105, 106; Olson 1989: 14).

Increasingly, the reports from the field dealt with their transgressions. On January 16, 1898, three Hamidiye officers in the Diyarbekir region were reported to be illegally "collecting taxes, going astray, and oppressing the local population." Orders were sent out for their arrest and court-martial in Diyarbekir (BBA Y. Mtv. 171/85, 22 Şaban 1315/16 Jan. 1898, Imperial Chief of Staff Rìza Paşa to Palace). Practically all the eastern *vilayets* reported untoward activity by the Hamidiye. On March 2, 1899, it was reported from Erzurum that three Hamidiye officers had been involved in plundering villages and killing peasants (BBA Y. Mtv. 187/46, 19 Şevval 1316/2 Mar. 1899. Imperial Chief of Staff Rìza Paşa to Sublime Porte). On March 30, it was reported from Erciyes that a Hamidiye captain, Abdul Aga, was actively involved in plunder (BBA Y. Mtv. 188/88, 18 Zilkade 1316/30 Mar. 1899, Imperial Chief of Staff Rìza Paşa to Sublime Porte). Almost all the cases reported dealt with transgressions against Muslims. This leads one to suspect that infringements against Christians were not reported or not considered transgressions. One of the rare cases where the British Embassy became involved (the British were the self-appointed protectors of the Ottoman non-Muslims) probably involved Armenians. A Hamidiye lieutenant colonel, Hacì Bey, from the Artuş tribe, was reported to "have indulged in brigandage and shed much blood which has gone unpunished." The vilayet of Mosul was ordered to arrest him "and punish him in an exemplary fashion." The people who had been wronged were told that they could bring their complaints to the courts of Cizre and Mardin (BBA Y. Mtv. 190/43, 7 Muharrem 1317/18 May 1899, Imperial Chief of Staff Rìza Paşa to Sublime Porte).

As the century neared its end, Istanbul became increasingly concerned that the Hamidiye command was proving more of a liability than an asset. The imperial chief of staff continued to report that various Hamidiye tribal commanders "did not show the necessary characteristics of command and responsibility." Some had registered as Hamidiye commanders despite the fact that "they were too old to mount a horse"; others had been found to be wanting in morals and responsibility. Even more serious was that the regular officers and troops who had been attached to the Hamidiye units had taken up their bad habits. It was ordered that a register be compiled of "those who had been seen to be of objectionable behavior" and that these be brought before courts martial in administrative centers such as Van and Erzurum (BBA Y. Mtv. 191/155, 23 Safer 1317/6 July 1899, Chief of Staff Receiver's Office no. 421).

Another aspect of the state's policy in the eastern Anatolian provinces was to conduct a census of the population in order to "standardize" it. The Kurdish tribes to be included in the Hamidiye regiments were to be provided with Ottoman identity cards (*nüfus tezkeresi*) noting the name, religious affiliation, and abode of the bearer, and births and deaths were to be recorded systematically. The first identity cards began to be issued in the urban areas after the 1885 census (Duben and Behar 1991: 19). Although this sounded fine on paper, it was very difficult to put into practice, given the "state of savagery of most of the tribes" (BBA Y.A. Res. 110/69, Selh-i Şaban 1318/22 Dec. 1900, Council of State memorandum no. 2,390).

As the twentieth century dawned, Istanbul came to realize that the Hamidiye were truly getting out of hand. Complaints continued to come in, often involving the Porte in disputes with foreign powers, such as that dealing with the "excesses of a Hamidiye commander against Russian subjects in Erzurum." The military authorities were increasingly concluding that "those regiments which are not immediately useful should be discharged" (BBA Y. Mtv. 253/111, 21 Tesrin-i Sani 1319/4 Dec. 1903, Yıldız Palace Imperial Secretariat). Yet the Armenian crisis continued to keep eastern Anatolia boiling. By the end of 1903, the Porte shifted to the more flexible policy of summoning the Hamidiye regiments to points of trouble only when they were needed and then discharging them (BBA Y. Mtv. 252/363, 21 Ştaban 1321/12 Nov. 1903).

The Hamidiye were also counterproductive in their tendency to recreate the old system of tribal consolidation. The policy of co-opting the tribes against the elevation of powerful local leaders was basic to the whole Hamidiye project. Now this danger seemed to be worse than ever, because the tribes were now armed and, to some extent, trained by the state (Duguid 1973: 152).

Yet the Young Turks, who deposed Abdülhamid in 1909, continued his Kurdish policies in much the same vein. The name of the Kurdish troops was changed from Hamidiye Alayları to Aşiret Alayları, Tribal Regiments, and they continued to grow in the period leading up to the Great War. It is a sublime irony that the military strongman of the Committee of Union and Progress, Mahmut Şevket Paşa, considered changing their name to Oguz Alayları, after the legendary Oguz tribe, the semimythical stem tribe of the first Turks (Olson 1989: 10).

The Hamidiye policy is usually seen as a failure, and a costly one at that. Most of the Hamidiye were Sunni Muslims, and their protection by the state often provided the opportunity for them to oppress and kill their Shiite brethren, the Zaza Kurds, as well as the Alewis. Yet some recent research has pointed out, "The Hamidiye Regiments were an important stage in the emergence of Kurdish nationalism from 1891 to 1914, serving as a fulcrum of Kurdish power for over two decades" (Olson 1989: 12). It is clear from the evidence that apart from using these regiments as irregular cavalry, the Ottoman center hoped to mobilize them as a reliable population of Muslims, loyal Ottoman protocitizens. Yet, paradoxically, just as Abdülhamid's Islamist policies served as the crucible of Kurdish nationalism, just as they did for Turkish nationalism. Some of the Hamidiye regiments were later to fight in the Balkan wars and the First World War. They would experience at first hand the challenge to Turkish power in the Balkans, and many would actually empathize with their Turkish fellow officers. As expressed by a recent historian of Kurdish nationalism, "The Hamidiye gave an opportunity for the Kurds to experience and attempt to fathom the wider world" (Olson 1989: 12).

Some Concluding Comments

Why do members of minorities sometimes become ideologues of majority views? A good example is Ziya Gökalp, one of the leading ideologues of the young Turkish republic, who grew up in Diyarbekir during the Hamidiye era. Gökalp became a militant opponent of the Hamidiye policies, which he saw as an extension of despotism. Yet this did not make him a Kurdish nationalist. Quite the contrary, he became an ardent supporter of the Young Turks as well as a committed Kemalist (Erişirgil 1984: 55–58).

An instructive episode from the early days of the Young Turk era is Gökalp's confrontation with Sati Al-Husri, a prominent pedagogue and thinker, who was assimilated to the extent that many of his Turkish contemporaries forgot, or chose to forget, that he was Syrian. The famous controversy was over education. Satì Bey contested the idea of a national curriculum, which Gökalp adamantly defended. When asked by a colleague why he had used strong language against Satì Bey, Gökalp replied, "Satì Bey is an Arab, I am Turkish" (Erişirgil 1984: 147–48). Like Şemseddin Sami, the Albanian who was a convinced Ottomanist, Gökalp pushed for a purified Turkish content in school curricula.

The main difference between the Ottoman and the republican approaches to the "minorities question" is that the republic had infinitely more bargaining power vis-à-vis the outside world and the material means to attempt to ethnically homogenize its population. What the Kemalists did was to take the Ottoman policies to their logical conclusion. In Turkey today, whether it was worth the cost is an open question.

12

Minority/Majority Discourse

THE CASE OF THE KURDS IN TURKEY

KEMAL KIRIŞCI

In the past many viewed Turkey as an ethnically homogeneous country. Students of political development attributed this view to the relative success of the founding fathers of Turkey in developing a strong sense of national identity. This image of Turkey is fast changing as a result of the increased salience of ethnicity in the post–cold war world. Today Turkey is at the epicenter of a troubled region and faces both foreign and domestic policy challenges. There is one common denominator in a majority of the foreign policy issues to which Turkey has had to respond: they result from conflicting ethnic identities and demands (Kirişci 1995). Among these issues are the mass influxes of refugees from Bulgaria in 1989 and from Iraq in both 1988 and 1991, the ethnic cleansing of Bosnian Muslims, the civil war in Chechnya, and the violent ethnic conflict between Armenians and Azeris.

Domestically, Turkey is facing a growing Kurdish ethnic assertiveness, which is challenging its image as a country of "Turks" alone. Increased emphasis on ethnicity has made the conflict between successive Turkish governments' efforts to construct a nation based on a Turkish identity and Kurdish ethnic assertiveness more conspicuous. This conflict has intensified since 1984, when the Kurdistan Workers Party (PKK) started a campaign of violence to achieve its objective of establishing an independent Kurdish state in southeastern Turkey (Robins 1993; Barkey 1993; Kirişci and Winrow 1997). Clashes between government forces and the PKK have so far left more than 26,000 people dead.

One way to better understand this conflict might be to examine the substance and evolution of the discourse in Turkey on Kurdish and Turkish national identities. However, this will inevitably invoke many conceptual and historical phenomena of a very complex nature. The analysis in this chapter should be considered exploratory; more research will be needed before it becomes possible to fully understand the causes of the Kurdish problem in Turkey, if indeed it ever does. (For a detailed study, see Kirişci and Winrow 1997.) The chapter is divided into three sections. The first section will examine the meanings of "minority" and "ethnicity" in Turkey, both in general terms and in reference to Kurds. The second section will look at the origins of Turkish nationalist discourse, and the third will analyze the origins of Kurdish consciousness and the evolution of political discourse on Kurds.

The Question of Minorities in Turkish Political Discourse

The present minority policy of the Turkish government is rooted in the 1923 Lausanne Treaty, which formed the legal basis for the international recognition of Turkey as an independent state. This treaty employs the term "minority" only in relation to non-Muslim peoples living in Turkey, without specifying them by language, geographical area, or religion. Articles 37 to 45 of the treaty stipulate basic principles for the protection of minorities, which include the right to use their own language, run their own schools, and maintain their social and religious institutions (Birsel 1933: 593–95).[1]

The use of religion as the sole criterion for the definition of a minority group comes from the Ottoman *millet* system. "Millet," which is the Turkish word for "nation," had a very different meaning during the Ottoman era than it does in our time. Nationality in the Ottoman system was determined on the basis of a person's membership in a religious community. Hence, Muslims basically belonged to the "community of Islam" and were the subjects of the sultan, who was also their caliph (B. Lewis 1962: 329). They identified themselves as Muslims, irrespective of whether, ethnically, they were Albanians, Arabs, Bosnians, Circassians, Kurds, Laz, or Turks. For most Muslims ethnic and national identity, in the Western senses of the words, were not as salient as religious affiliations—at least until the turn of the century. Under the millet system, the identities of non-Muslims were also functions of the religious communities they belonged to. For example, they would have been considered Greek by virtue of belonging to the Greek Orthodox Church, or Jewish if they professed Judaism.

The Lausanne Treaty projected for all Muslim citizens of Turkey a Turkish national identity. The founding fathers of the Turkish republic aimed at transforming the theocratic and cosmopolitan Ottoman society into a modern, secular, and homogeneous society. They envisaged achieving this through Turkish nationalism, which would forge a sense of Turkishness and create a common civic culture. Other than those citizens of Turkey who belonged to the non-Muslim minorities, everyone was considered to be a Turk. Hence, for the Turkish state these Turks constituted the majority.

Such definitions of "minority" and "majority," combined with an intense effort to construct a Turkish national identity, were not particularly conducive to the emergence of a discourse on diverse ethnic identities. Furthermore, the onset of the cold war made it even more difficult to develop such a discourse. This was a period in which one's allegiance in Turkey tended to be expressed both at the level of the bloc one belonged to, and the other at the level of the country. Anyone who challenged the view of an ethnically homogeneous and unified Turkey easily risked being labeled a traitor, a supporter of the opposing communist camp. The little discourse that did exist challenging the status quo worldview focused on a class-determined stratification of identities. Such views were generally suppressed and perceived by the Turkish state as divisive and threatening to the unity of Turkey.

The public was also discouraged from developing any interest in Turkish "minorities" or "outer Turks" in other countries. The founders of the Turkish Republic took this approach in their efforts to distance themselves from pan-Turkism. Some Ottoman intellectuals and statesmen had advocated pan-Turkism to achieve the unification of Turks in Anatolia with those who had fallen under Russian rule (Landau 1981; Ağaoğulları 1987). After the establishment of the Turkish Republic, however, most people in Turkey, with the exception of small extreme right-wing groups, failed to develop an awareness of Turks outside Turkey. Where such an awareness did exist, it was usually restricted to Turkish workers in Germany, Turkish Cypriots, and, to some extent, Turks in western Thrace. Those who expressed interest in Turkish communities outside Turkey were often viewed by authorities with as much disdain and suspicion as those who talked about ethnicity in Turkey. By and large, most of the Turkish public became conditioned to thinking of their own country and others as being homogeneous.

The end of the cold war seems to have significantly eroded this view of a world divided into neatly identifiable states populated by people sharing homogeneous national identities. The collapse of communism and the ensuing violent conflicts exposed people in Turkey to a completely different world and political discourse. In 1989, with the influx of more than 300,000 Bulgarian Turks, the public was made aware of the existence of Turks in a neighboring country that they had long assumed to be homogeneous. Similarly, the 1988 and 1991 mass influxes of Kurdish refugees from northern Iraq played an important role in precipitating open discussion about Kurds in general as well as Kurds in Turkey. Simultaneously, the public in Turkey, through the media, became exposed to a wide range of ethnic communities, ranging from the Chechen to the Meshketian Turks, that claimed common bonds to Turks.

As the Turkish government, in a significant departure from past practice, announced the existence of a "Turkish" world stretching from the Adriatic Sea to the Great Wall of China, for many people in Turkey their ethnic and cultural roots as Albanians, Abhazians, Azeris, Bosnians, Circassians, Kazakhs, Kyrgyz, Kurds, Laz, Tatars, and so forth acquired growing salience. Subsequently, during a NATO meeting in Brussels in January 1994, the Turkish prime minister, Tansu Çiller, claimed that there were 24 ethnic groups in Turkey (*Cumhurıyet*, Jan. 13, 1994). This number falls short of the 47 ethnic groups that a study called *Ethnic Groups in the Republic of Turkey* cites (Andrews 1989: 47).

According to Gurr and Scarritt (1989: 380–81), " 'minorities' are groups within larger politically-organized societies whose members share a distinctive collective identity based on cultural and ascriptive traits recognized by them and by the larger society. There are many possible bases for separate group identity: common historical experiences, religious beliefs, language, ethnicity, region of residence, and in caste-like systems, traditionally prescribed occupations. Communal minorities . . . usually are distinguished by several such traits." Clearly, then, there is a rich ethnic diversity in Turkey. But if each ethnic group were to be defined as a minority, this inevitably would raise the question, "Who is a Turk?" and make it rather difficult to identify who the majority might be in Turkey. A conceptual definition of the majority seems very much to depend on the nature of the minority identity one is looking at.

Eriksen's conceptualization of ethnicity might be helpful in differentiating between Kurds and other ethnic groups in Turkey. Eriksen argues that ethnicity "is essentially an aspect of a relationship, not a property of a group" (1993: 11–12). Then, for the purposes of this chapter, it is the nature of the relationship between a minority ethnic group and the majority that becomes critical. Glazer and Moynihan discuss how individuals can hold different identities depending on the context and level of generality (1975: 117–19). It seems, at least compared to a growing number of Kurds, that "Turks" of Abhazian, Albanian, Bosnian, Circassian, Pomak, or other ethnic origins prefer to emphasize their Turkish national identity. Such Turks might be considered to be a part of the majority because they find it expedient not to politicize their ethnic differences.

The same may also apply to some Kurds in Turkey. After all, a prominent advocate of Turkish nationalism, Ziya Gökalp, is widely believed to have been of Kurdish origin. In a 1923 essay about his "national identity," however, he reasoned, "I would not hesitate to believe that I am a Turk even if I had discovered that my grandfathers came from the Kurdish or Arab areas (of Anatolia); because I learned through my sociological studies that nationality is based solely on upbringing" (1959a: 43–44). Gunter lists the names of a number of prominent Turkish government figures of possible Kurdish origin who would not have achieved such high offices if they had not held a strong Turkish national identity. These personalities include former presidents Fahri Korütürk, Cevdet Sunay, and Turgut Özal (Gunter 1990: 7–8). One can add to this list former Turkish foreign minister Hikmet Çetin, who served in the government between 1991 and 1994.

In recent years, however, an increasing number of Kurds and Kurdish leaders in Turkey have emphasized their identities in a political manner. A growing number of Kurds are now articulating demands for the recognition of their ethnic differences with respect to culture, language, and identity. A smaller group of radical Kurds are advocating nationhood or local autonomy. Clearly, the difference between Kurds and other groups in Turkey is that Kurds are, as a group, "the focus of political mobilization and action in defense of . . . self-defined interests" (Gurr 1993: 7). Therefore, for the purposes of this study, Kurds will be treated as the "minority," and the other ethnicities living in Turkey will be considered to be constituting the "majority."

There is no definitive account of the origins of the Kurds as a people. According to a widely supported theory, they "are the mixture of the Median branch of the Aryans (the Iranians being the Persian branch) with indigenous populations, to which the Guti belonged. These people have been influenced by later invaders, including Armenians, Semites (Arabs and Assyrians), Turks, Turcomans, and Persian Iranians, but have absorbed them" (Arfa 1968: 1). The Kurds speak a number of distinct dialects, depending on the area they come from (Bruinessen 1992: 21–22), but "the perception of a common language as an integral part of the Kurdish nation remains very strong among Kurdish nationalists" (Entessar 1992: 5). The Kurds in Turkey mostly use the Zaza and Kurmanji dialects.

Traditionally, the Kurds lived in a geographical area that included parts of Iraq, Iran, the former Soviet Union, Syria, and Turkey. There are no clear, generally recognized boundaries for this area (ibid.: 1–2; Bruinessen 1992: 11–13). Although many publications on Kurds in Turkey include maps giving the impression that they all live in a specific geographical area, this is very misleading. Former Turkish president Turgut Özal argued, during an interview, that 60 to 65 percent of Kurds lived outside southeastern Anatolia, and that 20 to 25 percent of them lived in Istanbul alone.[2] A combination of social, economic, and political factors has led an ever-growing number of Kurds to migrate to urban centers in western Turkey. The areas generally inhabited by Kurds in Turkey also overlap with areas where As-syrian, Arab, Circassian, Turkish, Turcoman, and other ethnic communities have traditionally lived (Nestmann 1989).

Estimates of the Kurdish population vary widely. The most recent figures range from as low as 10–11 million to 20–25 million. There are no reliable statistics on the number of Kurds in Turkey. Today, the most commonly cited figures vary from approximately seven to twelve million. A recent demographic analysis of Turkey's ethnic composition based on the 1965 census puts their number at seven million (Mutlu 1995: 49). Considering that Turkey's current population is slightly over 60 million, the size of the Kurdish community would be near 12 percent. However, many regard this figure as very low. Both in and outside of Turkey, the most frequently cited figure seems to be twelve million, which is consistent with Bruinessen's calculations that the Kurds constitute 19 percent of the population of Turkey (Bruinessen 1992: 14).

Origins of Turkish Nationalist Discourse

At a time when Europeans referred to the Ottoman Empire as Turkey and to its subjects as Turks, "the Turks thought of themselves primarily as Muslims; their loyalty belonged . . . to islam and to the Ottoman house and state" (B. Lewis 1962: 2). As Deringil notes in his chapter in this volume as well as in an earlier study (1993: 167), a certain degree of consciousness about a distinct Turkish identity had existed prior to the twentieth century. Yet, as Gökalp notes, "before [1908], there were Turks, but there was no idea 'we are the Turkish nation' in the collective consciousness of that people: in other words, there was no Turkish nation at that time" (1959b: 62).

The origins of Turkish national consciousness can be traced back to a reformist movement in the Ottoman Empire. This movement, originally started by two Kurds, a Tatar, and a Circassian in 1889, aimed to develop a sense of Ottoman patriotism transcending religious and ethnic differences (Zürcher 1984: 13). It was hoped that a multidenominational nationalism could be nurtured to save the Ottoman Empire from disintegrating under the pressure of nationalist uprisings in the Balkans. The movement, which became known as the Committee of Union and Progress (CUP), fast began to show signs of an ideological disagreement between those advocating Ottomanism and those favoring Turkism. Once the CUP came to power in 1908, these differences grew more apparent as the government became dominated by those favoring centralization and the official use of the Turkish language.

After the defeats suffered in Libya against the Italians and the 1912–13

Balkan War, some Turkish nationalists started to take a more radical approach than ever, arguing for the establishment of a state that would unite all Turks. Yusuf Akçura, himself an immigrant from Russia, was probably the best-known advocate of this idea (Arai 1992; Landau 1981). (Interestingly, it was to Ziya Gökalp that most people attributed pan-Turkist ideas because of his much-quoted verse, "The fatherland for Turks is not Turkey, nor yet Turkistan; The fatherland is a vast and eternal land: Turan!" [quoted in Arai 1992: 31].) However, after the signing of the Sevres Treaty, which divided the remaining territories of the defeated Ottoman Empire among Britain and its allies after World War I, the foreign occupation of the core of Turkey and the arrival of the Greek army with the ambition of annexing parts of Anatolia had the immediate effect of narrowing the focus of Turkish nationalism.

Smith's observation that "at the gateway of every nationalism stands the foreigner" (1973: 47) applies well to the Turkish case. The focus of the Turkish nationalist movement quickly shifted from the CUP's goal of saving the state, meaning the Ottoman Empire, to constructing a Turkish national identity. The concern was no longer how to reform and modernize the Ottoman Empire, but how to liberate Anatolia, the very heartland of Turks. The new political discourse emphasized national resistance and the need to replace the Ottoman imperial regime—a regime that the nationalists argued had done nothing but exploit the people of Anatolia, keeping them in a state of permanent destitution. Mustafa Kemal (Atatürk) became the principal figure in mobilizing support for this approach.

At the time the National Pact was being adopted in 1920, advocates of Turkish nationalism still emphasized the importance of Islam and the multiethnic nature of the country. Issues concerning the form of rule and national identity had yet to be resolved. As Lewis notes, "The Pact still speaks of 'Ottoman Muslims' and not of Turks, and the word Turk appears nowhere in the document" (B. Lewis 1962: 346). The purpose of the pact was simply to identify the territorial extent of this new country, which was to replace the Ottoman Empire, and mobilize the maximum possible support to defeat the occupiers and achieve independence. It was not until after Turkey's victory in its war for independence that the unresolved issues were placed on the agenda.

Important developments followed the signing of the Lausanne Treaty in 1923. The outcome of the struggle between the modernists and the traditionalists would determine the character of this new state. The traditionalists were mainly members of the former Ottoman elite who favored allegiance to the sultan and Islam. Their preference was a decentralized, multiethnic, Muslim Turkey that would have a parliament while remaining a monarchy. The modernists led by Mustafa Kemal, on the other hand, were committed to a centralized, modern, and secular Turkish republic, and the development of a strong sense of patriotism and national identity would be central to its making.

Soon after the treaty, the modernists prevailed, persuading the Grand National Assembly to declare Turkey a republic. This success was followed by the introduction of a nationalist program to develop a Turkish identity powerful enough to completely dissociate the young republic from its predecessor, the Ottoman Empire. The program included the abolition of the caliphate and the initiation of radical reforms aimed at building a centralized modern state, but establishing a sense of national consciousness remained its first priority.[3] In many ways the success of all the reforms was dependent on this nation-building process. As Steinbach (1984: 85) argues, "Nationalism was the principal formula Atatürk used in turning a multiethnic conglomeration into a national state for 'Turks' . . . for whom Islam had been the foundation of state and society."

Originally, Atatürk's approach stressed territorial nationalism rather than Turkish ethnicity. This was a form of nationalism that was based not on the predominance of an ethnic or racial group, but on a sense of civic duty and loyalty to the state (Smith 1973: 36; Greenfeld 1992: 11). He must have been long aware of the challenge Turkey was going to face in this respect, since he noted, during a speech at the newly gathered Grand National Assembly in 1920, "Not only Turks live in Turkey, but Circassians, Kurds, Laz, and Arabs too, and the Turkish nation consists of these Muslim peoples" (quoted in Andrews 1989: 36). Ziya Gökalp seems to have provided an appropriate conceptual basis for Atatürk's approach when he indicated that a "nation is not a racial, ethnic, geographical, political, or voluntary group or association. Nation is a group composed of men and women who have gone through the same education, who have received the same acquisitions in language, religion, morality, and aesthetics" (1959b: 137).

Anderson notes the significance of education and communication in developing a sense of belonging to an "imagined community" (1991). It is thus no wonder that considerable emphasis was placed on unifying the education system in Turkey and introducing policies that would nurture a sense of Turkishness among the inhabitants of the country. "The Law for the Unification of Instruction was a fundamental step in the establishment of a unified, modern, secular, egalitarian and national education system. Its nation building role was especially vital in a country where identity was often Islamic rather than national, and which was fragmented into numerous tribal, racial and linguistic units" (Winter 1984: 186).

Institutions were established to support the nation-building process. The Turkish Language Institute was set up with the belief that the Turkish language needed to be purified of foreign words—mostly Arabic and Persian—and used as a vehicle to foster sentiments of national solidarity. Similarly, the Turkish Historical Society became instrumental in creating historical "myths" to instill a sense of attachment to the Turkish *patrie*. It advocated the theory, known as the Turkish History Thesis, that different peoples ranging from Hittites to Kurds and even Molokans (Andrews 1989: 36) were in reality people of Turkic descent who had migrated out of central Asia, "the cradle of all human civilizations" (quoted in B. Lewis 1962: 353).[4] For Atatürk, who was the main initiator of this thesis, it was critical for the construction of Turkish national identity (Tuncay 1981: 300–303). Dumont may well be correct that the long-term ethnic consequences of these policies were not well thought out at the time (1984: 29). In the early days of the republic, however, it was simply assumed that the Turkish language and a modern political culture would be sufficient to mold the various ethnic identities into an all-encompassing Turkish identity.

In the mid-1920s, opposition to Atatürk's policies of modernization (particularly from religious circles), coupled with his immediate followers' conviction that Turkey continued to face serious domestic and foreign challenges to its integrity and security, hardened their resolve in nation building. The situation evolved into a vicious cycle in which opposition to government policies brought about stricter measures, which in turn resulted in more resistance against these policies. The government was relatively successful in neutralizing religious opposition. Likewise, a majority of the ethnic groups went along with the nation-building policies with very little resistance.[5] The most violent opposition to Atatürk's policies came from the eastern parts of Turkey—mainly populated by Kurds—where it took the form of rebellions.

These rebellions deeply affected the political discourse concerning the Kurdish issue (see Kutschera 1979; Arfa 1968). This discourse centered on the denial of a Kurdish ethnicity. Great efforts were made to assimilate the Kurds and to try to prove that they were in reality of Turkish origin but had lost their Turkish identity due to foreign influence. Essentially, this discourse remained unchanged until very recently. The following section will briefly analyze the origins of Kurdish consciousness and the evolution of the discourse on the "Kurdish problem" in Turkey.

Kurdish Consciousness and the Turkish Political Discourse on Kurds

Olson (1989) takes the origins of Kurdish nationalism back to the 1870s, when Şeyh Ubaydallah attempted to set up an independent Kurdish state in the "Kurdistan" domains of the Ottoman Empire. He argues that Şeyh Ubaydallah was conscious of the existence of a separate Kurdish nation. What should be questioned here is whether the sheikh succeeded in constructing a sense of Kurdish nationhood among the people he claimed to be of Kurdish origin. As Stokes notes, "Before national consciousness is possible, consciousness in general has to emerge" (1993: 29). Clearly, just as an average Arab, Albanian, or Turk was not aware of his nationality, a Kurd living in Kurdistan, in the absence of an effective nationalist leadership, could not have developed a sense of otherness from his coreligionists. After all, as the founders of the Turkish republic discovered, almost half a century after Şeyh Ubaydallah, mobilizing national consciousness to supplement an entrenched Islamic identity is not an easy task.

The situation was no different for the members of the Ottoman elite who were of Kurdish ethnic background. It has already been pointed out that two of the founders of the CUP movement were Kurdish. They remained strong supporters of reforming the Ottoman Empire around an Ottoman national identity. Many who worked for this cause were conscious of their ethnic identity. In fact, they even published several newspapers and magazines in Kurdish in Istanbul, Cairo, and Geneva. Also, a number of Kurdish political organizations were formed at that time. By and large, the publications and members of these organizations advocated modernization and education for the eastern provinces of the Ottoman Empire—but always under the banner of Ottomanism. When Kurdish nationalist ideas did start to emerge, they did so in reaction to the CUP-led Ottoman government policies, which were becoming centralized and Turkified (Kutlay 1992; Olson 1989: 7–25).

Politically, however, the Kurdish elite was very much divided in a manner not dissimilar to its Turkish counterpart. As the Ottoman Empire was collapsing, some of the elite continued to support the ancien régime. Many Kurds who had served in the empire remained attached to their Ottoman identity and loyal to the sultan and the caliph. Another group, including renowned individuals such as Ziya Gökalp and Süleyman Nazif, became ardent advocates of Turkish nationalism.[6] In fact, many local Kurdish tribal and religious leaders supported the national resistance struggle led by Atatürk—although they seem to have done so in the belief that the state replacing the Ottoman Empire would be one with an Islamic identity and decentralized authority (see Olson 1989: 26–51). And finally, there were those who aspired to a separate Kurdish state.

One of the early manifestations of this last view was the participation of a Kurdish delegation, led by the former Ottoman ambassador to Stockholm, Şerif Paşa, in the Paris Peace Conference in 1919. Şerif Paşa called for the establishment of an independent Kurdistan alongside an independent

Armenia in eastern Anatolia (Kutlay 1992: 305–6; Karul 1992: 83). This was followed by similar demands from other Kurdish nationalist circles. The president of the Kurdish Society for Progress and Mutual Aid (Kürt Teavün ve Terakki Cemiyeti), Seyit Abdulkadir, also advocated a state in parts of eastern Anatolia and northern Iraq. This coincided with a 1920 rebellion started by the Koçgiri tribe, which demanded the recognition of yet another Kurdish state (Karul 1992: 83; Olson 1989: 28–33). These attempts were disjointed and drew criticisms from other Kurdish leaders (see Kutlay 1992; Karul 1992; Bruinessen 1992; Olson 1989). In fact, as Olson points out, "many Kurds were probably unconvinced of the inherent strength of their nationalism" (1989: 34).

The greatest challenge to the existence of the newly formed Turkish republic came in the form of a major rebellion in the spring of 1925 led by Şeyh Said. The origins of this rebellion lay in the establishment of a Kurdish nationalist party called the Azadi in 1923 (Bruinessen 1992: 280). The Azadi, founded by experienced Kurdish army officers, succeeded in mobilizing support among the Zaza-speaking tribes and particularly from an important Kurdish religious leader, Şeyh Said. They were opposed to the new Turkish government's policies toward Kurds and found the abolition of the caliphate and the introduction of a modern education system based on Turkish particularly offensive. They demanded an independent national government, planned to achieve it through a rebellion, and hoped to receive British assistance (ibid. 280–83; Olson 1989).

It is clear that the leaders of this movement were conscious of their Kurdish identity and had articulated a nationalist political agenda—even if it did include a heavy dose of religious discourse. As for the Kurds in general, however, it is difficult to say that they had a strong sense of nationhood. As both Bruinessen (1992) and Olson (1989) note, the Şeyh Said rebellion had a very strong religious dimension, which was evident in the fact that it was led by a prominent religious figure. Furthermore, it gained very little support from Kurdish groups other than the Zaza-speaking tribes, such as the Kurmanji-speaking tribes.

Today, Kurdish nationalists have incorporated the Şeyh Said rebellion into their discourse as a manifestation of Kurdish nationalism, while many Turks consider it a religious revolt led by reactionaries whose authority and power were undermined by the new Turkish state.[7] It is the grandson of Şeyh Said, Abdülmelik Fırat, former member of the Turkish Parliament, who seems to offer the best conceptualization of what the rebellion represented. He argues that it was a reaction to the undermining of the traditional Islamic worldview, which emphasized a religious identity rather than an ethnic one. Hence, he observes that the rebellion resulted from the frustration felt by Kurds, who asked themselves,

> what holds us together, with the state being the state of the Turks, and the country being the country of the Turks . . . with the caliphate gone, with the ban on thinking along the rules of Islam, that is to say, with *ümmet* [religious community] no longer being the factor holding us together. . . . In that case, what we need is to establish a state and a country of our own, where we could freely express our religion, by breaking away from these people who are forcing their race on us. (*Aktüel*, Dec. 11, 1991)

Clearly, the Şeyh Said rebellion coincided with a period when two worldviews clashed severely, one stressing modern nationalism and secularism, the other religion and traditionalism. The leaders of the Turkish Republic saw a unified language and education as critical elements in developing a strong sense of national consciousness, which they considered essential in the making of a modern state. The fact that they did not see Islam as a unifying factor was considered a threat by the advocates of the traditional worldview. The Şeyh Said rebellion was the most important manifestation of opposition to the new order in that it threatened the very foundation of the nascent Turkish state, its secular and Turkish identity. The rebellion reinforced the concerns of the governing elite, leaving them in a state of insecurity.

Their reaction reflected this sense of insecurity. The rebellion seemed like an effort to return to the old order, which they had been struggling to replace for a long time. Hence, they not only were swift in repressing the rebellion itself, but also used the occasion to purge all those whom they considered suspect in terms of commitment to their view of modern Turkey (see Zürcher 1984). Furthermore, they introduced a series of additional reforms to consolidate the modern, national, and secular state they had in mind. These reforms ranged from the introduction of a European-based civil code to the replacement of the Arabic script by a Latin one. Most, if not all, of these reforms were perceived as offensive by those who preferred the old order, so much so that the advocates of the Latin script were accused of giving the West an opportunity to declare "that the Turks have adopted . . . foreign writing and turned Christian" (quoted in G. L. Lewis 1984: 198).

Resentment did not come only from Islamic circles; rebellions in eastern Anatolia continued throughout the period leading up to the Second World War. As the reaction to the new policies increased, the government grew even more committed to its idea of developing a sense of nationhood. In 1930, the ruling Republican People's Party (RPP) defined the nation as "a social and political formation comprising citizens linked together by the community of language, culture and ideal" (quoted in Tunaya 1952: 585). The critical language and culture were Turkish, and the ideal was a modern, unified, and secular Turkey. In this context, anyone who lived within Turkey as a citizen was considered a Turk. Other national identities could not be tolerated and had to be overcome. This position was clearly stated by Recep Peker, a leading ideologue of the RPP, when he declared, "We consider as ours [Turkish] all those citizens who live among us, who belong politically and socially to the Turkish nation, and among whom ideas and feelings such as 'Kurdism,' 'Circassianism' and even 'Lazism' and 'Pomakism' have been implanted. We deem it our duty to banish, by sincere efforts, those false conceptions" (quoted in Alp 1937: 253–54).

The establishment and the work of the Turkish Language Institute and the Turkish Historical Society must be seen in the context of these efforts to inculcate a sense of Turkish nationhood. The strongest reaction came from mostly Kurdish-populated areas of eastern Anatolia. The Şeyh Said rebellion was only the first of a series of Kurdish rebellions that the government had to cope with. Although none of these rebellions was of a purely Kurdish-nationalist nature, they nevertheless constituted a major source of insecurity for the government in terms of maintaining Turkey's stability and unity. Hence, it was not surprising that the tasks of these two institutes included proving that Kurds were Turks and working to instill this "scientific" reality into the hearts and minds of "confused" Kurds. Accordingly, Kurds were "mostly comprised of Turks who had changed their language," and the term "Kurd" was "the name of a community that spoke a broken Persian and that lived in Turkey, Iraq and Iran" (quoted in Andrews 1989: 36 n)—a definition based on the infamous Turkish History Thesis or Sun Language Theory. The reference to Kurds as "mountain Turks" was the product of the Turkish nationalist discourse originating from this theory.[8]

By the time the Second World War broke out, it seemed that the Turkish government had succeeded in consolidating the Turkish republic. It would be very difficult, however, to estimate what proportion of Kurds became assimilated as a result of these policies. By the 1950s, when Turkey made a major move toward democracy, there did not seem to be any major signs of Kurdish nationalism. Bruinessen notes that the "assimilation policies were not without effect. Many individuals have for all practical purposes been Turkicised and do not consider themselves as Kurds any more. Most of the Kurds who migrated to the big cities up to the 1960s were rapidly assimilated, and their children do not know Kurdish any more. In several rural areas, too, Turkish has to a considerable extent replaced Kurdish, at least outside the family situation" (1989: 620).

Yet, paradoxically, the modernization of Turkey opened the way for the emergence of a new form of consciousness among some of the Kurds who had moved to the cities and become educated. The first signs of this development appeared in the late 1950s and were mainly couched in a leftist and class-based discourse, which ended when a group of Kurdish intellectuals was arrested in 1959. They were tried following the 1960 military intervention, which was based on the military's belief that the government was weakening the very pillars of the Turkish republic. The military reacted harshly to what it saw as a threat to the unity of the Turkish state, banishing a large group of Kurdish leaders from eastern Anatolia to the west and introducing a new law to change the names of villages from Kurdish to Turkish. These measures, according to Karul, were critical in causing Kurdish nationalist ideas to surface again once the liberal 1961 constitution came into force (1992: 92–93).

The 1961 constitution, as Ahmad notes, brought into being a more liberal political environment: "people had more civil rights, the universities greater autonomy, and students the freedom to organize their own associations" (1993: 136). In this environment, Kurdish ethnicity fast began to receive attention from a number of organizations. The Turkish Workers Party, which was set up in 1961 and won seats in Parliament during the 1963 elections, recognized the existence of a Kurdish people in eastern Anatolia during its fourth party congress. As Entessar notes, this was a revolutionary development in itself, because it was "the first time in modern Turkey that a Turkish political party had openly recognized the existence of the Kurds as a persecuted minority" (1992: 90). The party leadership organized meetings in eastern parts of the country to raise public consciousness of what it termed the "eastern and Kurdish reality."

Also, a number of cultural and student organizations that had emerged in the 1960s and 1970s started to promote Kurdish ethnicity (see Ballı 1991; Gunter 1990; Entessar 1992). Originally, the goal seemed to be getting the Turkish government to recognize the Kurdish language and Kurds' cultural rights. However, the demands of a group led by Abdullah Öcalan, the present leader of the PKK, and his supporters later took a radical tone. In 1977, the group produced a document titled "The Path of the Kurdish Revolution" that depicted the Kurdish-populated areas of Turkey as a colony. The document also argued that the Kurdish feudalists and bourgeoisie had chosen to collaborate with the Turkish ruling classes to exploit the Kurdish peasantry and working class. This necessitated a radical revolution, which would have to lead to the creation of an independent Marxist-Leninist Kurdistan for the Kurdish peasantry and proletariat to enjoy true independence (Gunter 1990).[9] This document later became the program of the PKK after it surfaced on the political scene in Turkey in 1978.

The political discourse used by these organizations was very different from the one that had prevailed among the Kurds of Turkey before the Second World War. The emphasis was clearly on a revolutionary and radical rhetoric. The denial of the Kurdish identity and the lack of economic development in eastern Anatolia were attributed to capitalism and imperialism. This argument provided a basis of solidarity for Turkish and Kurdish revolutionaries. The Federation of Turkish Revolutionary Youth, notorious for its support of violence, encouraged the "struggle against fascism and imperialism, for ideological independence and the liberation of peoples, including that of Turks and Kurds" (Landau 1974: 86). Kurdish Marxist revolutionaries seemed to have more in common with their Turkish comrades than with more traditional nationalist Kurds.

During the 1960s and 1970s, the more traditional Kurdish-nationalist views were represented by the Turkey branch of the Kurdish Democratic Party. Their demands, in general, were limited. They called for cultural rights and for autonomy rather than full independence. They maintained a close relationship with the traditional Kurdish leadership in northern Iraq. This moderate approach was considered compromising by the leftist Kurdish groups, which tended to see the traditional Kurds as belonging to the capitalist class. The class-based Marxist-Leninist rhetoric of the radical groups had little respect for any Kurd who was not revolutionary. For these groups, Kurdish ethnic identity was mainly expressed in terms of an economic class structure. Hence, for what Bruinessen has termed the "left wing of the emerging Kurdish movement" (1984: 8), the traditional Kurdish nationalists were rivals who impeded their struggle.

Although the 1961 constitution has been hailed as the most liberal constitution that Turkey has had so far, it nevertheless did not allow any of the above organizations to operate legally for very long. The ban on advocating Marxism-Leninism and propagating ideas deemed threatening to the indivisibility of Turkey and Turkish identity provided the basis on which the Constitutional Court shut down the Turkish Workers Party. The military intervention of March 1971 forced many of the Kurdish and Turkish radical groups to go underground. As Bruinessen points out, however, "towards the end of the 1970s, it seemed that this (Kurdish in general) nationalist movement was changing the self-perception of a considerable section of the Kurds. People who had long called themselves Turks started re-defining themselves as Kurds" (1989: 621).

The economic chaos, political instability, and violence that characterized the late 1970s in Turkey paved the way for another military intervention in September 1980. The military saw the salvation of Turkey in the reintroduction of what it regarded as strict Atatürkist policies. The political discourse derived from these policies put clear emphasis on the "Turkishness of Turkey," the unity of the Turkish nation, and the territorial integrity of Turkey. This was followed by a major backlash against the conspicuous growth in the 1970s of expressions of Kurdish ethnicity and Kurdish-nationalist ideas. The 1982 constitution manifested this backlash in a number of ways.

The constitution defined one of the fundamental tasks of the Turkish state as the safeguarding of "the independence and integrity of the Turkish Nation, the indivisibility of the country, the Republic" (Article 5). This effectively made it illegal to express any idea that could be interpreted by the authorities as amounting to a recognition of a separate Kurdish ethnic identity. The constitution also introduced an article (Article 26) on the "dissemination of thought" that made it illegal to use a "language prohibited by law." Subsequently, in October 1983, Law 2932 was introduced explicitly to ban the use of Kurdish for the dissemination of information. In addition, the constitution made the establishment of associations and political parties very complicated and banned political parties from supporting activities "in conflict with the indivisible integrity of the state" (Article 68).

The constitution also revitalized the Turkish Language and Turkish History institutes. One important service expected from them was the reintroduction of the political discourse of the 1930s that had argued that Kurds were Turks. Articles and books claiming common ancestry for Turks and Kurds as well as arguments that a separate Kurdish language did not exist proliferated during this period. According to this political discourse, efforts to distinguish the Kurdish identity from the Turkish one were simply fabrications on the part of Western intelligence agencies and separatist groups, both seeking to divide the country. When, in 1988, a number of Social Democrat members of the Turkish Parliament voted in favor of the "Minority Languages" report of the Council of Europe, they were accused of having fallen prey to the conspiracies of European countries to create a Kurdish minority in Turkey where one did not exist (see *Tercüman*, Oct. 5, 1988).

In a national referendum, this constitution received the approval of an overwhelming majority of the voters. Nevertheless, the approval rates in some of the eastern provinces of Turkey were considerably lower than the high average for the country as a whole. Harris argues that "the prospect of increased limitations on ethnic expression may have played a part in inducing five provinces predominantly inhabited by Kurds in eastern Turkey to show the highest rejection rate of any areas of the country in the referendum on the 1982 constitution" (1985: 18–19). These areas very quickly slid into widespread violence once the PKK began to launch terrorist operations in 1984. The Turkish government emphasized the use of force to restore order and neutralize the PKK's demands for a separate state, and the spiral of violence and counterviolence seems to have fueled the emergence of Kurdish national consciousness. Hence, it is not surprising that Abdülmelik Fırat argued that military operations in eastern parts of the country played a greater role in enhancing Kurdish national consciousness than the propaganda work of the PKK (*Aktüel*, Dec. 11, 1991).

The 1980s were also characterized by a massive migration of Kurds to urban centers in western parts of Turkey. The process of assimilation of Kurds in the big cities of the west had already started to weaken in the

1980s. A large proportion of the newly urbanized Kurds, especially the young, experienced a greater awareness of their Kurdish identity. The migration process also showed many Kurds that vast economic disparities existed between the west and the east of the country. The revelation of the underprivileged circumstances they had previously lived in brought about a heightened awareness of a distinct Kurdish identity. The literature on nationalism emphasizes the importance of communication in the development of national consciousness. The 1980s were also a period when communication technologies in Turkey advanced significantly, thus facilitating the dissemination of information about Kurdish ethnicity.

Anderson notes that "imagined communities" of nationhood are often born in exile. When Kurdish ethnicity began to assert itself in Turkey, the feeling of "otherness" became even more acute among the large number of Kurdish asylum seekers who had fled to Europe (Anderson 1991). These Kurds often joined the many Kurdish cultural and political organizations that proliferated in Belgium, France, Sweden, Switzerland, and Germany. Most of these organizations remained under the control or influence of the PKK. Hence, the discourse employed by the Kurds in exile became one that defined the Kurdish problem as the product of Turkish colonialism and the repression of the Kurdish national identity. The discourse advocated an armed liberation struggle to establish an independent Kurdish state. By and large, this discourse dominated the scene on Kurdish ethnicity until 1990, when the Turkish government introduced a radical change to its stand by recognizing the "Kurdish reality" in Turkey.

The change had been in the offing for some time. Increasing numbers of books and publications were appearing in Turkey focusing on Kurdish ethnicity and challenging the standard official discourse on the topic. A growing number of journalists, politicians, and citizens had become increasingly critical of the official denial of a Kurdish identity in Turkey. Turgut Özal, after securing his election as president of Turkey, became the first high-ranking Turkish official to hint that Turkey was soon going to see major changes with regard to Kurdish ethnicity. In June 1989, his assertion that he most probably had Kurdish blood became a first step in paving the way for the eventual recognition of the Kurdish reality in Turkey. The first concrete step in that direction occurred when, in April 1991, the ban on the Kurdish language was lifted.

The 1991 elections brought to power in November a coalition government that included the Social Democrat Populist Party (SHP), which had formed an electoral pact with the People's Labor Party (HEP).[10] The government program promised major reforms for eastern Anatolia that would also address the "Kurdish problem." In December 1991, Deputy Prime Minister Erdal Inönü called for recognition of the cultural identity of

Turkey's Kurdish citizens. Subsequently, in March 1992, Prime Minister Süleyman Demirel openly announced that he recognized the reality of a Kurdish ethnic presence in Turkey (*Turkish Daily News*, Mar. 18, 1992).

This positive atmosphere did not last long, however; the PKK incited people to violence during the March 1992 Newroz celebrations, and the security forces responded in a harsh manner. Since then, violence has continued unabated, except for a brief lull in the spring of 1993, when the PKK declared a unilateral cease-fire. The cease-fire collapsed in June when the PKK stopped a bus in eastern Anatolia and executed discharged soldiers on their way home. Since then, the government has essentially been committed to a policy of first bringing terrorism under control and destroying the PKK before considering anything else. The Democracy Party (DEP), the continuation of HEP after the latter had been closed by the Constitutional Court, in June 1994 met the same fate as its predecessor for supporting the PKK and advocating separatism.

In spite of the present hard-line approach toward real (terrorist) and perceived (ideal) threats to the integrity of the Turkish state, governmental discourse on the Kurdish problem has not slipped back to what it was before 1990. The larger political system in Turkey has been experiencing a lively debate on the need to amend the 1982 constitution or even to replace it with a more flexible and liberal one.[11] The remarks of the president of Turkey, Süleyman Demirel, in the context of this debate reveal the distance that has been covered on Kurdish identity in Turkey since the not-so-distant days when Kurds were defined as "mountain Turks." In May 1994 he noted, "the idea of a racially biased state system is a thing of the past. Citizenship cannot be expressed in relation to a race but should be expressed through constitutional rights—and this can be termed as constitutional citizenship [*anayasal vatandaşlık*]. If we try to define the nation on a racial basis, we risk disintegrating the state" (*Hürriyet*, May 22, 1994).

Conclusion

A century ago, in 1894, the notion of a separate Kurdish or Turkish national identity did not exist among the ordinary people of Anatolia. As the grandson of Şeyh Said puts it, "There were no Kurds and Turks then" (*Aktüel*, Dec. 11, 1991); the unifying factor was Islam. Today, the situation is a very different and complex one. A growing number of Kurds are becoming politically assertive about their ethnic identity, while some Kurds—to paraphrase Horowitz—continue "to conveniently forget their identity" (1985: 51). There are also other Kurds who recognize their ethnic differences but do not politicize them. On the other hand, some among the Turkish public continue to insist that in Turkey everyone is a "Turk," while others recognize the rich ethnic diversity of the country.

Greenfeld argues that "an essential characteristic of any identity is that it is necessarily the view the concerned actor has of himself or herself. It therefore either exists or does not exist: it can not be asleep and then be awakened" (1992: 13). Clearly, this suggests that a person of Kurdish origin may well feel himself or herself Turkish—a good case in point might be Ziya Gökalp. Conversely, a person who may have felt Turkish for a long time may well cease to feel Turkish and prefer to be identified as Kurdish. After all, Connor warns us, assimilation cannot be assumed to be unidimensional (1987: 198). Under these circumstances, one is inevitably confronted with a very fluid situation in which it may be difficult to clearly define who fits into a minority group and who constitutes a majority in one particular country. This, in turn, seems to make the task of understanding ethnic conflicts much more complex and puzzling. The key to unraveling this puzzle may well lie in capturing the cognitive processes behind Gellner's observation, "Nationalism is not the awakening of nations to self-consciousness: It invents nations where they do not exist" (Gellner 1964: 169).

PART VII

AMERICANNESS

13

Studying Mainstreams and Minorities in North America

SOME EPISTEMOLOGICAL AND ETHICAL DILEMMAS

RICHARD HANDLER

THIS chapter examines the anthropologist's role in configuring minority/majority discourses. Questions about ethnographers' relationships to the people they study, and about the depiction of such relationships in ethnographic texts, have been raised repeatedly in the last decade. Raised, but hardly resolved: indeed, one has the feeling that our discipline evades such questions, even when the act of raising them is professionally trendy—perhaps because to answer them would in turn raise serious doubts about our positioning within the class, race, and gender hierarchies of contemporary society. I do not expect to resolve such questions here; my aim is more modest. I will survey a range of positions that anthropologists can take in ethnographic work that involves minority/majority politics, using examples from my own experience in Quebec and the United States, as well as Maryon McDonald's work in Brittany. In the end, I will reaffirm what, perhaps, most anthropologists know but don't like to admit: that when it comes to the politics of their field sites, ethnographers have no place to hide.

Before turning to the ethnographic examples, it will be useful to consider the terms "minority" and "majority" as cultural concepts. They belong to modern discourse, to the cultural universe of individualism. They refer to aggregates, but aggregates of a particular type. They presuppose, first, that individual human persons are the fundamental social units; second, that those persons are indivisible, unitary units and, therefore, countable; and third, that the activities of counting and aggregating such units can proceed unproblematically on the basis of discernible similarities and differences, so that, fourth, majorities and minorities, as groups, are internally homogeneous, clearly bounded, and externally differentiated one from another.

Beyond those presuppositions, it is useful to distinguish two somewhat different usages of the pair "majority/minority" in American culture. The first comes from our notions of democracy and electoral politics. In this context, "majority" and "minority" refer to people who agree about a particular issue; that is, to temporary aggregates of persons (usually, of voters) who hold the same opinion with respect to one specific question or referendum. The second usage comes from American notions of ethnic identity and ethnic politics. Here "majority" and "minority" indicate a numerical relationship between two (or more) groups of individuals who are citizens of the same nation-state, yet are thought to differ in their cultural identity. The numerical relationship may be described as greater to lesser, or more to fewer. According to historian Philip Gleason, the first usage was common in the nineteenth century, but the second usage only became established, via social scientists, in the mid-twentieth century (1991: 393–98).

Notice that the second way of using the pair "majority/minority" erases the contextual specificity that is important in the first usage. In other words, the ethnic usage of "majority/minority" naturalizes difference. The similarities that unite the individual members of an ethnic aggregate are not taken to be contextually specific, like the fact of agreeing about a particular issue. Rather, they are thought to be essential features of each group member's personality or being. Indeed, in the ethnic usage, electoral aggregates are thought naturally to follow from ethnic aggregates, since people who are alike culturally, it is presumed, will always see issues in the same way and vote together accordingly.

Notice further that in both usages, the relationship between majority and minority is hierarchical. In the first usage, the majority dominates the minority, in the sense of winning a vote or confirming a choice, but this hierarchy is temporary, as, indeed, are the minority and majority aggregates. In the second usage, however, hierarchy is naturalized and rendered permanent. The majority becomes the norm, the valued (and usually, therefore, unmarked) category, from which the minority is understood to differ. Indeed, when Louis Wirth formulated one of the first American (as opposed to European) social-scientific definitions of "minority group" in 1945, he presupposed that minorities "are singled out from the others in the society in which they live for differential and unequal treatment and . . . therefore regard themselves as objects of discrimination" (1945: 348–50). According to Gleason, Wirth's definition set a pattern in American social science in which the notion of "minority" has been closely associated with the ideas of victimization and assimilation: "If being a victim of hatred and prejudice was intrinsic to minority status, it would seem almost perverse for minorities to wish to perpetuate their own existence. In that sense . . . formulations . . . like Wirth's . . . were unconsciously predicated on the American assumption that minorities ought naturally to disappear into the larger society" (Gleason 1991: 399–400).

The term "minority," then, naturalizes contextual cultural and historical differences, precisely as the term "culture" has become a synonym for "race" (Segal and Handler 1995) in the "new cultural politics of difference" (West 1990). This makes the term "minority" extremely tricky to use if one's aim is the critical analysis of cultural and racial hierarchies, as the following discussion will suggest.

When anthropologists study majority/minority situations, they more frequently focus on naturalized ethnic-racial minorities than on those that result from ongoing, changing political coalition building. This is perhaps because the anthropological culture concept, and our disciplinary praxis mandating that the appropriate unit of study for an anthropologist is "a culture," incline us toward the study of "ethnic minorities," which we consider to be cultures or almost cultures. At any rate, the examples to which I now turn all involve anthropologists and naturalized minority/majority groups.

My first example is the work I did in Quebec between 1975 and 1986. Recall that Quebec is one of ten Canadian provinces and that Canada has a population of 28 million people, of whom 8 million are French speakers. Of those latter, 7 million reside in Quebec, which has a population of 8 million. The majority/minority configuration of Canadian society grew out of the competitive colonialisms of England and France in eighteenth-century North America. To simplify, French Canada was conquered by English Canada in 1759, and Canada, as a "dominion" of Great Britain and gradually as a sovereign nation, developed as an "English" polity with an entrenched "French" minority. That minority was located principally in Quebec, but Quebec itself always had an entrenched "English" minority, just as several other provinces (Saskatchewan, New Brunswick) had important "French" minorities. This rough sketch does not, of course, do justice to other minorities—Native Americans or twentieth-century immigrant communities, for example.

I worked in Quebec at a moment of high nationalist fervor, when a separatist political party succeeded for the first time in gaining control of the provincial government. Separatism—or *indépendentisme*, the term that Quebecois nationalists preferred in the 1970s—implies a reversal of the prevailing Canadian majority/minority configuration. An independent Quebec, a Quebec separated from Canada, would no longer be a minority French province in an English country but a majority French nation with its own minorities (immigrants and "anglos" in cosmopolitan Montreal and Native Americans in the far north).

Since the early nineteenth century, French Canadian nationalists have complained of oppression at the hands of the English majority, specifically of the relegation of French Canadians to the bottom of the economic hierarchy and the disregard of French cultural, linguistic, and religious rights. But the sociology and politics of oppression were never simple, since, as many French Canadian nationalists would admit, the French elites (clerical and political) played a key role in maintaining Canada's ethnic hierarchy. By the time I got to Quebec, ethnic oppression was not easy to glimpse, since Francophones controlled the provincial government and even the Quebec business world had been largely (although not completely) "Frenchified." What I want to suggest is that an adequate analysis of this situation required a sophisticated method for examining the interplay of ethnicity, class, and the politics of majority/minority configurations.

In the late 1970s, I lacked those tools. Recall that I had begun this work before cultural studies, feminist theory, and African American studies had made much of an impact on anthropology. The prevailing models for dealing with the intersection of class and ethnicity were, I thought, reductionist: both Marxism and utilitarianism "explained" ethnicity in terms of "interests" that could be imputed to ethnic politicians or to the class fragments thought to be central in any particular ethnic movement. These theoretical approaches rarely asked about the constructedness of any of the elements of their models (interests, classes, ethnic groups). As I argued (1988: 23–26), they thereby took for granted or even naturalized precisely those ideological (and social-scientific) constructs that needed to be questioned.

I was also unprepared in another way to deal with Quebec nationalism. Anthropologists have never been comfortable studying mass rather than localized phenomena, and that was even truer twenty years ago than it is now. In Quebec I studied a mass ideology, nationalism. It was easy enough to gain access to that ideology, since it was propagated constantly and in multiple media. But I didn't have good tools to raise the sorts of questions that today's cultural studies ask or at least pretend to ask: how is an ideology enunciated, translated, and received or resisted at varying positions in a social formation? Lacking such tools, I concentrated on ideological texts and on the translation of those texts from one institutional context to another (for example, from a political party to a government bureau such as the Department of Cultural Affairs). But I never came to understand, to my satisfaction, what nationalism or ethnic identity meant to individuals at various moments of their lives.

The result was that my Quebec work took shape as a deconstruction of nationalist ideology and of the anthropological culture theory associated with it. This, of course, aroused the ire of many Quebecois (for references, see Handler 1993). It also put me in the odd position, for an anthropologist, of criticizing rather than affirming the natives' beliefs. And it left me unable to position myself vis-à-vis the difficult ethical and political questions that majority/minority oppression raises. Concentrating on debunking the essentialist claims of nationalist culture theory, I had nothing to say about either cultural or class oppression.

Now, I would like to compare this Quebec work with the work of Maryon McDonald in Brittany, as reported in her superb book "*We Are Not French*" (1989). McDonald studied the Breton nationalist movement in France at exactly the same moment that I was working in Quebec, and her book appeared one year after mine. So: two minority/majority configurations in French-language settings, but the place of French in the language hierarchy was reversed, since McDonald was studying a situation in which French was the dominant national language and the minority Breton movement had defined itself in linguistic opposition to French. Moreover, unlike the Quebec nationalist movement, the Breton movement never enjoyed significant popular or electoral support. Indeed, McDonald focused precisely on the disjunction between the ideology and sociopolitical resources of the urban intellectuals who constituted the Breton movement, on the one hand, and those of the rural Breton population on whose behalf the militants claimed to speak, on the other (Badone 1992; Handler 1991a).

In such a comparison, it is easy to show the discrepancy between the intellectuals' version, usually romanticized, of peasant culture and the lives and values of rural people. Indeed, one can fall into a trap in making such comparisons, for they usually take the form of debunking the intellectuals' fantasies while at least implying that "real peasant culture" is "authentic" (cf. Bruner 1994). The problem is that "authenticity" is not a helpful concept—all cultures, and all ideological models of a particular culture, are, I would argue, equally authentic or inauthentic, that is, equally constructed. As Jocelyn Linnekin and I once wrote, "all genuine traditions are spurious [and] . . . all spurious traditions are genuine" (Handler and Linnekin 1984: 288). One analyzes the disjunction between intellectual and rural cultures not to award prizes of authenticity, but to say something about the social construction of those differing models.

In McDonald's case, what she wants to say about that disjunction is, in the broad sense, political; and when she says it, I hear in her tone a barely suppressed rage. Consider, for example, her description of a harvest festival, the *fest-noz*, that was revived and objectified by militants in the 1960s. According to McDonald, "the *fest-noz* is now commonly regarded as an ancient and peculiarly Breton and Celtic folk-custom. The term is relatively new to much of Lower Brittany. It seems to have originated in a small area of central Finistere . . . where it described a special celebration . . . that followed collective agricultural work, principally the potato and beet harvests in September. With the mechanization of agriculture . . . the *fest-noz* virtually died out." After nationalist intellectuals revived it, McDonald continues, "the *fest-noz* became a paying affair, often subsidizing militant groups or activities, in which scruffy dress, heavy drinking, pot, and left-wing politics have mingled easily with often struggling conversations in a hastily learnt Breton. Large circles of sweating youths perform simple dance steps, shuffling round and round in newly bought clogs, in rustic celebration of a harvest they have not brought home" (1989: 144).

I can think of very few ethnographies that employ such cutting irony—or is it satire?—as this, and, indeed, students in my graduate course on nationalism have attacked McDonald for ridiculing her natives, the Breton militants. Why, they ask, does McDonald have the right to speak with such contempt of these nationalist intellectuals?

I defend McDonald, because I think her work plainly has an answer to that question. McDonald argues that the militants, with their higher social status, greater education (most are college graduates), greater social resources, and better understanding of how to manipulate mass media, are able to define a publicly presented version of Breton culture that the peasants are powerless to contest, but to which they must respond. As an example, McDonald tells the story of two peasants, Thérèse and her son Iffig. Asked by a folklore-collecting militant to sing some real Breton songs, Iffig was ashamed at his inability to do so; then,

> a few weeks later, he bought himself a record player and set it up, among the grain and potatoes, in his attic bedroom. He went to a supermarket . . . bought some records of modern Breton songs, and then played them in his attic, trying to learn them. It was very difficult: he found he could hardly understand them.
>
> It might seem a telling comment on the "Breton culture" of militants that a native Breton-speaking peasant . . . should have to spend hard-earned money, and shut himself in his attic, in order to try to acquire the culture lived and defended in his name. (p. 297)

Iffig's mother, Thérèse, was more actively exploited by the militants. To understand her case, you must know that for Breton peasants, French was a language of upward mobility to which they aspired: a responsible mother tried to ensure that her children would speak French, at least in addition to Breton. McDonald reports that to Thérèse's dismay, her and her father's local reputation for French competency was eclipsed when the militants fetishized her as a repository of Breton folk culture:

> In the very simplicity of her surroundings, Thérèse has been suddenly launched into super-modernity, through an urban and educated world. The recommendation that she knew Racine or La Fontaine . . . was gradually displaced; instead, she was said to know Breton well, and to know many Breton proverbs, songs, and stories. Increas-

ing numbers of young Breton enthusiasts were directed to her, gathering material for essays, theses, articles; then journalists from within the movement sought her out.

This led to "the bright lights of regional television" and to the playing of a role, McDonald tells us, that Thérèse "never fully understood":

> The press interviewed her repeatedly, and she was flattered. But she was launched into a discourse over which she had no control. Why did they keep writing that she had never been further from home than a few kilometres in her whole life? Did they not know that she had travelled to Leon markets regularly? And why did a television journalist cut her off when she insisted her father had known good French? What was the film about anyway? (p. 299)

What I interpret as barely concealed rage in McDonald's voice finds its justification, it seems to me, in this ethnography: the militants have objectified the very people for whom they claim to be struggling, and that objectification becomes a social force which intrudes on those peoples' lives but over which they have no control. The militants have social and political power, based on class and education, which they wield, in effect, over the peasants. As McDonald puts it, "The Breton-speaking peasant can find glamour in a structure of values in which the educated sophisticate plays a definitive role. Shift the focus elsewhere, however, and the . . . peasants who cannot speak French very well and grasp the loop of enthusiasms in which they are revalued fall back into the wild." For the peasants it is, McDonald concludes, "a world in which the power and centre of definition have always been elsewhere" (p. 302).

There is a further point. McDonald argues that the militants use the rhetoric of minority oppression and victimization to claim the moral high ground in public debate. Speaking more generally of the "Celtic" movements of France and Great Britain, she writes:

> Modern Celts have . . . appropriated the morally privileged half of whatever contemporary oppositions have presented themselves, and they are now self-defining minorities. As such, they are morally opposed to the majority world, and since part of the privilege of the self-consciously "Celtic" movements is to assume oppression . . . at the hands of this majority, they are morally exempt from responsibility not only for the actions of the majority, but also for their own (violence included). (p. 116)

McDonald does not construct a calculus of oppression, but she suggests that Brittany's economic plight (its relative lack of "development") is also found in other areas of France and that it must be understood in terms more complicated than simple ethnic oppression (p. 86).

Now, this discussion of the moral high ground and victimization returns us to the Quebec case, for, as you will recall, I never came to terms with the reality of oppression, whether ethnic, political, or cultural, in Canadian society. In any case, how does one measure oppression, and, in particular, how does one measure it in terms of presumed homogeneous aggregates like minority groups—especially when we know that such aggregates are not homogeneous in terms of other axes of oppression, or of hierarchy, such as class and gender?

The reality of oppression seems incontrovertible in the next case, that of African Americans. But that does not make the position of the anthropological analyst any less ambiguous. I turn now to my ongoing research at Colonial Williamsburg, America's largest outdoor history museum. As many readers will know, this is an institution founded with Rockefeller money in the 1920s; it is a restored and reconstructed late-eighteenth-century (that is, American colonial) town, administered by what is now a medium-sized nonprofit corporation called the Colonial Williamsburg Foundation. The museum has come to stand for an upper-class, colonial-revival patriotism that canonizes the rugged individualism and cultural elegance of Georgian, Revolutionary America. As such, it has been heavily criticized by intellectuals from the center leftward for being "a Republican Disneyland" (to use an insider joke), an institution that celebrates the values and culture of a ruling elite and whitewashes history by ignoring slavery, class oppression, and the violence and injustice perpetrated by that elite (Wallace 1986).

In the past fifteen years there has been a major effort on the part of a new generation of social historians at Williamsburg to make the museum's celebratory history more critical. That effort has centered on a new, "leaner" look for the museum's interiors, a scruffier outdoor appearance (unmown grass, peeling paint, unpaved streets), and the inclusion of slaves in Colonial Williamsburg's cast of characters (Gable, Handler, and Lawson 1992; Gable and Handler 1993b; Wells 1993). The history of slavery has been developed by a new unit within the institution, the Department of African-American Interpretation and Presentation (AAIP). This is a comparatively small unit, comprising about a dozen interpreters, as compared to the three or four hundred costumed interpreters who present the "mainstream" story to the public on the restored museum-town's streets.

The small size of the AAIP suggests one of the main problems the unit confronts: it is drastically underfunded and understaffed compared to other units within the museum. And, indeed, AAIP programming remains somewhat marginal compared to the array of programs and sites that convey the mainstream story, although this has been changing slowly (Lawson 1995). These comparisons of staff size and resources suggest that an administration that publicly proclaims its determination to "tell the full story" of colonial America, a story that includes African Americans (Colonial Williamsburg 1985), has thus far been unwilling to put its money where its mouth is. I will return, below, to consider why this is the case—a question not easy to answer.

An even stickier question concerns the content of the African American history that is presented. Here it is important to note that the AAIP is an all-black department, and its staff has a large measure of control over the stories it constructs and conveys to the public. Though the history the department presents is more critical than anything else presented at Colonial Williamsburg, it for the most part fits very well with mainstream American ideology about ethnicity and race.

Let me first give two examples of what I consider to be critical history that AAIP presents. On a two-hour walking tour called the Other Half Tour, an interpreter leads a small group of visitors (perhaps twenty) through the backstreets of the city and talks about Africa, the middle passage, the initiation of slavery in the American colonies, and the gradually elaborated laws that made that institution ever harsher. By keeping outdoors and in backstreet areas, the Other Half Tour suggests the exclusion of African Americans from the mainstream property holding and prosperity that all of the museum's interior spaces celebrate. A particularly poignant discussion of oppression and exclusion occurs in the Palace Gardens, an ornate, beautifully manicured space meant to re-create the pomp and power of the English Crown. In the gardens, Other Half interpreters talk to their audiences about the horrors of the middle passage. Using volunteers from the somewhat discomfited audience—when none come forward, some are drafted—the interpreters explain the difference between "loose pack" and "tight pack" on the slave ships. I quote from the dissertation of one of my associates in this research, Anna Lawson:

> The guide invited the children in the group to come to the front and make a line, adding if needed enough adults to have five or six people, standing side by side—i.e., shoulder to shoulder. She then asked the rest of the tour members to imagine the line with the people lying on their backs and every other person upside down, or side by side head to foot. This, the guide explained, was called "loose pack," one way of arranging slaves in the hold of a slave ship. She next had the volunteers turn so that they formed a line facing one direction. She pushed them together, so that each was touching the back of the person in front and explained that this arrangement was called "tight pack." Then she asked, "Which ship would you rather be on?" (1995: 118)

Lawson goes on to talk about the ironic contrast between this gruesome story and the lovely garden setting in which it is told, although, interestingly, she was unable to ascertain, even through direct questioning of the tour's creators, whether the irony was intended (p. 119).

A second example of AAIP history that criticizes the celebratory story told elsewhere in the museum concerns miscegenation. The simultaneous presence and absence of this topic is a staple at Southern historic sites (Lawson and Gable 1993). Thomas Jefferson's Monticello is the paradigmatic example. Stories abound concerning Jefferson's relationship to his "slave-mistress," Sally Hemings, but because the stories are not "documented" to the Monticello Foundation's satisfaction, the museum stubbornly refuses to tell them (Gable and Handler 1994; Brodie 1974). Still, visitors to Monticello expect and want to hear about this topic, either because they believe the institution is hiding the truth, or because they believe that great men have feet of clay that should be exposed.

Similar stories exist at Colonial Williamsburg, focused on one of the museum's most elegant houses, that which belonged to George Wythe, Jefferson's mentor. As is widely known, Wythe freed his slaves after the death of his wife and lived for many years thereafter with his cook, Lydia Broadnax. These circumstances continue to give rise to rumors of a love relationship between Wythe and Broadnax, rumors that Wythe's "official" biographers heatedly deny (Blackburn 1975; Brown 1981). Colonial Williamsburg, too, denies them, following those biographers in asserting that the rumors lack documentation. AAIP staff, however, are willing to lend credence to stories about Wythe and Broadnax. More importantly, on Other Half tours, they occasionally criticize the foundation for "hiding the truth." On such occasions, they tell visitors that they will not hear about Wythe and Broadnax inside the Wythe House, implying that a cover-up or, at the least, an exclusionary history, is presented there (Lawson and Gable 1993).

When questioned, AAIP staff members take a range of positions with respect to the significance of the Wythe-Broadnax liaison. Some see it—and, more generally, the miscegenation for which it stands—as evidence of the power that masters wielded over slaves and of the types of exploitation that slavery entailed. Others take it as evidence for an overcoming of interracial boundaries, for common ancestry and a common history. In any case, AAIP staff members criticize Colonial Williamsburg for omitting these possible significances, and for omitting significant roles for African Americans, from the version of colonial history that the museum tells.

Miscegenation and the middle passage are two fragments of a subversive history that are atypical of AAIP presentations and, as far as we could tell, utterly absent from the work of the mainstream interpreters at Colonial Williamsburg. When it came to black history, what was typical was what I will call benign multiculturalism. By this I mean that the museum presents Williamsburg's African American population as just another immigrant group in the American saga. Like new Americans from elsewhere, African-Americans are portrayed as individuals in possession of a vibrant ancestral culture, yet in the process of "becoming Americans," as the Foundation's guiding theme between 1985 and 1995 was labeled (Colonial Williamsburg 1985). The emphasis is on individual initiative leading to property ownership, whether of the burgeoning consumer wealth of the late eighteenth century—a theme that the museum, through its obsession with objects, dotes on—or of cultural property and respectability. Given this approach, the most common portrayal of slavery at Williamsburg shows dynamic, assertive individuals making the best of a bad situation. The bad situation is acknowledged—slaves were owned like cattle, visitors are told—but then passed over: this narrative is above all an individual success story (Handler 1989). It is not about the systemic use of power to exploit and oppress members of socially stigmatized categories.

Why Colonial Williamsburg draws the fangs of a critical history is one of those sixty-four-thousand-dollar questions in social theory. The standard answer, of course, is "hegemony": the museum is an elite institution that tells a history that reinforces elite interests. That answer is not so much wrong as it is oversimplified, but it is beyond the scope of this chapter to attempt a more complex answer. I want simply to make one additional point here: the AAIP staff as well as the museum's intellectuals—mostly white, male curators and historians who profess allegiance to a critical social history—acquiesce in the eviscerated African American history that Colonial Williamsburg purveys.

This last observation leads back to my initial inquiry concerning the position of the ethnographer vis-à-vis minority/majority configurations. For while I and my research associates advocate a history that tackles the horror of slavery, as well as its legacy in today's racism, the minorities at Colonial Williamsburg—the AAIP staff—have largely failed to provide such a history. We are on delicate ground here. First, one might properly ask us whether some change isn't better than none at all. That is, one might note that the history told at Colonial Williamsburg in the 1990s differs markedly from that told there during, say, the 1950s. That the current Williamsburg story is not as radical as outside critics might like is not a reason to sneer at the positive changes that have occurred. Given institutional inertia and the social forces arrayed against them, it is noteworthy that the social historians and AAIP interpreters have achieved as much as they have.

My response to this cannot be developed here; it will have to await the fuller report of our ethnographic findings concerning the stories that are actually told on the ground at Colonial Williamsburg. Suffice it to say that we ourselves were surprised at how *little* the Williamsburg story differs from past versions. True, blacks have been added to it, but the underlying message of individualism and opportunity for the worthy remains the same as it was in the time of John D. Rockefeller, Jr.

If we are right about this, it means that somewhere in our published results will have to appear a critique of the AAIP, one that claims its work has largely been co-opted by the hegemonic ideology of individual achievement. I have gone out on a limb several times arguing a similar point: that most nationalist and ethnic ideologies of liberation reproduce the mainstream ideology and hence, in the long run, will do nothing to change the global political order (Handler 1988, 1991b). And the response is familiar as well: such critiques deconstruct the nationalist ideologies of the dispossessed while leaving intact that of the dominant political order. In the end, one could argue that my ideas may be epistemologically correct but politically incorrect.

There is another problem. In the ethnography of the failure of black history at Colonial Williamsburg, Anna Lawson (1995) has tried to give a meticulous account of the varying aspirations and personalities of the AAIP staff members, as well as of the obstacles they face in their work. That is, without minimizing her political critique, she has tried to reveal the human dimension of subaltern voices caught in a rhetorical machine—the museum—that seems to leave them little space to operate. At her dissertation defense, the only African American on her committee criticized her sharply for making excuses for the AAIP. For this historian, black history at Colonial Williamsburg was what he called "coon science" and, as such, utterly without redeeming features.

There is yet another twist to the Williamsburg research, and this brings me to my final example. Our critique of Colonial Williamsburg brings us into painful conflict with our sponsors there, the social historians who challenged their institution to allow us to carry out our research. I would characterize these historians as not only of the mainstream, but of the majority and the elite. They are corporate vice presidents, and by most measures of wealth, occupation, and education, they would be considered upper-middle- to upper-class. Despite my personal liking for these people, and despite their sponsorship, the results of our work must argue that they have been largely co-opted by the institutional culture in which they work. I say this because, again, despite their professed commitment to bringing a critical history to Williamsburg's streets, our research tells us they not only have failed, but refuse to acknowledge their failure.

Such a conclusion is not what these historians expected. As one of them has written, in an essay celebrating the "coming of age" of American history museums, concerning our anthropological study of Colonial Williamsburg:

> After considerable soul-searching, Williamsburg agreed to be Handler's [and Gable's and Lawson's] Samoa, even after a sister institution got cold feet and backed out of [their] proposal for a two-part comparative study. We concluded that we had more to learn than lose from [their] observations. All the same, I daresay that my colleagues would not have risked potentially embarrassing "bad press" if

they had not been confident that the educational philosophy that guides the Foundation's work is responsible and defensible. (Carson 1991: 94)

Recently, our debate with our sponsors has continued in the prestigious *Journal of American History*, as Colonial Williamsburg's vice president for research has had to respond to an article we published there (Gable and Handler 1994; Carson 1994).

This ongoing debate has taught me that being a critic of the majority position is not particularly more comfortable than debunking minority nationalisms. Many of the people who, from our perspective, collude in the reproduction of nationalist ideology at Colonial Williamsburg work there with good intentions and, beyond that, are aware of the seriousness of the issues that racism presents. They are not in any simple sense on the wrong side, yet their work ultimately, we believe, reinforces a conservative ideology they themselves would reject. As for us—ethnographers of the majority, this time, rather than of a minority—we find that our research still entails a dubious ethics and puts us in an uncomfortable position vis-à-vis our subjects, however well placed, socially, they may be.

There are two related conclusions to this chapter. The first concerns the notion that the majority is monolithic. When we speak about black history (or minority history) versus mainstream history at Colonial Williamsburg (and note that "mainstream" is a native term), we set up the image of two opposing factions or processes that are internally homogeneous. But, of course, "the mainstream" is not homogeneous in a medium-sized nonprofit corporation with an annual budget of $140 million. It is a hierarchical organization in which not only race but also class and gender structure the chain of command and the routines of work. Mainstream history—the upbeat story of America's founding as a nation and of the positive contributions made by various individuals and groups to that process—is constructed and conveyed not only by managers and professionals but by the "front line," a museum proletariat, as it were. These people are poorly paid and rather tightly monitored in their work. Many are divorced, middle-aged women with harrowing personal histories, retired people, or college students—in any case, people without much political or economic clout.

These museum workers both resist and reproduce the corporate culture in which they work. They have plenty of gripes about their working conditions and their bosses' behavior and about the changing contents of the histories they are told to tell. But resistance aside, many of these workers are quite loyal to Colonial Williamsburg. Our critique of the museum angers and hurts them as well as their bosses. It challenges what they see as their professionalism, an attribute that they value highly as they try to improve their status vis-à-vis educators in other institutions. Our critique of the majority, then, is taken as a personal affront by many of the subalterns within the institution, who, at least in this context, identify more with a hegemonic order than with a critique of it (cf. Gable and Handler 1993a).

To give but one example: in our analysis of frontline interactions between museum interpreters and visitors, we have found that an ethos of what we call "good vibes" is used by the corporation to discipline workers in a way that becomes naturalized for them. The concept of good vibes (which is increasingly common in service industries) regulates the ways in which employees must interact, in a "friendly" manner, with visitors/customers. The trick of good vibes, as a mechanism of corporate discipline, is that it controls workers by means of their relations with visitors. Thus the workers' angers and frustrations become focused on the visitors, whom they must always tolerate in good-humored fashion, instead of on the corporate regime that enforces such conduct. When we tried to make this argument in a workshop for some veteran interpreters, they threw it back at us. We told them that the corporation forces them to be "nice" to visitors, to which one elderly woman responded, "Do you mean we're not naturally nice?"—that is, do you mean we have to be forced to be nice? In this example, our critique of corporate routines, which we saw as oppressive to museum workers, challenged the workers' conceptions of themselves and was accordingly rejected by them.

All this is hardly surprising, but it raises questions about the ethnographer's positioning vis-à-vis people who are variously positioned within a majority institution. It is almost as if we are like Maryon McDonald's Breton militants, trying to convince the masses that they are oppressed.

This brings me to the second conclusion to this chapter, concerning what I called the "dubious ethics" of fieldwork. Despite all the talk about dialogue, anthropologists are still mostly in the position of using other people's words in ways beyond the control of those others. Indeed, our critical, analytical insights depend upon being able to see what others fail to see, or upon creating new meanings for old scripts. When I look back at my Colonial Williamsburg fieldwork I am discomfited by the gap between the fairly amicable relations I had with people in the field, on the one hand, and their angered or bewildered response to the published results of that fieldwork, on the other. In the field, we all entered into those social relations in good faith. I was genuinely fascinated by Colonial Williamsburg and eager to learn as much about the place as I could. The natives were often eager to tell their stories, however much they may have edited or altered them for my benefit. But the natives didn't understand the critical framework into which their words would be made to fit—or, perhaps, to say it more fairly, they didn't understand how much they might have been revealing about their world.

The dubious ethics of fieldwork cannot be remedied simply by picking the right side, by sticking up for the underdog, or (to return to the terms that frame this chapter) by championing minority causes. Both minorities and majorities are socially constructed, contingent, and, above all, never homogeneous. Anthropological knowledge will never unproblematically represent "the" majority or minority position. Our work will always offend, contradict, or hurt some people, even some of those whose cause we believe is just.

14

The Illusion of Paradise

PRIVILEGING MULTICULTURALISM IN HAWAI'I

JONATHAN Y. OKAMURA

COMPARED to seemingly homogeneous societies such as Japan and Korea, Hawai'i appears especially diverse in its cultures. The population includes twelve major groups, which are, in approximately decreasing order of size, whites, Japanese, Filipinos, Native Hawaiians, Chinese, Portuguese, African Americans, Koreans, Okinawans, Puerto Ricans, Samoans, and Vietnamese. Furthermore, multiculturalism is celebrated and boasted about in Hawai'i and is valued as a societal asset rather than viewed as a source of social discord or conflict as it is in Malaysia and Turkey. Race and ethnicity are not perceived as fostering the disuniting or balkanization of Hawai'i.

This chapter discusses various aspects of Hawai'i as a multicultural society, particularly the prevalent view that the islands represent an especially harmonious and tolerant setting of race and ethnic relations. Recent ethnic conflicts in Los Angeles and other major American cities, Bosnia, the Middle East, and Rwanda certainly have contributed to the continuing perception that Hawai'i is indeed a special place in its appreciation and accommodation of cultural diversity. I shall critically review various dimensions of what has been referred to as the "Hawai'i multicultural model" (S. Yim, "Hawaii's Ethnic Rainbow: Shining Colors, Side by Side," *Sunday Star-Bulletin & Advertiser*, Jan. 5, 1992: B1–B2) and discuss the challenge that the Hawaiian sovereignty movement poses to majoritarian views of multiculturalism in Hawai'i.

The Promise of Hawai'i

One need not search very long or far for overly positive depictions of contemporary ethnic relations in Hawai'i. Academics, journalists, and novelists have all contributed to the reification of Hawai'i as a multiracial paradise. In recent years Hawai'i has been characterized as "the nation's experiment in multiculturalism" (Dan Boylan, quoted in S. Yim, "Hawaii's Ethnic Rainbow," Jan. 5, 1992: B1), a " 'freak'—a multiethnic society that really works" (Kent 1994), a "best-case scenario" of ethnic relations (Center for Research on Ethnic Relations n.d.: 1), an "ethnic rainbow of shining colors, side by side" (S. Yim, "Hawaii's Ethnic Rainbow," Jan. 5, 1992: B1), and "living proof that a community composed of minority groups . . . can still peacefully develop a unifying common culture required to prevent a Tower of Babel" (Grant and Ogawa 1993: 139). In these glorious portrayals, emphasis is also placed on the "unique" nature of race relations in Hawai'i compared to other interracial settings throughout the world.

These glowing descriptions of race and ethnic relations in Hawai'i are not new; they unfortunately represent a continuation of a trend that began in the 1920s. Romanzo Adams (1926: 213), the pioneer of race relations studies in Hawai'i, was perhaps the first to characterize the islands as a "racial melting pot." Adams (1934: 148) also expressed his view of the uniqueness of race relations in Hawai'i with his argument that an "unorthodox race doctrine" of equality prevailed (unorthodox, that is, from the perspective of whites at that time). Robert Park, who had a substantial influence on sociologists at the University of Hawai'i engaged in race relations research (e.g., Andrew Lind and Bernhard Hormann), referred to Hawai'i as "the most notable instance of a melting pot of the modern world" in his introduction to Lind's *An Island Community* (1938). Echoing Gunnar Myrdal's *An American Dilemma* (1944), Wittermans (1964: 154) maintained that there was an "overall ideology largely accepted by all ethnic categories" or a "Hawaiian creed" consisting of the "belief that Hawaii's multiracial population lives and works in perfect interracial harmony," a belief found to have moral overtones. Lind (1969: 9), for many years the foremost scholar of race relations studies in Hawai'i, expressed agreement with Adams in his observation that "the important and distinctive fact about Hawaiian race relations is, of course, the existence of a code of equalitarian relations which is deeply rooted in and has developed out of customary conduct of a similar nature."

Beyond the continued glorification of Hawai'i as a racial paradise, there is also the recent effort to advance the "Hawai'i multicultural model" as an example for emulation by the rest of the United States and the world.

Among the objectives of the Center for Research on Ethnic Relations at the University of Hawai'i are "to determine why ethnic harmony exists in Hawai'i" and "to export principles of ethnic harmony to the mainland and the world" (n.d.: 1). This center apparently does not think that a worthy research issue would be first to determine whether ethnic harmony exists and then to elucidate its scope and nature. Perhaps in an effort to transmit ethnic-harmony principles, the University of Hawai'i Department of American Studies, in conjunction with the Asian American Studies Center at the University of California, Los Angeles, has been offering a summer course entitled "Multiculturalism at Work: Is Hawai'i the Model?" since 1992 to students from both California and Hawai'i. Others have maintained that "if America's mushrooming minority populations are to live together in harmony, perhaps they should take a close look at our multicultural test tube" (S. Yim, "Hawaii's Ethnic Rainbow," Jan. 5, 1992: B1).

This belief that Hawai'i can serve as an exemplary model of race and ethnic relations for other societies also is not new and was expressed over 30 years ago by Lawrence Fuchs (1961: 449) in his well-known social history, *Hawai'i Pono*: "Hawaii illustrates the nation's revolutionary message of equality of opportunity for all, regardless of background, color, or religion. This is the promise of Hawaii, a promise for the entire nation and indeed, the world, that peoples of different races and creeds can live together, enriching each other, in harmony and democracy." Fuchs perhaps can be credited with introducing the notion of "harmony" into the discourse on Hawai'i race relations; however, at least some observers seem to be obsessed with this term and tend to use it without much reflection, and certainly without much definition. Thus, what exactly constitutes the multicultural model of Hawai'i needs to be clarified.

The Hawai'i Multicultural Model

The primary elements of the Hawai'i multicultural model reviewed below are not necessarily included by all of the scholars and journalists whose writings I discuss. Neither do all of them explicitly advocate the "Hawai'i multicultural model" in those specific terms. I have included as proponents of the model those who maintain that race and ethnic relations in Hawai'i can serve as an example or model for the rest of the United States or who argue that these relations are essentially based on tolerance, harmony, and equality, in marked contrast to more conflictual relations in the continental United States or elsewhere. The dimensions of the multicultural model include

1. a "tradition of tolerance and peaceful coexistence" (S. Yim, "Hawaii's Ethnic Rainbow," Jan. 5, 1992: B1) that can be traced to the traditional Hawaiian value of *aloha* (Grant and Ogawa 1993: 146–48);
2. "harmonious" race and ethnic relations evident in "cordial" and "low keyed" social relationships and in relatively high rates of intermarriage compared to those of the continental United States (Boylan 1993: xii; Center for Research on Ethnic Relations n.d.: 1; Grant and Ogawa 1993: 139; editorial, "Racial Trends: Hawai'i Will Be a Special Place," *Sunday Star-Bulletin & Advertiser*, Dec. 6, 1992: B2);
3. "equalization of opportunity and status" in the ethnic stratification order (Lind 1980: 90); and
4. a shared "local" culture and identity evident in "multicultural lifestyles" and based on "points of commonality" (Grant and Ogawa 1993: 149–50; Ogawa 1981: 7).

I will discuss each of these interrelated elements in turn.

The Tradition of Tolerance and Peaceful Coexistence

The notion that Hawai'i has a unique tradition of tolerance and peaceful coexistence can be traced back to Adams (1936: 5–6) and his concern with "mores of racial equality" evident in social rituals of etiquette, which he stated symbolized equality of social status. Adams (1934: 150) maintained, incorrectly in my view, that the origin of these racial mores and of the general pattern of race relations as he described them could be found in the initial interactions between Hawaiian royalty and Europeans and Americans, which were supposed to have been based on mutual "respect and deference." One can only wonder how such deferential attitudes and behaviors on the part of foreigners so quickly resulted in the decimation of Native Hawaiians, the destruction of their traditional culture, and the seizure of their land.

Kirkpatrick (1987: 310), although not an advocate of the Hawai'i multicultural model, has noted the "cultural emphasis on tolerance and acceptance" referred to in popular terms as the "aloha spirit." Grant and Ogawa (1993: 146–48) refer to *aloha kanaka* (love for people) as the "Native Hawaiian legacy of tolerance," particularly concerning race and intermarriage, that had the effect of curtailing the prejudices of the various groups immigrating to Hawai'i. Certainly, in their openness to outsiders, Native Hawaiians historically have had a major role in establishing the "benign" quality of race and ethnic relations in the islands (Kent 1994: 3). As a cultural value applied to ethnic relations, aloha is not simply a survival from precontact Hawai'i but has become very much a part of the social norms of ethnic relationships. These norms stipulate that ideally such relationships should be cordial and without prejudice against others of differing ethnicity. As noted by Kirkpatrick (1987: 314), one reason ethnic conflict is likely to be "muted" in Hawai'i is that it is viewed as "fouling the nest." Obviously, the everyday reality of race and ethnic relations does not always correspond to normative behavioral prescriptions, and indeed there are ethnic antagonism and hostility which are commonly expressed covertly or indirectly, as through the telling of ethnic jokes. Certainly a distinctive feature of race and ethnic relations in Hawai'i has been and continues to be the relative absence of collective violence in which groups seek literally to kill one another. While individual acts of ethnoviolence are not uncommon, there have been only two major incidents of group violence, both of which occurred during the difficult labor organizing movement prior to World War II: the "Hanapepe massacre" in 1924, in which sixteen striking Filipino plantation workers and four policemen were killed and many others wounded, and the "Hilo massacre" in 1938, in which 50 striking dockworkers were injured but no one was killed (Fuchs 1961: 235, 238).

From another perspective, Franklin Odo (quoted in S. Yim, "Hawaii's Ethnic Rainbow," Jan. 5, 1992: B1) has argued that the emphasis on tolerance and acceptance serves as a means of obscuring the more negative aspects of race and ethnic relations in Hawai'i: "It's kind of a mythology that allows us to cover up bad interethnic, interracial relations." This perhaps is the primary reason for the continued insistence that tolerance and congenial coexistence obtain among ethnic groups despite obvious evidence and knowledge to the contrary; it allows multicultural Hawai'i to avoid acknowledging and addressing the differential power and status among groups and the resulting resentment and tensions that have been generated (Okamura 1994: 165).

Harmonious Social Relations

The relatively high rate of intermarriage in Hawai'i compared to the continental United States is often cited as evidence of the harmonious nature of race and ethnic relations. From some of Adams's publications (1936, 1937), it appears that his arguments concerning racial equality in Hawai'i were primarily based on what were perceived as comparatively high rates of interracial marriage during the 1920s and 1930s. (In fact, those outmarriage rates of 19.2 percent between 1920 and 1930 and 22.8 percent between 1930 and 1940 [Lind 1980: 114] are about one-half of recent rates of intermarriage in Hawai'i. Recent figures indicate that 45.4 percent of marriages in which at least one spouse is a state resident are outmarriages [Hawai'i State Department of Business 1993: 87].) But Adams was comparing Hawai'i outmarriage rates with the undoubtedly lower rates on the U.S. mainland, where in some states, such as California, laws had been passed that prohibited marriage between certain racial groups. Intermarriage in Hawai'i prior to World War II was significantly affected by demographic factors, that is, a relative lack of women among Chinese and Filipinos and small numbers of Puerto Ricans and Koreans. Furthermore, not all groups were participating in interracial marriage to the same extent. The outmarriage rate of females of the dominant group, that is, haole women, has always been substantially lower than that for Hawai'i as a whole. For example, it was 10.7 percent in 1930–40 (Lind 1980: 114), and it was 27.2 percent in 1989, when the intermarriage rate for Hawai'i was 44.3 percent ("Who Marries Whom," *Honolulu Star-Bulletin*, Apr. 22, 1991: D4).

Clearly, Adams considered the prevalence of outmarriage highly significant for the nature of ethnic relations in Hawai'i. His "Summary Statement" of race relations in Hawai'i is concerned with intermarriage and the social status of the progeny of those marriages (1936: 5–6). In Adams's view, comparatively high rates of interracial marriage were indicative of, perhaps even equated with, racial equality and harmony in the wider society of Hawai'i. Perhaps more than any other factor, the prevalence of outmarriage has contributed to both sociological and popular notions of Hawai'i as having exceedingly harmonious and tolerant race and ethnic relations.

Intermarriage, even at high rates, does not, however, encompass or even represent the scope and nature of ethnic relations in society. While clearly influenced by the structure of ethnic group relations, intermarriage nonetheless is still fundamentally an interpersonal relationship. There has been a decided tendency to overemphasize the significance of outmarriage on the overall quality of interethnic relations in Hawai'i. High rates of intermarriage may indicate an ethnically tolerant society but not necessarily a harmonious or egalitarian one.

Rather than continuing to be harmonious, Odo and Yim (1993: 227, 229) contend that race relations "aren't as good as they used to be" and that ethnic tensions are growing. Odo (cited in editorial "Racial Trends," Dec. 6, 1992: B2) maintains that, rather than other states following the Hawai'i example, the opposite could occur, with outbreaks of mainland-type racial conflicts. Perhaps the major contributing factor in these developments is the increasing lack of socioeconomic opportunities in Hawai'i, which has created harsh competition for jobs, housing, education, and other benefits and privileges. While the expansion of the economy from the 1960s to the 1980s provided avenues for upward social mobility for the descendants of some of the immigrant plantation groups and thereby fostered ethnic stability, the continuation of such opportunities appears increasingly less likely given the state's overdependence on tourism, an industry dominated by low-wage, low-mobility, and low-security jobs. As Kent (1994: 3) observes,

> Our one-crop (tourism) economy stagnates. Few middle class jobs are generated. The gap between the wealthy and poor widens. Announcements of openings for "affordable" housing spawn mob scenes. While young middle class Asians find themselves on the downward escalator, working class Native Hawaiians, Filipinos and Samoans (those largely excluded from the economic gains of the last generation) are trapped in a slow growth, high cost/low wage, limited opportunity economy.

Such an economy cannot ensure continued ethnic stability in the immediate future, let alone a satisfying quality of life for Hawaii's people.

Equality of Opportunity

Lind is the principal advocate of the equal-opportunity dimension of the Hawai'i multicultural model, although, as noted above, Adams (1934: 148) and Fuchs (1961: 449) also have argued for it in the past. Despite much evidence to the contrary, which he acknowledges, Lind (1980: 90) has argued that there has been a "steady trend toward an equalization of opportunity and status across ethnic lines with reference to the occupational life of the Islands. *Obvious inequalities*, based in part on the order of arrival, the length of residence in Hawaii, and the cultural traditions of each group, still exist and will continue for some time in the future, but the difference becomes less apparent with each passing decade" (emphasis added). In perhaps his last published article on race and ethnic relations in Hawai'i, Lind (1982: 148) continued to maintain that it was possible for ethnic groups "brought here at the very bottom of the economic ladder to move upward, some of them to the very top," despite his acknowledgment that clear differences in income, occupational, and educational status obtain among groups.

My analyses of ethnicity and ethnic relations in Hawai'i (1982, 1990, 1996) have taken issue with the equality-of-opportunity thesis supposedly evident in socioeconomic mobility. I have maintained, to the contrary, that institutionalized inequality and differential access to socioeconomic positions are more characteristic of the social status order than is equality of access and status. Certainly, if one's time frame extends back to the turn of the century, when Chinese and Japanese laborers were leaving the plantations in large numbers and entering urban occupations, then it could be said that socioeconomic mobility has occurred over time, at least for those two groups. But if the time frame is restricted to the past two decades following the poststatehood economic boom of the 1960s, and if Native Hawaiians, Filipinos, Samoans, and other disadvantaged minorities are included in the analysis, then whether socioeconomic mobility has obtained for these latter groups, and thus whether upward mobility is the dominant process in the social status order, can be legitimately questioned. Native Hawaiians, Filipinos, and Samoans continue to be underrepresented at the upper levels of the occupational scale as professionals, executives, and technical workers, but overrepresented in lower-level positions as laborers and service workers (Okamura 1996). They also have comparatively lower levels of educational attainment, particularly in higher education, which indicates that significant occupational mobility is not especially likely for them in the short term.

The 1990 U.S. census data on socioeconomic status did not indicate much change in the ethnic stratification order in Hawai'i (Okamura 1996). The economy of Hawai'i during the 1980s became even more dependent on tourism than it was during the 1970s, with tourism increasing its leading share of the gross state product to 38 percent (Okamura 1994: 167). A tourism-dependent economy implies that jobs are being created primarily in service, sales, and construction categories rather than in white-collar positions that can provide significant avenues for occupational and income mobility for subordinate ethnic groups. And certainly a slumping tourist industry, such as has been the case since 1991 and is likely to occur again at regular intervals in the future, has even more of a negative impact on socioeconomic mobility.

In truth, social-status mobility is possible in Hawai'i, but it is limited through competitive achievement primarily to individuals based on merit and personal qualifications, rather than being open to minority groups as an institutionalized social process. As haoles, Chinese, and Japanese continue to maintain their dominant positions in the social stratification order, fewer viable avenues and means for both individual and group mobility are available for subordinate ethnic minorities.

In arguing that the ethnic stratification order in Hawai'i may not be as static as I have maintained it is, Grant and Ogawa (1993: 154) cite the Filipinos as a group on the verge of "assimilation into the economic and educational structures of island society." However, twenty years ago the Filipinos already were being referred to as "the next group to make it" and as a "sleeping giant" soon to be aroused to assume their political and economic place in Hawai'i. With substantial numbers of Filipinos as well as other minorities, especially immigrants, employed in the tourist industry, their prospects for upward social mobility may well be limited by factors in the global economy, particularly the continued Japanese and other multinational investment in Hawai'i that creates only service-industry jobs, rather than by their supposed "relative lack of experience or concern with financial success" (Lind 1982: 139).

Localism as Multiculturalism

Local culture in Hawai'i is often described in terms consistent with elements of the Hawai'i multicultural model, that is, harmony and tolerance among ethnic groups based on a shared culture. Ogawa (1981: 7) has argued that "the local culture of Hawai'i has been recognized since the 1920s as a prime example of the ability of diverse peoples to live harmoniously together" and that "the Island culture, the way of interacting, is very low keyed and shaped by consideration for others." Yet even a cursory review of Hawai'i history in the 1920s (as in other decades) provides numerous examples of ethnic conflict rather than harmony: plantation strikes by Filipino and Japanese workers in 1920 and 1924, racist efforts to close the Japanese-language press and language schools, and especially harsh negative stereotyping and prejudice against Filipinos. Also, in 1921, in testimony to a committee of the U.S. House of Representatives, the secretary of the Hawaiian Sugar Planters Association declared in clearly unharmonious terms, "The Territory of Hawaii is now and is going to be American; it is going to remain American under any condition and we are going to control the situation out there. The white race, the white people, the Americans in Hawaii are going to dominate and will continue to dominate—there is no question about it" (U.S. Congress 1921: 300–301).

More recently, Grant and Ogawa (1993: 150) have contended that local culture has resulted from a cultural "blending process" involving a "negotiation of . . . points of commonality" that provide a "common ground of understanding." These points of commonality are described as including certain food preferences, particular customs and traditions, ethnic joke telling, shared folk beliefs (Ogawa 1981: 7), and extended family relationships (Grant and Ogawa 1993: 150). They claim that the "cultural history of the Hawaiian islands in the last century has been a continuous process of finding points of commonality, negotiating the ties by which diversity can be maintained while acting together with mutual reward and comfort" (ibid.). Elsewhere I have argued that, except for certain customs and traditions, the above points of commonality are essentially trivial and can hardly provide the basis for a shared culture among ethnic groups in Hawai'i, or anywhere else, for that matter (1994: 164). Moreover, while there may well be some points of commonality, the history of Hawai'i over the last century also manifests much evidence of ethnic conflict, such as the overthrow of the Hawaiian monarchy in 1893, the numerous sugar and pineapple workers' and dockworkers' strikes from 1909 through 1958, and the emergence of the anti-Japanese backlash in the mid-1970s.

I also have criticized the notion of "blending" in the development of local culture insofar as that culture is said to include those of various ethnic groups in Hawai'i (1980, 1994). It is more likely that a common culture emerged over time as a cumulative result of social interactions among individuals from different ethnic groups at work, school, church, in the home (including through intermarriage), in the community, and in leisure activities, through which they gained familiarity with and knowledge of each other's cultural values, beliefs, norms, and practices, without there being any necessary blending or mixing of distinct cultures. Perhaps the most symbolic aspect of local culture and identity, Hawai'i creole, or pidgin English, is hardly the result of a blending of the languages or even individual words of the various local groups in Hawai'i. Pidgin is basically English with numerous Hawaiian loanwords; it has very few linguistic contributions from other ethnic groups that commonly speak it. Local culture cannot simply be compared to a "mixed plate lunch" of individual food items from different ethnic groups (see Grant and Ogawa 1993: 149). If it can be reduced to such a trivial notion, then we may as well accept local comedian Frank DeLima's characterization of Hawai'i as a "chop suey nation . . . all mixed up" (1991: v).

Rather than points of commonality, Odo and Yim (1993: 225) emphasize "ethnic pressure points," the neglect of which, they argue, has resulted in the deterioration of ethnic relations in Hawai'i. These pressure points include (1) the difficulty that Hawai'i society has in relating to newcomers, such as whites and African Americans from the continental United States and Asian and Pacific Islander immigrants; (2) social problems created by the tourism-based economy that employs large numbers of those immigrants and mainland newcomers; (3) developing tensions generated by the changing image and status of Japanese Americans; and (4) the potential for the Hawaiian sovereignty movement to be perceived as a threat to other ethnic groups. These pressure points pertain to significant areas of differential power, privilege, and status in contemporary ethnic relations that cannot be dismissed through appeals to a romanticized notion of a historical "acting together with mutual reward and comfort."

My perspective on local identity emphasizes its historical origin in the common working-class background prior to World War II of the groups that are considered local, that is, Native Hawaiians and the immigrant plantation groups, rather than arguing in terms of a blended or mixed culture (Okamura 1994: 162–63). The groups that perceive themselves and are perceived as local shared a subordinate social status in opposition to the dominant haole planter and merchant oligarchy. Since the mid-1960s, local identity has gained greater significance and has come to represent the common identity of people in Hawai'i who have an appreciation of and a commitment to the land, peoples, and cultures of the islands (Okamura 1980: 131; 1994: 174). Local culture and identity have emerged as expressions of resistance and opposition to external forces of development and change that are perceived as threatening the quality of life in the islands and that have marginalized Hawaii's people. Like Japanese identity and culture, as discussed by Yoshino in this volume, local culture and identity are representations of cultural nationalism that have been enhanced by processes of internationalization, ironically by Japanese (and other) investment in Hawaii's economy.

Localism, the view that a distinct local culture and identity are shared and valued by various peoples in the islands, might be considered the Hawai'i variant of multiculturalism insofar as it is inclusive of a wide diversity of ethnic groups. Local culture and identity, however, are not inclusive of all groups; they exclude groups such as haoles, African Americans, immigrants and other newcomers, the military, and tourists.[1] Localism is thus fundamentally a limited, if not divisive, form of multiculturalism, since it establishes and maintains categorical boundaries between local and nonlocal groups. Rather than being a universal, all-inclusive category, "local" is a relative designation insofar as groups and individuals consider themselves or are considered as local in relation to others who are not so perceived (Okamura 1994: 165).

Privileging the Model

Proponents of the Hawai'i multicultural model have a highly limited, if not distorted, perspective on race and ethnic relations in the islands. Because of their overriding concern with establishing the uniqueness or at least the distinctiveness of the Hawai'i situation so that it can be advanced as a model for emulation in other parts of the United States, they ignore or are blind to disturbing aspects of local race and ethnic relations, including ongoing racism and prejudice, institutional discrimination, and increasing ethnic tensions and hostilities that have become all-too-common features of everyday life. Recent violent confrontations between Filipino and Samoan students and between African American and local students in the public schools are a disturbing indication of the extent to which local ethnic relations are approximating the situation on the U.S. mainland.

Advocates of the multicultural model have an especially superficial understanding of Hawai'i history. They believe it can be summarized as a collective, mutually rewarding search for commonalities, and thus they systematically omit the struggles against, and resistance to, haole domination and control carried on by Native Hawaiians and the immigrant plantation groups for well over a century. In their zealous efforts to project ethnic tolerance and harmony into the past, despite history indicating otherwise, model proponents reject evidence of ethnic conflict and antagonism. I would not deny that relations among groups and individuals of differing race and ethnicity are qualitatively "better" in Hawai'i than in the continental United States and elsewhere, but that premise should not lead us to overlook Hawai'i's problematic areas of intolerance and inequality.

It should be no surprise that none of the above-cited supporters of the Hawai'i multicultural model are Native Hawaiian, Filipino, or Samoan or from another disadvantaged group. Advocacy of the model maintains the current structure of ethnic relations in Hawai'i, particularly the subjugation of the above groups. Given their majority status, proponents of the model are in a privileged position from which they can advance their perspective of race and ethnic relations and have it accepted as the dominant view. A decentered perspective from minority groups at the political and economic margins of Hawai'i society would be quite opposed to the multicultural model promoted from the center. It is extremely doubtful that these groups would agree that tolerant, accepting, harmonious, and egalitarian relations characterize their historical and contemporary experiences in Hawai'i. The Native Hawaiian sovereignty movement provides such a decentered view of multiculturalism in Hawai'i (see below).

Majorities as Minorities

One reason often cited for the seemingly harmonious and egalitarian quality of race and ethnic relations in Hawai'i is that "no one race is a majority" or, conversely, that all the racial and ethnic groups are minorities (Grant and Ogawa 1993: 139; Boylan, cited in S. Yim, "Hawaii's Ethnic Rainbow," Jan. 5, 1992: B1). Even comedian Frank DeLima (1991: v), who makes his living perpetuating if not creating ludicrous stereotypes of various ethnic groups in Hawai'i, has observed, "Nobody is in the majority here. We are all part of at least one minority group." This use of the terms "majority" and "minority" obviously pertains to numerical representation rather than to the more commonly understood sociological definitions that refer to political and economic status. While Waikiki comedians can be excused for not knowing any sociology, the extent to which both academics and journalists in Hawai'i misuse and misunderstand these terms, which are quite familiar to students in introductory sociology courses, is surprising. It results in declarations such as " 'Minorities Rule' Still Holding True in Isles" (*Honolulu Advertiser*, June 14, 1991: A1) and "Hawai'i never had a white majority" (*Sunday Star-Bulletin & Advertiser* 1992: B2). These statements are true in terms of population, but not in relation to social status; haoles dominated Hawai'i economically by the mid-nineteenth century, once private ownership of land had been established through the Great Mahele (land division) in 1848–50,[2] and dominated the island politically as well after the overthrow of the Hawaiian monarchy in 1893.

Numerical population rather than social status is emphasized in the discursive use of the terms "majority" and "minority" precisely because it obscures the obvious socioeconomic-status inequalities among ethnic groups (see Okamura 1990, 1996) and is thus consistent with the view of Hawai'i as an egalitarian model of ethnic relations. Viewed in terms of these status inequities, Hawai'i as an ethnically stratified society is quite comparable to other such societies, including the continental United States, and therefore the claim to the uniqueness of the Hawai'i situation is less valid. The emphasis on demographic population rather than social status, especially in reference to the term "majority," also masks the monopoly of political and economic power wielded by haoles as an oligarchy of planters, merchants, and politicians during much of Hawaii's history from the late nineteenth century to the middle of the present century. During this period, while haoles never constituted a numerical majority of the population, their small numbers (6,200 in 1890, according to Lind 1980: 34) did not prevent them from dethroning the Hawaiian queen and establishing their own republic. Through Republican control of the territorial government following annexation by the United States in 1898, haoles could be said to have dominated Hawai'i politically until 1954, when the multiethnic Democratic Party for the first time gained majority control of both houses of the territorial legislature from the haole-dominated Republican Party.

Consistent with the emphasis on demography rather than political status, the possibility of a single group composing a numerical majority of Hawaii's population is viewed by some as a danger to the "balanced" structure of race and ethnic relations. When longtime governor John A. Burns was asked by a journalist (possibly in the 1960s) what the one situation was that he saw as threatening the harmony of race relations in Hawai'i, he responded by writing "51%" on a piece of paper (Grant and Ogawa 1993: 152–53). He is said to have explained that if any one ethnic group were to emerge as a numerical majority, the supposed balance in ethnic relations would be substantially upset because the group would be able to dominate elections and thereby establish public policy for the others, thus generating ethnic conflicts. Similarly, Boylan (quoted in S. Yim, "Hawaii's Ethnic Rainbow," Jan. 5, 1992: B1) contends, "Our political model is no one constitutes that 50.1 percent that's necessary to oppress anyone else. . . . Whoever has wanted to govern in this state has had to form a coalition across ethnic lines."

The above reasoning gives far too much weight to demographics alone. Japanese Americans have been stereotyped as "dominating" local politics (F. Odo, "The Rise and Fall of the Nisei," *Hawai'i Herald*, Aug.-Nov. 1984), even though their proportion of the state population is less than one-fourth and has been steadily declining since 1920 (Lind 1980: 134). However, while Japanese Americans represented the largest group in both houses of the state legislature in 1994, notably a numerical majority in the Senate (including one Republican), by no means does that numerical dominance result in Japanese American control of state government. The simple reason is that these legislators do not vote, let alone cooperate, with one another as a unified bloc. As evident from the "anti-Japanese backlash" (Kotani 1985: 174) that emerged in the 1970s, when Japanese Americans held most of the major statewide elective positions in Hawai'i, ethnic tensions and animosities arise when a group is perceived to have more than its fair share of political and economic power relative to its proportion of the population, rather than when it constitutes a numerical majority of the population.

A more significant factor in the maintenance of ethnic stability than the fact that no ethnic group constitutes a population majority is that, at least since 1954, no such group, no matter what its size, has wielded both political and economic power. The pre-1954 monopolization by haoles of the political and economic orders generated substantial resentment and hostility against them on the part of most groups in Hawai'i, which unfortunately continues to the present, although Haoles compose one-third of the state population.

Another reason advocates of the multicultural model emphasize that the emergence of a group with a numerical majority of the population would pose a threat to ethnic harmony is that no group is anywhere near that proportion; this implies that ethnic relations must be harmonious. According to the 1990 U.S. census, Hawaii's population of 1.1 million includes whites (33.4 percent), Japanese (22.3 percent), Filipinos (15.2 percent), Native Hawaiians (12.5 percent), Chinese (6.2 percent), African Americans (2.5 percent), Koreans (2.2 percent), Samoans (1.4 percent), and Vietnamese (0.5 percent) (Hawaii State Department of Business 1993: 44). Figures from the Hawai'i Health Surveillance Program survey of the state Department of Health, which uses ethnic classification procedures different from the primarily self-identification principles used by the U.S. Census Bureau, indicate that the white percentage of the population is even smaller (23.2 percent), although whites are still the largest group (ibid.: 42).[3]

The Native Hawaiian Challenge: Multiculturalism or Nationalism

The Native Hawaiian movement for sovereignty and for recognition of the unique rights of the indigenous people of Hawai'i represents a critical challenge to the Hawai'i multicultural model and to general conceptions of race and ethnic relations in Hawai'i, particularly in terms of majority-minority relations. In constructing and asserting their collective identity as *na kanaka maoli*, the "real" or native people of Hawai'i, Native Hawaiians are distinguishing themselves from the other groups, who are all immigrants. As the indigenous people of Hawai'i, Native Hawaiians also are emphasizing that they are not merely another disadvantaged ethnic minority, such as Filipinos or Samoans, and that they do not necessarily share a common local culture and identity with other groups. Furthermore, in claiming certain rights and privileges, particularly *ea*, or sovereignty, for themselves as the native people of Hawai'i, Native Hawaiians are challenging the very structure of race and ethnic relations and are seeking a political and economic status that cannot readily be accommodated by the multicultural model of Hawai'i.

There is a very strong cultural basis for the assertion of the identity of Native Hawaiians as *na kanaka maoli* that is evident beginning with its expression in the Hawaiian language rather than in English. Since the early 1970s there has been a veritable renaissance of Hawaiian culture (Kanahele 1982: 25) that is manifest in the revitalization and expression of cultural values, beliefs, customs, and practices. Hawaiian traditional dance, music, arts and crafts, religious rituals and beliefs, and health and healing practices have flourished as *kupuna* (elders) have passed on their knowledge and experience to younger generations. The Hawaiian language, which is not widely spoken within the Native Hawaiian community because of the historical prohibition on its use, continues to gain new speakers each year through the efforts of Native Hawaiians to converse in the language among themselves and through the offering of courses in schools and at the University of Hawai'i.

This substantial interest in, adherence to, and articulation of their culture, especially its more traditional aspects, distinguish Native Hawaiians from other ethnic groups in Hawai'i. The latter (except for recent immigrants among some groups) have become largely acculturated to the local variant of American culture in the islands. While Native Hawaiians historically also have undergone acculturation processes, they have a far greater appreciation and concern for the maintenance and practice of their traditional culture, much of which was forcibly taken away from them, than other ethnic groups have for their respective cultural traditions and beliefs. The longer-established immigrant groups, such as the Chinese, Japanese, Koreans, and Portuguese, do maintain certain traditional cultural practices, but rather than being part of everyday culture, these are commonly associated with rites of passage that commemorate significant life-cycle events. The latter include particular birthdays (fortieth among the Japanese), marriage (wedding practices among all groups), death (traditional funeral beliefs and practices among all groups), New Year's Day (family meal among the Chinese), and certain religious holidays (Holy Ghost day among the Portuguese). Ethnic groups in Hawai'i also have specific values, beliefs, and practices regarding family and kinship, marriage, language, and religion, and it is these institutions of the "domestic or private domain" (Smith 1969: 39) that provide the cultural basis for the maintenance and assertion of their distinct ethnic identities given the prevailing acculturative and assimilative forces in the larger society.

Unlike those other ethnic groups, however, Native Hawaiians have extended their cultural construction and expression of distinctiveness into institutions of the "public domain" (Smith 1969: 39), that is, government, the economy, law, and education. Briefly, in terms of government, there is the effort to establish a sovereign nation or an independent nation-state; in the economy, Hawaiian values emphasize respect for and the sacredness of nature, particularly land, rather than the exploitation and commodification of nature for profit that is characteristic of Western values (Trask 1984–85: 125); in law, Native Hawaiians claim special legal rights, such as the right to practice traditional religious beliefs and rituals, which has been granted to other Native American peoples under federal law; and in education, the state government has established the *Punana Leo* preschools and the "language immersion" elementary schools, in which Native Hawaiian students are taught using their language as the medium of instruction. There are no comparable manifestations of institutional distinctiveness in both the private and public domains among other groups in Hawai'i, which is an indication that Native Hawaiians cannot readily be categorized with them as merely one of numerous ethnic groups.

The more recent origins of the sovereignty movement can be traced to the early 1970s and the establishment of several Native Hawaiian organizations with defined political objectives, such as protesting land abuses and obtaining rights to a land base (Trask 1984–85: 122). The movement then progressed to occupations of restricted areas, most notably the island of Kaho'olawe, which until 1990 was used for bombing practice by the U.S. Navy, and ultimately to declarations of sovereignty and independence in the 1980s.

The sovereignty movement has gained tremendous momentum over the past decade with the emergence of numerous Native Hawaiian organizations that advocate various modes of sovereignty, particularly independence. The largest of these organizations (23,000 registered citizens) is Ka Lahui Hawai'i (The Hawaiian Nation), which was established in 1987 at an islands-wide constitutional convention. Ka Lahui Hawai'i has a formal constitution with executive, legislative, judicial, and *ali'i nui* (chiefly) branches of government and elected officials, including a *kia'aina* (governor), and representatives from each island. Its approach to sovereignty is referred to as the "nation within a nation" model, insofar as Ka Lahui

Hawai'i seeks to gain recognition of a Hawaiian nation under current U.S. law that grants Native American peoples the right to self-governance (Ka Lahui Hawai'i 1991: 4). The land base for this nation would consist of half of the 1.4 million acres of ceded lands currently under state government control, the 190,000 acres of land administered by the state Department of Hawaiian Home Lands, and additional lands to be granted in compensation for the overthrow of Queen Liliuokalani in 1893 ("The Makings of a Nation," *Honolulu Star-Bulletin*, Jan. 12, 1993: A6).[4]

Other sovereignty organizations seek complete independence for the entire Hawaiian archipelago, including uninhabited islands to the northwest, and the establishment of a nation-state in which only Native Hawaiians would have the right to vote and hold office. Some organizations have provisions for non-Hawaiians to become citizens, but without the full rights held by Native Hawaiians. In short, the sovereignty movement consists of a variety of groups that operate on different fronts (local, national, and international) and with different strategies and goals.

Given the substantial support within the Native Hawaiian community for some form of sovereignty and the tremendous progress made by sovereignty groups in organizing and mobilizing that support, it is not surprising that the state government should have entered the debate. In 1991 the state legislature created the Sovereignty Advisory Council, which included fourteen sovereignty organizations as members. The council's sovereignty plan, submitted the following year, was rejected by the state, very likely because it did not ensure state control of the sovereignty process. In 1993 the state legislature established the Hawaiian Sovereignty Advisory Commission, which has nineteen members, including representatives of various state government agencies, appointed by the governor. Several sovereignty groups, particularly those seeking to establish an independent Hawaiian nation and Ka Lahui Hawai'i, declined to nominate representatives to serve on the commission because they viewed it as a state instrument for controlling a sovereignty movement that had begun as a grassroots community initiative.

Some sovereignty organizations also are critical of the Office of Hawaiian Affairs (OHA) and its role in the sovereignty process. OHA is a state agency, created in 1978, and is governed by an all-Native Hawaiian board of trustees, who are elected by Native Hawaiian voters. It has been criticized as an "extension of the state" and as a "powerless" mechanism for Hawaiian self-governance because it lacks control over Hawaiian trust lands (e.g., the Hawaiian Home Lands trust) (Trask 1992: 251). OHA's position statement on sovereignty declares that it "advocates the right of the Hawaiian people to elect a model of nationhood of their own choosing" without formally committing itself to any particular mode of sovereignty ("Elbowroom Is Shrinking Fast in Isles," *Honolulu Star-Bulletin*, Apr. 22,

1994: A1). Nonetheless, the OHA board of trustees recently approved providing $900,000 to the Hawaiian Sovereignty Elections Council (see below) to support its activities during fiscal year 1995. This amount was to be matched by a similar appropriation from the state legislature, contingent on the allocation of OHA funds ("Sovereignty Council Budget Is $1.8 Million," *Ka Wai Ola O OHA*, Aug. 4, 1994: 4).

After conducting public meetings throughout the islands to determine the views and concerns of Native Hawaiians regarding sovereignty, the Hawaiian Sovereignty Advisory Commission was renamed the Hawaiian Sovereignty Elections Council by the state legislature in 1994. The council conducted voter registration and sovereignty education activities for a vote held in 1996. Native Hawaiians voted affirmatively that they should "elect delegates to propose a Native Hawaiian government."[5]

Given substantial state intervention in the sovereignty process, the governor of Hawai'i, himself a Native Hawaiian, said in 1994, "There are few today who doubt that sovereignty will happen. It is a matter of how, when, and in what form" ("Hawaiian Self-Rule," *Honolulu Advertiser*, Apr. 24, 1994: A3). However, other Native Hawaiians have questioned state participation in, if not direction of, a movement that ultimately concerns their political and economic future. Dr. Kekuni Blaisdell, spokesperson for Ka Pakaukau (the Roundtable, a coalition of fourteen sovereignty groups) and a professor of medicine at the University of Hawai'i, argues, "Self determination means we determine, not [U.S.] Senator Inouye, OHA or the state" ("Makings of a Nation," *Honolulu Star-Bulletin*, Jan. 12, 1993: A6).[6] Gladney, in this volume, emphasizes the importance of these conflictual power relations in the "ongoing dialogue" between the state and local ethnic minorities for understanding the present resurgence of cultural nationalisms.

While the state's sovereignty initiative is proceeding, various sovereignty organizations are actively involved in their own community efforts. Until its eviction by the state government in June 1994, the 'Ohana Council had for fifteen months occupied a public beach at Makapu'u, where 150 members and their supporters built a village with taro patches and a stone *ahu*, or religious shrine. 'Ohana Council members, who consider themselves citizens of the "Independent Nation-State of Hawai'i," were relocated as a community to an undeveloped site in Waimanalo, where the state has given them a long-term lease of 69 acres of agricultural land. Ka Pakaukau, in 1993 conducted Ka Ho'okolokolonui Kanaka Maoli (The People's International Tribunal), at which the U.S. government was found guilty of crimes against the Native Hawaiian people. Kekuni Blaisdell reported on the tribunal's proceedings in July 1994 at the annual meeting of the United Nations Working Group on Indigenous Peoples in Geneva. Hui Na'auao, a coalition of more than 40 Hawaiian organizations, not all of which are formally concerned with sovereignty, continues to conduct sovereignty education workshops throughout the islands.

Rather than viewing themselves as an integral part of multicultural Hawai'i along with other ethnic groups, Native Hawaiians (at least those who are in favor of some form of sovereignty) are advancing their unique and therefore privileged status as the native people of Hawai'i. The Native Hawaiian movement thus poses a critical challenge to the multicultural model of Hawai'i and its liberal emphases on tolerance, harmony, equality of opportunity, and a shared local culture and identity. A Native Hawaiian graduate student, Kamana'opono Crabbe, comments, "We [in Hawai'i] talk a lot about the aloha spirit, and people on the mainland think this is paradise. But we native people are the ones who are suffering" ("Native Hawaiians Push to Extend and Deepen University's Diversity," *Chronicle of Higher Education*, Aug. 3, 1994: A29). In pointing to the historical injustices and abuses they have suffered and continue to endure as a colonized people, Native Hawaiians are asserting that they have not benefited from or participated in the various dimensions of the Hawai'i multicultural model, and therefore that multicultural Hawai'i and multicultural America hold little promise for them. Indeed, the basic premise of American multiculturalism—that the United States is a nation of immigrants—is seen as the primary obstacle to Native Hawaiian self-determination: "More than any single actor or agency, the general American ideology that 'everyone is deserving of the same treatment because everyone is an immigrant' works against the recognition and settlement of Hawaiian claims" (Trask 1992: 256–57). Even such an outspoken advocate of multiculturalism as Takaki (1993: 116) could be said to have neglected Native Americans in his notion of "different shores" whence "migrants departed" in the creation of multicultural America, "places such as Europe, Africa, and Asia."

Historically, the emergence and development of multicultural Hawai'i through the arrival of Europeans and Americans and the subsequent importation of plantation laborers from all over the world have resulted not simply in multicultural lifestyles and points of commonality but in Native Hawaiians becoming a "conquered people, their lands and culture subordinated to another nation. Made to feel and survive as inferiors when their sovereignty as a nation was forcibly ended by American military power, Hawaiians were rendered politically and economically powerless by the turn of the century" (Trask 1992: 245).

As a result, in their own homeland, Native Hawaiians rank relatively low in occupational status, income, and educational attainment (Okamura 1996); have the highest rates of diabetes, hypertension, heart disease deaths, cancer deaths, obesity, suicide (among males), and incarceration in Hawai'i prisons (40 percent of inmates), and have the shortest life expectancy ("Special Report: Status of Hawaiians," *Honolulu Star-Bulletin*, Jan. 4, 1993: A6). Given these tragic historical and contemporary conditions, the goal of restoration of the sovereign Hawaiian nation under native control is understandable.

Conclusion

A significant difference between multiculturalism in Hawai'i and multiculturalism on the U.S. mainland pertains to the major challenges that have arisen in opposition to them. In Hawai'i, multiculturalism generally has not been opposed by one of its principal foes in the continental United States, that is, individualism (see Ravitch 1990; Schlesinger 1991). As Schlesinger argues, "Most Americans continue to see themselves primarily as individuals and only secondarily and trivially as adherents of a group." According to Schlesinger, the separation of American society into "fixed ethnicities nourishes a culture of victimization and a contagion of inflammable sensitivities" that threatens the "brittle bonds of national identity that hold this diverse and fractious society together" (1991: 2, 21, 64). Consequently, according to multiculturalism's opponents, group rights and privileges are not to be recognized and provided for.

Multiculturalism in Hawai'i may have escaped the individualism counterargument because of the dominant view that Hawai'i society is composed of a diversity of groups rather than individuals. The Hawai'i multicultural model reinforces this view insofar as it contends that it is essentially groups or individuals as members of groups, rather than individuals per se, that enjoy harmonious and tolerant social relations, intermarry, benefit from socioeconomic mobility, and share a common local culture and identity.

Multiculturalism in Hawai'i also has not been opposed by conservative perspectives, such as individualism, because it is basically a conservative position itself. Despite its liberal rhetoric of tolerance, acceptance, and equality of opportunity, multiculturalism in Hawai'i represents an argument for stability and continuation of the status quo rather than for substantial change in the current structure of race and ethnic relations. This conservative orientation is quite evident in majoritarian responses to the Hawaiian sovereignty movement that emphasize elements of the Hawai'i multicultural model, such as the aloha spirit, and that depict the sovereignty movement as a dangerous threat to ethnic harmony. A recent editorial on sovereignty in one of the Honolulu daily newspapers begins with a glowing tribute to the Hawai'i multicultural model: "Every person who lives in these Islands has experienced the 'aloha spirit,' that warm feeling that comes from being part of a special place" ("Hawaiian Self-Rule," *Honolulu Advertiser*, Apr. 24, 1994: A3). The editorial then issues a warning that, if not handled "wisely," the sovereignty issue "could destroy our spirit of aloha and divide Hawai'i along racial lines." While maintaining that "the Hawaiian community doesn't want this newspaper or political candidates telling them what to do or how," the editorial nonetheless proceeds to outline a "sovereignty plan that benefits all of Hawaii's people" (instead of a plan that will primarily benefit Native Hawaiians); it includes participation by the state and federal governments. Others have accused Hawaiian-sovereignty advocates of engendering for Hawaii's people a "reputation for hate" in their "breach of the old unwritten compact that responsible leaders of all our diverse ethnic groups strive to work things out harmoniously when problems arise" ("Preservation of Aloha Spirit Is Essential," *Honolulu Star-Bulletin*, Sept. 20, 1994: A11). The unfortunate paradox of multiculturalism in Hawai'i is that its seemingly strongest advocates also provide, wittingly or unwittingly, the greatest resistance to the realization of a truly multicultural society that is tolerant, egalitarian, and just.

Notes

1. YOSHINO, THE DISCOURSE ON JAPANESE IDENTITY

1. By "nationalism" I mean both the sentiment among a people that they constitute a community with distinctive characteristics and the project of maintaining and promoting that distinctiveness within an autonomous state. Cultural nationalism attempts to regenerate the national community by creating, maintaining, and strengthening a people's cultural identity when it is felt to be lacking, inadequate, or threatened, whereas political nationalism emphasizes the nation's collective experience as a political reality by achieving or trying to achieve a representative state for its community.

2. An origin or ancestral myth is not always primarily important. Anthony Milner argues that the Malays recognized no single common ancestor but were capable of expressing a vague sense of cultural unity (1982: chap. 1). For the subsequent development of Malay identity, see Milner's chapter in this volume.

3. On Indian and Turkish cultural nationalism, see Yoshino (1992: 40–46). Interesting accounts of Turkish nationalism are also found in the chapters by Deringil and Kirişci in this volume.

4. Frequent cross-cultural contacts were the norm among European aristocrats before the age of nation-states. Cosmopolitanism was then replaced by nationalism. Although we are thus not without a precedent in this sense, contemporary globalism is characterized by its infiltration into many regions of the world and many social classes.

5. In actuality, the objectifying and nonobjectifying approaches are not mutually exclusive. For example, English people often express their ideas of Englishness by suggesting English values in the context of institutions and practices. They may mention various institutions, such as the aristocracy, Oxbridge, or the countryside, to refer to English values embodied in these institutions. For example, they may speak of cricket as something that embodies the English values of fair play and, perhaps, a leisurely pace of life.

6. Among the numerous scholars who provided a theoretical backing for the view of Japanese as group oriented, Nakane (1967) and Doi (1971) are two of the

most prominent. Nakane developed the theory of "vertical society," Doi the theory of *amae*.

7. The term "racialism" is sometimes used in a very different sense. For example, Miles (1984: 245) understands racialism as "denoting the practices which embody or express racism."

8. The only criterion of nation as "imagined community" that does not apply to race is sovereignty.

9. By contrast, "ethnicity" signifies "a possibility for change which 'race' precludes" (Wallman 1986: 229).

10. The word "race" (*jinshu*) as such is not normally used to refer to Japanese people.

11. The Westerners' sense of difference is fundamentally that of superiority, which is understandable, as racism arose in the West as an ideology to rationalize colonialism. By contrast, the Nihonjinron on the whole presented the image of the Japanese as being very different without explicitly claiming superiority, though some of the literature discussed the strengths of Japanese society. Explicit claims of Japanese superiority were not so common as non-Japanese readers, who may equate the Western style of racism with racial thinking in general, might have supposed. (This does not mean that the sense of superiority is absent among the Japanese; that sense is evident in their attitude toward the Korean minority and other Asians in Japan.)

12. The interviews were conducted in a fairly large provincial city in central Japan, a city with a population of several hundred thousand, from October 1986 to September 1988; pilot and supplementary studies were conducted on a number of visits before and after this period. I focused on educators (schoolteachers and principals) and businessmen because these two groups have a profound influence on Japanese society at large. For a detailed analysis of the findings, see Yoshino (1992: chaps. 6–10).

13. Another interpretation identified the Nihonjinron as an attempt to reaffirm and reinvent national identity threatened by Westernization and rapid industrialization. There was also an interpretation that viewed the Nihonjinron as an ideological instrument of class domination by which the dominant class, of which thinkers are part, manipulates the subordinate class by propagating a popular ideology of the uniquely homogeneous and harmonious social culture of Japan.

14. One exception was business elites, who were well-read in theories of Japanese society.

15. Because the Nihonjinron frequently discussed Japanese social culture in the context of management and business practices, they also attracted readers by providing them with ideas and insights considered useful at the workplace. Since these concerns are especially relevant to business elites, business elites were typical consumers of the Nihonjinron.

16. These manuals were published by major Japanese companies such as Mitsubishi, Nippon Steel, Taiyō Kōbe Bank, Nissho Iwai, Toshiba, and so on.

17. Reproducers' intentions of improving intercultural communication are stated in the editorial comments in their cross-cultural manuals. For example, the then president of Taiyō Kōbe Bank (now Sakura Bank) stated that the aim of its hand-

book was to "make a contribution, if modest, to the promotion of an understanding of Japan and the Japanese at a time when comprehension is badly needed to ease mounting trade tensions [and also to] help Japanese students who are destined to live in an era of internationalization, by providing hints about how things Japanese may be expressed in good English" (Taiyō Kōbe Bank 1988: 4). The Nippon Steel Corporation (1984: 11) published its handbook "in the hope of making some further contribution to mutual understanding between the people of Japan and the people of other countries throughout the world." Mitsubishi Corporation (1983: 6) intended its handbook to "help smooth the way for better international communication."

18. The Japanese sense of uniqueness therefore should not be confused with ethnocentrism, which is the belief that one's group is central and most important.

19. This useful concept of "boundary dissonance" was developed by Wallman (1978: 212).

2. OHNUKI-TIERNEY, THE SELF AND THE INTERNAL AND EXTERNAL OTHERS

1. Recent scholarship on those engaged in economic activities involving the sea and the mountains reveals that they too became marginalized. It has added to the complexity of the mosaic of Japanese society. See Amino (1994), Miyata (1993), and Ōbayashi (1983).

2. There have been two types of "foreigners": the elite and the unskilled laborers. Both are "minorities" but are treated enormously differently by the Japanese, who in other contexts nonetheless lump all of them together as, for example, Koreans. See DeVos and Wagatsuma (1966) for a list of minorities in Japan.

3. My work on the Ainu (Ohnuki-Tierney 1974, 1981, 1987) did not deal with their minority status within Japanese society, however.

4. For the archaeological chronology, see Pearson (1992).

5. The name of the grain soul is Masakatsu Akatsu Kachihaya Hiame no Oshihomimi no Mikoto (Kurano and Takeda 1958: 111, 125). Another name for the grandson-cum-first emperor is Amatsu Hiko Hiko Ho no Ninigi no Mikoto, which portrays rice stalks with succulent grains (ibid.: 125). This episode is referred to "as the descent of the heavenly grandson."

6. *Gokoku* means literally "five grains," but the number five meant "many" or "various" in ancient Japan.

7. Note that the Deity of the Rice Paddy has only the nigimitama, or peaceful soul, and drought or flood, which destroys rice paddies, is an act of the Mizu no Kami (Water Deity) rather than an expression of the aramitama (violent spirit) of the Deity of the Rice Paddy.

8. The prototype of Japanese deities was "stranger deities"—a belief in a deity who visits a settlement from outside (see Ohnuki-Tierney 1987).

9. See, for example, the illustrations by Katsushika Hokusai (1760–1849) for "One Hundred Poems by One Hundred Poets." The most common motif by far relates to rice and rice agriculture. Twenty-six prints out of 89 show rice farmers at work, sheaves of harvested rice, or flooded rice paddies. They are numbers 1,

5, 8, 9, 12–14, 17, 19, 20, 22, 23, 30, 39, 44, 47, 65, 68, 70, 71, 77–79, 83, 84, and 90. (For details of my interpretation, see Ohnuki-Tierney 1993.) These woodblocks were titled *Hyakunin isshu uba ga etoki* (Pictures of one hundred poems by one hundred poets, explained by the wet-nurse). They are illustrations of the well-known collection of one hundred poems (*Hyakunin isshu*; lit. One hundred poems, one poem each) selected and completed in 1235 by Fujiwara no Teika (1162–1241), as Hokusai interpreted them from the perspective of the mid-eighteenth century. Hokusai, who started to work on this series at age 76, completed prints for only 27 of the 100 poems but also left many line drawings. Eighty-nine of them are reproduced in the collection by Morse (1989).

Similar motifs appear in the woodblock prints by Andō (Utakawa) Hiroshige (1797–1858) in his "Fifty-Three stations along the Tōkaidō" (Tōkaidō gojū-san-tsugi) (Gotō 1975), as well as in "Sixty-Nine stations along the Kiso road" (Kiso kaidō rokujū-kyū-tsugi) (Gotō 1976), which contains prints by both Hiroshige and Keisai Eisen (1790–?).

10. The masters of these woodblock prints were most likely not the agents of the construction of agrarianism. Note that they produced various other types of woodblock prints. For example, Hokusai produced a famous series of woodblock prints in which the aristocrats (*kuge*) and warriors were caricatured, often by commoners (see Shimizu 1991: 10–14).

11. Note also that the concepts of the *hare* (sacred), the *ke* (profane or day-to-day), and *kegare* (impurity) have been the most important principles of Japanese cosmology and ethos. These notions too derive from agrarian cosmology (Sakurai 1981).

12. A broader picture is the impact of modernity among the intellectuals who assigned dual nature to both the urban and the rural. Thus, while Toulouse-Lautrec celebrated the decadence of Paris, others decried the decay of urban life and exalted the beauty of rural France. Likewise, the masters of the woodblock prints celebrated the urbane but decadent world of the geisha, while others sought refuge in the "uncontaminated" rice paddies. For further details, see Ohnuki-Tierney (1993).

13. These include deer, horses, oxen, and various birds, such as *tsuru* (cranes), *sagi* (herons), *kiji* (pheasants), and *hōō* (phoenixes). Although Buddhistic paintings did portray animals, they were not "wild animals" but were tamed within the context of Buddhistic culture. There were "imaginary animals," including *komainu* (lion-dogs), whose sculptures diffused from China and are placed at the entrances to shrines; Mu'chi's gibbon (see Ohnuki-Tierney 1987); and various other animals depicted by Japanese artists on the basis of original Chinese paintings or as they were described in stories whose setting is outside of Japan.

14. It is hard to pinpoint the birth of a nation, as Anderson (1991) argues. "Japan" or the "Japanese" came into being through long and complex historical processes.

15. See Ohnuki-Tierney (1993) for controversy over the continuity of population from the Jōmon hunting-gathering period to the Yayoi period.

16. These periods consist of the Palaeolithic period (50,000 B.P.–11,000 B.C.) and the Jōmon period (11,000 B.C.–250 B.C.).

17. From this perspective, the seemingly simple change of a national holiday,

April 29, from the Shōwa emperor's birthday, as it originated, to "Green Day" (*Midori no hi*) has a deeper meaning. The holiday continues to be based on the symbolic equation of nature with plants, expressed in *midori* (green), since, as we saw in the myth-histories, the deities, who were ancestral to the imperial family, transformed wilderness into rice paddies, which are green in the spring. On this day, the stock market and public institutions are closed.

18. The "conquest of nature" that lies behind the European hunting tradition does not contradict the view of animals expressed in the biblical tradition. The relationship between humans and nonhuman animals in Japanese cosmology contrasts sharply with the official cosmology expressed in the Old Testament, in which God presides over both humans and animals and is the creator of a classificatory system: culture (humans) and nature (animals) constitute his dyad. As the product of God, the classification or order is sacred and good, whereas its absence is blasphemous—a major sin against God, and thus evil. Humans and animals, therefore, are clearly separated by a sharp line which is guarded by taboos (for a detailed discussion of this topic, see Ohnuki-Tierney 1981: 108–11). In visual representations, religious paintings were succeeded by secular paintings, in which hunting scenes, game, and other subjects related to hunting were depicted, such as in seventeenth-century Flemish painting.

We note here that meat in many western European countries has been class- and gender-linked. Game meat was a symbol of the upper-class people in preindustrial Europe. In the nineteenth century, wild animal meat remained prestigious, while the bourgeoisie ate the meat of domesticated animals. Prestige accrued to hunting (and in fact continues to do so). The food of the lower class and in rural Europe continued to be dominated by dark bread, soup, eggs, and dairy products (Mennell 1985: 62–63). Furthermore, the symbolic opposition between animals and plants is gendered, beginning with the Greco-Roman tradition, through the biblical tradition. Both Greek mythology and the Bible are replete with differential treatment of animal and plant foods: the former receive more prestige and, thus, are assigned to men. In Greek mythology Hercules is the prototype of "man the hunter," whereas Deianira represents "woman the tiller." In the Bible the Lord's preference for Abel over Cain is symbolically expressed through his contrasting treatment of the animal offering from Abel, a keeper of sheep, and the fruit of the ground offering from Cain, a tiller of the ground. Abel and Cain represent a highly complex structure of thoughts, but Cain's association with agriculture and plant food seems to be embedded in a culture that values animals more highly (for details of this argument, see Ohnuki-Tierney 1993: 119–20). Meat is a male food, at least until recently, and hunting is a very masculine activity in many Western countries. Thus even today wild nature, inhabited by wild animals, is important and is part and parcel of those countries' fascination with hunter-gatherers.

Pastoralism, with its emphasis on the economic importance of domesticated animals, has occupied an important symbolic place in many Western cultures. In *Les Très Riches Heures du Duc de Berry* by Le Duc Jean de Berry (1340–1416), housed in Musée de Cluny in Paris, for example, a number of illustrations for each month of the year depict farmers working in the field side by side with those tending the grazing animals. Pastoralism that idealizes "a simplified life in the country" (Frye

1971 [1957]: 43) has a far-reaching effect on the way people in various Western cultures think not only of nature but also of religion, as exemplified in a series of metaphors, such as Christ the lamb, the pastor and the flock, and so forth (Frye 1971 [1957]). With the growing importance of agriculture, grazing land became agricultural land, creating tension between the two modes of using the land—agriculture and pastoralism.

The importance of animals in some European cultures had profound implications. The animal-centered view, or the prejudice against plant food, is found in the views of even prominent scholars. After explaining the caloric advantage of agricultural products, Braudel quite frankly expresses his prejudice: "Now fields were cultivated *at the expense* of hunting-ground and extensive stock-raising. As centuries passed a larger and larger number of people were *reduced to* eating vegetable foods . . . *often insipid and always monotonous*. . . . In ancient Greece it was said that 'the eaters of barley gruel have no desire to make war.' An Englishman centuries later (1776) stated: 'You find more courage among men who eat their fill of flesh than among those who make shift with lighter foods' " (Braudel 1973: 68; emphasis added).

19. Professor Freeman feels strongly that the designation should be "special-status *group*." I am using "people" most of the time in this book primarily to avoid the inference that the special-status *group* is a well-delineated social group throughout history. The use of "people" also frees me from having to use a long phrase such as "members of/individuals from the special-status group."

20. Of these categories, the first three are proposed by Noguchi, while the other four are proposed by Ninomiya, who specifies that these occupations were held by the special-status people during the Kamakura (1185–1392) and the Muromachi (1392–1603) periods.

21. The term "shokunin" as the designation for craftsmen and other "professionals" was first recorded in 1367 (Amino 1980: 105–8; Amino 1983: 186–99), indicating the consolidation of these people as a social group by the mid-fourteenth century.

22. In western Japan, the emperor granted these privileges to these shokunin, since it was he who directly controlled all boundary areas, while regional lords governed their own territories. In eastern Japan, although some of them received these privileges from the emperor, many received them from Minamoto-no-Yoritomo, the shogun (Amino 1980: 133–45). What is not clear, however, is which types of shokunin enjoyed this status and privilege, since there seem to have been a wide range and variety of shokunin at this time. Amino (1984) points to two categories of these privileged nonresidents: the *kugonin*, comprised of certain categories of shokunin, including blacksmiths, and the jinin, religious-cum-artistic specialists, who provided religious services at shrines but who also engaged in cross-regional trading.

23. There has been controversy over the residential pattern of the special-status people. Many scholars claim that they did not have permanent settlements but traveled from village to village. Ochiai (1972: 66–67), citing Yanagita, however, emphatically states that many were not outsiders but members of a community. I suggest that the special-status people in the artistic/religious category were tempo-

rary visitors to farming communities, but that those who engaged in occupations removing impurity were permanent members of settled communities, occupying spatially peripheral areas.

24. Kuroda (1972) does not include the hijiri in the hinin category, but points out that various types of special-status people were lumped together as hijiri-kojiki or kojiki-hinin.

25. The institution of the *tonseisha* (hermit) provided the opportunity for artists or religious specialists with unusual talents to remove themselves physically from the community by living in the mountains to continue their religious or artistic pursuits. Although physically removed from the society, they often achieved their social status because of their reputations. *Amigō* was a similar institution. It referred to a special title given to distinguished artists. Graced with this title, artists enjoyed prestige and respect regardless of their ascribed status. See Hayashiya 1980: 134–40 (for tonseisha), 161–86 (for amigō); Noguchi 1978: 95 (for amigō); Yokoi 1982: 14, 70, 336, 351 (for amigō), 35, 228–30, 284 (for tonseisha).

Although a comparison between the special-status people in Japan and "outcastes" and "untouchables" elsewhere in Asia is beyond the scope of this paper, it should be noted here that, as Kailasapathy (1968: 95) documents, the minstrels (the *pānar*) in India were one of the four noble clans and were held in high esteem until medieval times, when the caste system was formed and the word "pānar" came to mean a lower caste.

26. Biographies of many of the artists and architects during this period recorded their "humble origin," that is, that they belonged to the special-status group. Examples include Zen-ami (1393–1490?), who designed the Fushimi castle for Hideyoshi; Kanami (?–1384) and Zeami (?–1443), the father-son pair who developed the *sarugaku* (the forerunner of the Noh play); and Noami (1397–1471) and other masters of the tea ceremony (Noguchi 1978: 94–95). For an exhaustive treatment of artists during this period, see Hayashiya (1981).

27. For India the concept of "caste" by Dumont (1970) has invited a great deal of controversy.

28. A curious exception to this rule is the *gōmune*, a type of religious street entertainer, whose status was that of the common people and remained as such (Takayanagi 1981: 208–12).

29. See, for example, Bloch (1961 [1949]) and Dumont (1970) for scholarly controversies over the term "feudal" and debates about whether or not the Japanese system was truly a feudal one.

Note also that the Early Modern period saw the establishment of hierarchy among the special-status people themselves, although its development had already been foreshadowed during the Medieval period. For example, Danzaemon in Edo controlled the special-status people in several regions beside his own district in Edo of 46,210 square meters (55,328 square yards) and 232 families; his compound was 8,593 square meters (10,215 square yards). His power and wealth were said to be equal to those of a feudal lord (T. Harada 1971: 428; Takayanagi 1981: 37–57).

Outside their own society, all the "outcaste" members, including Danzaemon, suffered extreme discrimination. For example, Danzaemon frequented one of the most exclusive restaurants in Edo, where there was a special room used solely by him. If for some reason he was fed in a room used by other guests, the owners removed the tatami after his use and replaced it with a new one so that the "polluted" tatami would not contaminate other guests (T. Harada 1971: 428).

It is noteworthy that in contrast to the inflexibility with which the special-status people were defined during this period, there was considerable mobility across the castes/classes of warriors, farmers, craftsmen, and merchants. Some individuals even voluntarily moved down the social ladder. For example, Ishida Baigan, the founder of the Shingaku school of thought, which had a profound effect upon the morality of the common people during the Early Modern period, was of peasant extraction but entered the merchant class before he became a full-time preacher/lecturer (Bellah 1970 [1957]: 134).

30. Note, however, that the definition of "productivity" was problematic. While some people devalued merchants and to a certain degree artisans because they were non-productive in the agrarian sense, others, including prominent Kokugakuha scholars such as Ishida Baigan (1685–1744) and Motoori Nobunaga (1730–1801), considered merchants productive as long as they did not profit only for themselves but delivered services to others and for the economy of the nation at large.

31. More accurate figures for the population are hard to come by. The government census is probably inaccurate; its 1973 figure of 1,048,566 (Ueda 1978a: 3–6), for example, is probably too small.

32. For publications on the contemporary situation, see Buraku Kaihō Kenkyūsho (1978a, 1978b). See also several articles in DeVos and Wagatsuma (1966). None, however, deals with the most recent scene.

33. Most important, the cultures of the Hokkaido, Sakhalin, and Kurile Ainu were very different. To choose but the most conspicuous example, the Hokkaido Ainu, who inhabited ecozones rich in natural resources such as deer and salmon, were hunter-gatherers with permanent settlements with well-established political organizations, while the Sakhalin Ainu annually moved from the summer to the winter settlement, and the Kurile Ainu moved their settlements more frequently (for details of intracultural variation, see Ohnuki-Tierney 1976). Likewise, the history of contact with outsiders was very different for each of these Ainu groups. For example, because of relative isolation and the absence of diffusion of technology from neighboring groups, the Kurile Ainu continued to use stone and bone implements and manufactured pottery long after the Hokkaido and Sakhalin Ainu started to use metal goods traded from their neighbors.

34. The problem of the cultural, biological, and linguistic identity of the Ainu not only is intriguing in itself but also holds one of the keys to a broader anthropological problem—the peopling of both the Old and New Worlds, since the Ainu land is situated at a strategic location through which early migrants may have passed from the Old World to the New.

35. The definitive works on the history of Ainu colonization by the Japanese are those by the late Shinichirō Takakura in his *Ainu Seisakushi* (History of the Ainu policy), published in 1932, and *The Ainu of Northern Japan: A Study in Conquest and Acculturation*, which was translated into English by John A. Harrison and published in 1960. They were two pioneers, in Japan and the United States, who made invaluable contributions to the field.

36. The Sakhalin Ainu fought valiantly until 1308, when they too finally submitted to the sovereignty of the Yuan dynasty, the Mongolian dynasty that ruled China, to whom the Ainu started to pay tribute. The tribute system together with trade with other peoples along the way merged with the Japanese–Hokkaido Ainu trade during the fifteenth century. As a result, Japanese ironware reached the Manchus, and, conversely, Chinese brocade and cotton made their way to Osaka in western Japan. The Ainu were severely victimized through this trade not only by the Japanese and the Manchus, but also by other peoples who participated in the trade as middlemen.

37. The impact of the Japanese government on the Ainu was intensified with the establishment of the Meiji government in Japan in 1868. Waves of Japanese immigrants were sent to southern Sakhalin to exploit its resources. In 1875 southern Sakhalin came under Russian control, only to be regained by the Japanese in 1905. There were numerous events with devastating effects upon the Ainu and their way of life during these decades. The move between 1912 and 1914 by the Japanese government to place the Ainu, except those on the remote northwest coast, on reservations uprooted the Sakhalin Ainu, with drastic effects upon their way of life. With the conclusion of World War II, southern Sakhalin was reclaimed by the U.S.S.R. and most of the Ainu were resettled in Hokkaido. (Sakhalin north of 50° N had remained under Russian control all this time.)

38. Except for those who had been living there, no Ainu were allowed to live in this territory. Conversely, no Japanese were allowed to live in the rest of Hokkaido. During this time, the major routes of contact took the form of trading, either the Ainu visiting the Matsumae or the Japanese visiting the trading and fishing posts set up along the coast in the Ainu territory over which the Matsumae had an exclusive right. The trade between the two peoples later changed character when Japanese merchants began to exploit the Ainu. There were numerous revolts by the Ainu against the oppression by the Japanese. Most fatal for the Ainu was the revolt by a famous Ainu political leader, Shakushain, who rose to the forefront of the Ainu resistance in the middle of the 1660s. His force was crushed in the end when the Matsumae samurai broke the truce, slaying Shakushain and his retinue. The event marked the last large-scale resistance by the Ainu.

39. The land allotted to the Ainu was rented at a low cost to local Japanese, often resulting in a permanent shift in ownership. The land reform by the occupation forces at the end of World War II contributed to further deterioration of the situation, since it resulted in taking land away from Ainu who were absentee landlords. (For details of the history of the Hokkaido Ainu, see Takakura 1953, 1960.)

40. For a technical use of the term Ainu-e, see Sasaki (1990: 156–63). For reproductions of these paintings, see Izumi (1968a), Sasaki (1990), and Takakura (1953).

41. Sasaki (1990: 193) notes that Akechi Hidemitsu had this type of eyes.

42. Space does not allow me to elaborate the way the Japanese attempted to enlighten and civilize the Ainu, but there are a number of quite revealing points. For example, in a photo housed in the Peabody Museum at Harvard University, a male Ainu is shown with a pair of *geta* (for the significance of feet, including the notion of the bare foot, see Ohnuki-Tierney [1981]).

43. The Ainu are said to be physically distinguishable from the Japanese. However, it would be difficult to identify them on the basis of physical appearance. The

difference, I think, was accentuated by their style of hair, attire, and so forth rather than physical characteristics per se, especially since intermarriage has made phenotypes of the Ainu similar to those of the Japanese. My argument here relates only to their appearance. For references to their "racial" identity, see Ohnuki-Tierney (1974) and Hanihara (1992).

3. KENDALL, WHO SPEAKS FOR KOREAN SHAMANS?

Research in Korea was supported by the Korean Research Foundation and the Belo-Tanenbaum Fund of the American Museum of Natural History. I am grateful for the comments I received on this paper at the conference "Configuring Minority/Majority Discourse: Problematizing Multiculturalism" at the East-West Center and at an earlier workshop, "Gender and Narrative in Korea," sponsored by the Social Science Research Council. Comments by Nancy Abelmann, Cho Hae-joang, Dru Gladney, Richard Handler, and David McCann have been particularly helpful to me in writing and revising this paper.

1. "Han" is also homophonous with the "han" of grievance and resentment, the core emotion imputed to the historically victimized Korean masses, as discussed below and by Cho (this volume). Working between Chinese ideographs and indigenous sounds and scripts, Korean vernacular language is replete with mingled associations and puns.

2. Both Kim Seong Nae (1991) and I (Kendall 1988) have described the telling of Korean shaman lives as a creative act.

3. Tano, the fifth day of the fifth lunar month, initiates the summer season of intense agricultural activity. Celebrations of Tano were particularly important in northern Korea.

4. The banner draped over the performance area proclaimed the "First Sacrifice to the Spirit of X Mountain and Tano Festival."

5. Yongsu's Mother, the shaman of whom I have written in great detail (Kendall 1985, 1988), grumbles that this mixing of central and northern spirits is inappropriate and makes for a more difficult kut, but that such kut are "real" (*chinja*) insofar as the shaman's spirits are invoked and manifested. She contrasts them with her experiences performing in a folk art revival where the shaman's utterances are totally scripted and the performer does not expect the aid of inspiration.

6. I saw similarly lackluster attempts to encourage *communitas* at another revived ritual. This is in contrast to the spontaneous and sometimes intrusive frolicking of participants at village kut (Kendall 1985: chap. 1).

7. In a common folklore motif, scholar and shaman appear as fundamental opposites (Brandt 1971: 28; Kendall 1985: 30–34).

8. By 1994 there were at least four such associations and another was about to be announced. In the summer of 1994, I interviewed representatives of three of them. My remarks here are a summary and gross simplification of encounters that I will describe in more detail in a future essay.

9. Shamans of central and northern Korea have histories akin to those of shamans in many other societies. They experience a "calling" through strange dreams and

waking visions, by hearing voices, and by odd compulsions to bizarre behavior and distracted wandering. Through a process of initiation by more experienced shamans, they learn to serve the spirits and to transmit the will of the spirits—experienced as visions, dreams, and intuitions—to client households through inspired personifications of the spirits in the performance of ritual. The shamans of southern Korea, like the performers of the Chindo sikkim kut, are born into their profession and grow up amid the music, dance, and song of shaman performance. The daughters of these shaman (*tanggol mudang*) families learn their profession from their mothers-in-law when they marry the sons of shaman families, who then perform as their musicians.

10. For more about this ritual, the performers, and the formation of the National Treasure team, see Howard (1989).

11. In Korea, as elsewhere, one must recognize that the construction and ideological content of gendered realms is historically and sociologically contingent—both class bound and time bound—and understand that the "private" is a place where many significant things transpire (Nicholson 1986; Yanagisako 1987). For discussions of gender and space in Korea, see Kendall (1985), Kendall and Peterson (1983), and Sorensen (1983, 1988: chaps. 4 and 5).

12. A great deal could be said about the ways in which contemporary Korean women maintain the public face of Korean men through such "private" activities as investments (Moon 1990).

13. Male shamans (paksu mudang) become symbolic women when they dress in women's clothing before putting on the spirits' costumes to perform kut.

14. For a more complete discussion and additional sources, see Kendall (1985: chap. 2) and Kendall (n.d.).

15. The Park Chung Hee regime enacted policies to contain the cost and duration of elaborate Confucian rites, fostering economies of time and money in the name of development. At the same time, the government lionized historical Confucian figures, renovated shrines, and appropriated a Confucian discourse to its own patriotic ends (Kendall 1994; Kim, Yi, Yi, and Ha 1983; Kim K. 1988: 7–9).

16. See, for example, virtually any English-language publication of the Korean Overseas Information Service. Cho (this volume) notes a conservative swing in the 1990s matched by a resurgence of interest in the Confucian heritage.

17. A case can also be made for an older indigenous tradition of folklore scholarship. Some Korean scholars find the indigenous roots of Korean ethnology and folklore studies in the seventeenth- and eighteenth-century writings of those scholars of the Practical Learning School who conducted empirical investigations of local conditions and practices (Janelli 1986: 25).

18. Richard Bauman has argued that "from the invention of the concept in the late eighteenth century, folklore has always been about the politics of culture. Whether motivated by a romantic vision of traditional, preindustrial ways of life, or as a critical corrective to the discontents of modernity, or by a rationalist impulse to expose the irrational, supernaturalist foundations of folklore as impediments to progress, students of folklore have valorized certain ways of life over others in the service of larger political agendas" (quoted in Bauman and Sawin [1990, 288]). See also Linke (1990).

19. Ch'oe Nam-sôn was not the first to describe Tan'gun as the progenitor of contemporary shamans. Boudewijn Walraven notes that the *Mudang naeryôk* (History of the mudang), dated to 1885, makes this link while it disparages then-contemporary shaman practices (Walraven 1993: 10).

20. As a measure of what it meant to live in the city of Seoul in those years, a group of historians notes that to appreciate the transformation of urban life in the colonial period "one need only compare photographs of Seoul in the late Chosôn period with similar photographs taken in the mid-1930s. The former show a city that seems distant and alien to the modern eye—less a city, in fact, than an overgrown village of thatched-roof cottages that the famous nineteenth-century explorer Isabella Bird Bishop likened to an 'expanse of overripe mushrooms.' By contrast, pictures of Seoul in the 1930s show a city that is distinctly modern and familiar" (Eckert et al. 1990: 390).

21. Note, however, Chungmoo Choi's very important work with urban shamans in the 1980s. Although many folklorists have interviewed shamans who happen to live in cities, to my knowledge, Choi's is the first work that regards these women as producers of culture in a changing social milieu rather than as informants perpetuating a tradition preserved from another time and place.

22. Shamans received this designation relatively late, in the 1980s, after the system had been in place for almost two decades.

23. Soon-Hwa Sun (1991) provides a fascinating interview with a young shaman whose exorcism of the dead was at odds with the political expectations of students who hired her to send the soul of a fallen comrade to paradise.

24. Boudewijn Walraven (1994) notes that even here, the rare male shaman has been a privileged informant. Given the greater ease with which male researchers could work with male shamans and the ability of some male shamans to produce written texts in an age before tape recorders, their songs are disproportionately represented among published shaman texts.

25. This perception of women as the passive receptacles of culture is not restricted to the shaman world. See Park Heh-rahn's (n.d.) critical discussion of the portrayal of the female singer in the recent and extremely popular film *Sôp'yônje.*

26. Descriptions of Korean shaman ritual in the work of Chungmoo Choi (1987, 1989), Kim Seong Nae (1989), and myself (1977, 1985) have emphasized the emergent quality of shaman ritual in counterpoint to a preponderance of structural studies, but we write outside the tradition of Korean folklore studies.

27. See, for example, how bitterly the shaman "Yongsu's Mother" resents her lack of an education and how this sense of her own lost opportunity colors her relationship with the "student" anthropologist (Kendall 1988).

28. Both Youngsook Kim Harvey (1979) and I (1988) have recorded the lives of female shamans who see themselves as having experienced profound suffering because they were born female, but at the same time, these women invoke supernatural agency to account for the particular and important things that have happened to them, that set them apart from other women. In these stories, gender limitations inspire rage, but not the rage that carries the hope that things might be otherwise. The assumption is very different from that of the feminist scholar who assumes that

gender limitations are a plastic cultural construct, something that can be overcome through conscious recognition and collective action.

29. The laundering of "superstitious" practices into a nationalist text has broad implications for the development of Korean popular religion and for the role of women within it. As producers of popular culture, the geomancers who came to "help" the shamans at the Tano Kut were themselves in an ambiguous position. Although associated with learning and tradition, they also represent those elements of neo-Confucianism that have been least easily digested by those who self-consciously define themselves as modern: the technologies of person, time, and place associated with fortune-telling and auspicious arrangements of buildings and graves. Geomancy seems to have gained a foothold in middle-class consciousness by infusing its interpretation of the landscape with nationalistic meanings—witness recent press discussions on the proposed destruction of the colonial capitol building, sometimes complete with geomancy maps. Intellectual movements such as Chungsan'gyo attempt an overarching and intrinsically Korean cosmic vision that acknowledges shaman practice while purporting to offer a "higher way." I suspect that we are witnessing the reconstruction of a Korean popular religion acceptable to an educated and nationally conscious middle class, in the manner of religious cults among urban Chinese (Jordan and Overmyer 1986) and Indian devotional sects (Babb 1990).

30. At first, three regional shaman kut were designated as Intangible National Treasures, but in two of these cases (including the Chindo sikkim kut), the male musicians in hereditary mudang teams were designated as official spokespersons and group leaders.

31. Her vocabulary and consciousness may be attributed, in part, to the fact that she counts some feminist scholars among her clients and acquaintances.

32. Princess Pari, the seventh daughter of a sonless king and queen, was cast away as a sacrifice to her father's disappointment. Her parents were stricken with a fatal illness for their crime, but Princess Pari braved the perils of the underworld to find the elixir that would restore them. She refused the kingdom her parents would have bestowed upon her and returned to the underworld to guide lost souls. The tale is sung during the kut for the dead (T. Kim 1966; Kendall 1985: 154; Sorensen 1988).

33. Hershatter also discusses Chinese intellectuals who saw the prostitute as a sign and symptom of a weak and exploited China. She sees these men as another kind of subaltern: elite relative to most members of their society, but subaltern in quasi-colonial circumstance. In this they are analogous to the cultural nationalists who found new meanings in Korean shaman practice.

4. CHO, CONSTRUCTING AND DECONSTRUCTING "KOREANNESS"

I am thankful to Laurel Kendall, Evelyn McCune, Michael Robinson, and Laura Nelson for giving valuable suggestions and improving my English. I also thank Dru Gladney for inviting me to the Workshop on Configuring Minority/Majority Discourse, for which this paper was prepared. I learned much about the context in which new narratives have been made in the United States and had a chance to look at my own society from a proper distance. Finally, I want to thank my father, who has always helped me to visualize the colonial era, of which I have little experience. He gives me firsthand information from his memories and warns me not to write a history with my postcolonial "fantasies."

1. The Chosôn dynasty, the last kingdom of Korea, took neo-Confucianism as the state ideology and upheld it for five hundred years. Through the successful instrumentalization of the ideology, the ruling class gained legitimacy and maintained its status as Confucian scholar-officials and their "pure" descendants. The Confucian elite of Chosôn were famous for their strict observance of the neo-Confucian tradition of Zuxi, in some ways surpassing the practices of their Chinese counterparts. While Qing scholars such as Yang Ming Xue revised Zuxi's Confucianism to produce a much more practical version, Korean scholars adhered to Zuxi's teachings, with their heavy emphasis on ritualistic performances.

2. The number of hard-core Confucianists is small. According to 1992 statistics, less than one-half percent (420,000) of the population claimed to believe in Confucianism, while 51.2 percent (12,000,000) were Buddhist, 10 percent (2,300,000) were Catholic, and 34 percent (8,000,000) were Christian but not Catholic (Korean Statistical Bureau 1993: 300). However, about half of those who reported that they did not have a religion and even many of those who claimed to have other religions are likely to have internalized Confucian values as social norms and may emphathize with the Confucian revival.

3. Here, relatives are defined as kin within the distance of four *chon*. The distance between child and parent is calculated as one chon, that between child and grandparent as two chon, that between child and uncle or aunt as three chon, and that between child and cousin as four chon. The relatives here include those on both the mother's and the father's side, which shows the progressiveness of the Ministry of Education, at least in this regard.

4. "Sôp'yônje" refers to a subgenre of p'ansori, a performing art transmitted from the late Chosôn dynasty. In p'ansori, narratives are dramatized by a vocalist and a drummer. To the untrained audience, the vocal line may sound tragic and painful. Indeed, the music expresses the sorrow and wisdom attained after experiencing all the sufferings of life.

5. "Han" is a difficult word to translate. It refers to a state of emotion characterized by the accumulated anger, resentment, grief, and unburned desires born out of historical experience. Nancy Abelmann (1993: 162–63) emphasizes the historical dimension by saying that "han" connotes "the collective and the individual genealogical senses of the hardship of historical experience." Abelmann further elaborates, "'*Han* assumes that historical experience does not need to be individually or consciously part of the rationale by which people explain their actions or motivations." What makes han powerful, Abelmann points out, is its latency: "when experience is not the source of self-conscious action, *han* is only further 'building up,' becoming a greater force to fuel an eventual 'blow-up.'" There is a danger in taking han as an essential quality, as though it can explain Koreans' peculiarity in mobilizing mass uprisings in their history of resistance. Han can be a useful con-

cept, however, in understanding a history in which "the state of emergency was not the exception but the rule" (Benjamin 1973).

6. "Chosenjin" connotes a lazy people of a lowly species. Koreans have often accused themselves of having a slave mentality (*noye kunsong*). One can often hear negative comments on Koreanness from taxi drivers or from our neighbors, who say, as if they were not Koreans, "There is no hope in our society unless Koreans change their national character."

7. Of course, there are also voices of feminists, the labor movement, and young people. The voices of the feminist and labor movements are weak, however, following the overall decline of the revolutionary spirit in the 1980s. There seems to be a popular sentiment that it is time to get over any kind of organized social movement of the enlightenment spirit. As a reaction to the hyperpolitical movements of the 1980s and to the authoritarian culture, young people prefer to be "free individuals" and engage in creating a rather private and ahistorical discursive space. Between their parents' generation's endless craving for material wealth and the utopian slogans and militant protests of their elder siblings, many youngsters express a desire to have an easy and enjoyable life. They search for a new identity, but indulging in the hybrid commercial culture seems to be the only choice left for them. A desire to conjure something out of the hypermodern or postmodern present is strongly felt everywhere. To the younger generation, the postmodern indicates a departure from both feudalism and colonial modernity.

8. Regarding the issue of constructing, instead of deconstructing, Koreanness, I want to probe into the self-contradictory attribute of the "strategic use of positive essentialism" that Spivak (1988) has discussed. In a society where talk about culture has been insignificant, privileging culture is not simple but complex and politically enabling. It has a value in constructing the clear-cut subject position with a different meaning from the antihumanist decentering of the subject in the West.

6. GLADNEY, MUSLIM AND CHINESE IDENTITIES IN THE PRC

1. See particularly the *Foreign* Affairs issue rebutting Huntington (vol. 72, no. 4, Fall 1993), which contains critical readings by Fouad Ajami, Kishore Mahbubani, Robert Bartley, Liu Binyan, Jeane Kirkpatrick, and others. Elsewhere, Richard Cooper (1994) adds to the growing critique by arguing that conflict arises not between cultures but between rivals for political control "within as well as between civilizations." Liu Binyan (1994: 20) notes that the so-called Confucian civilizations on either side of the Formosa Strait have many more issues dividing than ideologies uniting them.

2. Walter Mair (1994: 10) argues that the "Islamic challenge [will] be one that is ultimately fought within the borders of its own civilization," which, though reifying "Islamic" civilization, at least admits that the potential for conflict between Muslim groups is as great as, if not greater than, tensions between Muslims and non-Muslims, as the Iran-Iraq and Gulf Wars evidenced. The Malay Muslim scholar Chandra Muzaffar (1994) suggests that reifying "Islamic" civilization as unified or predominantly Arab also neglects the fact that the largest numbers

of Muslim populations today are spread across the multinational populations of South and Southeast Asia.

3. The Chinese term "minzu" can be glossed as "nationality," "ethnic group," "nation," or "people," and it has meanings related to all these different English renderings. In China, the term is reserved for only those peoples recognized by the state as separate nationalities; unrecognized peoples are merely referred to as "peoples" (*renmin*). I will deal with the origin of the term below.

4. The publication in *Minzu Yanjiu* (*Nationality Research*) of several papers given at the 1986 national conference in Shanghai where Stalin's principles were discussed reveals that, though the principles are beginning to be questioned for the first time, they are still held as most appropriate for China.

5. Eric Hobsbawm repeats this widely accepted idea of Chinese and Asian majority monoethnicity in his classic work, *Nations and Nationalism Since 1780*: "China, Korea, and Japan . . . are indeed among the extremely rare examples of historic states composed of a population that is ethnically almost or entirely homogeneous." He continues: "Thus of the (non-Arab) Asian states today Japan and the two Koreas are 99% homogeneous, and 94% of the People's Republic of China are Han" (1991: 66 n. 37).

6. This is taken from the English version (Keyes 1984) of the original conference paper, which has now been published in Russian.

7. Bai Shouyi literally made the closing argument to an internal debate that had been taking place throughout the Nationalist period as to whether the Hui should be known as Hui min or believers in Hui jiao. This took place when many Hui intellectuals traveled to Japan and the Middle East and were caught up in the nationalist fervor of the republican period, publishing magazines and questioning their identity in a process that one Hui historian, Ma Shouqian (1989), has recently termed a "new awakening at the end of the nineteenth century and beginning of the twentieth century."

8. For a discussion of the problematic nature of these central Asian identifications in the Soviet Union, see Wimbush (1985). Elsewhere, I have attempted to describe the 1940s Soviet influence on the Chinese identification of the Uygur—a generic label applied to the settled, oases-dwelling, Muslim, Turkic-speaking peoples of the Tarim Basin, who had not used that ethnonym to refer to themselves until it was applied by the state (see Gladney 1990).

9. In *Red Dust*, Nym Wales, the wife of Edgar Snow, reproduces her fascinating Yenan interviews with several of the Long Marchers. Hsu Meng-ch'iu, official historian of the Long March, described how, after narrowly escaping slaughter at the hands of the "fierce Lolos" and "wild Tibetans" in Sichuan, the "Red Army marched on to north Shensi [Shaanxi], pursued by three cavalry elements—those of Ma Hung-k'uei, Ma Hung-p'ing, and Chiang Kai-shek. Because of the speed of the cavalry, many Red troops in the rear were cut off and captured" (in Wales 1952: 74). The first two were (Hui) Muslim warlords who controlled most of Ningxia and Gansu. Hsu also records several graphic accounts of "barbarians" sweeping down out of the mountains upon the hapless Long Marchers, screaming "Woo-woo-woo" in unintelligible dialects—reminiscent of American Western accounts of encounters with Native Americans.

8. MILNER, CONSTRUCTING THE MALAY MAJORITY

1. For a thought-provoking discussion of "collective identities as objectifications in need of semiotic exploration" (in the context of Israel), see Dominguez (1989: 12).

2. For the influence of British racial ideology on Sinhalese nationalism, see Gunawardana (1990).

9. KELLY, ASPIRING TO MINORITY

1. Consider Taylor's quick slide from the dulcet tones of the panhistoric (of course without an actual survey of world political discourse) to a chauvinist assertion about the priority of the United States in world political history: "But through all the differences of interpretation, the principle of equal citizenship has come to be universally accepted. Every position, no matter how reactionary, is now defended under the colors of this principle. Its greatest, most recent victory was won by the civil rights movement of the 1960s in the United States" (Taylor et al. 1992: 38). To be fair to Taylor, but also to suggest the extraordinary ambivalence about his own capacity for judgment that runs through his work—he is unable to abjure the role of knower, even when announcing that he is doing so—we must contrast this clean judgment about the U.S. civil rights movement with his final point: "Above all is an admission that we are very far away from that ultimate horizon from which the relative worth of different cultures might be evident" (p. 73). Let us leave aside Taylor's certainty about what is above all, despite his announcement of his own limits. At least, I hope to show in this chapter that the particular vision of a universal human political possibility that organizes liberal democracy is not, in fact, universally accepted in our actually existing world.

2. My account of this debate comes principally from a single source, the *Pacific Islands Monthly* of July 1994. I recognize the perils of relying on a single source to depict political events, but I also feel a responsibility to seek to connect scholarship to contemporary events. Handler (this volume) describes many of the ethical complexities involved in ethnographic study of contemporary ethnic and nationalist politics.

3. Even this last matter is complex: new Fiji banknotes and coins still bear the portrait of the British queen, about which she professes to be charmed, and Fiji's current rulers would surely rejoin the Commonwealth if invited. Such an invitation would be tendered over India's dead body.

4. Even Fiji's half-and-half ethnic demographics are not unique, and several other British colonies, in particular, provide close comparisons. Malaysia's political history, in so many ways comparable to Fiji's, makes Fiji look simple in its history of community oppositions and national imagining—see Shamsul (this volume) and Milner (this volume). More generally, one would be hard pressed to assimilate any case described in this volume, even those in which a national majority is clearly constituted, to the general scheme of a "pirated" model of national identity provided by Anderson without at least equally accommodating Anderson's scheme to the dynamics of the case. In particular, see Ohnuki-Tierney's chapter in this volume and Ohnuki-Tierney (1987, 1993) for delineation of an intense, long-run social

alterity dialogue in and about Japan that absorbs and engulfs the idea of nation in its own workings.

5. In Fiji, at least since independence, Diwali is celebrated as the day of Ram's return from exile to righteous rule as firmly as it is celebrated as the night Laksmi comes to earth to inhabit clean homes and hearts. For more on the political uses of Ramayan narrative and on the current battles over the scope and shape of the sacred in Fiji, see Kelly (1991, 1995).

6. This visiting team included then-major general Rabuka, the leader of the coups, who was also at that time minister for home affairs. (Later, other government officials forced him to choose between public office and the army, and since then, so far he has remained out of the army.) Rabuka gave "personal assurances," amid the public clamor on both sides, that (quoting the official, English-language government press release) "security forces would ensure that law and order was maintained." However, Rabuka was also well known as a Methodist lay preacher who had predicted that peace will come to Fiji when the Indo-Fijians have all converted to Methodism.

7. Specifically, they created a Senate in the Parliament that was constituted by appointment rather than public election, gave the party forming a government only one more seat in the Senate than the opposition, and set aside eight seats in the Senate for appointees of the indigenous Fijian "Great Council of Chiefs." Further, they exempted a list of laws from amendment except with approval of six of these eight senators, specifically, the laws safeguarding indigenous Fijian land rights (the right to perpetual kin-group ownership of 83 percent of Fiji's land) and otherwise concerned with matters of indigenous Fijian custom. Regardless of what party won elections and formed a government, government support for chiefly privileges and indigenous land rights could not be eroded. Still, the army, which the colonials had restricted to indigenous Fijian membership, told the world that the coups were necessary to protect the indigenes from their enemies.

8. Consider, for example, Weber's famous definition of sociology (1978: 4): "Sociology . . . is a science concerning itself with the interpretive understanding of social action and thereby with causal explanation. . . . We shall speak of 'action' insofar as the acting individual attaches a subjective meaning to his behavior. . . . Action is 'social' insofar as its subjective meaning takes account of the behavior of others and is thereby oriented in its course." In the Weberian social universe, it is meanings all the way down.

9. Many would add, especially the Indo-Fijian rich and middle class, though I know of no statistics to prove this.

10. KAPLAN, DISCOURSES AGAINST DEMOCRACY IN FIJI

1. As I will describe below, in 1984 a new party, the Fiji Labour Party, formed to challenge racial politics in Fiji. In the 1987 elections the Labour Party formed a coalition government with the National Federation Party, a party primarily supported by Indo-Fijians. Within a few months, a Fijian army colonel led a military coup, claiming to represent Fijian interests. He first reinstated the Fijian chiefly

leaders of the party that lost the election. Since then, the colonel (now brigadier general) has himself become Fiji's prime minister.

2. Of course, much more should be said about the ways in which Fijian chiefs fit British god and government into their own ritual-political projects. Macnaught (1982) is interesting on this, as is, of course, Sahlins (1985).

3. An ironic article in *DomoDomo*, bulletin of the Fiji Museum, notes that South Asian "Lascars" off of whaling and China-trade ships intermarried with high-chiefly Fijian women in the early nineteenth century.

4. Part of the silencing of this potential contradiction is gendered. As long as the children are of Fijian mothers, they are not legally entitled to *mataqali* (kin-group) membership and property, since colonial regulation insisted on patrilineal transmission of kin/property group membership. For an interesting contrast, the census category of "part European" really requires study. British discourse saw Indians and Fijians as sensual, with Indians sinister and Fijians childlike, and British discourse is highly gendered, with a masculine gaze on an effeminate or feminine other (Indians) or, sometimes, a civilized adult male gaze on a boyish, untamed warrior masculinity (Fijians). Thus, on the one hand, the British portrayed "others" as sensual and erotic, evading and denying, as John Kelly (1991) has pointed out, the vast history of colonial male sexual predation and participation in the colony. On the other hand, it is very interesting that the census category "part European," clearly invoking European participation in "racial" boundary crossing/reconstruction/deconstruction, was insisted upon (see 1946 debates). This may have been largely because the concern was with the children of European men who were married to non-European women, or children who were not raised in villages by their mothers and mothers' kin.

11. DERINGIL, SELF-IMAGE AND SOCIAL ENGINEERING IN TURKEY

1. I am using "protonationalism" in the sense in which it is used by Eric Hobsbawm (1992).

2. The BBA is the Prime Ministry Archives in Istanbul. This chapter uses the following abbreviations for collections of documents in these archives:

Y.A. Res. (Yıldız Arşivi Resmi Maruzat)

YEE (Yıldız Esas Euraki)

Y. Mtv. (Yıldız Arşivi Mülenevvi Malumat)

3. It is worth noting here that Süleyman Hüsnü Paşa had written a world history (*Tarih-i Alem*) dealing with matters ranging from the "big bang" to the sequence of Chinese dynasties. See Taneri (1963).

4. It is also worth noting that the man whom Süleyman Hüsnü Paşa recommended to write the chapter on Christianity, Moulvi Rahmetullah, is referred to by Snouck Hurgronje (1931) as "the highly revered assailant of Christianity, Rahmat Ullah an exile from British India (living in the Hicaz)."

5. The Hicaz had a special status and considerable autonomy. One of its privileges was that its population was exempted from military service.

6. It is interesting to note that a recent work on the topic, like all other works to date, only guesses that the Hamidiye were designed on the cossack model, because of obvious similarities. See Karaca (1993: 173). It is now clear from the evidence that the government took the cossack example literally, to the point of sending officers to be trained in Russia.

12. KIRIŞCI, THE CASE OF THE KURDS IN TURKEY

1. For an English version of the Lausanne Treaty see Israel (1967: 2305–68).

2. Assembly of the Western European Union, 38th ordinary session (second part), Document 1341, *Turkey*, Nov. 6, 1992, p. 4.

3. Some of the more significant reforms of the period included the 1924 Law on the Unification of Education, the 1924 Village Law, the 1928 Hat Law, the law replacing the Arabic script with a Latin script, and the introduction of the civil code to replace practices derived from Islamic law.

4. For references to some of the main works advocating this theory, see Akural (1984: 147). Molokans were a very small population of Russian descent who lived near Kars in eastern Anatolia until the 1960s, when they decided to return to the Soviet Union (Andrews 1989: 134–36).

5. The only exception, other than the Kurds, seems to have been the Circassians. But their reaction was not so much against Turkish nationality as against the secularization of Turkey, because, as Andrews notes, "their presence in Turkey was justified only, in their eyes, by its role as the land of the Caliphate" (1989: 37). Subsequently, however, the Circassians became integrated and adopted a Turkish national identity. On Circassian ethnicity in Turkey, see Andrews (1989: 167–71). See Olson (1989: 32) for references to Circassians joining Kurdish rebellions in 1920.

6. Süleyman Nazif too was one of the early members of the CUP. Unlike Abdullah Cevdet and other Kurds, however, he chose to join the Turkish nationalists. He played an important role in the organization of the Turkish national resistance movement that paved the way for establishment of the Turkish republic.

7. For a Kurdish nationalist representation of the rebellion, see Kendal (1980). For representations of the rebellion as a foreign-instigated reactionary revolt, see Toker (1968) and Mumcu (1991).

8. For a basic Turkish history book that argues that Kurds are Turks, see Fırat (1948). Giritli (1989) offers an extensive bibliography of literature that has employed the Sun Language Theory in treating the identity of Kurds. For criticism of the theory that Kurds are Turks, see Beşikçi (1991b).

9. For a Marxist analysis by a radical Turkish academic of the idea of Kurdistan as a colony, see Beşikçi (1991a).

10. The HEP was set up in 1990 by a group of nationalist Kurdish members of Parliament, most of whom had been expelled from the SHP for having attended a conference on Kurdish national identity in Paris in October 1989.

11. In July 1994 the prime minister of Turkey, Tansu Çiller, argued that the constitution could be changed to allow for private education and radio/television

broadcasting in Kurdish as long as Turkish remained the official state language (*Hürriyet*, July 7, 1994).

14. OKAMURA, PRIVILEGING MULTICULTURALISM IN HAWAI'I

I would like to thank Vicente Rafael for the eloquent and provocative comments he made as the discussant of my paper when it was presented at the Configuring Minority/Majority Discourse conference and for providing me with a lengthy written version of those comments. I also express my appreciation to Franklin Odo for his very useful suggested revisions of my paper.

1. There are haoles who are considered local, but these are individuals rather than representing a significant category of the population.

2. The Great Mahele was a series of decrees and acts that resulted in the following division of land in Hawai'i: 1.6 million acres (39 percent of the total) to 250 chiefs as their private lands; 1.5 million acres (36 percent) as government lands; 1 million acres (24 percent) to Kamehameha III, then the king, as his private lands; and 28,600 acres (1 percent) to 8,200 commoners (of the 80,000 total) as their private property (Fuchs 1961: 15–16).

3. The U.S. Census Bureau has predicted that by the year 2020 whites will constitute 48 percent of Hawaii's population and that Hawai'i will be the second fastest growing state in the nation during the next three decades ("Elbowroom Is Shrinking Fast in Isles," *Honolulu StarBulletin*, Apr. 22, 1994: A1). These predictions are based solely on demographic projections, however, and do not take into consideration the more significant economic factors that would limit Hawai'i's population growth through in-migration from the continental United States. These factors include the high cost of living, especially housing; the wage scale, which is lower than that of the U.S. mainland; and the relatively fewer professional, managerial, and other white-collar positions.

4. The ceded lands were initially transferred to the U.S. government in 1898 when Hawai'i was annexed. The lands were then ceded to the state government in 1959 at the time of statehood. These lands are sometimes referred to as "5(f)" lands in reference to the section in the Admissions Act that provided for statehood. According to this section, one of the purposes for which the proceeds from the use of the ceded lands are to be used is to benefit Native Hawaiians.

5. According to the Hawaiian Sovereignty Elections Council (1997), a final list of 81,507 Native Hawaiian registered voters received ballots that asked, "Shall the Hawaiian people elect delegates to propose a Native Hawaiian government?" Approximately 37 percent of these voters returned valid ballots; of these, 73.3 percent voted "yes" and 2.7 percent voted "no."

6. As chairman of the U.S. Senate Subcommittee on Indian Affairs, Daniel K. Inouye of Hawai'i proposed legislation regarding sovereignty and also has aligned himself with the state's sovereignty initiative.

References Cited

INTRODUCTION

Anderson, Benedict. 1991. *Imagined Communities: Reflections on the Origin and Spread of Nationalism*. 2d ed. London: Verso.

Chatterjee, Partha. 1986. *Nationalist Thought and the Colonial World: A Derivative Discourse*. London: Zed.

Clifford, James, and George Marcus, eds. 1986. *Writing Culture: The Poetics and Politics of Ethnography*. Berkeley: University of California Press.

Cohn, Bernard S. 1987. "The Census, Social Structure and Objectification in South Asia." In Bernard S. Cohn, ed., *An Anthropologist Among the Historians and Other Essays*. Delhi: Oxford University Press.

Dirlik, Arif, ed. 1993. *What's in a Rim: Critical Perspectives on the Pacific Region Idea*. Boulder, Colo.: Westview Press.

Dominguez, Virginia R. 1986. *White by Definition: Social Classification in Creole Louisiana*. New Brunswick, N.J.: Rutgers University Press.

Fischer, Michael M. J. 1986. "Ethnicity and the Post-Modern Arts of Memory." In Clifford and Marcus, *Writing Culture*.

Frankenberg, Ruth. 1993. *White Women, Race Matters: The Social Construction of Whiteness*. Minneapolis: University of Minnesota Press.

Gladney, Dru C. 1994. "Representing Nationality in China: Refiguring Majority/Minority Identities." *Journal of Asian Studies* 53(1): 92–123.

Greenfeld, Liah. 1992. *Nationalism: Five Roads to Modernity*. Cambridge: Harvard University Press.

Gurr, Ted Robert. 1993. *Minorities at Risk: A Global View of Ethnopolitical Conflicts*. Washington, D.C.: United States Institute of Peace.

Handler, Richard. 1988. *Nationalism and the Politics of Culture in Quebec*. Madison: University of Wisconsin Press.

Hobsbawm, Eric. 1992. *Nations and Nationalism Since 1780*. 2d ed. Cambridge: Cambridge University Press.

Hobsbawm, Eric, and Terence Ranger, eds. 1983. *The Invention of Tradition*. Cambridge: Cambridge University Press.

Huntington, Samuel P. 1993. "The Clash of Civilizations?" *Foreign Affairs* 72(3): 22–49.

Keyes, Charles, Laurel Kendall, and Helen Hardacre, eds. 1994. *Asian Visions of Authority: Religion and the Modern States of East and Southeast Asia*. Honolulu: University of Hawai'i Press.

Kotkin, J. 1993. *Tribes: How Race, Religion, and Identity Determine Success in the New Global Economy*. New York: Random House.

Rafael, Vincent. 1989. *Contracting Colonialism*. Ithaca, N.Y.: Cornell University Press.

Thomas, Nicholas. 1992. *Colonialism's Culture: Anthropology, Travel, and Government*. Princeton, N.J.: Princeton University Press.

White, Geoffrey. 1991. *Identity Through History*. Cambridge: Cambridge University Press.

Young, Robert J. C. 1995. *Colonial Desire: Hybridity in Theory, Culture, and Race*. London: Routledge.

1. YOSHINO, THE DISCOURSE ON JAPANESE IDENTITY

Anderson, Benedict. 1983. *Imagined Communities: Reflections on the Origins and Spread of Nationalism*. London: Verso.

Banton, Michael. 1970. "The Concept of Racism." In S. Zubaida, ed., *Race and Racialism*. London: Tavistock.

——— 1983. *Racial and Ethnic Competition*. Cambridge: Cambridge University Press.

Barzun, Jacques. 1965 [1937]. *Race: A Study in Superstition*. New York: Harper & Row.

Benedict, Ruth. 1983 [1942]. *Race and Racism*. London: Routledge & Kegan Paul.

Bocock, Robert. 1974. *Ritual in Industrial Society: A Sociological Analysis of Ritualism in Modern England*. London: Allen and Unwin.

Bourdieu, Pierre. 1992 [1984]. *Distinction*. London: Routledge.

Cohen, Percy. 1976. "Race Relations as a Sociological Issue." In G. Bowker and J. Carrier, eds., *Race and Ethnic Relations*. London: Hutchinson.

Dikötter, Frank. 1994. "Racial Nationalisms in East Asia." *ASEN Bulletin* 6: 8–10.

Doi, Takeo. 1971. *Amae no kōzō* (Structure of dependence). Tokyo: Kōbundō. Trans. as *The Anatomy of Dependence* by J. Bester. Tokyo: Kodansha International, 1973.

Eisenstadt, S. N. 1972. "Intellectuals and Tradition." *Daedalus* (Spring): 1–19.

Firth, Raymond. 1973. *Symbols: Public and Private*. London: Allen and Unwin.

Hamaguchi, Eshun. 1980. "Nihonshakairon no paradaimu kakushin o mezashite" (Toward a paradigmatic change in the theories of Japanese society). *Gendai Shakaigaku* (*Reviews of Contemporary Sociology*) 7(1): 29–45.

Husband, Charles. 1982. "Introduction: 'Race,' the Continuity of a Concept." In Charles Husband, ed., *"Race" in Britain*. London: Hutchinson.

Kedourie, Elie, ed., 1971. *Nationalism in Asia and Africa*. London: Weidenfeld and Nicolson.

Kushner, David. 1977. *The Rise of Turkish Nationalism, 1876–1908*. London: Frank Cass.

Lee, Chansoo, and George DeVos. 1981. *Koreans in Japan: Ethnic Conflict and Accommodation.* Berkeley: University of California Press.

Miles, Robert. 1984. "Racialism." In E. Ellis Cashmore, ed., *Dictionary of Race and Ethnic Relations.* 2d ed. London: Routledge.

Milner, Anthony. 1982. *Kerajaan: Malay Political Culture on the Eve of Colonial Rule.* Tucson: University of Arizona Press.

Mitsubishi Corporation. 1983. *Japanese Business Glossary/Nihonjingo.* Tokyo: Tōyō Keizai Shinpōsha.

Nakane, Chie. 1967. *Tate shakai no ningen kankei: tan'itsu shakai no riron* (Human relations in vertical society: A theory of a unitary society). Tokyo: Kōdansha.

Nippon Steel Corporation, Personnel Development Office. 1984. *Nippon: The Land and Its People.* 2d ed. Tokyo: Gakuseisha.

Sampson, Anthony. 1982. *The Changing Anatomy of Britain.* Sevenoaks: Hodder and Stoughton.

Shils, Edward. 1972. "Intellectuals, Tradition, and the Traditions of Intellectuals: Some Preliminary Considerations." *Daedalus* (Spring): 21–33.

Taiyō Kōbe Bank. 1988. *The Nipponjin/The Scrutable Japanese.* Tokyo: Gakuseisha.

Tanizaki, Junichirō. 1974 [1934]. *Bunshō Dokuhon* (Manual of prose composition). In *Tanizaki Junichirō Zenshū* (Collected works of Tanizaki Junichirō), vol. 21. Tokyo: Chūō Kōronsha.

Van Heerikhuizen, Bert. 1982. "What Is Typically Dutch? Sociologists in the 1930s and 1940s on the Dutch National Character." *The Netherlands' Journal of Sociology* 18: 103–25.

Wallman, Sandra. 1978. "The Boundaries of 'Race': Process of Ethnicity in England." *Man* 13(2): 200–215.

——— 1981. "Refractions of Rhetoric: Evidence for the Meaning of 'Race' in England." In R. Paine, ed., *Politically Speaking: Cross-cultural Studies of Rhetoric.* Philadelphia: Institute for the Study of Human Issues.

——— 1986. "Ethnicity and the Boundary Process in Context." In J. Rex and D. Mason, eds., *Theories of Race and Ethnic Relations.* Cambridge: Cambridge University Press.

Watanabe, Shōichi. 1974. *Nihongo no kokoro* (The soul of the Japanese language). Tokyo: Kōdansha.

White, Merry. 1992. *The Japanese Overseas: Can They Go Home Again?* Princeton, N.J.: Princeton University Press.

Yoshino, Kosaku. 1992. *Cultural Nationalism in Contemporary Japan: A Sociological Enquiry.* London: Routledge.

2. OHNUKI-TIERNEY, THE SELF AND THE INTERNAL AND EXTERNAL OTHERS

Akisada Yoshikazu. 1978. "Suiheisha undō to yūwa seisaku" (The Suiheisha movement and the Yūwa policy). In Buraku Kaihō Kenkyūsho, ed., *Buraku mondai gaisetsu*, pp. 161–88.

Amino Yoshihiko. 1980. *Nihon chūsei no minshūzū—heimin to shokunin* (Portrait of the folk in medieval Japan—the common people and the "professionals"). Tokyo: Iwanami Shoten.

——— 1983 [1978]. *Muen kugai raku—nihon chūsei no jiyū to heiwa* (*Muen*, *Kugai*, and *Raku*—freedom and peace in medieval Japan). Tokyo: Heibonsha.

——— 1984. "Chūsei no tabibitotachi" (Travelers during the Medieval period). In Amino et al., eds., *Hyōhaku to teijū* (Wandering and settlement), pp. 153–266. Tokyo: Shōgakkan.

——— 1994. *Nihon shakai saikō: ama to rettō bunka* (Rethinking Japanese society: People of the sea and cultures of archipelago). Tokyo: Shōgakkan.

Anderson, Benedict. 1991. *Imagined Communities*. London: Verso.

Bellah, Robert. 1970 [1957]. *Tokugawa Religion: The Values of Pre-Industrial Japan*. Boston: Beacon Press.

Berque, Augustin. 1990. *Nihon no fūkei seiyō no keikan soshite zōkei no jidai* (Comparative study of landscape in Japan and Europe). Tokyo: Kōdansha.

Bloch, Marc. 1961 [1949]. *Feudal Society*. Trans. L. A. Manyon. Chicago: University of Chicago Press.

Bolitho, Harold. 1977. *Meiji Japan*. Cambridge: Cambridge University Press.

Braudel, Fernand. 1973 [1967]. *Capitalism and Material Life, 1400–1800*. London: Weidenfeld and Nicolson.

Brettell, Richard R., and Caroline B. Brettell. 1983. *Painters and Peasants in the Nineteenth Century*. New York: Rizzoli International Publications.

Buraku Kaihō Kenkyūsho, ed. 1978a. *Buraku mondai gaisetsu* (Introduction to *Buraku* problems). Ōsaka: Kaihō Shuppansha.

——— 1978b. *Buraku mondai yōsetsu* (Outline of *Buraku* problems). Ōsaka: Kaihō Shuppansha.

Burke, Kenneth. 1955. *A Grammar of Motives*. New York: George Braziller.

DeVos, George, and H. Wagatsuma, eds. 1966. *Japan's Invisible Race: Caste in Culture and Personality*. Berkeley: University of California Press.

Donoghue, John. 1966. "The Social Persistence of Outcaste Groups." In DeVos and Wagatsuma, *Japan's Invisible Race*, pp. 138–52.

Dumont, Louis. 1970 [1966]. *Homo Hierarchicus*. Trans. M. Sainsbury. Chicago: University of Chicago Press.

Frye, Northrop. 1971 [1957]. *Anatomy of Criticism*. Princeton, N.J.: Princeton University Press.

Gladney, Dru C. 1994. "Representing Nationality in China: Refiguring Majority/Minority Identities." *Journal of Asian Studies* 53(1): 92–123.

Gluck, Carol. 1985. *Japan's Modern Myth: Ideology in the Late Meiji Period*. Princeton, N.J.: Princeton University Press.

Gotō Shigeki. 1975. *Tōkaidō gojū-san-tsugi* (Fifty-three stations along the Tōkaidō). Tokyo: Shūeisha.

——— 1976. *Kiso kaidō rokujū-kyū-tsugi* (Sixty-nine stations along the Kiso road). Tokyo: Shūeisha.

Hanihara Kazuro, ed. 1992. *Japanese as a Member of the Asian and Pacific Populations*. International Symposium, 1990. Kyoto: International Research Center for Japanese Studies.

Harada Nobuo. 1993. *Rekishi no naka no kome to niku—shokumotsu to tennō sabetsu*

(Rice and meat in history—food, emperor and discrimination). Tokyo: Heibonsha.

Harada Tomohiko. 1971. "Danzaemon yuishogaki kaidai" (Introduction to "The report by Danzaemon"). In T. Harada, K. Nakazawa, and H. Kobayashi, eds., *Nihon shomin seikatsushiryō shūsei* (History of the lives of the common people in Japan), vol. 14 (*Buraku*): 427–28. Tokyo: Sanichi Shobō.

——— 1978a. "Buraku no zenshi" (An early history of *Buraku*). In Buraku Kaihō Kenkyūsho, ed., *Buraku mondai yōsetsu*, pp. 16–23.

——— 1978b. "Kinsei hōken shakai to buraku keisei" (The feudal society of the Early Modern period and the formation of *Buraku*). In Buraku Kaihō Kenkyūsho, ed., *Buraku mondai yōsetsu*, pp. 24–33.

Harootunian, Harry. 1988. *Things Seen and Unseen: Discourse and Ideology in Tokugawa Nativism*. Chicago: University of Chicago Press.

Hayashiya Tatsusaburō. 1980 [1973]. *Nihon geinō no sekai* (The world of performing arts in Japan). Tokyo: Nihon Hōsō Shuppan Kyōkai.

——— 1981. "Chūsei geinō no shakaiteki kiban" (The social foundation of arts during the Medieval period). In Nihon Bungaku Kenkyū Shiryō Kankōkai, ed., *Yōkyoku kyōgen* (*Yōkyoku* and *kyōgen*), pp. 201–9. Tokyo: Yūseidō Shuppan.

Hokkaidōchō (Government of Hokkaido), ed. 1934. *Hokkaidō kyū-dojin hogo enkakushi* (History of the protection of the natives of Hokkaido). Sapporo: Hokkaidōchō.

Howell, David L. 1994. Ainu Ethnicity and the Boundaries of the Early Modern Japanese State. *Past and Present* 142: 69–93.

Inoue Hisashi et al. 1978. *Shinpojūmu Sabetsu no Seishinshi Josetsu* (Introduction to a conceptual history of discrimination—a symposium) (1977). Tokyo: Sanseidō.

Izumi Seiichi. 1968a. *Kinsei Wajin Gaka ni yotte Egakareta Ainu no Sekai* (The world of the Ainu: Through the drawings by Japanese painters, 1775–1886). Tokyo: Kashima Kenkyūjo.

——— 1968b. "Minzokushi to shiteno Ainu-e" (The *Ainu-e* as ethnography). In Izumi, *Ainu no sekai*, pp. 9–16.

Kailasapathy, K. 1968. *Tamil Heroic Poetry*. Oxford: Clarendon Press.

Kawasoe Taketani. 1980 [1978]. *Kojiki no sekai* (The world of *Kojiki*). Tokyo: Kyōikusha.

Kurano, Kenji, and Yūkichi Takeda, eds. 1958. *Kojiki Norito* (*Kojiki* and *Norito*). Tokyo: Iwanami Shoten.

Kuroda Toshio. 1972. "Chūsei no mibunsei to hisen kannen" (The social stratification during the Early Medieval period and the concept of baseness). *Buraku mondai kenkyū* 33: 23–57.

Mennell, Stephen. 1985. *All Manners of Food: Eating and Taste in England and France from the Middle Ages to the Present*. Oxford: Basil Blackwell.

Mertz, John P. 1997. "Internalizing Social Difference: Kanagaki Robun's *Shank's Mare to the Western Seas*." In Helen Hardacre, ed., *New Directions in the Study of Meiji Japan*, pp. 219–28. Leiden-Brill.

Miyata Noboru. 1993. *Yama to sato no shinkōshi* (History of beliefs in the mountains and homestead). Tokyo: Yoshikawa Kōbundō.

Morinaga Taneo. 1967 [1963]. *Rūnin to hinin—zoku Nagasaki bugyō no kiroku* (The exiled and the *hinin* outcastes—the records of the commissioner of Nagasaki *bugyō*, cont.). Tokyo: Iwanami Shoten.

Morita Yoshinori. 1978. *Kawara makimono* (The scrolls of the "riverbanks"). Tokyo: Hōsei Daigaku Shuppankyoku.

Morse, Peter. 1989. *Hokusai: One Hundred Poets*. New York: George Braziller.

Murakami Shigeyoshi. 1977. *Tennō no saishi* (Imperial rituals). Tokyo: Iwanami Shoten.

Murasaki Yoshimasa. 1983. *Sarumawashi jōgeyuki* (The upward and downward travels of monkey trainers). Tokyo: Chikuma Shobō.

Murphy, Joseph. 1997. "Conception of Equality in Izumi Kyōka's *Kechō*." In Helen Hardacre, ed., *New Directions in the Study of Meiji Japan*, pp. 246–69. Leiden: Brill.

Newby, Howard. 1979. *Green and Pleasant Land?* London: Hutchinson.

Ninomiya Shigeaki. 1933. "An Inquiry Concerning the Origin, Development, and Present Situation of the *Eta* in Relation to the History of Social Classes in Japan." *Transactions of the Asiatic Society of Japan* 10: 47–154.

Noguchi Michihiko. 1978. "Chūsei no shomin seikatsu to hisabetsumin no dōkō" (The life of common people and movements of the discriminated people during the Medieval period). In Buraku Kaihō Kenkyūsho, ed., *Buraku mondai gaisetsu* (Introduction to *Buraku* problems), pp. 86–99. Osaka: Kaihō Shuppansha.

Ōbayashi Tarō, ed. 1983. *Sanmin to ama* (People of the mountain and people of the sea). Tokyo: Shōgakkan.

Ochiai Shigenobu. 1972. *Mikaihō buraku no kigen* (Origin of *Buraku*). Kobe: Kobe Gakujutsu Shuppan.

Ohnuki-Tierney, Emiko. 1974. *The Ainu of the Northwest Coast of Southern Sakhalin*. New York: Holt, Rinehart & Winston. Republished 1984. Prospect Heights, Ill.: Waveland Press.

——— 1976. "Regional Variation in Ainu Culture." *American Ethnologist* 3(2): 297–329.

——— 1981. *Illness and Healing among the Sakhalin Ainu—A Symbolic Interpretation*. Cambridge: Cambridge University Press.

——— 1984. *Illness and Culture in Contemporary Japan: An Anthropological View*. Cambridge: Cambridge University Press.

——— 1987. *The Monkey as Mirror: Symbolic Transformations in Japanese History and Ritual*. Princeton, N.J.: Princeton University Press.

——— 1993. *Rice as Self: Japanese Identities Through Time*. Princeton, N.J.: Princeton University Press.

——— In press. "We Eat Each Other's Food to Nourish Our Body: The Global and the Local as Mutually Constituent Forces." In Raymond Grew, ed., *Food in Global History*. Boulder, Colo.: Westview Press.

Pearson, Richard. 1992. *Ancient Japan*. New York: George Braziller.

Pollack, David. 1986. *The Fracture of Meaning: Japan's Synthesis of China from the Eighth Through the Eighteenth Centuries*. Princeton, N.J.: Princeton University Press.

Price, John. 1966. "A History of Outcaste: Untouchability in Japan." In DeVos and Wagatsuma, *Japan's Invisible Race*, pp. 6–30.

Said, Edward W. 1978. *Orientalism*. New York: Random House.

Saigō Nobutsuna. 1984 [1967]. *Kojiki no sekai* (The world of the *Kojiki*). Tokyo: Iwanami Shoten.

Sakurai Tokutarō. 1981. Kesshū no genten—minzokugaku kara tsuikyū shita shochiiki kyōdōtai kōsei no paradaimu (The source of solidarity—folklorists' search for a paradigm for the structure of corporate groups in various regions). In K. Tsurumi and S. Ichii, eds., *Shisō no bōken* (Explorations into thought structure), pp. 187–234. Tokyo: Chikuma Shobō.

Sasaki Toshikazu. 1990. "Ainu-e ga egaita sekai" (The world drawn in the Ainu-e). In Sapporo Gakuin Daigaku Jinmongakubu, ed., *Ainu bunka ni manabu* (Lessons from Ainu culture), pp. 147–213. Sapporo: Sapporo Gakuin Daigaku Seikatsu Kyōdō Kumiai.

Shimizu Isao. 1991. *Manga no rekishi* (A history of cartoons). Tokyo: Iwanami Shoten.

Takakura Shinichirō. 1932. *Ainu seisakushi* (History of policy toward the Ainu). Tokyo: Nihon Hyōronsha.

——— 1953. *Ezo fūzokuga ni tsuite* (On ethnographic drawings of the Ezo). Kyōdo Kenkyū Shiryō, Series no. 3. Sapporo: Hokkaidō Kyōdo Kenkyūkai.

——— 1960. "The Ainu of Northern Japan: A Study in Conquest and Acculturation." Trans. J. A. Harrison. *Transactions of the American Philosophical Society*, n.s., 50(4). Philadelphia: American Philosophical Society.

Takayanagi Kinpō. 1981. *Edo jidai hinin no seikatsu* (The life of the *hinin* outcastes during the Edo period). Tokyo: Yūzankaku Shuppan.

Taki Kōji. 1990 [1988]. *Tennō no shōzō* (Portraits of the emperor). Tokyo: Iwanami Shoten.

Ueda Kazuo. 1978a. "Buraku no bunpu to jinkō" (Distribution of buraku settlements and population). In Buraku Kaihō Kenkyūsho, ed., *Buraku mondai gaisetsu*, pp. 3–10.

——— 1978b. "Kinsei hōken shakai to mibunsei" (The feudal society of the Early Modern period and the hierarchical system). In Buraku Kaihō Kenkyūsho, ed., *Buraku mondai gaisetsu*, pp. 100–118.

——— 1978c. "Kodai senminsei to buraku kigensetsu" ("The base people" in ancient Japan and the origin of the *Buraku*). In Buraku Kaihō Kenkyūsho, ed., *Buraku mondai gaisetsu*, pp. 73–85.

Williams, Brackette F. 1989. "A Class Act: Anthropology and the Race to Nation Across Ethnic Terrain." *Annual Review of Anthropology* 18: 401–44.

Williams, Raymond. 1973. *The Country and the City*. Oxford: Oxford University Press.

Yanagita Kunio. 1982 [1940]. "Kome no chikara" (Power of rice). *Teihon Yanagita Kunioshū* (Collected works of Yanagita Kunio), 14: 240–58. Tokyo: Tsukuma Shobō.

Yokoi Kiyoshi. 1982 [1975]. *Chūsei minshū no seikatsu bunka* (The life of the common people during the medieval age). Tokyo: Tōkyō Daigaku Shuppankai.

3. KENDALL, WHO SPEAKS FOR KOREAN SHAMANS?

Abu-Lughod, Lila. 1990. "Can there be a feminist ethnography?" *Women and Performance: A Journal of Feminist Theory* 5: 25.

——— 1991. "Writing Against Culture." In R. G. Fox, ed., *Recapturing Anthropology: Working in the Present*, pp. 137–62. Santa Fe, N. Mex.: School of American Research Press.

——— 1993. *Writing Women's Worlds: Bedouin Stories*. Berkeley: University of California Press.

Allen, Chizuko T. 1990. "Northeast Asia Centered Around Korea: Ch'oe Namsôn's View of History." *Journal of Asian Studies* 49(4): 787–806.

Anderson, Benedict. 1983. *Imagined Communities: Reflections on the Origin and Spread of Nationalism*. London: Verso.

Babb, Allan. 1990. "New Media and Religious Change." *Items* 44(4): 72–76.

Bauman, Richard, and Patricia Sawin. 1990. "The Politics of Participation in Folklife Festivals." In I. Karp and S. Lavine, ed., *Exhibiting Cultures: The Poetics and Politics of Museum Display*, pp. 288–314. Washington, D.C.: Smithsonian Institution Press.

Behar, Ruth. 1993. *Translated Woman: Crossing the Border with Esperanza's Story*. Boston: Beacon Press.

Brandt, Vincent S. R. 1971. *A Korean Village: Between Farm and Sea*. Cambridge: Harvard University Press.

Chang Chu-gun. 1974. "Mingan sinang" (Folk beliefs). In D. Yi, K. Yi, and C. Chang, eds., *Han'guk minsokhak kaesôl* (Introduction to Korean ethnology), pp. 128–97. Seoul: Minjung Sogwan.

Ch'oe Kil-song [Kil Seong Choi]. 1974. "Misin t'ap'ae taehan ilgoch'al" (A study on the destruction of superstition). *Han'guk minsokhak* (*Korean Folklore*) 7: 39–54.

Choi, Chungmoo. 1987. "The Competence of Korean Shamans as Performers of Folklore." Ph.D. dissertation, University of Indiana.

——— 1989. "The Artistry and Ritual Aesthetics of Urban Korean Shamans." *Journal of Ritual Studies* 3(2): 235–49.

——— 1991. "Nami, Ch'ae, and Oksun: Superstar Shamans in Korea." In Ruth-Inge Heinze, ed., *Shamans of the 20th Century*, pp. 51–61. New York: Irvington Publishers.

Choi In-Hak. 1987. "Non-academic Factors in the Development of Korean and Japanese Folklore Scholarship." Paper presented at the annual meeting of the American Anthropological Association, Chicago, November.

Chow, Rey. 1991. *Woman and Chinese Modernity: The Politics of Reading Between West and East*. Theory and History of Literature, vol. 75. Minneapolis: University of Minnesota Press.

Clark, Donald N. 1986. *Christianity in Modern Korea*. Lanham, Md.: University Press of America for the Asia Society.

Clifford, James. 1983. "On Ethnographic Authority." *Representations* 1(2): 118–46.

Commission on Theological Concerns of the Christian Conference of Asia, ed. 1981. *Minjung Theology: Peoples as the Subjects of History*. Maryknoll, N.Y.: Orbis/Zed/CCA.

Eckert, Carter J., Ki-baik Lee, Young Ick Lew, Michael Robinson, and Edward W. Wagner. 1990. *Korea Old and New: A History*. Cambridge: Ilchokak for the Korea Institute, Harvard University.

Guillemoz, Alexandre. 1992. "What Do the *Naerim Mudang* from Seoul Learn?" Paper presented at the Conference on Korean Shamanism Today, London, Dec. 10–12.

Hardacre, Helen. 1989. *Shinto and the State, 1868–1988*. Princeton, N.J.: Princeton University Press.

Harvey, Youngsook Kim. 1979. *Six Korean Women: Biographies of Shamans*. St. Paul, Minn.: West.

Hershatter, Gail. 1993. The Subaltern Talks Back: Reflections on Subaltern Theory and Chinese History. *Positions* 1(1): 103–30.

Howard, Keith. 1989. *Bands, Songs, and Shamanistic Rituals: Folk Music in Korean Society*. Seoul: Royal Asiatic Society, Korea Branch.

Hung, Chang-tai. 1985. *Going to the People: Chinese Intellectuals and Folk Literature, 1918–1937*. Cambridge: Council on East Asian Studies, Harvard University.

Irigaray, Luce. 1985. *Speculum of the Other Woman*. Trans. G. C. Gill. Ithaca, N.Y.: Cornell University Press.

Janelli, Roger L. 1986. "The Origins of Korean Folklore Scholarship." *Journal of American Folklore* 99(391): 24–49.

Janelli, Roger L., and Dawnhee Yim Janelli. 1982. *Ancestor Worship and Korean Society*. Stanford, Calif.: Stanford University Press.

Jordan, David K., and Daniel L. Overmyer. 1986. *The Flying Phoenix: Aspects of Chinese Sectarianism in Taiwan*. Princeton, N.J.: Princeton University Press.

Kapferer, Bruce. 1983. *A Celebration of Demons: Exorcism and the Aesthetics of Healing in Sri Lanka*. Bloomington: Indiana University Press.

Kendall, Laurel. 1977. "Caught Between Ancestors and Spirits: Field Report of a Korean *Mansin's* Healing *Kut*." *Korea Journal* 6: 8–23.

——— 1985. *Shamans, Housewives, and Other Restless Spirits: Women in Korean Ritual Life*. Honolulu: University of Hawai'i Press.

——— 1988. *The Life and Hard Times of a Korean Shaman: Of Tales and the Telling of Tales*. Honolulu: University of Hawai'i Press.

——— 1994. "A Rite of Modernization and Its Postmodern Discontents: Of Weddings, Bureaucrats, and Morality in the Republic of Korea." In C. F. Keyes, L. Kendall, and H. Hardacre, eds., *Asian Visions of Authority: Religion and the Modern States of East and Southeast Asia*, pp. 165–92. Honolulu: University of Hawai'i Press.

——— 1996. "Initiating Performance: The Story of Chini, a Korean Shaman." In C. Laderman and M. Roseman, eds., *The Performance of Healing*, pp. 17–58. New York: Routledge.

——— N.d. "Transformations of the Primal: Talking About Women's Spirituality in the Republic of Korea." Manuscript.

Kendall, Laurel, and Mark Peterson. 1983. "Traditional Korean Women: A Reconsideration." In L. Kendall and M. Peterson, eds., *Korean Women: A View from the Inner Room*, pp. 5–22. New Haven, Conn.: East Rock Press.

Kim, Kwang-ok. 1988. "A Study on the Political Manipulation of Elite Culture." Paper presented to the Fifth International Conference on Korean Studies, Academy of Korean Studies, June 30–July 3.

——— 1994. "Rituals of Resistance: The Manipulation of Shamanism in Contemporary Korea." In C. F. Keyes, L. Kendall, and H. Hardacre, eds., *Asian Visions of Authority: Religion and the Modern States of East and Southeast Asia*, pp. 195–219. Honolulu: University of Hawai'i Press.

Kim Kwangon, Yi Kwanggyu, Yi Hyônsun, and Ha Hyogil, eds. 1983. "Kônjônhan kajông ûiye chunch'ik" (The wholesome family ritual code). In *Kajông ûirye taebaekkwa* (Great compendium of family ritual), pp. 338–54. Seoul: Hando Munhwasa.

Kim Seong Nae. 1989. "Chronicle of Violence, Ritual of Mourning: Cheju Shamanism in Korea." Ph.D. diss., University of Washington.

——— 1991. "Han'guk musoge nat'anan yôsôngch'ehôm: kusul saengaesaûi sôsabunsôk" (Personal experiences in Korean shaman practices: Analysis of an oral narration of life history). *Han'guk yôsônghak (Korean Women's Studies)* 7: 7–43.

Kim, T'ae-gon. 1966. *Hwangch'on Muga Yôngu* (A study of shaman songs of the Yellow Springs). Seoul: Institute for the Study of Indigenous Religion.

——— 1972. "The Influence of Shamanism on the Living Pattern of People in Contemporary Korea." In T. Kim, ed., *The Modern Meaning of Shamanism*, pp. 71–80. Iri: Folklore Research Institute, Wôn'gwang University.

Linke, Uli. 1990. "Folklore, Anthropology, and the Government of Social Life." *Comparative Studies of Society and History* 32(1): 117–48.

Mani, Lata. 1987. "Contentious Traditions: The Debate on SATI in Colonial India." *Cultural Critique* 11: 119–56.

Moon, Okpyo. 1990. "Urban Middle Class Wives in Contemporary Korea: Their Roles, Responsibilities and Dilemma." *Korea Journal* 30(11): 30–43.

Nicholson, Linda J. 1986. *Gender and History: The Limits of Social Theory in the Age of the Family*. New York: Columbia University Press.

Nolte, Sharon, and Sally Ann Hastings. 1991. "The Meiji State's Policy Toward Women, 1890–1910." In G. L. Bernstein, ed., *Recreating Japanese Women, 1600–1945*. Berkeley: University of California Press.

Ong, Walter J. 1982. *Orality and Literacy: The Technologizing of the World*. New York: Methuen.

Park Heh-rahn. N.d. "Gender Critique of Sopyonje: On National Sentiment, Modernity and Tradition." Manuscript.

Robinson, Michael E. 1988. *Cultural Nationalism in Colonial Korea, 1920–1925*. Seattle: University of Washington Press.

Rosaldo, Michelle Zimbalist. 1974. "Woman, Culture, and Society: A Theoretical Overview." In M. Z. Rosaldo and L. Lamphere, eds., *Woman, Culture, and Society*, pp. 17–42. Stanford, Calif.: Stanford University Press.

Sanjek, Roger. 1990. "On Ethnographic Validity." In R. Sanjek, ed., *Fieldnotes: The Makings of Anthropology*, pp. 385–418. Ithaca, N.Y.: Cornell University Press.

Sorensen, Clark W. 1983. "Women, Men, Inside, Outside: The Division of Labor in Rural Central Korea." In L. Kendall and M. Peterson, eds., *Korean Women: A View from the Inner Room*, pp. 63–80. New Haven, Conn.: East Rock Press.

——— 1988. *Over the Mountains Are Mountains*. Seattle: University of Washington Press.

Spivak, Gayatri Chakravorty. 1988. "Can the Subaltern Speak?" In Cary Nelson and Lawrence Grossberg, eds., *Marxism and the Interpretation of Culture*, pp. 271–313. Urbana: University of Illinois Press.

Sun, Soon-Hwa. 1991. "Women, Religion, and Power: A Comparative Study of Korean Shamans and Women Ministers." Ph.D. dissertation, Drew University.

Thompson, Laurence G. 1975. *Chinese Religion: An Introduction*. 2d ed. Encino, Calif.: Dickenson Publishing Co.

Visweswaran, Kamala. 1988. "Defining Feminist Ethnography." *Inscriptions* 3(4): 27–44.

Walraven, Boudewijn. 1993. "Our Shamanistic Past: The Korean Government, Shamans, and Shamanism." *Copenhagen Papers in East and Southeast Asian Studies*, 5–25.

——— 1994. "Gender in Shamanic Narratives." Paper presented to the Workshop on Gender and Narrative in Korea, New York, March.

Williams, Brackette F. 1990. "Nationalism, Traditionalism, and the Problem of Cultural Inauthenticity." In R. G. Fox, ed., *Nationalist Ideologies and the Production of National Cultures*. American Ethnological Society Monograph Series, no. 2.

Wolf, Margery. 1992. *A Thrice-Told Tale: Feminism, Postmodernism, and Ethnographic Responsibility*. Stanford, Calif.: Stanford University Press.

Yanagisako, Sylvia Junko. 1987. "Mixed Metaphors: Native and Anthropological Models of Gender and Kinship Domains." In J. F. Collier and S. J. Yanagisako, eds., *Gender and Kinship: Essays Toward a Unified Analysis*, pp. 86–118. Stanford, Calif.: Stanford University Press.

Yanagita, Kunio. 1970 [1945]. *About Our Ancestors*. Tokyo: Ministry of Education.

Yang, C. K. 1961. *Religion in Chinese Society*. Berkeley: University of California Press.

4. CHO, CONSTRUCTING AND DECONSTRUCTING "KOREANNESS"

Abelmann, Nancy. 1993. "Minjung Theory and Practice." In H. Befu, ed., *Cultural Nationalism in East Asia*. Berkeley: University of California Press.

Academy of Korean Studies. 1994. *The Universal and Particular Natures of Confucianism*. Eighth International Conference on Korean Studies. Seoul: Academy of Korean Studies.

Allen, Chizuko T. 1990. "Northeast Asia Centered Around Korea: Ch'oe Namson's View of History." *Journal of Asian Studies* 49(4): 787–806.

Benjamin, Walter. 1973. "Theses on the Philosophy of History." In Walter Benjamin, *Illuminations*. London: Fontana.

Chatterjee, Partha. 1986. *National Thought and the Colonial World: A Derivative Discourse*. Minneapolis: University of Minnesota Press.

——— 1993. *The Nation and Its Fragments*. Princeton, N.J.: Princeton University Press.

Cho, Hae-joang. 1990. "Yogyojok chongtong puwhal undong kwa sahae pyon-dong" (Confucian revivalism and social change). Vols. 10–11, *Yonsei Sociology*.

——— 1994. "*Sôp'yônje* ũi Munwhasajõk Ũimi" (A Cultural Critique of *Sôp'yônje*). Vol. 2, *Kũlilki wa Samilki* (Reading text, reading lives). Seoul: Ttohana ũi Munwha.

Cho, Sun. 1994. "Yokyo hwa kyongje paljon" (Confucianism and economic development). In *Kongja sasang kwa 21 segi* (Confucian thought and the 21st century), pp. 75–88. Seoul: Dong-a Daily News Company.

Chung, Chai-sik. 1994. "Transcending the Clash of Civilization." *Theology & Public Policy* 6(1): 11–21.

Dirlik, Arif. 1994. "Confucius in the Borderlands: Global Capitalism and the Reinvention of Confucianism."

——— 1995. "Asia-Pacific Identities: Culture and Identity Formation in the Age of Global Capital." Symposium proposal.

Em, Henry H. 1995. "Overcoming Korea's Division: Narrative Strategies in Recent South Korean Historiography," *Positions* 1(2): 450–85.

Funabashi, Yoichi. 1993. "The Asianization of Asia." *Foreign Affairs* 72(6): 77–85.

Huntington, Samuel P. 1993. "The Clash of Civilizations?" *Foreign Affairs* 72(3): 22–49.

Kendall, Laurel. 1994. "A Rite of Modernization and Its Postmodern Discontents." In C. F. Keyes, L. Kendall, and H. Hardacre, eds., *Asian Visions of Authority*, pp. 165–92. Honolulu: University of Hawai'i Press.

Kim, Chung-yol. 1994a. *Uyga uynri kanguy* (Lectures on Confucian ethics). Seoul: Eymun.

——— 1994b. "Isybil segi hwa dongyang cholhak" (The 21st century and Asian thought). In *Kongja sasang kwa 21 segi* (Confucian thought and the 21st century), pp. 75–88. Seoul: Dong-a Daily News Company.

Kim, Il-gon. 1994. "Confucian Culture in the Economy and Management of East Asian Countries." In Academy of Korean Studies, *The Universal and Particular Natures of Confucianism.*

Kim, Pyong-gwan. 1994. *Kongja sasang kwa isibilsegi* (Confucian thought and the 21st century). Seoul: Dong-a Ilbo sa.

Koo, Hagen. 1993. *State and Society in Contemporary Korea*. Ithaca, N.Y.: Cornell University.

Korean Statistical Bureau. 1993. "Hanguk ni Sahoyjipyo." Seoul: T'onggyechong.

Kristof, Nicholas D. 1993. "The Rise of China." *Foreign Affairs* 72(6): 59–73.

Mahbubani, Kishore. 1995. "The Pacific Way." *Foreign Affairs* 74(1): 101–11.

Park, Heh-rahn. 1994. "Gender Critique of Sopyonje: On National Sentiment, Modernity and Tradition." Manuscript.

Robinson, Michael. 1984. "National Identity and the Thought of Sin Ch'aeho: *Sadaejuui* and *Chuch'e* in History and Politics." *Journal of Korean Studies* 5: 121–42.

——— 1993. "Enduring Anxieties: Cultural Nationalism and Modern East Asia." In H. Befu, ed., *Cultural Nationalism in East Asia*, pp. 167–86. Berkeley: University of California Press.

Spivak, Gayatri Chakravorty. 1988. "Can the Subaltern Speak? Speculations on

Widow Sacrifice." In Cary Nelson and Lawrence Grossberg, eds., *Marxism and the Interpretation of Culture*. Urbana: University of Illinois Press.
Tanaka, Stefan. 1993. *Japan's Orient: Rendering Pasts into History*. Berkeley: University of California Press.

5. HSIEH, IMAGES OF THE MAJORITY PEOPLE IN TAIWAN

Barth, Fredrik. 1969. "Pathan Identity and Its Maintenance." In Fredrik Barth, ed., *Ethnic Groups and Boundaries*, pp. 117–34. Boston: Little, Brown.
Bawan Danaha. 1991. "Ye tan Yuan Zhu Min de sheng cun quan li yu zun yan" (On the rights of existence and dignity of the indigenous people). *Lieren Wenhua* 15: 36–45.
——— 1992. "Chu cao' wen hua zhi yuan qi ji qi jing shen yi yi" (The origin of head-hunting culture and its inner meaning). *Lieren Wenhua* 17: 40–42.
Berreman, Gerald D. 1982 [1975]. "Bazar Behavior: Social Identity and Social Interaction in Urban India." In George DeVos and Lola Romanucci-Ross, eds., *Ethnic Identity: Cultural Continuities and Change*, pp. 71–105. Chicago: University of Chicago Press.
Bihao Lamang. 1991. "He Ping cun quan yi bei buo duo" (The rights of the villagers of He Ping have been deprived). *Lieren Wenhua* 7: 19.
Chen, Chih-wu. 1991. "Yuan Zhu Min wu wen hua you bu wei sheng: Tan cou lou de Han zu zong xin zhu yi?" (Do the indigenous people have no culture and ignore public health? On ugly Han chauvinism). *Lieren Wenhua* 13: 61–63.
Chen, Mao-t'ai. 1992. "Tai Wan Yuan Zhu Min de zu qun biao zhi yu zheng zhi can yu" (On ethnic emblems and political participation of Taiwan indigenous people). In Mao-Kuei Chang, ed., *Zu qun guan xi yu guo jia ren tong*. Taipei: Ye Qiang.
Chen, Yu-feng. 1993. "Shei lai gong wu—shi que wu tai de Yuan Wu Zhe" (Who is going to dance with us, *Yuanwuzhe* who have lost their platform?). In Chin-fa Wu, ed., *Yuan Wu Zhe: Yu ge Yuan Zhu Min wu tuan de cheng zhang ji lu*, pp. 98–105. Taichung: Chen Xing.
Chiang, Hsun. 1992. "Tian lai chang zan" (Marvelous singing as the situation of paradise). *Lieren Wenhua* 17: 58–59.
——— 1993. "Nan Wang cun gui lai: Xiang Yuan Wu Zhe zhi jing" (Returning from Nanwang Village: Salute to *Yuanwuzhe*). In Chin-fa Wu, ed., *Yuan Wu Zhe: Yi ge Yuan Zhu Min wu tuan de cheng zhang ji lu*, pp. 163–70. Taichung: Chen Xing.
DeVos, George. 1982 [1975]. "Ethnic Pluralism Conflict and Accommodation." In George DeVos and Lola Romanucci-Ross, eds., *Ethnic Identity: Cultural Continuities and Change*, pp. 5–41. Chicago: University of Chicago Press.
Eidheim, Harald. 1969. "When Ethnic Identity Is a Social Stigma." In Fredrik Barth, ed., *Ethnic Groups and Boundaries*, pp. 39–57. Boston: Little, Brown.
Geertz, Clifford. 1973 [1963]. "The Integrative Revolution: Primordial Sentiments and Civil Politics in the New States." In Clifford Geertz, *The Interpretation of Cultures*, pp. 255–310. New York: Basic Books.
Ho, Ts'ui-p'ing. 1993. "Dang ren lei xue jia yu dao Yuan Zhu Min" (When anthropologists meet the indigenous people), *Cheng Ping Yue Du* 12: 83–85.

Hsieh, Shih-chung. 1987a. *Ren tong de wu ming: Tai Wan Yuan Zhu Min de qun bian qian* (Stigmatized identity: On ethnic change of the indigenous people of Taiwan). Taipei: Zi Li Wan Bao.

——— 1987b. "Yuan Zhu Min yun dong sheng cheng yu fa zhan li lun de jian li: Yi bei mei yu Tai Wan wei li de cu bu tan tao" (Toward a theory of the initiation and development of indigenous movement: Case studies on North America and Taiwan). *Zhong Yang Yan Jiu Yuan Min Zu Xue Yen Jiu Suo Ji Kan* 64: 139–77.

——— 1990. "Di si shi jie' de jan gou: Yuan Zhu Min shi jie de qi ji yu wei ji" (The establishment of the fourth world: On the opportunities and crises of the indigenous world). In Shih-chung Hsieh and Pao-Kong Sun, eds., *Ren lei xue yan jiu: Qing zhu Ruey Yih-fu jiao shou jiu zi hua dan lun wen ji*, pp. 177–215. Taipei: Nan Tian.

——— 1992a. "Guan guang huo dong, wen hua chuan tong de shu mo yu qun yi shi: Wu Lai Tai Ya zu Daiyan ren tong de yan jiu" (Tourism, formulation of cultural tradition, and ethnicity: A study on *Daiyan* identity of Atayal in Wulai). *Kao Gu Ren Lei Xue Kan* 48: 113–29.

——— 1992b. "Pian li qun zhong de jing ying: Shi lun 'Yuanzhumin' xiang zheng yu Yuan Zhu Min jing ying xian xiang de guan xi" (The elites who lost their supporters: On the symbol of '*Yuanzhumin*' and its relation to phenomena of indigenous elites). *Dao Yu Bian Yuan* 5: 52–60.

——— 1992c. "Xing shi zi yuan de cao kong yu jing zheng: Fei Han zu qun zheng zhi yun dong de sheng cheng tiao jian" (On manipulation and competition of formal resources: Conditions of initiation of non-Han ethnic-political movement). *Kao Gu Ren Lei Xue Kan* 48: 99–112.

——— 1994a. "Guan guang guo cheng yu 'chuan tong' lun shu: Yuan Zhu Min de wen hua yi shi" (Touristic process and the discourse of "tradition": Cultural consciousness of the indigenous people). In *Yuan Zhu Min wen hua hui yi lun wen ji, xing zheng yuan wen hua jian she wei yuan hui bian ying*, pp. 1–18. Taipei: Council of Cultural Development.

——— 1994b. *Shan Bao guan guang: Dang dai shan di wen hua zhan xian de ren lei xue quan shi* (Tourism of Mountain People: On anthropological interpretation of the performance of indigenous culture in Taiwan). Taipei: Zi Li Bao Xi.

Hsu, Mu-chu. 1989. "Tai Wan Yuan Zhu Min de zu qun ren yun dong: Xin li wen hua yan jiu tu jing de chu bu tan tao" (On the ethnic identity movement of Taiwan indigenous people: A psychocultural approach). In Cheng-Kuang Hsu and Wen-Li Sung, eds., *Tai Wan xin xing shi Hui yun dong*, pp. 127–56. Taipei: Ju Liu.

——— 1991. "Ruo shi zu qun wen ti" (On inferior ethnic groups). In Kuo-shu Yang and Chi-cheng Yeh, eds., *Tai Wan de she Hui wen ti*, pp. 399–428. Taipei: Ju Liu.

Huang, Shih-ch'iao. 1966. "Ben sheng shan di ren min sheng huo gai jin cheng guo" (The accomplishment of improving the lives of the Mountain People). *Tai Wan Wen Xian* 17(1): 138–48.

Huang, Ying-kuei. 1989. "Jin liu nian lai Tai Wan di qu chu ban ren lei xue lun zhu xuan jie" (A review of anthropological literature in a recent six-year period). *Han Xue Yan Jiu Tong Xun* 8(4): 227–38.

Hung, T'ien-chun. 1993. "Shan lin gou huo zai ran qi: Zhi ci 'Tai Wan Yuan Wu Zhe'" (Re-burned powerful fire in mountain: Support the Taiwan *Yuanwuzhe*).

In Chin-fa Wu, ed., *Yuan Wu Zhe: Yi ge Yuan Zhu Min wu tuan de cheng zhang ji lu*, pp. 50–54. Taichung: Chen Xing.

I Sing. 1992. "Shan zhong de wen ming ren: Lie ren" (Hunters are civilized people in the mountains). *Lieren Wenhua* 17: 20–25.

Jilufugan Awu. 1991. "Gan yi bei, jin ku ming de Shan Di Ren" (Cheers, salute to unfortunate Mountain People). *Lieren Wenhua* 1(10): 11–15.

Kabi Kaliduoai. 1991. "Yuan Zhu Min de bei ge" (The tragic stories of the indigenous people). *Lieren Wenhua* 1 (11–12): 27.

Kao, Te-I. 1994. "Tai Wan Yuan Zhu Min shi xing zi zhi de zheng ce ke xing xin fen xi" (An analysis of the possibility of practicing ethnic autonomy in indigenous homelands). In Xing Zheng Yuan Wen Hua Jian She Wei Yuan Hui, ed., *Yuan Zhu Min wen hua hui yi lun wen ji*, pp. 251–73. Taipei: Council of Cultural Development.

Keyes, Charles F. 1973. "Ethnic Identity and Loyalty of Villagers in Northeastern Thailand." In John T. McAlister, Jr., ed., *Southeast Asia: The Politics of National Integration*, pp. 355–65. New York: Random House.

——— 1976. "Towards a New Formulation of the Concept of Ethnic Group." *Ethnicity* 3: 202–13.

——— 1981. "The Dialectics of Ethnic Change." In Charles F. Keyes, ed., *Ethnic Change*, pp. 8–30. Seattle: University of Washington Press.

——— 1992. "Who Are the Lue? Revisited: Ethnic Identity in Laos, Thailand, and China." Working paper, Center for International Studies, Massachusetts Institute of Technology.

Kuo, Hsiu-yen. 1985. "Dang qian shan di xing zheng zhong yao cuo si yu zhan wang" (On important policies and future development of the contemporary mountain administration). Manuscript.

"Lan yu yuan yun de qi shi" (An enlightening guidance from the indigenous movement in Orchid Island). 1991. *Lieren Wenhua* 8: 2.

Lin, Mei-hui. 1991. "Zai Hui ba! Tao Yuan" (So long! Tao Yuan). *Lieren Wenhua* 1(9): 35–40.

McKay, James, and Frank Lewins. 1978. "Ethnicity and the Ethnic Group: A Conceptual Analysis and Reformulation." *Ethnic and Racial Studies* 1(4): 412–27.

Moerman, Michael. 1965. "Ethnic Identity in a Complex Civilization: Who Are the Lue?" *American Anthropologist* 67: 1215–30.

Nagata, Judith A. 1974. "What Is a Malay? Situational Selection of Ethnic Identity in a Plural Society." *American Ethnologist* 1(2): 331–50.

——— 1981. "In Defense of Ethnic Boundaries: The Changing Myths and Charters of Malay Identity." In Charles F. Keyes, ed., *Ethnic Change*, pp. 87–116. Seattle: University of Washington Press.

P'eng, Hsiao-yen. 1994. "Zu qun shu xie yu min zu/guo jia: Lun Yuan Zhu Min wen xue" (Ethnic discourse and nation: On indigenous literature). In Xing Zheng Yuan Wen Hua Jian She Wei Yuan Hui, ed., *Yuan Zhu Min wen hua hui yi lun wen ji*, pp. 67–80. Taipei: Council of Cultural Development.

"Shei shi sha shou?" (Who is the killer?). 1992. *Lieren Wenhua* 16: 3.

Southall, Aiden W. 1976. "Nuer and Dinka are People: Ecology, Ethnicity, and Logical Possibility." *Man* 11: 463–91.

Tai Wan Sheng Zheng Fu Xin Wen Cu. 1971. *Gai shan Shan Bao sheng huo* (Improving the lives of Mountain People). Nantou: Provincial Government of Taiwan.

Trosper, Ronald L. 1981. "American Indian Nationalism and Frontier Expansion." In Charles F. Keyes, ed., *Ethnic Change*, pp. 246–70. Seattle: University of Washington Press.

Ts'ai, Chung-han. 1992. "*Di, Rong, Man, Yi, Shan Bao: Dou bu shi ren lei*" (Di, Rong, Man, Yi, and the Mountain People: All are not human beings). *Lieren Wenhua* 18: 14–15.

Van Den Berghe, Pierre L. 1978. "Race and Ethnicity: A Sociobiological Perspective." *Ethnic and Racial Studies* 1: 401–11.

——— 1981. *The Ethnic Phenomenon*. New York: Elsevier.

Walis Yugan. 1992. "Bian qian xia de Yuan Zhu Min: Dui bei qu Yuan Zhu Min da zhuan sheng de yan jiang shi lu" (The indigenous people in transition: A lecture for the indigenous college students in northern Taiwan). *Lieren Wenhua* 17: 50–55.

Wang, Chia-hsiang. 1993a. "Sheng qi gou huo lai sai xi" (Light a fire to start a competition of play performances). In Chin-fa Wu, ed., *Yuan Wu Zhe: Yi ge Yuan Zhu Min wu tuan de cheng zhang ji lu*, pp. 217–27. Taichung: Chen Xing.

——— 1993b. "Tai Wan Yuan Wu Zhe" (Taiwan *Yuanwuzhe*). In Chin-fa Wu, ed., *Yuan Wu Zhe: Yi ge Yuan Zhu Min wu tuan de cheng zhang ji lu*, pp. 55–62. Taichung: Chen Xing.

——— 1993c. "Xi wang zhi lu: Ji 'Yuan Wu Zhe' di yi ci tu de xun yan" (A journey of hope: The first time to perform around the entire island by the Yuanwuzhe). In Chin-fa Wu, ed., *Yuan Wu Zhe: Yi ge Yuan Zhu Min wu tuan de cheng zhang ji lu*, pp. 69–97. Taichung: Chen Xing.

Wu, Chin-fa. 1992. "Huan gei Yuan Zhu Min zun rong de 'min'" (Give back a respectful name to the indigenous people). *Lieren Wenhua* 18: 28.

——— 1993. "Yuan Wu Zhe de zhan dou" (A fight of the *Yuanwuzhe*). In Chin-fa Wu, ed., *Yuan Wu Zhe: Yi ge Yuan Zhu Min wu tuan de cheng zhang ji lu*, pp. 30–33. Taichung: Chen Xing.

Yang, Pai-yuan. 1968. "Jing ru wen ming ling yu de ben sheng shan di fu nu" (The mountain women who have been promoted to a civilized sphere). *Tai Wan Wen Xian* 19(4): 163–69.

Yijiang, Baluer, and Lawagao Laigelake. 1992. "Tai Wan Yuan Zhu Min zu de fa zhan shi" (A history of the indigenous people of Taiwan). *Lieren Wenhua* 16: 30–41.

Yijiang Xilan. 1992. "Fan shu de ye ci bu shi qiu hai tang" (Leaves of yams are not begonia). *Lieren Wenhua* 18: 26–27.

"Yuan Zhu Min ku qi le" (Indigenous people are crying). 1992. *Lieren Wenhua* 18: 29.

"Yuan Zhu Min shi jian fen xi" (An analysis of the events regarding the indigenous people). 1991. *Lieren Wenhua* 13: 6–13.

"Yuan Zhu Min shi jian ji" (A record of the social events of the indigenous people). 1991. *Lieren Wenhua* 7: 16–17.

Zhong Guo Guo Min Dang Zhong Yang Wei Yuan Hui Di Wu Zu, ed. 1960. *Nong, yu min, kuang gong, Shan Bao sheng huo fang wen bao gao* (A report on the general lives of farmers, fishermen, miners, and Mountain People). Taipei: Nationalist Party.

6. GLADNEY, MUSLIM AND CHINESE IDENTITIES IN THE PRC

Allworth, Edward. 1980. "Ambiguities in Russian Group Identity and Leadership of the RSFSR." In Edward Allworth, ed. *Ethnic Russia in the USSR: The Dilemma of Dominance*, pp. 17–41. New York: Pergamon.

Anagnost, Ann S. 1986. "The Mimesis of Power." Paper presented at the conference "Anthropological Perspectives on Mainland China, Past and Present," Center for Chinese Studies, University of California, Berkeley, Nov. 22.

Anderson, Benedict. 1983. *Imagined Communities: Reflections on the Origin and Spread of Nationalism*. London: Verso.

Appadurai, Arjun. 1986. "Introduction: Commodities and the Politics of Value." In Arjun Appadurai, ed., *The Social Life of Things: Commodities in Cultural Perspective*, pp. 3–63. Cambridge: Cambridge University Press.

Bai Shouyi Djamal al-Din. 1951. "Huihui minzu de xingcheng" (The nature of the Hui nationality). *Guangming Ribao*, Feb. 17.

Bakhtin, M. Mikhail. 1981. *The Dialogic Imagination*. Ed. Michael Holquist, trans. Caryl Emerson and Michael Holquist. Russian ed. 1975. Austin: University of Texas Press.

——— 1984. *Problems of Dostoevsky's Poetics*. Ed. and trans. Caryl Emerson. Russian ed. 1963. Minneapolis: University of Minnesota Press.

Banister, Judith. 1987. *China's Changing Population*. Stanford, Calif.: Stanford University Press.

Bentley, G. Carter. 1987. "Ethnicity and Practice." *Comparative Studies in Society and History* 1: 24–55.

Blake, C. Fred. 1981. *Ethnic Groups and Social Change in a Chinese Market Town*. Honolulu: University of Hawai'i Press.

Bourdieu, Pierre. 1977. *Outline of a Theory of Practice*. Cambridge: Cambridge University Press.

Chiang Kaishek. 1947 [1943]. *China's Destiny*. New York: Roy.

Chow, Rey. 1993. *Writing Diaspora*. Minneapolis: University of Minnesota Press.

Cohen, Ronald, and John Middleton. 1970. *From Tribe to Nation in Africa*. Scranton, Pa.: Chandler.

Cohn, Bernard S. 1971. *India: The Social Anthropology of a Civilization*. Englewood Cliffs, N.J.: Prentice-Hall.

Comaroff, Jean. 1994. "Defying Disenchantment: Reflections on Ritual, Power, and History." In Charles Keyes, Laurel Kendall, and Helen Hardacre, eds., *Asian Visions of Authority: Religion and the Modern States of East and Southeast Asia*, pp. 301–14. Honolulu: University of Hawai'i Press.

Connor, Walker. 1984. *The National Question in Marxist-Leninist Theory and Strategy*. Princeton, N.J.: Princeton University Press.

Cooper, Richard. 1994. "Will the Fault Lines Between Civilizations Be the Battle Lines of the Future?" *Centerpiece* (Winter/Spring): 9.

Dunlop, John B. 1983. *The Faces of Contemporary Russian Nationalism.* Princeton, N.J.: Princeton University Press.
Ekvall, Robert. 1939. *Cultural Relations on the Kansu-Tibetan Border.* Chicago: Chicago University Press.
Evans-Pritchard, E. E. 1940. *The Nuer.* Oxford: Clarendon.
Fallers, Lloyd. 1974. *The Social Anthropology of the Nation-State.* Chicago: Aldine.
Fei Xiaotong. 1981. *Toward a People's Anthropology.* Beijing: New World.
Forbes, Andrew D. W. 1976. "Survey Article: The Muslim National Minorities of China." *Religion* 6(2): 67–87.
Foucault, Michel. 1972. "Truth and Power." In Colin Gordon, ed., *Power/Knowledge.* New York: Pantheon Books.
——— 1980. *Knowledge/Power: Selected Interviews and Other Writings, 1972–1977.* Ed. and trans. Colin Gordon. New York: Pantheon.
Francis, E. K. 1976. *Interethnic Relations.* New York: Elsevier.
Friedman, Edward. 1994. "Reconstructing China's National Identity: A Southern Alternative to Mao-Era Anti-Imperialist Nationalism." *Journal of Asian Studies* 53(1): 67–91.
Furnivall, J. S. 1939. *Netherlands India.* Cambridge: Cambridge University Press.
Geertz, Clifford. 1968. *Islam Observed.* Chicago: University of Chicago Press.
Gellner, Ernest. 1983. *Nations and Nationalism.* Ithaca, N.Y.: Cornell University Press.
Gladney, Dru C. 1987. "Muslim Tombs and Ethnic Folklore: Charters for Hui Identity." *Journal of Asian Studies* 46(3): 495–532.
——— 1990. "The Ethnogenesis of the Uighur." *Central Asian Survey* 9(1): 1–28.
——— 1991. *Muslim Chinese: Ethnic Nationalism in the People's Republic.* Cambridge: Harvard University Press, Council on East Asian Studies.
——— 1994a. "Representing Nationality in China: Refiguring Majority/Minority Identities." *Journal of Asian Studies* 53(1): 92–123.
——— 1994b. "Salman Rushdie in China: Religion, Ethnicity, and State Definition in the People's Republic." In Charles Keyes, Laurel Kendall, and Helen Hardacre, eds., *Asian Visions of Authority: Religion and the Modern States of East and Southeast Asia*, pp. 255–78. Honolulu: University of Hawai'i Press.
——— 1995. "Economy and Ethnicity: The Revitalization of a Muslim Minority in Southeastern China." In Andrew Walder, ed. *Political Consequences of Departures from Central Planning: The Economic Origins of Political Change in Communist States*, pp. 242–66. Berkeley: University of California Press.
——— 1996. "Relational Alterity: Constructing Dungan (Hui), Uygur, and Kazakh Identities Across China, Central Asia, and Turkey." *History and Anthropology* 9(2): 445–77.
Goldstein, Melvyn C. 1990. "The Dragon and the Snow Lion: The Tibet Question in the Twentieth Century." In Anthony J. Kane, ed., *China Briefing, 1989*, pp. 129–67. Boulder, Colo.: Westview Press.
Harrell, Stevan. 1989. "The Invention of Ethnicity: The History of the History of the Yi." Presented at the Association for Asian Studies Meetings, Mar. 17–19, Washington, D.C.
Hobbes, Thomas. 1962 [1651]. *Leviathan.* New York: Fontana.

Hobsbawm, Eric. 1983. "Introduction: Inventing Traditions." In Hobsbawm and Ranger, eds. *Invention of Tradition.*

——— 1991. *Nations and Nationalism Since 1780.* Cambridge: Cambridge University Press.

——— 1992. "Ethnicity and Nationalism in Europe Today." *Anthropology Today* 8(1): 3–8.

Hobsbawm, Eric, and Terence Ranger, eds. 1983. *The Invention of Tradition.* Cambridge: Cambridge University Press.

Honig, Emily. 1992. *Creating Chinese Ethnicity.* New Haven, Conn.: Yale University Press.

Huizu Jianshi Editorial Committee. 1978. *Huizu jianshi* (Brief history of the Hui). Yinchuan: Ningxia People's Publishing Company.

Huntington, Samuel P. 1993a. "The Islamic-Confucian Connection." *New Perspectives Quarterly* 10(3): 19–35.

——— 1993b. "The Clash of Civilizations?" *Foreign Affairs* 72(3): 22–49.

Israeli, Raphael. 1978. *Muslims in China.* London: Curzon; Atlantic Highlands: Humanities Press.

——— 1984. "Muslims in China: Islam's Incompatibility with the Chinese Order." In Raphael Israeli and Anthony H. Johns, eds., *Islam in Asia*, vol. 2. Boulder, Colo.: Westview Press.

Jin Binggao. 1984. "The Marxist Definition of Nationality, Its Origin and Influence." *Central Nationalities Institute Journal* 3: 64–67.

Keyes, Charles F. 1981. "Introduction: The Dialectics of Ethnic Change." In Charles F. Keyes, ed., *Ethnic Change*, pp. 4–30. Seattle: University of Washington Press.

——— 1984. "The Basis of Ethnic Group Relations in Modern Nation-States." In V. I. Kozlov, ed., *Ethnic Processes in the USA and the USSR: Material of the Soviet American Symposium.* Moscow: INION, Academy of Sciences.

Leach, Edmund R. 1954. *Political Systems of Highland Burma.* Cambridge: Cambridge University Press.

Leslie, Donald Daniel. 1986. *Islam in Traditional China: A Short History to 1800.* Canberra: Canberra College of Advanced Education.

Lindbeck, J. 1950. "Communism, Islam and Nationalism in China." *Review of Politics* 12: 473–88.

Lipman, Jonathan N. 1988. "Ethnicity and Economics: The Tibetan-Muslim-Han Trading Network in Northwest China." Paper presented at the Association for Asian Studies Meetings, Mar. 26, San Francisco.

Liu Binyan. 1993. "Civilization Grafting: No Culture Is an Island." *Foreign Affairs* 72(4): 19–21.

Ma Shouqian. 1989. "The Hui People's New Awakening at the End of the Nineteenth Century and Beginning of the Twentieth Century." Paper presented at the conference "The Legacy of Islam in China: An International Symposium in Memory of Joseph F. Fletcher," Apr. 14–16, Harvard University, Cambridge, Mass.

Ma Weiliang. 1986. "Yunnan Daizu, Zangzu, Baizu, he Xiao Liangshan Yizu Diqu de Huizu" (The Hui of Yunnan's Dai, Tibetan, Bai, and Small Liangshan Yi Areas). *Ningxia Shehui Kexue* 1.

Mair, Walter. 1994. "Will the Fault Lines Between Civilizations Be the Battle Lines of the Future?" *Centerpiece* (Winter/Spring): 10.

Maybury-Lewis, David. 1984. "Living in Leviathan: Ethnic Groups and the State." In David Maybury-Lewis, ed., *The Prospects for Plural Societies*, pp. 220–31. Washington, D.C.: The American Ethnological Society.

Millward, James A. 1988. "The Chinese Border Wool Trade of 1880–1937." Paper presented at the Association for Asian Studies Meetings, Mar. 26, San Francisco.

Moerman, Michael. 1965. "Ethnic Identity in a Complex Civilization: Who Are the Lue?" *American Anthropologist* 67(5): 1215–30.

Muzaffar, Chandra. 1994. Interview in *Third World Network Features*. Penang. Reprinted in "The Clash of Civilizations? Responses from the World," *Centerpiece* (Winter/Spring): 8.

Pang, Keng-Fong. 1992. "The Dynamics of Gender, Ethnicity, and State Among Austronesian-speaking Muslims of Hui-Utat of Hainan Island." Ph.D. dissertation, University of California, Los Angeles.

Pillsbury, Barbara L. K. 1973. "Cohesian and Cleavage in a Chinese Muslim Minority." Ph.D. dissertation, Columbia University.

Rahim, Syed A. 1994. "Participatory Development Communication as a Dialogical Process." In Shirley A. White, K. Sadanandan Nair, and Joseph Ascroft, eds., *Participatory Communication: Working for Change and Development*. New Delhi: SAGE Publications.

Rousseau, Jean-Jacques. 1968 [1762]. *The Social Contract*. Trans. Maurice Cranston. London: Penguin.

Rubenstein, Richard L. 1978. *The Cunning of History: The Holocaust and the American Future*. New York: Harper & Row.

Salisbury, Harrison E. 1985. *The Long March: The Untold Story*. New York: Harper & Row.

Schwarz, Henry. 1971. *Chinese Policies Toward Minorities: An Essay and Documents*. Bellingham Western Washington State College.

Snow, Edgar. 1938. *Red Star Over China*. New York: Grove.

Sun Yatsen. 1924. *The Three Principles of the People: San Min Chu I*. Trans. Frank W. Price. Taipei: China Publishing Company.

Wales, Nym. 1952. *Red Dust: Autobiographies of Chinese Communists as told to Nym Wales*. Stanford, Calif.: Stanford University Press.

Weber, Max. 1978 [1956]. *Economy and Society*. 2 vols. Trans. Guenther Roth and Claus Wittich. Berkeley: University of California Press.

Wimbush, S. Enders. 1985. "The Politics of Identity Change in Soviet Central Asia." *Central Asian Survey* 3(3): 69–78.

Yang, Mayfair Mei-Hui. 1989. "The Gift Economy and State Power in China." *Comparative Studies in Society and History* 31(1): 25–54.

Yang, Muhammed Usiar Huaizhong. Forthcoming. "Sufism Among the Muslims in Gansu, Ningxia, and Qinghai." In Charles Li and Dru C. Gladney, eds., *Minority Nationalities of China: Language and Culture*. Amsterdam: Mouton.

Yanov, Alexander. 1987. *The Russian Challenge and the Year 2000*. Trans. Iden J. Rosenthal. Oxford: Basil Blackwell.

Yokoyama, Hiroko. 1988. "Ethnic Identity Among the Inhabitants of the Dali Basin

in Southwestern China." Paper presented at the 87th Annual Meeting of the American Anthropological Association, Nov. 16–20, Phoenix, Ariz.
Zhongguo Shaoshu Minzu. 1981. *Zhongguo Shaoshu Minzu* (China's Minority Nationalities). Beijing: People's Publishing Society.

7. SHAMSUL, "MALAYNESS" IN POSTWAR MALAYSIA

Ackerman, Susan, and Raymond Lee. 1988. *Heaven in Transition: Non-Muslim Religious Innovation and Ethnic Identity in Malaysia*. Honolulu: University of Hawai'i Press.
Andaya, Barbara, and Leonard Andaya. 1982. *A History of Malaysia*. London: Macmillan.
Anderson, Benedict. 1983. *Imagined Communities: Reflections on the Origins and Spread of Nationalism*. London: Verso.
Ariffin Omar. 1993. *Bangsa Melayu: Malay Concepts of Democracy and Community, 1945–1950*. Kuala Lumpur: Oxford University Press.
Chandra Muzaffar. 1979. *Protector? An Analysis of the Concept and Practice of Loyalty in Leader-Led Relationships Within Malay Society*. Penang: Aliran.
Chatterjee, Partha. 1986. *Nationalist Thought and the Colonial World: A Derivative Discourse*. London: Zed Press for the United Nations University.
Cho, Hae-joang. 1994. "Constructing and Deconstructing 'Koreanness.'" Paper presented at the Conference on Configuring Minority/Majority Discourse, Aug. 11–13, East-West Center, Honolulu, Hawai'i.
Das, Veena. 1986. "Gender Studies, Cross-cultural Comparisons and the Colonial Organisation of Knowledge." *Berkshire Review* 21: 58–76.
Eriksen, Thomas Hylland. 1993. *Ethnicity and Nationalism: Anthropological Perspectives*. London: Pluto.
Handler, Richard. 1994. "Studying 'Mainstreams' and 'Minorities' in North America: Some Epistemological and Ethical Dilemmas." Paper presented at the Conference on Configuring Minority/Majority Discourse, Aug, 11–13, East-West Center, Honolulu, Hawai'i.
Herzfeld, Michael. 1993. *The Social Production of Indifference: Exploring the Symbolic Roots of Western Bureaucracy*. Chicago: University of Chicago Press.
Hirschman, Charles. 1986. "The Making of Race in Colonial Malaya: Political Economy and Racial Ideology." *Sociological Forum* (Spring): 330–61.
——— 1987. "The Meaning and Measurement of Ethnicity in Malaysia." *Journal of Asian Studies* 46(3): 555–82.
Hobsbawm, Eric. 1983. "Introduction." In E. Hobsbawm and T. Ranger, eds., *The Invention of Tradition*. Cambridge: Cambridge University Press.
Hsieh, Shih-chung. 1994. "On Three Kinds of Definitions of Han Ren: Images of the Majority People in Taiwan." Paper presented at the Conference on Configuring Minority/Majority Discourse, Aug. 11–13, East-West Center, Honolulu, Hawai'i.
Jesudason, James. 1989. *Ethnicity and the Economy: The State, Chinese Business, and Multinationals in Malaysia*. Singapore: Oxford University Press.

Kamaruddin Jaafar. 1980. *Dr. Burhanuddin AlHelmy: Politik Melayu dan Islam.* Kuala Lumpur: Yayasan Anda.

Kaplan, Martha. 1994. "When 8,870 − 850 = 1: Discourses Against Democracy in Fiji Past and Present." Paper presented at the Conference on Configuring Minority/Majority Discourse, Aug. 11–13, East-West Center, Honolulu, Hawai'i.

Kelly, John. 1994. "Aspiring to Minority: An Indo-Fijian Tactic Against Violence." Paper presented at the Conference on Configuring Minority/Majority Discourse, Aug. 11–13, East-West Center, Honolulu, Hawai'i.

Kirişci, Kemal. 1994. "Minority/Majority Discourse: The Case of the Kurds in Turkey." Paper presented at the Conference on Configuring Minority/Majority Discourse, Aug. 11–13, East-West Center, Honolulu, Hawai'i.

Kua Kia Soong. 1985. *The Chinese Schools of Malaysia: A Protean Saga.* Kuala Lumpur: United Chinese School Committees Association of Malaysia.

——— 1987. *Polarization in Malaysia: The Root Causes.* Kuala Lumpur: Malaysian Chinese Research and Resource Centre.

Lau, Albert. 1991. *The Malayan Union Controversy, 1942–1948.* Singapore: Oxford University Press.

Mahathir Mohamed. 1991. "Malaysia: The Way Foward." Paper presented at the Inaugural Meeting of the Malaysian Business Council, Jan. 28.

Miles, Robert. 1989. *Racism.* London: Routledge.

Mills, Leonard. 1942. *British Rule in Eastern Asia.* London: Oxford University Press.

Milner, Anthony. 1982. *Kerajaan: Malay Political Culture on the Eve of Colonial Rule.* Association for Asian Studies Monograph. Tucson: University of Arizona Press.

——— 1991. "Inventing Politics: The Case of Malaysia." *Past & Present* 132: 104–29.

——— 1994. "Episodes in the History of Malayness." Paper presented at the Conference on Configuring Minority/Majority Discourse, Aug. 11–13, East-West Center, Honolulu, Hawai'i.

Okamura, John. 1994. "Multiculturalism in Hawaii: A Promise for Whom?" Paper presented at the Conference on Configuring Minority/Majority Discourse, Aug. 11–13, East-West Center, Honolulu, Hawai'i.

Potter, Jonathan, and Margaret Wetherell. 1987. *Discourse and Social Psychology: Beyond Attitudes and Behaviour.* London: Sage.

Roff, William. 1967. *The Origins of Malay Nationalism.* Kuala Lumpur: University of Malaya Press.

Rustam A. Sani. 1993. *Melayu Baru dan Bangsa Malaysia: Tradisi cendekia dan krisis budaya.* Kuala Lumpur: Utusan.

Said, Edward. 1985. *Orientalism.* Harmondsworth: Penguin.

Shamsul A. B. 1977. *RMK: Tujuan dan perlaksanaannya, suatu tinjauan teoritis.* Kuala Lumpur: Dewan Bahasa dan Pustaka.

——— 1986. *From British to Bumiputera Rule: Local Politics and Rural Development in Peninsular Malaysia.* Singapore: Institute of Southeast Asian Studies.

——— 1988. "Battle Royal: The UMNO Elections of 1987." In *Southeast Asian Affairs 1988.* Singapore: Institute of Southeast Asian Studies.

——— 1993. "The Making of an Islamic Revivalist Activist in Malaysia." Paper

presented at the Conference on Islam in Southeast Asia, Aug. 3–6, University of Hawai'i, Honolulu.
——— 1994. "Religion and Ethnic Politics in Malaysia: The Significance of the Islamic Resurgence Phenomenon." In Charles Keyes, Laurel Kendall, and Helen Hardacre, eds., *Asian Visions of Authority: Religion and the Modern States of East and Southeast Asia*. Honolulu: University of Hawai'i Press.
——— 1995. "Inventing Certainties: The Dakwah Persona in Malaysia." In Wendy James, ed., *The Pursuit of Certainty: Religious and Cultural Formulations*. London: Routledge.
——— 1996a. "Nations-of-Intent in Malaysia." In Stein Tonnesson and Hans Antloev, eds., *Asian Forms of the Nation*. London: Curzon.
——— 1996b. "UMNO: 50 Years," *Business Times* (Singapore), Apr. 27–28.
Shamsul A. B. and Vijai Balasubramaniam. 1994. "Federalism: The Sabah Dilemma." *Trends* (Institute of Southeast Asian Studies, Singapore) 43 (Mar. 26–27).
Smith, Anthony. 1981. *The Ethnic Revival*. Cambridge: Cambridge University Press.
Watson, Bill. 1994. "The Construction of the Post-colonial Subject in Malaysia." Paper presented at the Workshop on Comparative Approaches to National Identities in Asia, Nordic Institute of Asian Studies, May 26–28, Copenhagen.
Yoshino, Kosaku. 1994. "Culturalism, Racialism and Internationalism in the Discourse on Japanese Identity." Paper presented at the Conference on Configuring Minority/Majority Discourse, Aug. 11–13, East-West Center, Honolulu, Hawai'i.
Zawiah Yahya. 1994. "The Malays as a Colonial Construct." Paper presented at the Conference on Identities, Ethnicities, Nationalities: Asian and Pacific Contexts, July 7–9, La Trobe University, Melbourne.

8. MILNER, CONSTRUCTING THE MALAY MAJORITY

Abdul Hadi bin Haji Hasan. 1948. *Sejarah Alam Melayu*. Singapore: Malaya Publishing House.
Abdul Latiff Abu Bakar. 1987. *Puisi-puisi Kebangsaan, 1913–1957*. Kuala Lumpur: Dewan Bahasa dan Pustaka.
Anderson, B. R. O'G. 1991. *Imagined Communities*. London: Verso.
Ariffin Omar. 1993. *Bangsa Melayu: Malay Concepts of Democracy and Community, 1945–1950*. Kuala Lumpur: Oxford University Press.
Bakhtin, M. M. 1984. *The Dialogic Imagination*. Austin: University of Texas Press.
Banton, M. 1988. *Racial Consciousness*. London: Longman.
Brown, C. C. 1952. "Sejarah Melayu, or Malay Annals." *Journal of the Malaysian Branch of the Royal Asiatic Society* 25(2–3): 1–276.
Chandra Muzaffar. 1987. *Islamic Resurgence in Malaysia*. Petaling Jaya: Fajar Bakti.
Chatterjee, Partha. 1986. *Nationalist Thought and the Colonial World: A Derivative Discourse?* London: Zed.
——— 1993. *The Nation and Its Fragments: Colonial and Postcolonial Histories*. Princeton, N.J.: Princeton University Press.

Comaroff, J. 1987. "Of Totemism and Ethnicity: Consciousness, Practice and the Signs of Inequality." *Ethnos* 52(3–4): 301–23.
Crawfurd, J. 1967 [1820]. *History of the Indian Archipelago*. London: Frank Cass.
Cushman, J. W., and A. C. Milner. 1979. "Eighteenth and Nineteenth Century Accounts of the Malay Peninsula." *Journal of the Malaysian Branch of the Royal Asiatic Society* 52(1): 1–56.
Datoek Besar, R. A., and R. Roolvink. 1953. *Hikajat Abdullah*. Djakarta: Djambatan.
Dominguez, V. R. 1989. *People as Subject, People as Object*. Madison: University of Wisconsin Press.
Dumont, L. 1972. *Homo Hierarchicus*. London: Paladin.
Gladney, D. C. 1994. "Representing Nationality in China: Refiguring Majority/Minority Identities." *Journal of Asian Studies* 53(1): 92–123.
Gunawardana, R. A. L. H. 1990. "The People of the Lion: The Sinhalese Identity and Ideology in History and Historiography." In Jonathan Spencer, ed., *Sri Lanka: History and the Roots of Conflict*, pp. 45–80. London: Routledge.
Hikayat Dunia iaitu pada menyatakan darihal Benua Asia dan Africa serta dengan Tokong Tokong Pulau Tanah Melayu. 1855. Singapore: Bukit Zion.
Hirschman, C. 1987. "The Meaning and Measurement of Ethnicity in Malaysia: An Analysis of Census Classifications." *Journal of Asian Studies* 42(3): 555–82.
Huntington, S. P. 1993. "The Clash of Civilizations?" *Foreign Affairs* 72(3): 22–49.
Ibrahim Yaacob. 1941. *Melihat Tanah Air*. Kota Bharu.
——— 1975. *Melihat Tanah Air*. Kuantan: Timur.
Ileto, R. C. 1979. *Pasyon and Revolution*. Manila: Ateneode Manila University Press.
Kahn, J. S. 1992. "Class, Ethnicity and Diversity: Some Remarks on Malay Culture in Malaysia." In J. S. Kahn and F. Loh Kok Wah, eds., *Fragmented Vision: Culture and Politics in Contemporary Malaysia*, pp. 158–78. Sydney: Allen & Unwin.
Kapferer, B. 1988. *Legends of People, Myths of State: Violence, Intolerance, and Political Culture in Sri Lanka and Australia*. Washington, D.C.: Smithsonian Institution Press.
Kassim Ahmad. 1964. *Kisah Pelayaran Abdullah*. Kuala Lumpur: Oxford University Press.
Kessler, C. S. 1992. "Archaism and Modernity: Contemporary Malay Political Culture." In J. S. Kahn and F. Loh Kok Wah, eds., *Fragmented Vision: Culture and Politics in Contemporary Malaysia*, pp. 133–58. Sydney: Allen & Unwin.
Khoo Kay Kim. 1981. "Sino-Malaya Relations in Peninsular Malaysia before 1942." *Journal of Southeast Asian Studies* 12(1): 93–107.
Lee, Raymond. 1986. *Ethnicity and Ethnic Relations in Malaysia*. Monograph series. De Kalb: Northern Illinois University, Center for Southeast Asian Studies.
Matheson, V. 1979. "Concepts of Malay Ethos in Indigenous Malay Writings." *Journal of Southeast Asian Studies* 10(2): 351–71.
Means, G. P. 1976. *Malaysian Politics*. London: Hodder & Stroughton.
Milner, A. C. 1982. *Kerajaan: Malay Political Culture on the Eve of Colonial Rule*. Association for Asian Studies Monograph. Tucson: University of Arizona Press.
——— 1986. "Rethinking Islamic Fundamentalism in Malaysia." *Review of Indonesian and Malaysian Affairs* 20: 48–75.

——— 1991. "Inventing Politics: The Case of Malaysia." *Past & Present* 132: 104–29.

——— 1992. " 'Malayness': Confrontation, Innovation, and Discourse." In V. J. H. Houben, H. M. J. Maier, and W. Van der Molen, eds., *Looking in Odd Mirrors: The Java Sea*, pp. 43–59. Leiden: Rijksuniversiteit.

——— 1995. *The Invention of Politics in Colonial Malays: Contesting Nationalism and the Expansion of the Public Sphere*. Cambridge: Cambridge University Press.

——— 1996. "Malaysia." In A. C. Milner and Mary Quilty, eds., *Communities of Thought*, pp. 157–83. Melbourne: Oxford University Press.

Mohamad Abu Bakar. 1988. "Islam and Nationalism in Contemporary Malay Society." In Taufik Abdullah and Sharon Siddique, eds., *Islam and Society in Southeast Asia*, pp. 155–74. Singapore: Institute of Southeast Asian Studies.

Mohamad Suffian bin Hashim. 1972. *An Introduction to the Constitution of Malaysia*. Kuala Lumpur: Jabatan Chetak Kerajaan.

Nagata, J. 1981. "In Defense of Ethnic Boundaries: The Changing Myths and Charters in Malay Identity." In C. F. Keyes, ed., *Ethnic Change*, pp. 87–116. Seattle: University of Washington Press.

Ratnam, K. J. 1965. *Communalism and the Political Process in Malaya*. Kuala Lumpur: University of Malaya Press.

Reynolds, C. J. 1991. *National Identity and Its Defenders: Thailand, 1939–1989*. Monash Papers on Southeast Asia, no. 25. Clayton, Vic., Australia: Monash University.

Roff, W. R. 1967. *The Origins of Malay Nationalism*. Kuala Lumpur: University of Malay Press.

Rustam A. Sani. 1994. *Melayu Baru dan Bangsa Malaysia: Tradisi Cendekia dan Krisis Budaya*. Kuala Lumpur: Utusan.

Sennett, R. 1976. *The Fall of Public Man*. Cambridge: Cambridge University Press.

Senu Abdul Rahman. 1973. *Revolusi Mental*. Kuala Lumpur: Utusan Melayu.

Smail, J. 1961. "On the Possibility of an Autonomous History of Modern Southeast Asia." *Journal of Southeast Asian History* 2(2).

Tan Liok Ee. 1988. *The Rhetoric of Bangsa and Minzu: Community and Nation in Tension, the Malay Peninsula, 1900–1955*. Clayton, Vic., Australia: Centre of Southeast Asian Studies, Monash University.

Van Leur, J. C. 1955. *Indonesian Trade and Society*. The Hague: W. Van Hoeve.

Vasil, R. K. 1971. *Politics in a Plural Society: A Study of Non-Communal Political Parties in West Malaysia*. Kuala Lumpur: Oxford University Press.

Wan Hashim. 1983. *Race Relations in Malaysia*. Kuala Lumpur: Heinemann.

Williams, R. 1983. *Keywords: A Vocabulary of Culture and Society*. New York: Oxford University Press.

Zabedah Awang Ngah. 1964. *Renongan: Antoloji Esei Melayu Dalam Tahun, 1924–1941*. Kuala Lumpur: Dewan Bahasa dan Pustaka.

9. KELLY, ASPIRING TO MINORITY

Anderson, Benedict. 1991. *Imagined Communities: Reflections on the Origin and Spread of Nationalism*. 2d ed. London: Verso.

Bavadra, Timoci. 1990. *Bavadra, Prime Minister, Statesman, Man of the People: Selection of Speeches and Writings, 1985–1989*. Ed. 'Atu Bain and Tupeni Baba. Nadi: Sunrise Press.

Corrigan, Philip, and Derek Sayer. 1985. *The Great Arch: English State Formation as Cultural Revolution*. Oxford: Basil Blackwell.

Gladney, Dru C. 1994. "Representing Nationality in China: Refiguring Majority/Minority Identities." *Journal of Asian Studies* 53(1): 92–123.

Kaplan, Martha, and John D. Kelly. 1994. "Rethinking Resistance: Dialogics of 'Disaffection' in Colonial Fiji." *American Ethnologist* 21(1): 123–51.

Kelly, John D. 1988. "Fiji Indians and Political Discourse in Fiji: From the Pacific Romance to the Coups." *Journal of Historical Sociology* 1(4): 399–422.

——— 1991. *A Politics of Virtue: Hinduism, Sexuality, and Countercolonial Discourse in Fiji*. Chicago: University of Chicago Press.

——— 1995. "*Bhakti* and Postcolonial Politics: Hindu Missions to Fiji." In Peter van der Veer, ed., *Nation and Migration*. Philadelphia: University of Pennsylvania Press.

——— 1997. "Gaze and Grasp: Plantations, Desires, Indentured Indians and Colonial Law in Fiji." In Lenore Manderson and Margaret Jolly, eds., *Sites of Desire/Economies of Pleasure: Sexualities in Asia and the Pacific*, pp. 72–98. Chicago: University of Chicago Press.

Mintz, Sidney. 1981. "Ruth Benedict." In Sydel Silverman, ed., *Totems and Teachers: Perspectives on the History of Anthropology*, pp. 141–66. New York: Columbia University Press.

Ohnuki-Tierney, Emiko. 1987. *The Monkey as Mirror: Symbolic Transformations in Japanese History and Ritual*. Princeton, N.J.: Princeton University Press.

——— 1993. *Rice as Self: Japanese Identities Through Time*. Princeton, N.J.: Princeton University Press.

Pacific Islands Monthly. June 1993. "On the Brink of Anarchy: Papua New Guinea Is Thrown into Chaos As a Crime Wave Sweeps Through the Country," pp. 14–17.

——— July 1994. "Opposition Boycott: Indians Walk Out of Fiji Parliament After PM Warns of Bloody Coup," p. 18.

Parry, Jonathan, and Maurice Bloch, eds. 1989. *Money and the Morality of Exchange*. Cambridge: Cambridge University Press.

Sahlins, Marshall. 1993. "Cery cery fuckabede." *American Ethnologist* 20(4): 848–67.

Siegel, Jeff. 1987. *Language Contact in a Plantation Environment: A Sociolinguistic History of Fiji*. Cambridge: Cambridge University Press.

Stocking, George. 1987. *Victorian Anthropology*. New York: Free Press.

Taussig, Michael. 1987. *Shamanism, Colonialism and the Wild Man*. Chicago: University of Chicago Press.

Taylor, Charles, Amy Gutmann, Steven C. Rockefeller, Michael Walzer, and Susan Wolf. 1992. *Multiculturalism and "The Politics of Recognition": An Essay by Charles Taylor with Commentary*. Princeton, N.J.: Princeton University Press.

Thomas, Nicholas. 1991. *Entangled Objects: Exchange, Material Culture, and Colonialism in the Pacific*. Cambridge: Harvard University Press.

Wagner, Peter. 1994. "Survey Article: Action, Coordination, and Institution in Recent French Debates." *Journal of Political Philosophy* 2.

Weber, Max. 1978. *Economy and Society*, vol. 1. Berkeley: University of California Press.

Williams, Brackette F. 1989. "A Class Act: Anthropology and the Race to Nation Across Ethnic Terrain." *Annual Review of Anthropology*, pp. 401–44.

——— 1990. "Nationalism, Traditionalism, and the Problem of Cultural Inauthenticity." In Richard Fox, ed., *Nationalist Ideologies and the Production of National Cultures*. American Ethnological Society Monograph Series, no. 2. Washington, D.C.: American Anthropological Association.

10. KAPLAN, DISCOURSES AGAINST DEMOCRACY IN FIJI

Ali, Ahmed. 1986. "Fiji: Political Change, 1874–1960." In Lal, *Politics in Fiji*.

Burridge, Kenelm. 1980. *New Heaven, New Earth*. Oxford: Basil Blackwell.

Clammer, John. 1975. "Colonialism and the Perception of Tradition in Fiji." In Talal Asad, ed., *Anthropology and the Colonial Encounter*. London: Ithaca Press.

Corrigan, Philip, and Derek Sayer. 1985. *The Great Arch: English State Formation as Cultural Revolution*. Oxford: Basil Blackwell.

France, Peter. 1969. *The Charter of the Land*. Melbourne: Oxford University Press.

Gordon, Sir Arthur. 1879. "Paper on the System of Taxation in Force in Fiji." London: Harrison & Sons. (Copy at Newberry Library, Chicago.)

Kaplan, Martha. 1989a. "The 'Dangerous and Disaffected Native' in Fiji." *Social Analysis* 26: 20–43.

——— 1989b. "Luveniwai As the British Saw It: Constructions of Custom and Disorder in Colonial Fiji." *Ethnohistory* 36(4): 349–71.

——— 1990. "Christianity, People of the Land, and Chiefs in Fiji." In John Barker, ed., *Christianity in Oceania*, pp. 189–207. Association for Social Anthropology in Oceania Monograph no. 12. Lanham, Md.: University Press of America.

——— 1995. *Neither Cargo nor Cult: Ritual Politics and the Colonial Imagination in Fiji*. Durham, N.C.: Duke University Press.

——— N.d. "From Jew to Roman: Imaging Self and Other in Colonial Fiji." Manuscript.

Kelly, John D. 1988. "Fiji Indians and Political Discourse in Fiji: From the Pacific Romance to the Coups." *Journal of Historical Sociology* 399–422.

——— 1991. *A Politics of Virtue: Hinduism, Sexuality and Countercolonial Discourse in Fiji*. Chicago: University of Chicago Press.

——— 1995. "Threats to Difference in Colonial Fiji." *Cultural Anthropology* 10(1): 64–84.

Lal, Brij. 1985. "Kunti's Cry: Indentured Women on Fiji's Plantations." *Indian Economic and Social History Review* 22(1): 55–71.

——— ed. 1986. *Politics in Fiji: Studies in Contemporary History*. Laie: Institute for Polynesian Studies, Brigham Young University–Hawai'i.

Lattas, Andrew, ed. 1992. *Hysteria, Anthropological Disclosure and the Concept of the Unconscious: Cargo Cults and the Scientisation of Race and Colonial Power. Oceania* 63(1) (special edited edition).

Lawson, Stephanie. 1990. "The Myth of Cultural Homogeneity and Its Implications for Chiefly Power and Politics in Fiji." *Comparative Studies in Society and History* 32(4): 795–821.

Legislative Council of Fiji. 1946. *Debates*. Suva, Fiji: Government Printer. (Copy at National Archives, Suva.)

Macnaught, Timothy. 1982. *The Fijian Colonial Experience*. Pacific Research Monograph no. 7. Canberra: Australian National University.

Norton, Robert. 1977. *Race and Politics in Fiji*. New York: St. Martin's.

Sahlins, Marshall. 1985. *Islands of History*. Chicago: University of Chicago Press.

Sukuna, Ratu Sir Lala. 1983. *Fiji, the Three-Legged Stool: Selected Writings of Ratu Sir Lala Sukuna*. Ed. Deryck Scarr. London: Macmillan Education.

Thomas, Nicholas. 1990. "Sanitation and Seeing." *Comparative Studies in Society and History* 32: 149–70.

Toren, Christina. 1988. "Making the Present, Revealing the Past: The Mutability and Continuity of Tradition as Process." *Man* 23(4): 696–717.

Worsley, Peter. 1969. *The Trumpet Shall Sound*. New York: Schocken Books.

11. DERINGIL, SELF-IMAGE AND SOCIAL ENGINEERING IN TURKEY

Anderson, Benedict. 1991. *Imagined Communities*. London: Verso.

Berkes, Niyazi. 1964. *The Development of Secularism in Turkey*. Montreal: McGill University Press.

Deringil, Selim. 1991. "Legitimacy Structures in the Ottoman State: The Reign of Abdülhamid II (1876–1909)." *International Journal of Middle East Studies* 23(3): 345–59.

——— 1993. "The Ottoman Origins of Kemalist Nationalism: Namik Kemal to Mustafa Kemal." *European History Quarterly* 23(2): 165–91.

Duben, Alan, and Cem Behar. 1991. *Istanbul Households*. Cambridge: Cambridge University Press.

Duguid, Stephen. 1973. "The Politics of Unity: Hamidian Policy in Eastern Anatolia." *Middle Eastern Studies* 9(2) 139–55.

Erişirgil, Mehmet Emin. 1984. *Ziya Gökalp*. Istanbul: Alan Publishers.

Findley, Carter. 1989. *Ottoman Civil Officialdom*. Princeton, N.J.: Princeton University Press.

Fleischer, Cornell H. 1986. *Bureaucrat and Intellectual in the Ottoman Empire: The Historian Mustafa Ali (1541–1600)*. Princeton, N.J.: Princeton University Press.

Hanioglu, Şükrü. 1986. *Osmanli Ittihad ve Terakki Cemiyeti ve Jön Turkluk*. Istanbul: İletişim Publishers.

Hobsbawm, Eric J. 1992. *Nations and Nationalism Since 1870: Programme, Myth, Reality*. Cambridge: Cambridge University Press.

Hurgronje, Snouck. 1931. *Mekka in the Latter Part of the Nineteenth Century*. Leiden: E. J. Brill.

Karaca, Ali. 1993. *Anadolu Islahatì ve Ahmet Şakir Paşa, 1838–1899*. Istanbul: Eren Publishers.

Kodaman, Bayram. 1983. *Sultan II. Abdülhamid'in Dogu Anadolu Politikasì*. Istanbul: Ötüken Publishers.

Lewis, Bernard. 1961. *The Emergence of Modern Turkey*. London: Oxford University Press.

Olson, Robert. 1989. *The Emergence of Kurdish Nationalism and the Sheikh Said Rebellion, 1880–1925*. Austin: University of Texas Press.

Ramsay, William M. 1890. *The Historical Geography of Asia Minor*. Royal Geographical Society, Supplementary Papers. London.

Sami, Şemseddin. A.H. 1306, A.D. 1896. *Kamus-u Alam. Tarih ve Cografya Lügatìnì ve Tabir-i ashale-i kaffe-i esma-i hassayì camidir. Dictionnaire Universel D'Histoire et de Géographie par Ch Samy Bey Fraschery*. Istanbul.

——— 1897. *Kamus-u Türki* (Turkish-Turkish lexicon). Istanbul: İletişim Yayinlari.

Sonyel, Salahi Ramsdan. 1975. *Turkish Diplomacy, 1918–1923: Mustafa Kemal and the Turkish National Movement*. London: Sage.

Suny, Ronald Grigor. 1993. *Looking Toward Ararat: Armenia in Modern History*. Bloomington: Indiana University Press.

Taneri, Kemal Zülfü. 1963. *Süleyman Hüsnü Paşa'nìn Hayatì ve Eserleri* (The biography and works of Süleyman Hüsnü Paşa). Ankara: Sevil Publishers.

Türk Meşhurlari Ansiklopedisi (Encyclopedia of famous Turks). 1993. Istanbul.

12. KIRIŞCI, THE CASE OF THE KURDS IN TURKEY

Ağaoğulları, M. A. 1987. "The Utranationalist Right." In I. C. Schick and E. A. Tonak, eds., *Turkey in Transition: New Perspectives*. Oxford: Oxford University Press.

Ahmad, F. 1993. *The Making of Modern Turkey*. London: Routledge.

Akural, S. 1984. "Kemalist Views on Social Change." In J. Landau, ed., *Atatürk and the Modernization of Turkey*. Boulder, Colo.: Westview.

Alp, T. 1937. *Le Kemalisme*. Paris: F. Alacan.

Amnesty International. 1994. *Amnesty International Report*. New York: Amnesty International.

Anderson, B. 1991. *Imagined Communities*. London: Verso.

Andrews, P. A., ed. 1989. *Ethnic Groups in the Republic of Turkey*. Wiesbaden: Dr. Ludwig Reichert.

Arai, M. 1992. *Turkish Nationalism in the Young Turk Era*. Leiden: E. J. Brill.

Arfa, H. 1968. *The Kurds: An Historical and Political Study*. London: Oxford University Press.

Balım, Ç., Ersin Kallaycıoğlu, Cevat Karataş, Gareth Winrow, and Feroz Yasamee, eds. 1995. *Turkey: Economic, Political and Foreign Policy Challenges for the 1990's*. Leiden: E. J. Brill.

Ballı, R. 1991. *Kürt Dosyası*. Istanbul: Cem Yayınevi.

Barkey, H. 1993. "Turkey's Kurdish Dilemma." *Survival* 35: 51–70.

Beşikçi, I. 1991a. *Devletlerarası Sömürge Kürdistan*. Ankara: Yurt Kitap-Yayın.

——— 1991b. *Türk Tarih Tezi, Güneş Dil Teorisi Ve Kürt Sorunu*. Ankara: Yurt Kitap-Yayın.

Bilsel, C. (M. Cemil). 1933. *Lozan*. Istanbul: Ahmed İhsan Matbaası.
Bruinessen, van M. 1984. "The Kurds in Turkey." *MERIP Reports* 121 (Feb.): 6–12.
——— 1989. "The Ethnic Identity of Kurds." In Andrews, *Ethnic Groups*, pp. 613–21. Wiesbaden: Dr. Ludwig Reichert.
——— 1992. *Agha, Shaikh and State: The Social and Political Structure of Kurdistan*. London: Zed.
Chaliand, G., ed. 1993. *A People Without a Country: The Kurds and Kurdistan*. London: Zed.
Connor, W. 1987. "Ethnonationalism." In M. Weiner and S. P. Huntington, eds., *Understanding Political Development*, pp. 196–220. New York: Harper Collins.
Deringil, S. 1993. "The Ottoman Origins of Kemalist Nationalism: Namik Kemal to Mustafa Kemal." *European History Quarterly* 23: 165–91.
Dumont, P. 1984. "The Origins of Kemalist Ideology." In J. Landau, ed., *Atatürk and the Modernization of Turkey*. Boulder, Colo.: Westview Press.
Entessar, N. 1992. *Kurdish Ethnonationalism*. Boulder, Colo.: Lynne Rienner.
Eriksen, T. H. 1993. *Ethnicity and Nationalism: Anthropological Perspectives*. London: Pluto.
Fırat, M. S. 1948. *Doğu İlleri ve Varto Tarihi*. Istanbul: Saka Matbaası.
Gellner, E. 1964. *Thought and Change*. Chicago: University of Chicago Press.
Giritli, I. 1989. *Kürt Türklerinin Gerçeği*. Istanbul: Yeni Forum Yayıncılık.
Glazer, N., and D. Moynihan. 1970. *Beyond the Melting Pot*. Cambridge: Harvard University Press.
——— 1975. *Ethnicity: Theory and Practice*. Cambridge: Harvard University Press.
Gökalp, Z. 1959a. "My Nationality." In N. Berkes, ed., *Turkish Nationalism and Western Civilization*, pp. 43–45. Westport: Greenwood Press.
——— 1959b. "What Is a Nation." In N. Berkes, ed., *Turkish Nationalism and Western Civilization*, pp. 126–34. Westport, Conn.: Greenwood Press.
Greenfeld, L. 1992. *Nationalism: Five Roads to Modernity*. Cambridge: Harvard University Press.
Gunter, M. 1990. *The Kurds in Turkey: A Political Dilemma*. Boulder, Colo.: Westview.
Gurr, T. R. 1993. *Minorities at Risk: A Global View of Ethnopolitical Conflicts*. Washington, D.C.: USIP.
Gurr, T. R., and J. R. Scarritt. 1989. "Minorities' Rights at Risk: A Global Survey." *Human Rights Quarterly* 11: 380–81.
Harris, G. 1985. *Turkey: Coping with Crisis*. Boulder, Colo: Westview.
Horowitz, D. L. 1985. *Ethnic Groups in Conflict*. Berkeley: University of California Press.
Israel, F. 1967. *Major Peace Treaties of Modern History, 1648–1967*. New York: Chelsea House.
Karul, O. 1992. *"Kürt Gerceği" Dinmeyen Sancı*. Istanbul: Erdini Basım ve Yayınevi.
Kendal, N. 1980. "Kurdistan in Turkey." In Chaliand, *A People Without a Country*.
Kirişci, K. 1995. "New Patterns of Turkish Foreign Policy Behavior." In Balım et al., *Turkey*.
Kirişci, K., and G. Winrow. 1997. *The Kurdish Question and Turkey: An Example of a Trans-state Ethnic Conflict*. London: Frank Cass.

Kutlay, N. 1992. *Ittihat Terakki ve Kürtler*. Ankara: Beybun.

Kutschera, C. 1979. *Le Mouvement national Kurde*. Paris: Flammarion.

Landau, J. 1974. *Radical Politics in Modern Turkey*. Leiden: E. J. Brill.

——— 1981. *Pan-Turkism in Turkey*. Hamden, Conn.: Archon Books.

——— ed. 1984. *Atatürk and the Modernization of Turkey*. Boulder, Colo.: Westview.

Lewis, B. 1962. *The Emergence of Modern Turkey*. London: Oxford University Press.

Lewis, G. L. 1984. "Atatürk's Language Reform as an Aspect of Modernization in the Republic of Turkey." In Landau, *Atatürk and the Modernization of Turkey*.

Mumcu, U. 1991. *Kürt İslam Ayaklanması*. Istanbul: Tekin Yayınevi.

Mutlu, S. 1995. "Population of Turkey by Ethnic Groups and Provinces." *New Perspectives on Turkey* 12: 33–60.

Nestmann, L. 1989. "Die ethnische Differenzierung der Bevolkerung der Ostturkei in ihren sozialen Bezugen." In Andrews, *Ethnic Groups in the Republic of Turkey*, pp. 543–63.

Olson, R. 1989. *The Emergence of Kurdish Nationalism and the Sheikh Said Rebellion, 1880–1925*. Austin: University of Texas Press.

Özsoy, A., I. Koç, and A. Toros. 1992. "Türkiye'nin Etnik Yapısının Ana Dil Sorularına Göre Analizi." *Nüfus Bilim Dergisi* 14: 101–14.

Robins, P. 1993. "The Overlord State: Turkish Policy and the Kurdish Issue." *International Affairs* 69(4): 657–76.

Smith, A. 1973. "Nationalism." *Current Sociology* 21(3): 1–187.

——— 1993. "Ethnic Election and Cultural Identity." *Ethnic Studies* 10: 9–25.

Steinbach, U. 1984. "Atatürk's Impact on Turkey's Political Culture Since World War II." In Landau, *Atatürk and the Modernization of Turkey*.

Stokes, G. 1993. "Cognition, Consciousness, and Nationalism." *Ethnic Studies* 10: 27–42.

Toker, M. 1968. *Şeyh Sait İsyanı*. Ankara: Rüzgarlı Matbaası.

Tunaya, T. Z. 1952. *Türkiye'de Siyasi Partiler, 1859–1952*. Istanbul: Doğan Kardeş.

Tuncay, M. 1981. *T.C.'nde Tek-Parti Yönetimi'nin Kurluması (1923–1931)*. Ankara: Yurt Yayınları.

Winter, M. 1984. "The Modernization of Education in Kemalist Turkey." In Landau, *Atatürk and the Modernization of Turkey*.

Zürcher, E. J. 1984. *The Unionist Factor*. Leiden: E. J. Brill.

13. HANDLER, MAINSTREAMS AND MINORITIES IN NORTH AMERICA

Badone, Ellen. 1992. "The Construction of National Identity in Brittany and Quebec." Review of McDonald 1989 and Handler 1988. *American Ethnologist* 19: 806–17.

Blackburn, Joyce. 1975. *George Wythe of Williamsburg*. New York: Harper & Row.

Brodie, Fawn. 1974. *Thomas Jefferson: An Intimate History*. New York: Norton.

Brown, Imogene. 1981. *American Aristides: A Biography of George Wythe*. Rutherford, N.J.: Fairleigh-Dickinson University Press.

Bruner, Edward. 1994. "Abraham Lincoln as Authentic Reproduction: A Critique of Postmodernism." *American Anthropologist* 96: 397–415.

Carson, Cary. 1991. "Front and Center: Local History Comes of Age." In *Local History, National Heritage: Reflections on the History of the AASLH*, pp. 67–108. Nashville: American Association for State and Local History.

——— 1994. "Lost in the Fun House: A Commentary on Anthropologists' First Contact with History Museums." *Journal of American History* 81: 137–51.

Colonial Williamsburg. 1985. *Teaching History at Colonial Williamsburg*. Williamsburg, Va.: Colonial Williamsburg Foundation.

Gable, Eric, and Richard Handler. 1993a. "Colonialist Anthropology at Colonial Williamsburg." *Museum Anthropology* 17(3): 26–31.

——— 1993b. "Deep Dirt: Messing Up the Past at Colonial Williamsburg." *Social Analysis* 34: 3–16.

——— 1994. "The Authority of Documents at Some American History Museums." *Journal of American History* 81: 119–36.

Gable, Eric, Richard Handler, and Anna Lawson. 1992. "On the Uses of Relativism: Fact, Conjecture, and Black and White Histories at Colonial Williamsburg." *American Ethnologist* 19: 791–805.

Gleason, Philip. 1991. "Minorities (Almost) All: The Minority Concept in American Social Thought." *American Quarterly* 43: 392–424.

Handler, Richard. 1988. *Nationalism and the Politics of Culture in Quebec*. Madison: University of Wisconsin Press.

——— 1989. "Ethnicity in the Museum." In Susan Keefe, ed., *Negotiating Ethnicity*, pp. 18–26. Bulletin no. 8. Washington, D.C.: National Association for the Practice of Anthropology.

——— 1991a. Review of McDonald 1989. *Anthropological Quarterly* 64: 159–60.

——— 1991b. "Who Owns the Past: History, Cultural Property, and the Logic of Possessive Individualism." In Brett Williams, ed., *The Politics of Culture*, pp. 63–74. Washington, D.C.: Smithsonian Institution Press.

——— 1993. "Fieldwork in Quebec, Scholarly Reviews, and Anthropological Dialogues." In Caroline Brettell, ed., *When They Read What We Write: The Politics of Ethnography*, pp. 67–74. New York: Bergin & Garvey.

Handler, Richard, and Jocelyn Linnekin. 1984. "Tradition, Genuine or Spurious." *Journal of American Folklore* 97: 273–90.

Lawson, Anna. 1995. "Black History at Colonial Williamsburg: Mainstream Objects and Marginal Subjects." Ph.D. dissertation, University of Virginia.

Lawson, Anna, and Eric Gable. 1993. "Miscegenation in the Mainstream: The Museum Experience." Paper presented at 92d annual meeting of the American Anthropological Association, Washington, D.C., November.

McDonald, Maryon. 1989. *"We Are Not French": Language, Culture, and Identity in Brittany*. New York: Routledge.

Segal, Daniel, and Richard Handler. 1995. U.S. Multiculturalism and the Concept of Culture. *Identities* 1: 391–407.

Wallace, Michael. 1986. "Visiting the Past: History Museums in the United States." In Susan Porter Benson, Stephen Brier, and Roy Rosenzweig, eds., *Presenting the*

Past: Essays on History and the Public, pp. 137–61. Philadelphia: Temple University Press.

Wells, Camille. 1993. "Interior Designs: Room Furnishings and Historical Interpretations at Colonial Williamsburg." *Southern Quarterly* 31: 89–111.

West, Cornel. 1990. "The New Cultural Politics of Difference." *October* 53: 93–108.

Wirth, Louis. 1945. "The Problem of Minority Groups." In Ralph Linton, ed. *The Science of Man in the World Crisis*, pp. 347–72. New York: Columbia University Press.

14. OKAMURA, PRIVILEGING MULTICULTURALISM IN HAWAI'I

Adams, R. 1926. "Hawai'i as a Racial Melting Pot." *Mid-Pacific Magazine* 32(3): 213–16.

——— 1934. "The Unorthodox Race Doctrine of Hawai'i." In E. B. Reuter, ed., *Race and Culture Contacts*, pp. 143–60. New York: McGraw Hill.

——— 1936. "Race Relations in Hawai'i (A Summary Statement)." *Social Process in Hawai'i* 2(1): 5–6.

——— 1937. *Interracial Marriage in Hawai'i*. New York: Macmillan.

Boylan, D. 1993. Foreword to Kent, *Hawai'i*, pp. ix–xii.

Center for Research on Ethnic Relations. N.d. Prospectus. Honolulu: Social Science Research Institute, University of Hawai'i at Manoa.

DeLima, F. 1991. *Frank DeLima's Joke Book*. Honolulu, Hawai'i: Bess Press.

Fuchs, L. 1961. *Hawai'i Pono: A Social History*. New York: Harcourt, Brace & World.

Grant, G., and D. Ogawa. 1993. "Living Proof: Is Hawai'i the Answer?" *Annals of the American Academy of Political and Social Science (Interminority Affairs in the U.S.: Pluralism at the Crossroads*, special editor P. I. Rose) 530: 137–54.

Hawaiian Sovereignty Elections Council. 1997. "Hawaiian Sovereignty Elections Council Final Report." Honolulu: Sovereignty Elections Council.

Hawai'i State Department of Business, Economic Development and Tourism. 1993. *The State of Hawai'i Data Book, 1992*. Honolulu: Department of Business, Economic Development and Tourism.

Ka Lahui Hawai'i. 1991. "Ka Lahui Hawai'i, The Sovereign Nation of Hawai'i: A Compilation of Legal Materials for Workshops on the Hawaiian Nation."

Kanahele, G. S. 1982. "The New Hawaiians." *Social Process in Hawai'i* 29: 21–31.

Kent, N. J. 1993. *Hawai'i: Islands Under the Influence*. Honolulu: University of Hawai'i Press.

——— 1994. "Scouring the Melting Pot." *Honolulu Weekly*, Feb. 2: 3.

Kirkpatrick, J. 1987. "Ethnic Antagonism and Innovation in Hawai'i." In J. Boucher and D. Landis, eds., *Ethnic Conflict: International Perspectives*, pp. 298–316. Beverly Hills: Sage.

Kotani, R. M. 1985. *The Japanese in Hawai'i: A Century of Struggle*. Honolulu: Hawai'i Hochi.

Lind, A. W. 1938. *An Island Community: Ecological Succession in Hawai'i*. Chicago: University of Chicago Press.

——— 1969. *Hawai'i: The Last of the Magic Isles.* London: Oxford University Press.

——— 1980. *Hawaii's People.* 4th ed. Honolulu: University Press of Hawai'i.

——— 1982. "Race and Ethnic Relations: An Overview." *Social Process in Hawai'i* 29: 130–50.

Myrdal, G. 1944. *An American Dilemma: The Negro Problem and American Democracy.* New York: Harper.

Odo, F., and S. Yim. 1993. "Ethnicity." In R. W. Roth, ed., *Price of Paradise,* 2: 225–29. Honolulu: Mutual Publishing.

Ogawa, D. M. 1981. "Dialogue: What Is Local?" *Hawai'i Committee for the Humanities News* 2(1): 1, 7.

Okamura, J. Y. 1980. "Local Culture and Society in Hawai'i." *Amerasia Journal* 7(2): 119–37.

——— 1982. "Ethnicity and Ethnic Relations in Hawai'i." In D. Y. H. Wu, ed., *Ethnicity and Interpersonal Interaction: A Cross Cultural Study,* pp. 213–35. Singapore: Maruzen Asia.

——— 1990. "Ethnicity and Stratification in Hawai'i." Operation Manong Resource Papers, no. 1. Honolulu: Operation Manong, University of Hawai'i.

——— 1994. "Why There Are No Asian Americans in Hawai'i: The Continuing Significance of Local Identity." *Social Process in Hawai'i (The Political Economy of Hawai'i,* special editor I. G. Aoude) 35: 161–78.

——— 1996. "Institutionalized Inequality: Racial and Ethnic Stratification in Hawai'i." Manuscript.

Ravitch, D. 1990. "Multiculturalism: E Pluribus Plures." *American Scholar* 59(3): 337–54.

Schlesinger, A. M. 1991. *The Disuniting of America: Reflections on a Multicultural Society.* Knoxville, Tenn.: Whittle Communications.

Smith, M. G. 1969. "Institutional and Political Conditions of Pluralism." In L. Kuper and M. G. Smith, eds., *Pluralism in Africa,* pp. 27–65. Berkeley: University of California Press.

Takaki, R. 1993. "Multiculturalism: Battleground or Meeting Ground?" *Annals of the American Academy of Political and Social Science (Interminority Affairs in the U.S.: Pluralism at the Crossroads,* special editor P. I. Rose), 109–21.

Trask, H. K. 1984–85. "Hawaiians, American Colonization and the Quest for Independence." *Social Process in Hawai'i* 31: 101–36.

——— 1992. "*Kupa'a 'Aina*: Native Hawaiian Nationalism in Hawai'i." In Z. A. Smith and R. C. Pratt, eds., *Politics and Public Policy in Hawai'i.* Albany: State University of New York Press.

U.S. Congress. 1921. *Labor Problems in Hawai'i.* Washington, D.C.: House Committee on Immigration and Naturalization.

Wittermans, E. 1964. *Inter-ethnic Relations in a Plural Society.* Groningen, Netherlands: J. B. Wolters.

Index

In this index an "f" after a number indicates a separate reference on the next page, and an "ff" indicates separate references on the next two pages. A continuous discussion over two or more pages is indicated by a span of page numbers, e.g., "57–59."

Library of Congress Cataloging-in-Publication-Data
Making majorities : constituting the nation in Japan, Korea, China, Malaysia, Fiji, Turkey, and the United States / edited by Dru C. Gladney.
p. cm. — (East-West Center series on contemporary issues in Asia and the Pacific)
Based on a conference at the East-West Center—Pref.
Includes bibliographical references (p.) and index.
ISBN 0-8047-3047-4 (cl.) — ISBN 0-8047-3048-2 (pbk.)
1. Ethnicity—Case studies. 2. Majorities—Case studies. 3. Minorities—Case studies. I. Gladney, Dru C. II. Series: Contemporary issues in Asia and the Pacific.
GN495.6.M35 1998
305.8—dc21 97-42928

⊗ This book is printed on acid-free, recycled paper.
Original printing 1998
Last figure below indicates year of this printing:
07 06 05 04 03 02 01 00 99 98